W9-DEW-012

VISUAL BASIC™
FOR
COBOL
PROGRAMMERS

Written by
Greg Perry

Visual Basic for COBOL Programmers

Copyright © 1995 by Que® Corporation.

All rights reserved. Printed in the United States of America. No part of this book may be used or reproduced in any form or by any means, or stored in a database or retrieval system, without prior written permission of the publisher except in the case of brief quotations embodied in critical articles and reviews. Making copies of any part of this book for any purpose other than your own personal use is a violation of United States copyright laws. For information, address Que Corporation, 201 W. 103rd Street, Indianapolis, IN 46290.

Library of Congress Catalog No.: 95-68261

ISBN: 0-7897-0268-1

This book is sold *as is*, without warranty of any kind, either express or implied, respecting the contents of this book, including but not limited to implied warranties for the book's quality, performance, merchantability, or fitness for any particular purpose. Neither Que Corporation nor its dealers or distributors shall be liable to the purchaser or any other person or entity with respect to any liability, loss, or damage caused or alleged to have been caused directly or indirectly by this book.

98 97 96 95   4 3 2 1

Interpretation of the printing code: the rightmost double-digit number is the year of the book's printing; the rightmost single-digit number, the number of the book's printing. For example, a printing code of 95-1 shows that the first printing of the book occurred in 1995.

Screen reproductions in this book were created with Collage Plus from Inner Media, Inc., Hollis, NH.

Publisher: Roland Elgey

Associate Publisher: Joseph B. Wikert

Director of Product Series: Charles O. Stewart III

Managing Editor: Sandra Doell

Director of Marketing: Lynn E. Zingraf

Dedication

To Mr. Bob Enyart, a man who doesn't tell me what to think but who does teach me how.

Credits

Acquisitions Editor

Lori A. Jordan

Product Director

Bryan Gambrel

Production Editor

Caroline D. Roop

Copy Editors

Lori Cates

Patrick Kanouse

Mike La Bonne

Theresa Mathias

Susan Ross Moore

Jeff Riley

Technical Editor

John Winkelman

Operations Coordinator

Patricia J. Brooks

Acquisitions Coordinator

Angela C. Kozlowski

Book Designer

Sandra Schroeder

Cover Designer

Dan Armstrong

Graphic Image Specialists

Stephen Carlin

Jason Hand

Clint Lahnen

Michael Reynolds

Laura Robbins

Craig Small

Jeff Yesh

Production Team

Steve Adams

Claudia Bell

Aren Howell

Bob LaRoche

Steph Mineart

Kaylene Riemen

Kris Simmons

Mike Thomas

Scott Tullis

Indexer

Michael Hughes

Composed in *Stone* and *MCPdigital* by Que Corporation

Acknowledgments

There's one man who's been encouraging me from my first book at Que Corporation. Mr. Joe Wikert, you are the undisputed King of Que Corporation. I'm not sure why you keep asking me back for more books, but there must be *something* in my pages that you like, and I'm sincerely grateful.

My thanks also goes out to Lori Jordan. Lori is one of the best editors around because she believes in giving me the freedom and quiet that I need, but she's right there the few times I've wanted something from her end. I hope this isn't the last book that we work on, Lori.

I know that John Winkelman had the hardest job of all. John took my mess and fine-tuned it into code that actually works!

The others who worked so diligently on this book, namely Caroline Roop, Patrick Kanouse, Lori Cates, Mike La Bonne, Jeff Riley, Theresa Mathias, and Susan Ross Moore, please hear my sincere thanks.

Finally, I want to thank my beautiful bride Jayne (lovely and gracious as always), my parents Glen and Bettye Perry (supportive continuously), and the rest of my friends and associates (who always ask so little).

Trademarks

All terms mentioned in this book that are known to be trademarks or service marks have been appropriately capitalized. Que Corporation cannot attest to the accuracy of this information. Use of a term in this book should not be regarded as affecting the validity of any trademark or service mark.

About the Author

Greg Perry has written more than 30 books, including Que's best-selling *QBasic By Example,* Special Edition; *C By Example,* Special Edition; as well as Sams Publishing's *Absolute Beginner's Guide to Programming.* Perry has written numerous books covering diverse programming languages such as Visual Basic, QBasic, C, C++, Pascal, as well as books on applications such as Microsoft Access. After receiving a degree in Computer Science and a Masters in Finance, Perry programmed for a major Fortune 500 company where he became supervisor over the subsidiary's COBOL and 4th generation financial systems. In recent years, Perry taught programming at the college level until he quit to pursue writing and speaking full-time. Perry also practices the principles he authored in a rental property book by managing his rent houses around Oklahoma. In his spare moments, Perry travels the world looking for excitement, and finding good people, food, adventure, and history at least annually in Italy with his wife.

We'd Like To Hear from You!

As part of our continuing effort to produce books of the highest possible quality, Que would like to hear your comments. To stay competitive, we *really* want you, as a computer book reader and user, to let us know what you like or dislike most about this book or other Que products.

You can mail comments, ideas, or suggestions for improving future editions to the address below, or send us a fax at (317) 581-4663. For the on-line inclined, Macmillan Computer Publishing has a forum on CompuServe (type **GO QUEBOOKS** at any prompt) through which our staff and authors are available for questions and comments. The address of our Internet site is **http://www.mcp.com** (World Wide Web).

In addition to exploring our forum, please feel free to contact me personally to discuss your opinions of this book: on CompuServe, I'm at 75230,1556, and on the Internet, **bgambrel@que.mcp.com**.

Thanks in advance—your comments will help us to continue publishing the best books available on computer topics in today's market.

Bryan Gambrel
Product Development Specialist
Que Corporation
201 W. 103rd Street
Indianapolis, Indiana 46290
USA

Contents at a Glance

Contents

5 The Graphical Controls   **79**

II Point & Click Programming   **105**

6 Presto, No Code Required!   **107**

7 Capturing Events   **123**

8 VB's *IDENTIFICATION* and *ENVIRONMENT* Equivalents   **141**

Introduction

If I had the authority (which I don't!), I'd require that this book be stamped with the words, "Don't look back!" There are so many superb COBOL programmers in the world who are the cream of the crop, the masters of code, and the leaders in creating business programs. This book is for all of you who want to move from the world that you know so fluently into... well, into the world many of you are possibly hesitant to explore.

I began my career as a COBOL programmer and analyst. I know the fears that I had several years ago when I moved into the world of PC programming. I'm sure that I was more hesitant than you. In fact, I'm sure that it is safe to say that you have not hesitated at all and that you look forward to learning how to program in a microcomputer windowed environment such as Microsoft Windows. The odds are good that you've been using a PC for word processing, spreadsheets, and your personal financial needs (and games, right?). Probably, you've already explored PC-based languages such as QBasic.

The reason I'd add the "Don't look back!" stamp is that the graphical industry is not new anymore. From PCs to minicomputers to mainframe X-Terminals, the graphical user environments are becoming the mainstream environments. The text-based computer arena that was so important to our industry since the genesis of computers in the 1940s must now take a back seat. The windowing-graphical mode is now the standard and the requirement of most installations.

Perhaps the text mode is not actually taking a back seat. Perhaps, the text mode is *mentoring* the shift towards the graphical environment. For example, COBOL programmers are some of the most well-structured and disciplined coders in existence. COBOL programmers understand what it's like to work in a team environment. COBOL programmers know that a movement of code into the production code's area is a one-way movement and that those programs carry both good and bad with them. The user, of course, always finds the bad (bugs) and only sometimes mentions the good. Nevertheless, we shouldn't blame the user. If we do our job, our code will function as it should, bug free (*virtually* bug free), and it will handle the user's needs with ease so that the user is basically unaware that he or she is using a program.

The practices that you learned so well from the text world carry forward into Visual Basic and Windows. As this book shows, you will still code loops, look for efficiencies, and write structured code using Visual Basic, but your focus will no longer be on the user's processing needs alone. Your focus must now change to take on a new dimension—the user's interface. The graphical interface offered by Windows is rich for users but vast for programmers. Mastering Visual Basic means mastering the interface programming that comes with Windows.

Who Should Use This Book?

The title of this book says it all. This book was written for, designed with, and targeted to *COBOL programmers*. What more is there to say? If you know COBOL like the back of your hand, but you're not even sure if you can spell *PC*, you have the right book!

Perhaps you have attempted to write Windows programs before. Depending on the source of your teaching, you may not have had much success in moving from a text-based and *comfortable* COBOL environment to the ever-changing visual world of Windows programs. One of the reasons that you'll like this book's approach is that the book concentrates on moving you from the environment you now use to the environment of PC-based visual programming. The Visual Basic language is not really all that different from the COBOL language. The mode in which you write programs in Visual Basic, however, is extremely different. If you want help with the programming environment of Visual Basic, you'll get that help here.

This Book's Approach

If this were a book that took each COBOL statement and converted that statement to an equivalent Visual Basic statement, this book would waste your time and money. Even more important, that approach would not teach you the real world of Visual Basic programming.

This book uses the COBOL language as a stepping stone to the Visual Basic language when and where it can. Visual Basic and COBOL are like night and day, however. Although your disciplined background will quickly turn you into a superb Visual Basic programmer, your COBOL background will not necessarily make Visual Basic's programmer interface easier to handle. Visual Basic's user interaction is *nothing* like you've written for before.

Therefore, when this book discusses the language elements of Visual Basic, COBOL works as a great guide to show you quickly how a Visual Basic loop operates (or doesn't operate) like a related statement in COBOL. You'll find, nevertheless, that there are chapters in this book that mention COBOL only in passing. When your background will help you learn a part of Visual Basic, this book concentrates on that COBOL background and brings to light the similarities of COBOL and Visual Basic. However, when this book must teach you a new Visual Basic user interface control or discuss debugging using the interactive, online Visual Basic debugging windowing tools, there is nothing in COBOL that would help you move to the Visual Basic environment any faster. In fact, there are many places in this book where discussing too much COBOL would convolute the description.

Therefore, this is a book aimed strictly at COBOL programmers, but this is also a book *that teaches you Visual Basic*. When you finish this book, you may not call yourself a Visual Basic *expert* but you'll certainly be writing complete, fancy Windows applications in a fraction of the time that you used to write text-based programs in COBOL.

This Book's Disk

This book contains a disk that holds every application and data file mentioned in the book. You won't have to write one program as you read through this book. Instead, you can load an application from the disk and analyze the code and program as you read.

Before you rely too heavily on the disk, however, consider this: how did you learn COBOL? You wrote COBOL programs. Lots of COBOL programs! Do not load every chapter's application before reading the chapter. Work through the chapters, building the applications as described. If you get stuck, save your work and load the disk's programs to see what you did not understand. Use the disk's programs as a review guide to inform you of what you may have forgotten or misunderstood.

Unlike many books, this book's disk contains only uncompressed programs. Therefore, you don't need fancy (and often confusing) decompression programs to decompress and copy the book's files to a directory on your computer's hard disk. Instead, you can use the DOS COPY command or the Windows File Manager, to copy this book's files to your hard disk.

Since Visual Basic requires Windows, you're probably better off using the File Manager to copy the files. Before copying the files, however, you need to think about where you'll copy them. I would suggest creating a special directory just for this book's files. When this book requests that you load data or an application, you can specify the directory you created.

There's another way that might be a little easier, although not as organized. Find out on which disk drive and directory your Visual Basic program resides. To do this, you can start the File Manager and look for the directory named VB. Once you find the directory, copy the diskette's files to that directory.

Suppose that you found Visual Basic in the directory named VB which was located on drive D:. You would insert this book's disk into your floppy disk drive (probably named A:) and display the VB directory inside the File Manager. To copy the files, simply drag the File Manager's A: icon to the directory named VB. The first place that Visual Basic looks for its application files (until you or someone else changes the location) is in its primary program directory. Therefore, if you place this book's disk files in Visual Basic's directory, you'll have no trouble locating the files when you want to work with them.

There's one big assumption that I'm making here: I'm assuming that you understand the Windows File Manager and PC-based drives and directories. Not all COBOL programmers will understand this. You may need to find one of your company's PC gurus (*all* companies have them) and get some help, or try one of the Que books on Windows, *Easy Windows 3.11* or *Using Windows 3.11*. The fact that this book's applications are not compressed makes the job very easy, so if the person who helps you takes a long time and requests that you buy lunch, strike a better bargain!

Organization

This book is organized into these five primary parts:

Part I: From Mainframe to GUI

Introduces you to the world of PCs and Windows in case you are new to the environment. This part of the book explains what you'll be getting into and explores how Visual Basic takes the COBOL programmer a step forward in user programming.

Part II: Point & Click Programming

You'll begin creating Visual Basic applications in this part of the book. The amazing thing is that you'll create applications that are full-blown Windows applications and you'll write just a few lines of code! Whereas COBOL is a descriptive and wordy language, Visual Basic is succinct due to its graphical nature.

Part III: Primary Differences

Perhaps Part III is the only traditional section in this book. You'll see most of Visual Basic's major commands related to their COBOL equivalents when possible and contrasted when things don't match well between the two languages.

Part IV: Advanced VB Programming

Some of Visual Basic's advanced and esoteric commands and internal routines are discussed. You'll build more complete programs with the extra power that you learn about in this part of the book.

Part V: Your Next Step with VB

This part of the book is not the end but a springboard that takes you to the next level of Visual Basic programming. You'll learn how to add graphics and spreadsheet-like controls to your applications that would have taken months to accomplish (if even possible) in a traditional COBOL environment.

Appendix

There is just a single appendix that provides you with a comprehensive listing of the PC's ASCII. (Just when you thought you knew EBCDIC by heart, you'll see a new data representation!)

Conventions Used in This Book

The following typographic conventions are used in this book:

- Code lines, variable names, and functions are in monospace.

- Text that you type appears in **boldface**.

- Optional parameters on format lines are enclosed in square brackets ([ ]). You do not type the brackets when you include these parameters.

- Code continuation characters ➥ are inserted in lengthy code lines to indicate that the code continues to the next line.

- New terms are in *italic*.

The following sections help provide highlights when warranted:

Margin notes call your attention to important topics.

Note

Notes help clarify topics and tell you when exceptions might occur.

Tip

Tips offer shortcuts and efficiencies when possible.

Caution

Cautions describe problems that can arise if you're not careful.

Sidebars Detour

A sidebar provides an in-depth look at a topic related to the current chapter's topic. When your attention should be diverted to present another side of an issue or to explore a command further than was necessary in the regular text, these sidebars give you side comments.

Part I

From Mainframe to GUI

Chapter 1

Welcome to Visual Basic

Many COBOL programmers come from a background rich in mainframe tools that provide comfortable environments for writing the "COBOL way." Today, most banks, corporations, and educational institutions use applications that contain COBOL code. Over the years, batch processing, aided by JCL (*Job Control Language*, which did for mainframes what batch files now do for PCs), data access, transaction file processing, and almost every other business application, required the record-processing capabilities that COBOL offers.

You, a traditional COBOL programmer whose programs have made a tremendous impact on the world, are going to have to do an "about-face" when you migrate from COBOL to Visual Basic. Moving to Visual Basic requires not only a change in the language but also a change in your approach to the language. The Visual Basic programming environment requires a new atmosphere that's completely different from the typical COBOL-based text editor. With Visual Basic, you'll design, create, and test programs differently.

By the time you finish this book, you'll never view programming in the same way again. Maybe you need Visual Basic for your job, or perhaps you just want to begin writing Windows-based programs using the most popular and easiest programming tool around. Whatever the reason for making the switch, there's good news for anyone who decides to tackle the challenge— learning Visual Basic is lots of fun!

Here are some of the topics that are discussed in this chapter:

- The Visual Basic environment versus the traditional COBOL environment

- The strengths of Visual Basic

- The nature of writing today's graphical programs

- A brief history of Visual Basic

- The reasons for moving to Visual Basic

Get ready to ride the graphical programming wave...the water is warm!

Why Move to Visual Basic?

One of the primary reasons you're making the shift to PC programming is obvious when you consider the sheer number of personal computers in use today. PCs are blanketing the home computer market and are installed within networked and distributed computing throughout every major company in the world. Technology has finally allowed the PC catch up to the demands of day-to-day business.

The PC's single CPU offers advantages over the distributed resources that a mainframe gives. The PC provides instant interaction with its user. A terminal connected to a centralized computer cannot respond to each user as fast as a PC can respond to its user. Therefore, mainframe and minicomputer terminals do not allow the graphical interaction provided by single-user PCs.

Since the development of today's powerful PCs, especially those PCs networked to other PCs and to larger computers, programmers see the tremendous opportunity for end-user interfaces that were never before possible. The PC's on-board CPU enables the user to interact instantaneously with the mouse and keyboard while background processing sends and retrieves data to and from other centralized sources. These new and powerful interfaces require different programming challenges from those needed in the past.

As you know, *COBOL* is an acronym for *COmmon Business-Oriented Language*. Although large-computer COBOL was the mainstream business language for almost 40 years, the PC has made tremendous inroads into the corporate environment in the last decade. The traditional mainframe-based "programmer at each terminal" environment doesn't exist today. In its place is a variety of computers. Mainframes and minicomputers still exist, but often just as data repositories so that networked PCs can access the data through visual-based programming languages such as Visual Basic.

COBOL's Design

In 1958, the military, with the help of the late, great Ms. Grace Hopper, designed COBOL to be a language that helped the military solve problems in ways that non-military, business-oriented organizations could benefit from as well. Yes, the military requires business-like programming. Think of the inventory nightmares incurred by tracking the military's supplies, clothing, and people, as well as the accounting requirements needed to keep accurate records of all movements and costs.

Over the years, Ms. Hopper went on to become an admiral and COBOL grew in stature and rank as well. Until the development of COBOL, there were no real programming standards. No methods existed that unified the programming process. With the help of the ANSI committee (the *American National Standards Institute*), which set in stone all COBOL standards, most COBOL compiler vendors jumped on the bandwagon and offered ANSI-standard COBOL (called *ANS COBOL*). The industry's adherence to the ANSI standard ensured that companies and programmers who used COBOL wouldn't find themselves in quick obsolescence, as was the case before COBOL came along.

Sure enough, COBOL remained the leading programming language in business for almost 40 years. It was only when technology surpassed everyone's wildest expectations, with the advent of fast PCs and graphical interfaces, that COBOL shops began to seek other tools for writing their programs.

COBOL's strength is its explicit language. A descriptive keyword is used in place of a more cryptic symbol as is the case with FORTRAN (and later, with C) programs. One of the goals of the original COBOL design team was to make COBOL a language for non-programmers. Before COBOL, there were many programming languages, lots of versions of each, and virtually no standards. COBOL's language is explicit and contains scores of keywords that describe exactly what each statement does.

GUI stands for Graphical User Interface.

With COBOL, a person who has never programmed before can look at a program and, in theory, decipher the code and understand what the program is supposed to do. Everyone agrees, however, that COBOL's wordiness does make the language approachable and less technical for the thousands of people who have used it over the years.

Whereas COBOL's strength is its wordiness, Visual Basic's strength is its *lack* of wordiness. Visual Basic relies on the visual elements that are so important in today's GUI world. Instead of typing text in a text editor, you'll be using

Visual Basic programs are small.

the mouse to drag pictures across your screen when writing programs with Visual Basic. There is a comprehensive Visual Basic programming language that you'll need to master, but a Visual Basic program relies much less on its language commands than other programming languages do.

Windows is the platform for which Microsoft developed Visual Basic. It's true that some mainframe programmers fight the shift from the traditional COBOL transaction-processing text-based environment to a Graphical User Interface (GUI) environment such as Microsoft Windows. Obviously, you are interested in making this shift (or your boss is interested in you making the shift!) because you are reading this book.

Despite the fact that Visual Basic programs control data as well as complex graphical user interfaces, Visual Basic programs often require much less programming effort than equivalent COBOL programs. You will design your user interfaces much more quickly with Visual Basic than with COBOL. You are so accustomed to the four familiar COBOL divisions, ANSI standards, sequentially numbered labels, and page after page of readable, structured code, that you may wonder how only a little programming effort with the mouse and keyboard can produce today's robust graphical programs.

Caution

The COBOL listings you see here have been modified to work with the author's PC-based COBOL compiler. Although standard COBOL is used, your ENVIRONMENT DIVISION details will vary slightly from the book's, depending on your hardware.

Listing 1.1 shows a very simple COBOL program that asks the user for an hourly rate and number of hours worked, then computes and displays the gross pay. As you know, even this elementary task requires a relatively long COBOL listing. The program performs simple I/O with the ACCEPT and DISPLAY statements. If the program contained typical READ and WRITE statements instead, the program would be even longer due to the record layouts necessary to support these statements.

This book's disk contains each complete code listing in the book. The file name for each program listing resides in an IDENTIFICATION DIVISION comment. If you use a COBOL compiler that requires a different file name extension, change the .COB extension to the extension required by your compiler. Listing 1.1 is stored under EASYCALC.COB on the book's disk.

Listing 1.1   A COBOL Program Uses Lots of Text

```
        IDENTIFICATION DIVISION.
        PROGRAM-ID. EASY-GROSS-CALC.
        PROGRAM-ID.     EASYCALC.
        AUTHOR. Perry.
        *****************************************************************
        * Computes simple gross pay
        * Filename: EASYCALC.COB
        *****************************************************************
        ENVIRONMENT DIVISION.
        CONFIGURATION SECTION.
        SOURCE COMPUTER. IBM-PS/2.
        OBJECT COMPUTER. IBM-PS/2.
        INPUT-OUTPUT SECTION.
        *
        * Send the output to the DOS console
        * (the PC's screen) to keep things simple
        *
        FILE-CONTROL.
            SELECT OUTFILE ASSIGN TO "CON:".
        DATA DIVISION.
        FILE SECTION.
        FD  OUTFILE.
        01  OUT-REC.
            02  FILLER      PIC X(48).
        WORKING-STORAGE SECTION.
        01  WORK-AREAS.
            02  RATE        PIC S9999     VALUE IS ZERO.
            02  HOURS       PIC S99       VALUE IS ZERO.
            02  GROSS       PIC S9(5)V99  VALUE IS ZERO.
        01  DETAIL-LINE.
            02  FILLER      PIC X(18) VALUE 'Your gross pay is '.
            02  FGROSS      PIC $$,$$9.99.
            02  FILLER      PIC X(21) VALUE ', enjoy your weekend!'.
        *
        PROCEDURE DIVISION.
        Begin.
            OPEN OUTPUT OUTFILE.
            DISPLAY "What is the rate per hour? ".
            ACCEPT RATE.
            DISPLAY "How many hours did you work? ".
            ACCEPT HOURS.
        *
        * Calculate and print the Gross Pay
        *
            MULTIPLY RATE BY HOURS GIVING GROSS.
            MOVE GROSS TO FGROSS OF DETAIL-LINE.
            WRITE OUT-REC FROM DETAIL-LINE.
            CLOSE OUTFILE.
            STOP RUN.
```

To see the equivalent Visual Basic program, look at Figure 1.1 and Listing 1.2. A Visual Basic program almost always requires both a graphically designed Windows interface as well as some code that controls the program's data flow. Don't worry about understanding the details of the Visual Basic program at this point. The important thing for you to note is the difference in approach between COBOL and Visual Basic. Time and time again, this book returns to this kind of comparison, showing you how Visual Basic eases the traditional approach you have been used to for so long.

Fig. 1.1

A Visual Basic program consists of the user's I/O screen.

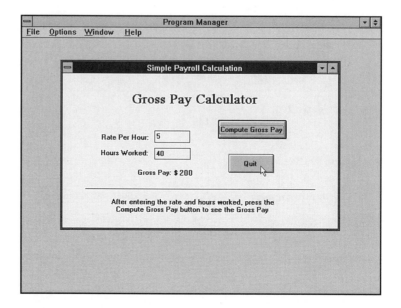

Note

When you write a new COBOL program, you almost always make a copy of an existing COBOL program and delete the portions that will change for the new one. A COBOL program requires too much effort to begin typing a new program from scratch each time. Visual Basic programmers, on the other hand, rarely want to use an existing Visual Basic program as a starting point for a new program. Visual Basic programs are often easier to write from scratch.

Listing 1.2 The Visual Basic Code that Augments the Window's Operation

```
Sub cmdGrossPay_Click ()
    lblGrossPay = txtRate.Text * txtHours.Text
End Sub

Sub cmdQuit_Click ()
    End    ' Exits the application
End Sub
```

Note

Notice that a Visual Basic program consists of both the output screen as well as code. The screen's window is an integral part of the program. By designing an application's window, you eliminate a lot of tedious coding you must do in a text-oriented language such as COBOL.

Figure 1.1's window title bar (the bar across the top of the window) contains a title that appropriately describes the running application. Remember to add these kinds of finishing touches to your own Visual Basic programs.

Tip

If you are new to Windows, you'll learn more about managing and navigating the windows on your screen in Chapter 2, "A Brief Windows Tour for Programmers."

As you will learn in the course of reading this book, Visual Basic offers all kinds of tools that enable you to design program windows such as the window in Figure 1.1. In the way that an artist uses a palette of paint colors, Visual Basic programmers use window-design tools to design and add elements to their programs. Figure 1.2 may look extremely busy (due to your newness to the Visual Basic environment); however, it gives you a glimpse of the design screen and tools used to create the previous gross pay application. (Your screen may appear slightly different from the one in Figure 1.2, depending on your version of Visual Basic.)

Although you haven't yet learned enough to load and run the Visual Basic application, you may want to come back to this gross pay application later. In case you do, these are the file names that make up the Visual Basic version of the program:

EASYCALC.MAK

EASYCALC.FRM

Fig. 1.2

Visual Basic
supplies many
screen-design
tools.

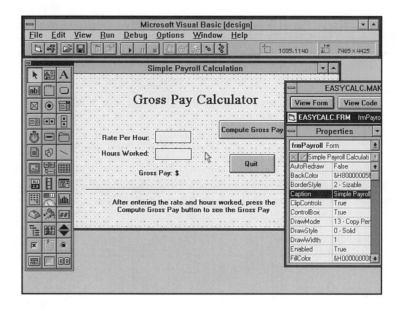

The first file, EASYCALC.MAK, is called a *project file* (perhaps you've heard of a similar term in the minicomputer world called a *makefile*). Often, more than one file makes up a Windows program. The project file contains a listing of every file needed to produce the complete running application. All project files end with the .MAK file name extension. The other file, EASYCALC.FRM, is the *form file,* which contains a description of the program's window as well as the code used in the program. You'll learn more about the files that make up a Visual Basic program as you progress through this book.

What Exactly Is Visual Basic?

This entire book answers the question, but you're ready for some initial insight. Visual Basic was created due to the need for a simple Windows programming tool. You can write Windows programs in virtually any programming language (even COBOL). Using a language other than Visual Basic, however, can be very difficult and extremely time-consuming. Although virtually all Windows programs share common elements, each program uses those common elements differently. This difference in control usage gives traditional text-based programmers nightmares.

Windows programming needs graphical tools.

As you'll see in the first few chapters of this book, users do not interact with a Windows-based program in the same way that they interact with text-oriented programs. Using a more traditional procedural programming language such as COBOL or FORTRAN to write a Windows program is akin to building a house with one arm tied behind your back.

The designers of Visual Basic moved away from the typical programming paradigm when they developed Visual Basic. They decided exactly which elements all Windows programs share. Visual Basic makes placing, using, and interacting with those Windows programming, graphic-controlling elements extremely easy.

The most important advantage that Visual Basic offers is a set of graphical tools that you use to produce graphical programs. Traditional text-based programming tools cannot adequately interpret the user's movements and interactions needed for Windows programs. Not only are text-based programming languages difficult for translating the needs of users into programs, but maintenance of such programs is virtually impossible. Where in the code do you look when the user's mouse movement over one part of the screen works properly, but not over another part of the screen? Visual Basic encapsulates the code for all possible mouse movements into specific areas of the program. The programmer can get to those areas with only a few keystrokes.

You may be more than a little confused at this point. This chapter refers to the visual tools in Visual Basic but also describes the code in a Visual Basic program. Where exactly does the code from Listing 1.2 fit with the graphical window portion of the program? How and more importantly *when* does this code execute?

Visual Basic's language handles data and control specifics.

Visual Basic's text-based code is required to control underlying details that are specific to each application. If you could write every program solely by moving and clicking pictures, you would, because doing so is much easier than writing one line of code. However, there are just too many application-specific details that cannot be captured with graphical tools alone. The Visual Basic language augments the graphical interface by handling data manipulation and program control. The next section explains more about how Visual Basic's code orchestrates the application's details.

A Short Background of the BASIC Language

The *Basic* in Visual Basic comes from a programming language, BASIC, that's been around since the early 1960s. BASIC stands for *Beginner's All-purpose Symbolic Instruction Code*. Although that acronym is almost as long as the language itself, the first word, *Beginner*, is the focus of the language. Professors at Dartmouth College designed the language so that beginners and non-computer types could master BASIC with relative ease.

(continues)

(continued)

BASIC was originally interpretive and never designed to be a compiled language. The authors of BASIC felt that the compilation process added an extra step that newcomers simply should not have to mess with. In eliminating compilation, however, they eliminated speed and power.

BASIC matured through the years, especially once Bill Gates and Microsoft started getting involved. BASIC was too slow and simple to be used for serious applications until Microsoft augmented the language and added powerful structured programming constructs and advanced data types. Microsoft has offered numerous BASIC interpreters and compilers over the years including MBASIC, BASICA, GW-BASIC, QuickBasic, QBasic, and now Visual Basic. Visual Basic was the first version used exclusively for writing Windows programs. (Microsoft sold a Visual Basic for DOS version a few months after releasing Visual Basic for Windows.)

The designers of Visual Basic could have used a language other than BASIC as the underlying control code. BASIC was a great choice, however, because of how quickly beginners can get up to speed with the language. There are other popular Windows programming tools on the market today that use C and C++ as the underlying control language, but these tools are almost out of reach for the introductory programmer. A programmer requires much more training before he or she can write Windows programs with C and C++, whereas a programmer can produce a Visual Basic program right away.

The Code in Visual Basic

Windows contains thousands of internal routines that Visual Basic uses to control I/O and common data manipulation. Sometimes, you need to tap into these routines. You can utilize the internal Windows routines through code written in the Visual Basic language.

When faced with a program requirement that cannot be described graphically, you'll have to resort to writing code. You write a *lot less* code using Visual Basic than you would otherwise write in another language. The code, written in an easy and structured BASIC-like style, interacts with the program's graphical elements and executes only when needed.

Calculations are excellent examples of why code is needed in addition to the program's graphical elements. There is no way to design graphical controls that handle every possible calculation needed in a program. Additionally, you need to manipulate and sort data in many different ways depending on the requirements of certain applications. The code handles these details.

> **Tip**
>
> Actually, Visual Basic's text editor offers a few advantages over the ISPF editor you may have used before on the mainframe. You'll be able to utilize familiar Windows cut, copy, and paste operations and control those operations with your mouse. Also, you may be surprised to learn that the text editor actually writes some of the program's code for you! The text editor supplies the starting and ending lines of the code, and you only need to fill in the blanks between.

You can write Visual Basic code that is just as structured as the COBOL code you write. You'll just have less code to structure because so much of a Visual Basic program is written without the traditional text. Every structured programming technique that you've mastered will pay off with Visual Basic, just as structured programming has paid off through the years with COBOL.

You can write structured Visual Basic code.

In a way, a well-written Visual Basic program is easier to follow and maintain than a program written in any other language; Visual Basic's programming interface keeps *routines* (similar to COBOL's *paragraphs*) separated. Each routine is a pocket of code that stays with whatever Windows graphical element the code controls. When you want to look at code that operates a pull-down menu, for example, you can use the mouse to move directly to that code without thumbing through page after page of a tedious listing.

> **Caution**
>
> You can rarely make a one-to-one comparison of a COBOL program and a Visual Basic program. The two environments are completely different and you must keep this in mind throughout this book.

The Graphical Nature of Visual Basic

Visual Basic programs almost always contain Windows elements such as command buttons, mouse selections, and pull-down menus that make up a true graphical Windows interface. COBOL's code, on the other hand, sequentially and specifically controls the order of actions the user can do. Unless you purchase a third-party and non-standard COBOL interface to Windows (none of which have done extremely well in the PC arena), COBOL's strength is best left to the text-based programs that perform traditional file processing and file-updating tasks.

To produce a program for Windows, you must find a tool that handles all the standard Windows I/O for you and frees you up for the more esoteric nature of Windows programming. In other words, you must use a programming tool designed to handle several possible user actions in several possible orders. Use a programming tool designed to streamline the work you'll be doing with graphical *icons* (those little pictures you see all the time in Windows).

As you'll soon see, when your program needs a Windows pushbutton control (called a *command button* in Windows terminology), you'll click a command button that the Visual Basic's toolbox contains, and Visual Basic will instantly put a command button in your application that you can then move to wherever you want. If you want a larger or smaller command button, use the mouse to resize the command button. If you want to change the command button's color, you don't have to write code to change the color; instead, you select a color from a color selection screen provided by Visual Basic.

Programmers often refer to Visual Basic as *VB*.

Note

Don't worry about standards. Although the ANSI committee probably will not adopt an ANSI Visual Basic standard anytime soon, Visual Basic is in use by thousands of programmers all over the world. Tons of Visual Basic programs reside on electronic bulletin boards, the Internet, and commercial online services such as CompuServe. Microsoft has released several versions of Visual Basic since its first introduction in the early 1990s. Each subsequent version has retained compatibility with the previous version while becoming even easier to use.

Visual Basic is its own standard.

Visual Basic has become a de facto standard by the sheer volume of Visual Basic programmers and the number of programs used every day all around the world.

The Real Reason To Learn Visual Basic

Here's a little secret that you want to keep just between us: Visual Basic is really fun! You'll be creating a huge portion of Visual Basic programs just by clicking and dragging the mouse over icons and Windows controls. You'll be designing powerful and colorful user interfaces in minutes instead of scribbling on layout pads as programmers did throughout the last 40 years of mainframe programming. You'll be using Visual Basic to access vast databases without knowing or caring what the exact database schema design looks like.

Perhaps I should slow down, however, and warn you that Visual Basic is a serious programming tool with which you can design comprehensive and extremely powerful programs. Despite the easy interface and the enjoyable nature of Visual Basic, it is not a toy computer language. Some people from the mainframe world approach Visual Basic with a little distrust and lots of cynicism, and that's understandable. Visual Basic turns the entire programming paradigm topsy-turvy.

At first it's hard to focus on Visual Basic as a whole. When you design a Visual Basic program, you often work on one part such as a menu option's controlling code, then move to a completely different part of the program such as the printer control before finally getting back to the rest of the menu. Visual Basic makes jumping from one program element to another easy. The nature of Windows programs often dictates a strange order of development. Always stay aware that you can write structured and well-written Visual Basic code without resorting to the time-tested top-down design that's worked so well in the COBOL world. Top-down design methodology is still a nice approach to breaking your problem into separate design components, but when you go to the keyboard to write the actual program, you'll find yourself building the program one part at a time, often in random order.

This Book's Approach

The challenge of teaching you Visual Basic isn't the language itself. As a matter of fact, only a little more than half of the book describes the conversion of COBOL commands into Visual Basic commands. As an experienced COBOL programmer, you simply don't need a tedious command cross-reference.

You'll see that Visual Basic contains loops just as COBOL does. Visual Basic contains variables that are nothing more than COBOL's DATA DIVISION's WORKING-STORAGE items. Visual Basic contains a CALL statement that mirrors COBOL's PERFORM statement.

You already know what a loop is, but you don't know how Visual Basic executes loops. You already know what I/O is, but you don't know how Visual Basic performs I/O. You already know the difference between numeric data and text data, but you don't know how Visual Basic programs tell the difference. This book compares and contrasts Visual Basic and COBOL.

> **Note**
>
> Actually, COBOL is an excellent language for introducing Visual Basic. You can take many COBOL commands and find similar matches in Visual Basic. You will discover that you will have no trouble understanding the Visual Basic commands and keywords.

A major part of this book, and a recurring theme throughout each chapter, will be to teach you the conceptual changes that you face as a Visual Basic programmer. As you probably have gathered by now, Visual Basic is not just a *different* programming language from COBOL, but rather a completely different *approach* to programming. Often, you won't be able to take a complete COBOL program and convert that program, line by line, to Visual Basic. Instead, you'll have to pick out various places where a COBOL program interacts with the user, then build an equivalent Visual Basic interface by directly moving and drawing graphical interface elements on the screen.

Only in the actual parts of the COBOL program's PROCEDURE DIVISION, which manipulates data through conversions and calculations, will there ever be a direct one-to-one code comparison between Visual Basic and COBOL. COBOL's strength lies in its screen and report I/O. Major portions of COBOL programs contain lots of code that handles I/O. Your Visual Basic programs simply won't have much code devoted to I/O specifics. Even a Visual Basic program that reads and writes data files requires relatively little I/O code.

Much of the time, this book will be teaching you the Visual Basic approach using your knowledge of COBOL as the teaching vehicle. Often, this book describes a section of code that you'd write in COBOL—perhaps showing you a snippet of COBOL code—and then teaches you how to approach the same problem in Visual Basic. The difference in language approaches makes a one-to-one comparison impossible. Therefore, you won't see many long COBOL listings in this book, because that would simply waste page space and your time. This book will convert you into a Visual Basic programmer by developing your visual approach to programming.

If you are one of those cautious (and perhaps a little skeptical) programmers approaching Visual Basic with a wary eye, I welcome your skepticism. It makes my job even more important. I began my career as a COBOL programmer; now I'm convinced that visual programming is in everyone's future and that Visual Basic is the easiest and best all-around tool to use for Windows programming.

What about Other Windows Programming Languages?

There's lots of debate right now among C, C++, and Visual Basic programmers as to which tool is the best to use for Windows program development. Here's a fact that even the C and C++ purists admit: while the debate rages on, Visual Basic programmers are cranking out complete, debugged, and productive programs, while the C and C++ programmers are still deciding what kinds of subroutines will best interact with certain mouse clicks.

It's true that Visual Basic programs often run more slowly than equivalent C and C++ programs. However, Visual Basic programs don't run much more slowly, and except in math-intensive and time-critical environments, most people never see the difference in speed. If the speed issue concerns you, however, keep the following in mind: computers get faster all the time, not slower. As computers get faster, the differences in runtime speed become unimportant. The costly part of programming is development and debugging time, and Visual Basic races past other Windows development languages by making you a productive programmer rather than one who labors over long program listings late into the night.

Visual Basic is the champ when it comes to being a complete Windows development tool that beginners as well as advanced programmers can use to turn out production-quality code with flair and relatively little effort.

Conclusion

Visual Basic's language is almost secondary to its graphical design interface. In other words, a large part of writing a Visual Basic program is *not* the coding of instructions, but rather the placement of graphical elements on the screen.

The rest of this book further explores the concepts introduced here. Remember that the most important step in moving from COBOL to Visual Basic is changing your programming philosophy. Visual Basic requires a shift in thinking due to the graphical nature of Windows and also due to the way that users respond to Windows programs. In the past, a program would lead users sequentially through the program's execution. In today's graphical world, the program must be able to respond to whatever the user decides to do next, whether that action involves a menu selection, a mouse move, or a command button click.

Chapter 2

A Brief Windows Tour for Programmers

If you have a working knowledge of Windows, either a little or a lot, you are ready to master Visual Basic. A book targeted to COBOL programmers cannot assume that its readers have a preliminary or complete mastery of Windows because many COBOL programmers work primarily in mainframe and mini-computer non-Windows environments.

This chapter takes you on a Windows tour and uses Visual Basic as the ve-hicle for the tour. Perhaps you have run Windows programs before but you have probably never started Visual Basic. Perhaps you have opened and closed windows in Windows applications, but not when using Visual Basic. This chapter's practice will not only ensure that each reader is on common ground for the rest of the book, but also will familiarize you early with the look and feel of the Visual Basic environment.

Here are some of the topics that will be discussed in this chapter:

- Starting Windows and Visual Basic

- Using the menu bar

- Selecting menu options using access keys

- Opening and closing windows

- Understanding the Control menu

- Using scroll bars and command buttons

- Exiting Visual Basic

> **Note**
>
> This chapter explores some of the fundamentals of Windows. If you know Windows well, you can probably skim this chapter with no sense of loss. Don't skip the chapter completely, however, because you learn how to start and exit Visual Basic as well as explore the first level of Visual Basic program management.

Make Sure You're Ready

This book is not written for PC and Windows experts. Although the more you already know about PCs and Windows, the faster you can utilize Visual Basic to develop programs; however, you don't have to be a PC guru to use this book. If you have never used a PC before, put this book aside now and seek some hands-on help through a local college course or a company training class. In addition, there are scores of wonderful books on the market that lead the beginning PC user by the hand from hardware setup to program operation.

> **Tip**
>
> Que publishes an excellent beginning tutorial for PC users titled, *Using Your PC*. If you are brand new to Windows, you'll also want to check out *Using Windows 3.11* for a complete Windows guided tour.

If you've never seen a Windows program in your life, Visual Basic may not be the best place to begin. You should have *some* hands-on Windows experience before starting to write Windows programs. Until you have used Windows programs, you will not know what your own programs should contain or what they should look like. Therefore, familiarize yourself with a Windows word processor, spreadsheet, and maybe even a game or two (Windows Solitaire is included with every version of Windows and is addictingly fun) before using this book to create new applications.

See Windows in a Nutshell

Windows provides a consistent interface.

Once you learn one Windows program, all the rest work the same. That's the *goal*, that is. In reality, *most* Windows programs work in a consistent manner. Every once in a while, you'll find one that does not follow a Windows-like pattern and you'll have to search through the documentation and online help files to find out how to operate the software. The section "Write True Windows Applications," describes the importance of a consistent Windows interface. For now, bear in mind that taking time to learn Windows will pay dividends because you'll reuse the Windows skills that you master from now on.

As you already know, the Windows environment is graphical. When users and programmers first approach Windows, especially from a text-based DOS or larger computer environment, they understandably hesitate to make the switch. It is especially true that programmers feel that they lose some control over their computing when faced with icons instead of a command-line prompt.

Microsoft did *not* design Windows to be difficult for either users or for programmers. You lose no functionality when moving to Windows. Sometimes, a command takes a little longer to execute due to the Windows layer between you and the hardware. This speed decrease is a particular thorn to programmers who want to squeeze out the most speed from every operation. Nevertheless, computers are getting faster all the time and the advantages and power that a GUI (Graphical User Interface) offers does indeed make up for some slight and usually negligible speed degradation.

Start with the Program Manager

When you first start Windows, either by an automatic startup command at power-up or by a command that you type at the DOS prompt, you are taken to the Windows *Program Manager*. The Program Manager provides you with an overview of programs that you can execute on your PC. For example, Figure 2.1 shows a sample Program Manager screen with several icons. One icon's title is always highlighted. In Figure 2.1, the Visual Basic 3.0 icon is highlighted.

The descriptions beneath each icon tell you what each icon represents. The icons are not specific program names but are *program groups*. A program group often, but not always, represents a set of related programs often located in the same directory on the disk.

Note

A file on a PC is analogous to a dataset on a mainframe.

Fig. 2.1

The Program
Manager offers a
high-level view of
what's available
on your PC.

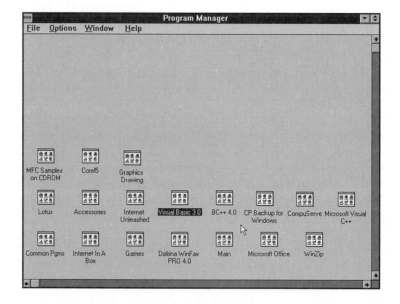

Locate the Visual Basic 3.0 icon in the Program Manager. This icon represents
a program group that contains one or more files related to that program
group. Depending on how the installer put Visual Basic on your PC, your
icon's description may differ slightly. Also, you may have a different version
of Visual Basic. If you have a different version, don't fret because all versions
of Visual Basic are compatible with one another and all offer programming
tools like the ones described in this book.

To see the available programs located within the Visual Basic program group,
double-click the Visual Basic 3.0 group icon. *Double-clicking* means that you
press and release the left mouse button rapidly twice in succession. When
you double-click a program group, it expands into an open window with the
programs related to that group. Figure 2.2 shows how your Visual Basic program group might look once you open the group icon.

The icons inside a program group almost always represent programs that
you can execute or text files that you can view. To execute a program, you
double-click the program's associated icon. In the next section, you'll start
Visual Basic by double-clicking the Visual Basic program's icon. If the icon
that you double-click happens to represent a text file, Windows will automatically start a Windows text editor and load the text file so you can read
the file's contents.

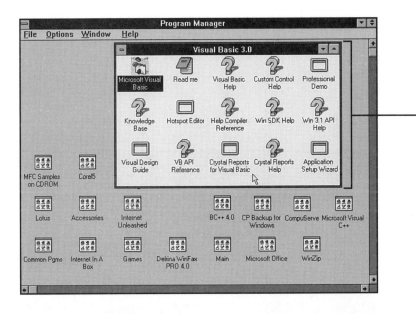

Fig. 2.2

The contents of the Visual Basic program group.

The Visual Basic program group contents

> **Note**
>
> Often, installation notes and last-minute additions to a program's documentation appear in text files that you find inside program groups. In Figure 2.2, the Read me icon represents a text file that offers Visual Basic release notes not found in the manuals. You may have a similar icon in your Visual Basic program group.

Start Visual Basic

As you can see from the Visual Basic program group, several files comprise the Visual Basic system. The file icon labeled Visual Basic is the most important and most common file that you'll execute. This file is the Visual Basic development system and compiler you need for the rest of this book.

To start Visual Basic, double-click the Visual Basic program icon. After a few moments, the Visual Basic screen appears as shown in Figure 2.3. Your screen may look slightly different depending on your version of Visual Basic and how Visual Basic is set up to display its initial screen.

> **Note**
>
> The Visual Basic screen can look fairly complicated at this point. Don't worry because you'll soon learn how to rearrange the screen to your liking. Most of the time, you'll only use a fraction of the buttons, menus, and tables that you see on the Visual Basic screen.

Fig. 2.3
Visual Basic's
startup screen.

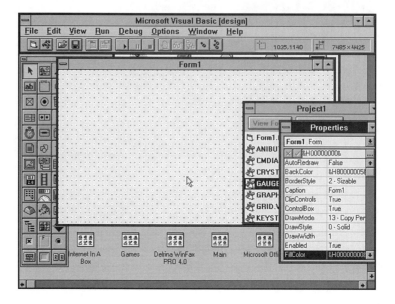

As you can see, there are several Program Manager icons that peek out from behind Visual Basic's screen. You can eliminate these icons from view in one of two ways:

■ Choose Options, Minimize on Use from the Program Manager's menu before starting Visual Basic (you learn how to select from Windows menus later in this chapter if you are uncertain how to do so).

or

■ Drag the icons from view using the mouse before or after starting Visual Basic.

Many programmers ignore the Program Manager icons that creep through the Visual Basic screen. Once you become more familiar with Visual Basic, its screen won't seem so busy and you will have no trouble distinguishing the different parts of the screen. The rest of this chapter's figures don't show the icons in the background so as to keep things simple at this point.

Keep in mind that this chapter will not take the time to explain what the parts of the Visual Basic screen are all about. For now, focus on the Windows operations described here, such as program execution from the Program Manager, menu selection, and mouse control. Chapter 4, "The Visual Basic Screen," describes each of the screen elements.

Learn a Startup Shortcut

If you're willing to make a one-time setup change to your version of Windows, you can launch Visual Basic from the Program Manager using a single keystroke instead of opening the Visual Basic program group and then double-clicking the Visual Basic program icon, as described in the previous section. There are master Windows gurus who don't know this trick!

Follow these steps to shorten the launch time for Visual Basic:

1. If you started Visual Basic in the previous section, choose the Exit command from the File menu (or press Alt+F, X) to return to the Program Manager. You learn in the next section that this menu option terminates Visual Basic.

> **Note**
>
> Use the Alt key in the same way you use a Shift key. That is, first press and hold the Alt key, then press the next letter. Alt+F indicates that you should press the Alt key (if your keyboard has two Alt keys, either will work) and then press F while still holding down the Alt key. As soon as you press F, release both the Alt and the F keys.

2. While the Visual Basic program icon is still highlighted, press the following keystroke: Alt+F, P. Pressing this keystroke is the same as choosing the Properties command from the File menu. This opens the Properties dialog box shown in Figure 2.4.

A *dialog box* enables you to send several kinds of data to Windows.

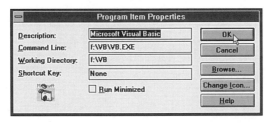

Fig. 2.4
Add a shortcut key to the icon.

3. Press the Tab key three times until the vertical cursor rests after the word None to the right of the <u>S</u>hortcut Key option.

4. Press the letter V. The Program Manager replaces the None message with Ctrl+Alt+V. This tells Windows to start Visual Basic whenever you press these three keys at the same time: Ctrl, Alt, and V.

5. Press Enter to close the dialog box.

With the Program Manager still active, press the Ctrl+Alt+V combination (first hold down Ctrl, then press Alt while still holding Ctrl, then press V while still holding the previous two keys, then release all three keys). Visual Basic starts as if you had double-clicked on the Visual Basic 3.0 group icon. From now on, you'll never have to open the Visual Basic program group to start Visual Basic. Once you start Windows, you only need to press Ctrl+Alt+V from within the Program Manager to launch Visual Basic.

Choose from Menus

Across the top of almost every Windows program is a *menu bar*. Depending on your version, your Visual Basic menu bar contains approximately eight menu options, from <u>F</u>ile to <u>H</u>elp. Many of these menu bar options are consistent with other Windows programs. For example, Microsoft Word for Windows contains five of the same menu options as shown in Figure 2.3 even though Word is very different from Visual Basic. Although the programs differ, they share common features such as file I/O and online help.

Windows menus are often called *pull-down* menus. When you choose one of the options from the menu bar, Visual Basic opens another menu using a drop-down menu list that looks a little like a pull-down shade on a real window. For example, if you select the <u>F</u>ile menu from the menu bar, Visual Basic opens the large pull-down menu shown in Figure 2.5.

The first step in seeing a pull-down menu is to select an option from the menu bar using one of these two methods:

■ Click the menu option with the mouse. To display the <u>F</u>ile menu, for example, move the mouse cursor so that it points anywhere within the menu bar's <u>F</u>ile menu option and click the left mouse button.

or

■ Press Alt and the underlined letter on the menu option's command. Therefore, you could select the <u>F</u>ile menu by pressing Alt+F.

Once the pull-down menu is displayed, you then must select from one of the options. Selecting an option issues a command. For example, File, Exit immediately terminates Visual Basic as you saw in the previous section. If a pull-down menu option's name ends with an ellipses (such as File, Open Project), Visual Basic displays a dialog box that requests additional information from you before it can execute the menu command.

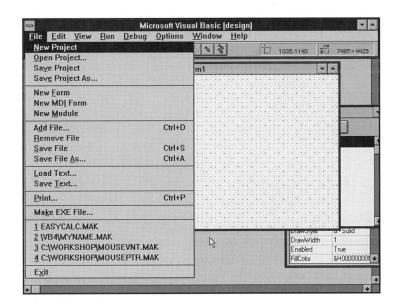

Fig. 2.5
The File pull-down menu.

Once a pull-down menu is displayed, there are three ways to select one of the commands:

- Press the up and down arrow keys to move the menu highlight bar up and down the commands on the pull-down menu. Once the command you want to execute is highlighted, press Enter to execute it.

- Point to the pull-down menu command you want to execute and double-click that command with the mouse button.

- Press the *access key* shortcut; however, not all pull-down menu commands have access keys. An access key enables you to execute a menu command without displaying a pull-down menu first. For example, in Figure 2.5's File menu, the Add File command has an access key listed to the right of the command, Ctrl+D. If you want to add a file (don't try this now), you can select Add File using one of the previous two methods, or you can press Ctrl+D without ever displaying the File menu.

Tip

If you display a menu and then decide that you want to display another menu instead, you can press the right or left arrow keys to open the menu to the right or left of the one currently pulled down.

To close a menu quickly, you can press Esc twice. The first time you press Esc, Visual Basic closes the pull-down menu but keeps the menu bar option highlighted. The second Esc keypress removes the menu bar highlight. If you choose another menu with the mouse while a menu is still pulled down, Visual Basic closes the first menu and pulls down the second. For example, if you choose the Options menu while the File menu is open, Visual Basic will close the File menu and open the Options menu. Close whatever menu you may have open now.

When you write your own Visual Basic applications, you'll be able to add menu bars to the applications that behave like the Visual Basic's menu bar. Your own users will be able to choose from your program's menus just as you do with Visual Basic.

Now you know everything there is to know about menus! Well, *almost* everything. At this point, you probably understand little or nothing about what you actually use the pull-down menus and their associated commands for. A great deal of this book explains what the menu commands are all about.

Review the Mouse

Before going too much further, you need to make sure that you use the mouse in a manner consistent with Windows standard usage. The mouse is a fairly easy pointing and selecting device, and there are only a few things you can do with the mouse. Table 2.1 explains every action possible.

Table 2.1 Mouse Operations

Operation	Description
click	Click the mouse button once.
double-click	Click the mouse button twice rapidly in succession.
move	Move the mouse without pressing a button. As you move the mouse, you see the mouse cursor (usually a pointing arrow) move across your screen.

Operation	Description
drag	When you *drag* a screen element such as an icon or window, you move that element across the screen using the mouse. While pointing to the screen element to drag, click *and hold* the mouse button. Without releasing the button, move the mouse, and the screen element will move with the mouse cursor. You are *dragging* the screen element. When the element gets to where you want it to reside, release the mouse and Windows will anchor the element at its new position.

Button, Button, Who's Got the Button?

Some mice have three buttons, some have two (the most common), and some have a single button. When you need to click or double-click a mouse button, click the leftmost button.

If you have a one-button mouse, you'll click the single button. Some Windows programs use a two-button or three-button mouse, but you drive most Windows programs with a single mouse button. Future versions of software promise to use the rightmost mouse button for certain kinds of selections, but very few programs use the right button at this time.

Arrange the Screen Elements

Rarely does a Windows program start up exactly the way you want it to. When you start Visual Basic, the program displays several windows that overlap each other. (These windows are sometimes called *window panes*, although the generic term *window* is used most often for these smaller windows.) This section explains how to accomplish such tasks as enlarging and closing a window, and moving a window to another part of the screen.

Arranging Specific Windows

Managing the smaller windows on a screen is a required skill for successful Windows program navigation. Before learning how to navigate and arrange windows, study Figure 2.6 to learn the parts of a typical window. Most windows you work with contain the elements labeled in the figure.

All windows share common features.

Fig. 2.6
The parts of a window.

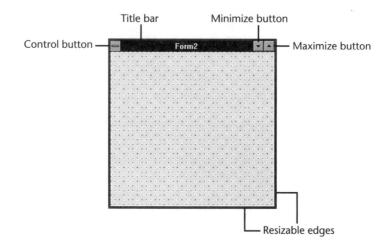

If a window is partially hidden by another window, you can bring the hidden window into full view (in effect, placing the hidden window on top of the other window) by clicking the mouse pointer on any unhidden region. In other words, if you can only see part of the Form window (the large white window with a dotted grid in the middle of the Visual Basic screen), you can point to the Form window and click the mouse to make the Form window appear.

Note

The title bar holds a form's title. Figure 2.6's Form window happens to have the title Form2. You can customize the title to hold any text you want.

You can move a window up, down, left, and right by dragging the window's title bar across the screen. Click and drag the Form window around your screen. As soon as you click on the window, it comes into full view. As you drag the mouse, the window goes with the movement. When you release the mouse button, the window stays fixed at the spot where you released the button.

Resizing a Window

If you press the Minimize button, the window will collapse. Depending on the window's importance and function, you may see an icon in the lower-left corner of your screen representing this minimized window. You can double-click the icon to bring the window back. If you do not see an icon when you minimize a window, you may have to issue a menu command to see the window again. Not all windows have Minimize (or Maximize) buttons, but many do.

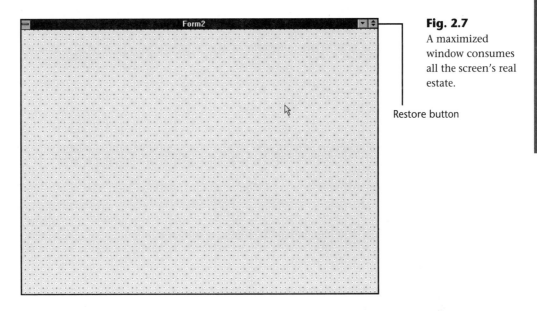

Fig. 2.7
A maximized window consumes all the screen's real estate.

Restore button

If you press the Maximize button, the window will immediately enlarge to consume the full screen width and height. Figure 2.7 shows how the maximized Form window looks.

Once you maximize a window, the Maximize button changes to a Restore button. You can see the Restore button in the upper-right corner of the Form window in Figure 2.7. Clicking the Restore button returns the window back to its original size before you enlarged it.

Tip

You can maximize a window by double-clicking anywhere within the title bar.

From Mainframe to GUI

Many times you will want to change the size of a window, but not completely enlarge or minimize it. Sometimes, you'll just want to lengthen a window or widen it a bit to hold graphics or text better. If you move the mouse cursor to any window's edge, the cursor changes to a double-headed arrow indicating that you can manually resize the window at that location. When you see the double-headed arrow, drag that edge of the window back and forth and the window size changes accordingly.

Caution

If you maximize a window, you will not be able to manually resize the window until you restore the window to its original pre-maximized size.

Note

Although you can resize a window with the keyboard instead of the mouse, this book does not explain the keyboard-movement commands. If you use Windows, you must master the mouse as soon as possible because the mouse offers greatly improved efficiencies when performing operations such as resizing and moving windows.

Using the Control Menu

The control button in the upper-left corner of every window opens the Control menu. Figure 2.8 shows the Form window's Control menu. The Control menu enables you to use the keyboard to access many of the window's resizing features more easily performed with the mouse. Almost every window's Control menu looks like the one in Figure 2.8 and contains the same commands.

Fig. 2.8
The window's
Control menu.

Control menu —

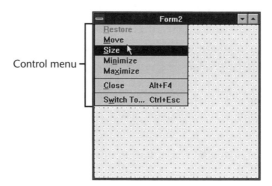

Table 2.2 lists each of the Control menu commands. The menu enables you to control the status of the open window.

Table 2.2 The Window's Control Menu Commands	
Option	**Description**
Restore	Restores a maximized window to its original (pre-maximized) size.
Move	Enables you to move the window with the keyboard.
Size	Enables you to resize the window with the keyboard.
Minimize	Minimizes the window.
Maximize	Maximizes the window to full screen.
Close	Closes the window completely.
Switch To	Displays a list of other programs running under Windows. By scrolling through this list, you can switch from Visual Basic to another program while keeping Visual Basic loaded. You then can switch back to Visual Basic by using the other program's Control menu.

Most Windows programs, including Visual Basic, include the control button in the upper-left corner of the screen and perhaps some open windows. If you use the Control menu on the program's primary window, the Control menu's actions apply to the program itself. For example, if you choose the Close command from Visual Basic's primary Control menu, Visual Basic will terminate and return to Windows.

The Gray Options... Don't Adjust Your Screen!

The Restore command in the Control menu in Figure 2.8 appears fuzzy or grayed out. Often, not all menu commands are available at the time you display the menu. In this case, the window is not maximized, so you cannot restore the window to a previous size. Therefore, Visual Basic grays out the Restore command to remind you that you cannot restore the window.

Visual Basic's pull-down menus often contain grayed-out options also. If you display the Debug menu, you'll see that many of the menu commands are grayed out. Only under certain conditions will Visual Basic activate these commands by darkening them and thereby enabling you to execute the commands.

Master Pushbuttons and Scroll Bars

Windows is full of all kinds of controls you can use to manipulate windows and other program elements. As a Visual Basic programmer, you'll soon learn how to employ and program a majority of the controls in use today. Often, these controls offer a visual representation of a real-world control panel.

Command buttons quickly execute commands.

Often, you'll see pushbuttons in Windows programs; these pushbuttons are called *command buttons*. Sometimes command buttons will contain icons such as the row of buttons directly below your Visual Basic menu bar. If you don't see a row of command buttons, choose the Toolbars command from the View menu (or press Alt+V, T) to bring the row into view. This row of pictured command buttons is called the *toolbar*. Command buttons can contain either icons or text. When you click a command button, you activate a specific command.

Figure 2.9 shows a window called the *Project window* which contains the View Form and View Code buttons. If you were to close Visual Basic's Form window, you could display the Form window again by clicking the View Form command button. A special window called the *Code window* opens when you click View Code.

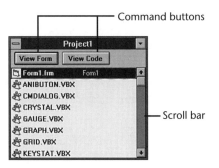

Command buttons

Scroll bar

Fig. 2.9
A window with both command buttons and a scroll bar.

As you work with Visual Basic, you'll often see command buttons that quickly execute certain commands. The command buttons save you time because you don't have to display and select from menu options or remember access keystrokes to execute certain commands.

Many windows contain *scroll bars* because a window doesn't always have enough room to display all the information needed. The window shown in Figure 2.9 contains rows of options from which you'll be selecting once you learn more about Visual Basic. There are more options than will fit in the window at its current size; therefore, Windows displays a vertical scroll bar at the right of the window. By clicking the down arrow, the window scrolls more options into view; the up arrow scrolls the window in the opposite direction. As you scroll, the box inside the scroll bar (called the *elevator bar*) moves up and down indicating the relative position of the scrolled window.

> **Note**
>
> Some windows contain *horizontal scroll bars* that enable you to scroll a window's contents left and right.

Scroll bars don't always apply to rows of options. Many times, a window contains text but the window isn't large enough to display the full text. Scroll bars enable you to scroll through that text. In a way, a scroll bar works as if the window were a camera panning across or up and down a scene. As a Visual Basic programmer, you'll be able to place scroll bars on your application's windows.

Write True Windows Applications

Now that you've mastered the fundamentals of Windows program navigation and control, you have also mastered Visual Basic as well. In other words, you'll be developing true Windows programs with Visual Basic. The applications you create will look and feel just like other Windows programs.

Although Windows is a little awkward for newcomers, you'll quickly overcome that awkwardness. Once a user finally masters his or her first Windows program, that user's knowledge extends to virtually every other Windows program on the market because most Windows programs contain similar controls and menu commands. Each application dictates exactly which menu items the program needs, but there are always common traits across programs. You'll be able to add menus that behave exactly the way Visual Basic's menus behave. You can even add your own access keys to certain menu options in your applications.

For example, you must give users a way to exit your program. You can add a command button to the program so the user can easily quit the application. However, almost every Windows program also provides an Exit menu option located on the File menu. By choosing File, Exit, most applications terminate. Therefore, you'll want to make sure that your application contains a File, Exit menu option as well.

Tip

Microsoft sells a publication called *The Windows Interface: An Application Design Guide* (Microsoft Part No. 28921). This booklet tells Windows programmers how to write applications that conform to recommended Windows standard appearances and actions. You may want to add a copy of this Microsoft publication to your library so you can ensure that the programs you write will follow the industry standard for Windows programs.

The more familiar a user is with your application, the more the user will like your program and use it often. If you write applications to sell, you'll certainly want to adapt your application to the look and feel of the Windows interface. Users don't want to learn a new interface for each program they use. The idea behind Windows is that users only need to learn the interface *once* for all programs.

Caution

When you develop a Visual Basic program, try to maintain the common Windows program design. As mentioned in this section, Visual Basic does all it can to help you produce a true Windows program. Avoid writing non-standard menu lists, designing strange-colored buttons, and creating ill-behaved programs that don't look or act like other Windows programs. When designing your program, don't stray too far from the look and actions of other Windows programs you have seen and used. Although each application is different, they all share common properties and interactions with their users.

Exit Visual Basic

When you're done with a Visual Basic session, be sure to exit Visual Basic completely before starting something else or before turning off your PC. By exiting Visual Basic, you ensure that your program is saved and that you don't inadvertently turn off the computer while Visual Basic is still saving a file.

Earlier, you learned that the File, Exit menu command terminates Visual Basic. Also, you can use the Visual Basic Control menu's Close command to exit Visual Basic. If you are going directly to the next chapter, you may not want to exit Visual Basic at this time, but make sure that you exit Visual Basic when you are finished with each Visual Basic session.

When you exit Visual Basic, the program often displays the dialog box shown in Figure 2.10. After starting Visual Basic, if you make any change, addition, or deletion to a form or Visual Basic application in any way, Visual Basic displays this dialog box. The dialog box is Visual Basic's last-ditch effort to remind you to save your changes.

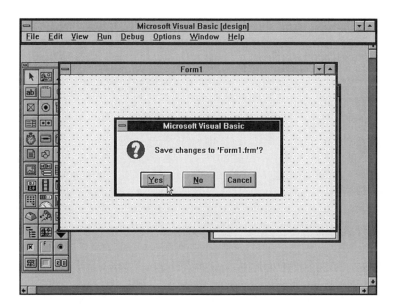

Fig. 2.10
This dialog box will appear if you haven't saved your changes.

The message that appears in Figure 2.10 indicates that a form named Form1 has been altered. The form name will vary depending on which form you are exiting. By clicking Yes, you tell Visual Basic that you want to save your changes, and Visual Basic will display a file saving dialog box where you can specify a file name under which to save the form. If you click No, Visual Basic exits and returns to Windows. If you click Cancel, Visual Basic will not terminate. If you want to terminate Visual Basic now, you can safely click the No button because you made no changes that you must save in this chapter.

Conclusion

This chapter quickly reviewed common Windows controls. A mastery of Windows techniques, such as menu, mouse, and window movements, is necessary to be productive as a Visual Basic programmer. You will only be able to create effective Windows programs when you understand how to use the controls common to all major Windows programs.

Perhaps all of this chapter's material was new to you. If so, you may need more help with Windows before working more with Visual Basic. The Windows environment is completely different from the environments that most COBOL programmers are used to. For those readers who needed this chapter's review, everybody should now understand the same basic Windows skills set. If you had no trouble with this chapter and if you're comfortable with Windows, you're ready to tackle the fundamentals of Visual Basic programming.

Chapter 3

Event-Driven Programs

One of the most difficult transitions you must make when moving from a COBOL environment to a Visual Basic environment is the event-driven paradigm. A Windows program is said to be *event-driven* whereas a traditional COBOL program is procedural and sequential in its approach to user interaction.

This chapter delves into the event-driven philosophy and begins to explore the programming considerations required by event-driven programs. All Visual Basic programs are, by their very nature, event-driven programs.

Here are some of the topics that are discussed in this chapter:

- What being *event-driven* means

- Why it is difficult for COBOL environments to capture and decode the event-driven process

- Why a graphical interface requires an event-driven paradigm

- How Visual Basic views events

- The modular approach of Visual Basic

- Visual Basic's program development cycle

This short chapter provides a foundation on which all your future Visual Basic programs will reside. By the time you finish this chapter, you'll be ready to tackle the Visual Basic specifics.

Change the Way You Think

This chapter is the only real *theory* chapter in the book. As a current COBOL programmer wishing to make the switch to Visual Basic, you are probably anxious to get into Visual Basic's language specifics. Unlike more traditional languages, in Visual Basic you cannot simply replace one command with another and expect to write programs in a new language. If this book started by teaching you Visual Basic without first explaining the nature of graphical programming, you'd soon be lost.

It is true that all programming languages are different. Even more traditional languages such as COBOL and FORTRAN have different strengths and weaknesses. COBOL is great for business applications, and FORTRAN's strength is its scientific and mathematical prowess.

Even though COBOL and FORTRAN are used to write different kinds of programs, a programmer who knows COBOL can pick up the FORTRAN manual and begin to write programs immediately. Where you would normally use COBOL's WRITE statement, you'd quickly see that FORTRAN also has a WRITE statement. Rather than defining the output format in a DATA DIVISION statement, FORTRAN defines the output with a FORMAT statement. Although you would not become a FORTRAN programming expert overnight, you could be productive in a matter of a couple of hours.

Even the brightest of programmers, however, has a much more difficult time making the programming transition to a GUI-based language such as Visual Basic. Programmers moving from COBOL to Visual Basic face the following two obstacles:

- The language differences between COBOL and Visual Basic.

- The philosophical differences between COBOL and Visual Basic. Programmers must approach a Visual Basic program differently from a more traditional language.

If Visual Basic were another more traditional text-based language, programmers would only face the challenge of a language conversion. The dual problem of the language conversion combined with the paradigm shift adds extra burden to anyone making the move.

In the past, how did your users inform your programs of their intent? In other words, if the user had the choice of adding, deleting, or printing records from a file, how did your COBOL program know what the user wished to do?

One of the primary methods by which a traditional program provides the user a series of choices is with a menu. Look at the screen shown in Figure 3.1. The menu is presenting the user a choice of several options from which to choose. The user has only five choices. The program cannot know in advance which choice the user is going to make; however, the program does know the user can and will only select from one of the five choices.

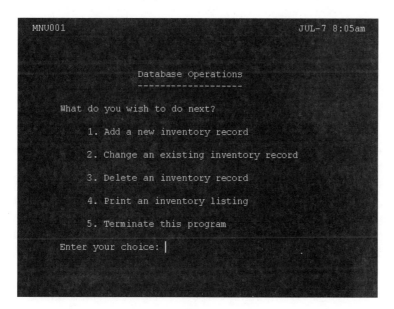

```
MNU001                                      JUL-7 8:05am



                     Database Operations
                     -------------------

        What do you wish to do next?

                1. Add a new inventory record

                2. Change an existing inventory record

                3. Delete an inventory record

                4. Print an inventory listing

                5. Terminate this program

        Enter your choice: |
```

Fig. 3.1
Displaying a traditional menu for the user.

There are several ways to code a user's menu selection using COBOL. Listing 3.1 shows one way using a GO TO...DEPENDING ON statement.

Listing 3.1 One Way COBOL Can Handle the User's Menu Selection

```
GO TO PARA-ADD,
   PARA-CHANGE,
   PARA-DELETE,
   PARA-PRINT,
   PARA-END
DEPENDING ON USER-ANS.
```

Of course, debate rages against using the GO TO statement in today's structured programming world. Programs can be structured and *still* contain GO TO statements despite popular opinion. GO TO...DEPENDING is very straightforward and clear and many COBOL programmers still use GO TO...DEPENDING today.

There are other ways to handle the user's menu selection without the GO TO statement, however. Listing 3.2 shows the menu code handled with an IF statement and PERFORM statements, which call appropriate routines.

Listing 3.2 *IF* Statement Takes Care of the User's Menu Selection

```
IF USER-ANS = 1
    PERFORM PARA-ADD
ELSE IF USER-ANS = 2
    PERFORM PARA-CHANGE
ELSE IF USER-ANS = 3
    PERFORM PARA-DELETE
ELSE IF USER-ANS = 4
    PERFORM PARA-PRINT
ELSE IF USER-ANS = 5
    STOP RUN
ELSE PERFORM ERROR-RTN.
```

An *event* is any action that triggers code execution.

In a way, even this traditional text-based menu shows an example of event-driven programming, albeit the example is archaic in today's GUI world. An event, which is the user's response in this case, determines the course of action. Events are anything, including keystrokes, that determine a running program's next course of action. The user's response determines what the program does next; therefore, this program's event is the user's keypress. The actual key pressed determines what the program will execute.

When you shift to Windows programming, many more events can occur in addition to keystroke events. A Windows event may also be a mouse movement, a mouse click, a menu selection (using either the keyboard or the mouse), a window movement by the user, or even a programmed internal clock timer that hits a preset time.

Not only are there more kinds of events that are possible in a Windows environment, but handling these events becomes arduous at best. Thankfully, Visual Basic supplies programmers with all kinds of tools to work with events. Although scores of events may occur in a program at any given moment, Visual Basic enables the programmer to concentrate only on a subset of selected events required for the program's next course of action.

Figure 3.2 presents you with the same programming scenario as the menu in Figure 3.1. Instead of a text-based environment, however, the menu routine has been converted to match a typical Windows-like environment. Study the figure and see if you can determine all the possible events that the user can trigger.

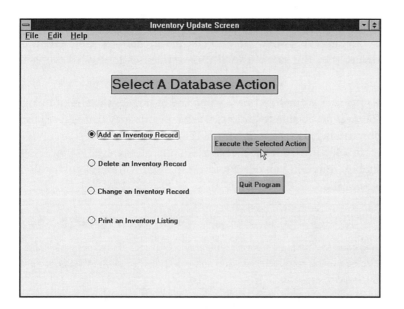

Fig. 3.2
Menu selection
from within a
Windows program.

From Mainframe to GUI

Note

The column of buttons, next to each of the four user options in Figure 3.2, are called, appropriately enough, *option buttons*. The user can select an option with a mouse click or keystroke.

Here are the possible events that can be triggered in Figure 3.2:

- The user can select one of the four option buttons.

- The user can press the top command button to execute the selected option button's command.

- The user can terminate the program by pressing the command button.

- The user can move the mouse over the screen.

- The user can click or double-click the mouse button.

- The user can display and possibly select from a pull-down menu.

- The user can restore the maximized program window.

- The user can minimize the window.

- The user can move the program window.

- The user can display and select from the program's Control menu.

Not all events are user-driven.

As you learn more about Windows, you'll see that there are several additional but less obvious events that can also take place. Many possible events aren't even triggered by the user but we'll stick to the user-controlled events for now.

What is the user going to do next when she or he sees the screen in Figure 3.2? You need to be able to anticipate what events may be triggered by the user. For instance, you cannot be sure that the user will select an option button before selecting from the menu. You know all the events that the user may choose from, but you don't know *if* the user will select any or all of the possible events.

Caution

Writing code to handle so many possible events becomes almost unmanageable unless you use the advanced programming tools provided by the Visual Basic programming environment.

The traditional approach to programming is not suitable for all the possible events. If you wrote an extremely lengthy GO TO...DEPENDING that handled all possible events, you would soon find yourself in page after page of GO TO labels, and even the best-structured program would rapidly end up looking like spaghetti code. Perhaps a long nested IF would even be worse.

When Windows senses an event taking place, it attempts to tell your running program about the event. Windows sends your running program a *message*; your program must interpret that message, determine which event the message stands for, and then act accordingly. There is a lot more work required than simply checking a working-storage location for one of five values as you can do with a text-based menu of five choices.

Part II of this book, "Point & Click Program Design," teaches you how to design Visual Basic programs to intercept these messages and act upon them using a modern approach. This approach greatly streamlines the process of checking for key events and enables your program to ignore all trivial events that you don't want to apply to your program. Visual Basic eliminates the primary message-passing and interpretation functions typically required by other Windows programming languages.

Visual Basic enables you to write routines (similar to COBOL's paragraphs) that execute *if and only if a certain event occurs*. Therefore you'll write a routine that you want Visual Basic to execute only if the user clicks a certain command button or selects the first option. You'll write a routine for each menu option that Visual Basic executes only if the user selects that menu command.

Visual Basic eliminates the need for multiple-choice testing for events, which greatly improves the readability of programs, reduces the amount of code you have to write, and reduces the amount of debugging and maintenance time in the future. People often find that they are more productive when they write Visual Basic programs than they are with virtually any other programming language available.

GUIs Require Event-Driven Programming

The very advantage of GUI programs—the graphical icons, buttons, options, menus, and other controls that the user selects with the mouse or keyboard—requires the paradigm shift away from text-based menu selections to event-driven programming.

Consider this real-world example. Look at the control panel on your VCR, and you'll see all kinds of buttons, dials, and controls. Do you always select the controls in the same order? Of course not. Sometimes you record, rewind, fast forward, and sometimes you eject the tape. Real-world control devices are not sequential in nature.

The whole world is event-driven.

The goal of Windows programs is to mimic the real world's kinds of controls and eliminate a layer of abstraction from computer programs. In other words, when the user is ready to do something, isn't it nice to be able to put a labeled command button on the screen that looks and acts just like a pushbutton that the user could push if the screen contained physical controls? Windows programs behave much more like the real-world systems they represent.

You Never Check for Events

As you can see, an event can happen at any time during a running Windows program session. There is no way to check for these events using the standard IF or GO TO...DEPENDING statements you are used to. If you knew exactly when a user triggered an event, you could use a more standard approach to your Visual Basic programs.

One of the difficult parts of Visual Basic programming that programmers from other environments face is that a programmer's program is not always in control of the user's next move. Windows is more than a pretty interface; it relieves you of the tedious burden of always checking for an event.

(continues)

(continued)

Concentrate your programming efforts on the user's interface and on the data-manipulation needed. Windows will let your program know when an event takes place. When Windows notices an event, the program executes the code you wrote for that event. You never have to check for an event or execute specific event-handling code directly. The event-handling may seem like magic to you at this point (it is magic compared to the old-fashioned ways), but you'll soon see how to set up a program so that Windows and Visual Basic work together.

Take a Modular Approach

When you finally get to the code-writing stage of your program, Visual Basic forces you to write in short code segments. If you've followed structured programming techniques in the past (you have, haven't you?), you haven't written COBOL programs with long single-paragraph PROCEDURE DIVISIONs but rather, you wrote PROCEDURE DIVISIONs with many small paragraphs. Each paragraph performed a single function.

Small routines are easy to maintain.

By breaking your program's PROCEDURE DIVISION into several smaller paragraphs, you make your program modular and easier to maintain. You can quickly locate specific places in your program without wading through page after page of long paragraphs. By its very nature, the code in a Visual Basic program is modular. You simply will not be able to write a lengthy Visual Basic program and insert all the program's code in one routine.

As you've seen throughout this chapter, Visual Basic is event-driven. When you're ready for the code-writing stage, you'll write a small section of code that handles each event you want to respond to. If you don't want to respond to an event, you simply don't write a routine for that event. For instance, there may be no reason to respond to a mouse movement in a particular program. If Visual Basic doesn't find a mouse-movement routine, Visual Basic ignores the mouse movement event when Windows says that event just occurred.

Instead of concentrating on when particular things happen as you've always done, you concentrate on what specifically happens if and when an event finally occurs. Sure, some events must occur before others. For example, Figure 3.3 shows a simple Visual Basic application that converts a user's number to one of three bases (octal, decimal, or hexadecimal). The starting base is

decimal so the user enters a decimal (base-10) number. The user types the
number in the Enter a number text box (the box is called a *text box control* in
Visual Basic terminology), and then clicks one of the three options to see that
number change to a different base.

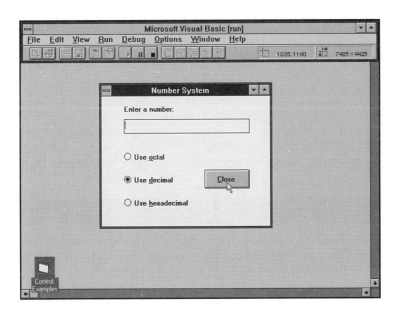

Fig. 3.3
Some events are
sequential by their
very nature.

Obviously, the user has to type a number in the text box *before* selecting one
of the options. It makes no sense to select a base before entering a number.
(This application will display 0 for any base if the user fails to enter a number
before clicking the base change.) You can control, with code, this kind of
event's occurrence. In other words, you can force the user to enter a number
before the user will be able to select an option from the list of bases. If the
user does not first enter a number, you can display an error message to the
user or your program will simply ignore the change until the user first types a
number.

As the programmer, therefore, you have complete control over your program
and the events if you want that control. Many times, however, you don't
need to order specific events. The user can click any command button,
choose any menu item, or select any option at any time. The application's
needs determine whether or not you want to limit the user's activities and
the order in which the user performs those activities.

> **Note**
>
> The program that contains the dialog box shown in Figure 3.3 comes with Visual Basic; it is one of the options in the make file called CONTROLS.MAK.

Visual Basic's Development Cycle

To write a Visual Basic program, follow these steps:

1. Define the problem you want to program.

2. Design the user interface. Decide exactly what screen or screens your user is to see and decide how you want the user to interact with that interface.

> **Tip**
>
> Remember how you used to lay out all your COBOL users' screens and reports on wide pads of paper before ever going to the keyboard? Visual Basic's interface tools are so flexible that you design the user interface at the keyboard. If you mess up, you can make an immediate adjustment because nothing is written in stone until you save the file, and even then you can easily change the design.

3. Determine how each of the interface elements (sometimes called *objects*) is to behave. You will soon see that you can control how an object looks and behaves through its *properties*.

4. Add code to handle each event that can take place as well as code your application needs for calculations and file I/O.

5. Test and debug the program.

6. Compile the program.

Keep in mind that the mainframe batch cycle and even the interactive online compile cycle will change dramatically now that you're using Visual Basic. You no longer have to leave the language to compile the program. In other words, you can test a Visual Basic program from within the Visual Basic environment. If you see a needed change, you can make the change right away.

Note

Look at the running program in Figure 3.3 again. You'll see that the form in the middle of the screen contains the program and that Visual Basic's menu bar and screen surround the running program. If the programmer wants to change the color of the form or reduce the size of a command button, the programmer only has to halt the running program and change that object's property.

Working with Visual Basic is therefore almost as easy as running Visual Basic-produced programs. Microsoft designed a powerful and friendly programming tool when they designed Visual Basic.

Conclusion

You now know that an event is any kind of action that possibly triggers another action in Visual Basic. Your Visual Basic programs can ignore or respond to events. Visual Basic can control the order of events or respond to events that occur in random order.

However, Visual Basic programs don't test for events using traditional decision-checking methodology. Instead of writing scores of nested IF statements or GO TO...DEPENDING statements, your Visual Basic code waits for Windows to tell the program that an event took place. When an event occurs that you want to respond to, such as a command button keypress of a menu selection, Visual Basic executes the code routine you wrote for that particular event.

All of this event-handling may seem difficult still, but the Visual Basic environment makes event-handling very simple indeed. You'll soon see how a few mouse clicks and keystrokes create programs that literally take hundreds of lines of traditional procedural-based programming statements.

Chapter 4

The Visual Basic Screen

Whereas the previous chapter familiarized you with common Windows program features and controls, this chapter describes every part of the Visual Basic screen. Here you'll learn about each window inside Visual Basic and you'll learn what many of the menu options do.

The reason this chapter is so important is that, in future chapters, you will need to refer to specific areas of the Visual Basic screen, such as the Properties window. You need to know what the Properties window is and how to display it. This chapter acts as an online reference, teaching you each of the Visual Basic-specific screen elements. When you're finished, you'll be working your way around the Visual Basic environment just as the pros do.

Here are some of the topics that will be discussed in this chapter:

- Identifying the screen's elements
- Understanding Visual Basic's major windows
- Explaining the toolbox
- Learning the difference between the toolbar and the toolbox
- Explaining the menu bar
- Navigating the online help system

Your patience with these introductory chapters will pay great dividends when you get to the second part of the book where you actually create your first Visual Basic program.

Exploring the Visual Basic Screen

If you don't have Visual Basic running, start Visual Basic now. Figure 4.1 shows a Visual Basic screen right after startup and labels the primary parts of the screen. Your screen may differ slightly depending on the version of Visual Basic that you use and the way you terminated Visual Basic previously.

The next section discusses all the labeled screen components from Figure 4.1.

Fig. 4.1
Identifying the screen's primary elements.

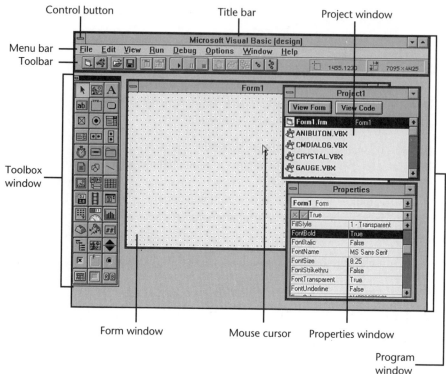

Mastering the Primary Windows

Figure 4.1 shows five of the primary Visual Basic windows. Not all of the windows are actually called windows, however. Here are the windows that you will work with most often:

Program window	Properties window
Form window	Toolbox window
Project window	Code Window

The Program Window

The Program window is the Visual Basic application itself. Windows programs run inside the Program window. The Visual Basic Program window consumes the entire screen (unless you resize the window) and holds the entire Visual Basic workspace. This book refers to the Program window as *Visual Basic* or the *Visual Basic program* or just the Program window. The Program window really is Visual Basic, and you rarely do anything more with the Program window than use it as a slate for writing programs.

The Form Window

The Form window is where you design your user's screen. An application can have more than one Form window, although the first applications that you create will use only a single Form window.

The Form window holds your application design.

> **Note**
>
> Many people write and use powerful Windows programs that require only one Form window. Often, the entire program can fit easily and logically within a single Form window.

The Form window contains a *grid* of dots. As you place program elements on the Form window (when you are creating your user's interface), the grid enables you to align lists and objects with other elements on the screen. Through menu options, you can adjust the space between the grid's dots to align items more closely or farther apart as you place items on the Form window. You can also turn off the grid if you don't want to see it.

> **Tip**
>
> If you don't want to use the grid, turn it off by choosing the Environment command from the Options menu (or by pressing Alt+O, E). This displays the Environment Options dialog box shown in Figure 4.2. Scroll down the list of options to highlight Show Grid. Press N to change the Show Grid value to No, or point to the line and click two times. It's best to leave the grid dots displayed when you first begin Visual Basic to help you align objects evenly.

If you want all screen objects to align to the grid every time you place or move the objects, make sure the Options, Environment, Align To Grid option value contains Yes instead of No.

Fig. 4.2

The grid no longer
shows on the form.

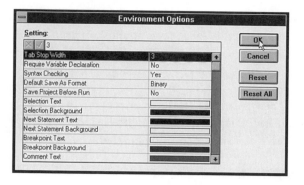

If you've turned off the automatic alignment to the grid, you can still align screen objects one at a time. The Edit menu contains the Align to Grid command, which turns on the grid-alignment feature for the currently highlighted object. When you select Align to Grid, Visual Basic automatically aligns the object, such as a command button, with the nearest grid dot. This alignment is a one-time alignment; that is, Visual Basic only aligns the current screen object but lets you later move that object to another place on the form that doesn't align.

The primary advantage of the Align to Grid command is you ensure that all screen elements align both vertically or horizontally. The disadvantage is that you have less control over the exact placement of visual elements. If you want to adjust objects with more precision than the grid allows, you can turn off the grid alignment and drag the objects to whatever location you prefer. You will get a great deal of practice with placing and aligning objects throughout this book.

The Project Window

The Project
window lists
related files.

The Project window exists for every Visual Basic application, although you may choose to close the window and hide its contents when designing a program. The Project window lists all files related to the application you create. For example, a Visual Basic application that contains two Form windows and some Visual Basic code may require three separate files to form the single application. Often a single-compiled Windows program requires compiling two or more files. The Project window lists every file needed by your application.

Only when you compile a Visual Basic program do those files get transformed and merged into a single executable program. Unless you compile

From Mainframe to GUI

the program, the application's separate files remain separate. The Project window lists the files needed to create the application at compilation time.

When writing COBOL programs, you often use the COPY statement to copy pre-written source code into your own COBOL program. For example, suppose that your company had a standard DATA DIVISION entry that described special credit records such as the one in Listing 4.1. Every credit-related COBOL program you write may need to use this same DATA DIVISION entry.

Listing 4.1   Library Code To Be Used in Multiple COBOL Programs

```
01  CREDIT-REC.
    02 CRED-ID          PIC X(6).
    02 CRED-AMT         PIC 9(5)V99.
    02 CRED-DATE        PIC 9(4).
    02 CRED-FLAGS.
        03 SOLD         PIC X.
        03 RETAIL-STORE PIC X.
        03 OVER-LIM     PIC X.
        03 PRE-APPROVED PIC X.
    02 CRED-RATE        PIC 9V99.
    02 CRED-NUM         PIC 999.
```

If the credit library code is called CREDLIB, every COBOL programmer would need the following statement in his or her program to include the library within their own program:

```
COPY CREDLIB.
```

Using the COPY statement ensures that every programmer's DATA DIVISION properly sets up the credit-related data descriptors. Using the copy library named CREDLIB eliminates typing errors and maintains consistency.

This credit copy library is simplistic. In the real world, companies actually use several libraries for COBOL source code, for ENVIRONMENT, DATA, and PROCEDURE DIVISION entries. Keeping track of these libraries becomes a chore. More importantly, when the library code changes, as often occurs when an accounting change takes place, a maintenance programmer must find every program within the company that uses the changed copy library and recompile those programs for the new change to take place. The bookkeeping needed for source code library maintenance is tremendous.

If COBOL programs had some way of maintaining a Project window, the maintenance programmer would need to look no further than the Project window to see if a program used a certain copy library or not. There are mainframe and minicomputer tools that do help automate the source code library maintenance, but none are as simple and elegant as the Project window.

The Project window displays the contents of the program's project file. When you want to work on a Visual Basic application, you won't have to load each related file individually; you only have to load the project file. Figure 4.3 helps visually demonstrate the Project window's job. Visual Basic makes sure that all related files are loaded for you while displaying a list of those files in the Project window.

Fig. 4.3
The Project window ensures that all related files load together

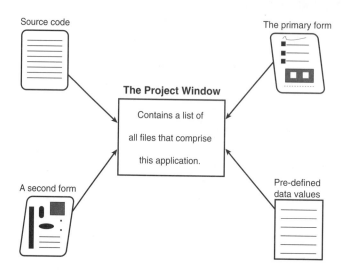

Tip

Close the Project window until you begin to create multi-file applications so the Project window does not take up screen space that you need when designing your form.

Double-click the Project window's control button (or choose Close from the Project window's Control menu) to close the Project window. Closing the window doesn't eliminate or erase the window; it simply hides the window from view so that you have more screen real estate space for more important windows such as the Form window.

If you need to see the Project window once again, choose the Project command from the Window menu. For this chapter, either close the Project window or hide it behind the Form window.

The Toolbox Window

The Toolbox window, often just called the toolbox, is really the most important part of Visual Basic programming. The toolbox contains pre-written Windows objects that you can add to your program, such as command buttons, text boxes, message boxes, timers, check boxes, icon placeholders, and more. Each of these screen objects is called a *control*. Therefore, when you place a command button in a Visual Basic application, you are placing a command button control in that application.

Chapter 6, "Presto, No Code Required!" discusses the toolbox in detail at a more appropriate place in your Visual Basic education. For now, keep these points in mind about the toolbox:

- The toolbox is also called the Toolbox window.

- As with any window, you can move and close the toolbox.

- The items in the toolbox, Visual Basic's controls, are pre-written components that you will place on your application's Form window when you design user interfaces.

Your toolbox may differ from the one shown in this book. Different versions of Visual Basic have different numbers of controls in the toolbox. Throughout this book, you'll see only the most common toolbox controls used in all major releases of Visual Basic. No matter how different your version's toolbox is, you'll be able to follow this book completely.

The Properties Window

Each control on the toolbox operates differently. For example, there is a command button control on the toolbox, which the user can click to trigger an event. Command buttons may have text or pictures on them. The toolbox also contains a label control. A label displays text on the screen but doesn't do anything else. The label can display text using any font, font size or color.

Every aspect of a control that makes that control unique (the control's color, size, action, and so on) is called a *property*. When you eventually place a control on your user's interface screen, that control's properties appear in the Properties window. If the Properties window is hidden, you can display it by pressing the F4 function key. Figure 4.4 shows the Properties window for a command button. All the properties relate specifically to command buttons.

Fig. 4.4

A command button's Properties window lists properties specific to command buttons.

Even the form has properties such as color, size, screen location, and title. Therefore your form may not yet contain controls but you can still see the Properties window. Go ahead and look at the Properties window now and scroll through the list of form properties. Figure 4.5 shows a Properties window listing form properties.

Fig. 4.5

The Properties window changes depending on the control.

You can close the Properties window by double-clicking the window's control button.

From Mainframe to GUI

The Code Window

There is another window called the Code window that you will be working with for a while. The Code window holds code that you write; it is the text editing area where you can edit, change, and navigate through Visual Basic code. Figure 4.6 shows the Code window with code shown inside the window. The View Code command button on the Project window enables you to see the Code window when you need to work with code.

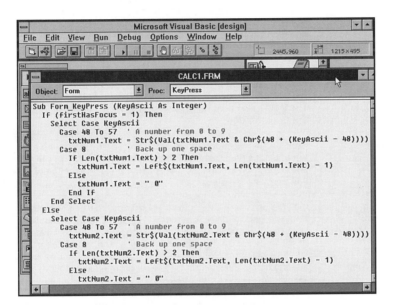

Fig. 4.6
The Code window is needed to hold the code you write.

Note

Don't be concerned with the code inside the Code window in Figure 4.6. The code comes from the CALC.MAK sample project file included with Visual Basic. This code is slightly cryptic and doesn't represent common code that you'll face as a newcomer to Visual Basic programming.

Explaining the Menus

Table 4.1 gives you a brief overview of the eight menu options located on the menu bar. As mentioned in the previous chapter, you'll find many of these same menu options on the menu bars of other Windows programs. The consistency enables you to master Visual Basic faster than if Microsoft used an unusual menu bar.

Table 4.1	The Menu Bar Options
Option	**Description**
File	Contains all Visual Basic file-saving and loading commands. The File menu contains project management operations, printer control, and provides a program exit.
Edit	Contains typical Windows copy, cut, and paste operations for both text code and visual controls. Visual Basic uses the Windows clipboard to store copied and cut material so you can transfer the material to other Windows programs that support the clipboard. The Edit menu also provides you with search and replace commands as well as the Align to Grid command for alignment of screen elements.
View	Provides commands that enable you to see the Code window and the Toolbox window when these windows are hidden from view. The View menu commands also enable you to navigate throughout Code window.
Run	Controls the execution of Visual Basic programs from within the Visual Basic environment. With the Run command, you can test and debug Visual Basic programs without leaving the Visual Basic environment.
Debug	Includes an online, interactive debugging tool that you control from the Debug menu. Chapter 9, "Debugging the Visual Basic Way," explains how to use these debugging menu commands. (If you've never used a debugging tool before, you're in for a treat. You'll be able to request a line-by-line program execution and look at and change data values as your program executes.)
Options	Enables you to change two sets of options. The Environment command enables you to control the way Visual Basic looks and works by changing screen colors, the grid, and Code window options. The Options menu also contains a Project command that enables you to control the way your project starts and behaves.
Window	Enables you to customize your form colors, design pull-down menus for the applications you write, and display hidden Project, Properties, and Toolbox windows.
Help	Provides you with all kinds of online advice and reference material. The electronic help system is so advanced that the only book you'll need with Visual Basic is *this* one! This chapter's last section, "Help Is on Its Way," explains how you can navigate the help system to find the aid you need.

> **Tip**
>
> If you want to know what version of Visual Basic you have, choose the About Microsoft Visual Basic command from the Help menu (or press Alt+H, A). Visual Basic will then display a dialog box that shows you a copyright screen, memory usage, and the version of your Visual Basic system. Figure 4.7 shows the About dialog box for Visual Basic version 3.0. To close the About box, click OK or press Enter or Esc.

Fig. 4.7
Use the About dialog box to find Visual Basic's version number.

Exploring the Toolbar

Although it's easy to do, don't mistake the toolbar with the toolbox. The toolbox is the window of controls from which you'll select as you build user interfaces. The toolbar is the row of icons directly beneath the menu bar.

> **Tip**
>
> If you don't see the toolbar, choose the Toolbar command from the View menu (or press Alt+V, T). Choosing the Toolbar command a second time hides the toolbar once again if you want to do so.

The toolbar is a row of pushbutton icons that performs common Visual Basic tasks. All of the toolbar's commands are available from elsewhere within the Visual Basic environment. However, some programmers prefer to use the toolbar while others prefer to use menus and access keys.

Figure 4.8 describes what each of the toolbar's command buttons stand for. The toolbar command buttons provide a shortcut to performing common tasks.

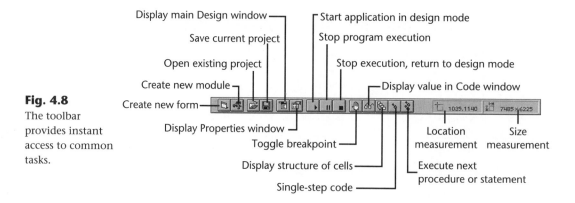

Fig. 4.8
The toolbar
provides instant
access to common
tasks.

You may be the kind of programmer who does not prefer to use the toolbar. Even if you aren't the "toolbar kind," go ahead and leave the toolbar on your screen for your first few Visual Basic applications. Often, this book will remind you that a toolbar button is available that performs the next step. Once you have written a few Visual Basic applications, you can then better decide if you want to leave the toolbar on the screen or free up additional screen space by hiding the toolbar.

Help Is on Its Way

**Online help
provides quick
advice while
programming.**

Visual Basic's online help system works a lot like the help systems in other Windows products. Visual Basic's help, however, does offer a few features that are unique to its programming environment. Therefore, if you are already comfortable with Windows-based help, you may want to skim the rest of this chapter. Don't skip the chapter, though, because you'll need to see how Visual Basic's help offers programmers an additional kind of online help system not usually available in more traditional user-oriented Windows programs.

A Brief Visual Basic Tutorial

One of the first online help features you can access is Visual Basic's online tutorial. Although the tutorial offers only a brief overview of the Visual Basic environment, the tutorial is a nice starting place to get more accustomed to the nature of Visual Basic's program development.

When you choose the Learning Microsoft Visual Basic command from the Help menu, Visual Basic displays the tutorial's opening screen, shown in Figure 4.9. The topics list a complete walkthrough of Visual Basic's major components that you use to design and write programs.

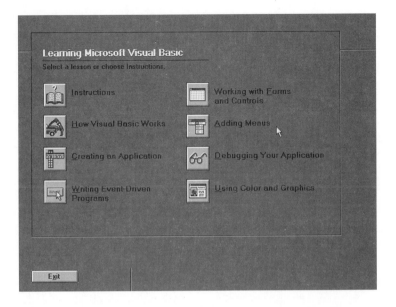

Fig. 4.9
Choosing the
Learning Microsoft
Visual Basic
command starts
the online tutorial.

From Mainframe to GUI

The tutorial enables you to skip around from option to option and take the lessons in any order you want. When you click a topic, such as Adding Menus, the tutorial leads you by the hand with a step-by-step explanation.

The major problem with the tutorial is its lack of depth. Beginning Visual Basic programmers will not learn a lot due to the tutorial's lack of detail and broad overview. Nevertheless, if you want to get a feel for your future as a Visual Basic programmer, you may want to explore some of the topics.

Context-Sensitive Help

The F1 function key provides *context-sensitive help* when you need it. Context-sensitive help means that you can get help on a particular command or task as you use Visual Basic. For example, anytime you display a menu, such as the Run menu, you can press F1. As soon as you do, Visual Basic assumes that you need help with menus. Therefore, Visual Basic displays the help screen shown in Figure 4.10.

When you use a help screen such as the one shown in Figure 4.10, Visual Basic offers cross-referenced topics. In other words, you can jump to additional help on any help subject that is underlined. The lines beneath the topics File Menu, Edit Menu, and so on, indicate that you can get more detailed help on these topics.

Fig. 4.10

Context-Sensitive menu help offers advice for your current activity.

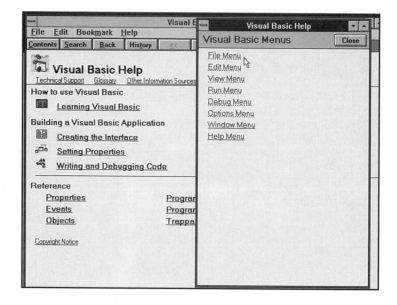

If a cross-referenced topic is underlined with a dotted line, such as the File Menu topic, that cross-referenced topic produces yet another menu of cross-referenced topics. For example, if you move the mouse cursor over the Edit Menu cross-referenced topic (the mouse cursor changes to a pointing hand) and click the mouse button, the help menu in Figure 4.11 appears.

> **Note**
>
> This cross-referenced online help is sometimes called *hypertext help* due to the electronically cross-referenced topics that you can jump between.

As you can see, every topic on the Edit Menu's cross-referenced help screen is underlined with a straight line. The straight lines indicate further cross-referenced topics. Instead of taking you to another menu of topics, however, you can jump to a description of that cross-referenced topic. Go ahead and click the Cut topic and Visual Basic displays a full-screen description of how you cut, copy, and paste text with Visual Basic. To exit the help screen, click Close and press Alt+F4 to return to the Visual Basic Form window.

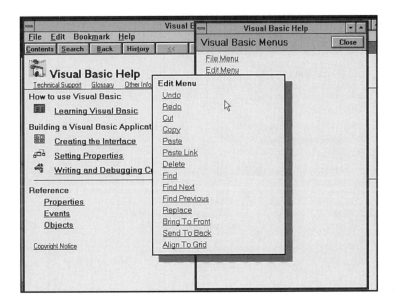

From Mainframe to GUI

Fig. 4.11
Additional help for
you to browse.

Viewing the Help Contents

The Help menu contains a Contents command. The Contents command
displays an overview of the entire Visual Basic online help system. In other
words, the Contents command gives you a table of contents for the rest of
the help screens.

Select the Contents command now, and you see the screen shown in Figure
4.12. If your contents screen is not as wide as the one in the figure, you may
want to double-click the title bar to maximize the window size to full screen.

There is a lot of advice available to you through the help contents screen.
Look at the three cross-referenced subjects directly beneath the Visual Basic
Help label. You see cross-referenced topics that tell you how to obtain technical support from Microsoft (be ready to stay on hold a while!), and to read an
online glossary. Click the Other Information Sources topic to find last-minute
helpful advice that comes in text files supplied with Visual Basic.

Note

The Help menu's Obtaining Technical Support command describes how you can
obtain help directly from Microsoft.

Fig. 4.12

The table of contents for the help system.

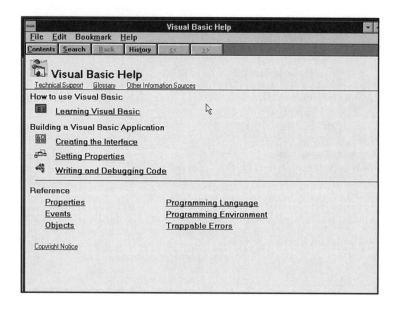

The glossary is one of the most overlooked features in Visual Basic's online help system. As a newcomer to the Visual Basic environment, you may sometimes forget what *control* or *property* means. Instead of digging through reference manuals or losing your place in this book, display the contents help screen and click the Glossary cross-reference.

When you choose the Glossary topic, Visual Basic displays an alphabetical listing of all glossary topics. Figure 4.13 shows the glossary screen. To move to a topic not listed, use the scroll bars to scroll down the list or click a letter command button at the top of the glossary. For example, to see the glossary entry for *shortcut key*, you can scroll to *shortcut key* or click the *S* command button to jump directly to the glossary entries that begin with S and then choose *shortcut key* from the list.

When you click a glossary entry, Visual Basic displays a description box that explains that entry in further detail.

Using Help While Writing Programs

The following three contents screen entries take you though guided descriptions that help you with aspects of application design and creation:

Creating the Interface

Setting Properties

Writing and Debugging Code

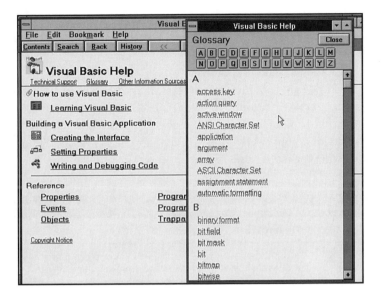

Fig. 4.13
Looking up a
definition in the
online glossary.

As with most of the help system, beginners may not get a lot of help from
these help topics. Although the topics are thorough, they aren't tutorials but
rather descriptions. This helpful application-creation advice helps most when
you use it for reminders and hints during the creation of your programs.

> **Note**
>
> The Learning Visual Basic topic, shown on the help screen (refer to Fig. 4.12), takes
> you on the guided tutorial described earlier in this chapter.

The Help References

The remaining help contents screen topics provide cross-references that will
be useful to you when you get into the "nitty-gritty" details of program
development. You may recall that a property is one aspect of an on-screen
control such as a command button. There are approximately two hundred
properties in all! No Visual Basic programmer can learn all of the possible
properties for all the controls. When you want to know more about a property, or when you forget the exact name of a property, you can click the help
contents Properties cross-reference topic and scroll to the property you want
to know more about.

One of the most important reference help topics is the one labeled Programming Language. Visual Basic is like COBOL in one respect: both languages are
large and there are several statements in each. The Programming Language

cross-reference topic displays a selection screen similar to the one for the Glossary, which you use to get help on any Visual Basic statement.

The Help Contents Toolbar

At the top of the help contents screen is a toolbar that stays with the help screens as you move from topic to topic. Table 4.2 describes each of the toolbar options. Unlike the Visual Basic toolbar, the help contents screen's toolbar contains command buttons with descriptions, so you don't have to remember what the icons stand for.

Table 4.2	The Help Contents Toolbar
Option	**Description**
Contents	A click here always takes you back to the help contents screen no matter how far down in the Help system you have strayed.
Search	The Search command button is one of the most useful commands. When you click Search, Visual Basic displays the Search dialog box shown in Figure 4.14. Scroll through the list or type the first few letters of a statement or object you want help with. Once you find the topic (by highlighting or selecting the topic), click the Show Topics button to get a list of every help subject related to your selection. You can immediately jump to that topic's help screen and then cross-reference other topics from there once you press the Go To command button.
Back	If you move from one cross-referenced topic to another, you can traverse backwards through the help screens you've already seen by clicking Back.
History	The History toolbar button displays a list of help topics that you have traversed in your current help session. Whereas Back takes you backwards through the list of help topics you have looked at, the History command button enables you to go back to *any specific* help topic you want to see by providing you with a list of all the topics you have traversed.
<< and >>	Often, a help topic covers more than one screen. These command buttons move you back and forth from screen to screen when a topic consumes more than one screen.

Note

The Help menu's Search For Help On command performs the same searching operation as the Help Content's Search command button described in Table 4.2.

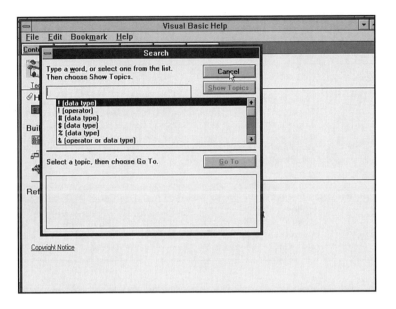

Fig. 4.14
Search for any
topic in help's
entire system.

I

From Mainframe to GUI

The Help Screen's Menu Bar

Table 4.3 describes what each of the help screen's menu bar options does.
The menu bar appears at the top of every help screen provided by Visual
Basic. There is so much online help, and so many ways to get online help,
that Visual Basic almost goes overboard in its advice. Nevertheless, Microsoft
was thinking of you when they provided so much online help.

Table 4.3	The Help Menu Bar
Option	**Description**
File	The File menu serves several purposes. You can load and view any Windows help file if you know the file name. Rarely will you *know* the file name of a help file, however. There are ways to create your own help files and you can use the File menu commands to look at your own files. More often, programmers use the Print command to print help screen text. The Print Setup command enables you to choose or specify printer settings before printing.
Edit	The Copy command enables you to copy selected help text to the clipboard. The Annotate command opens the dialog box shown in Figure 4.15. Use Annotate when you want to add your own text to certain help screens. You can type a message into the Annotate dialog box and save the message. Visual Basic then places a paper clip icon on that help page which you see every time you display that same help topic. When you click the paper clip icon, Visual Basic displays the annotated text you entered previously for that particular help topic. (You cannot control exactly where Visual Basic places the paper clip on the screen.)

(continues)

Table 4.3 Continued	
Option	**Description**
Bookmark	You can assign a specific name to any help screen using the Bookmark menu. When you assign a bookmark to a help screen, Visual Basic adds your bookmark name to the bottom of the Bookmark menu (the pull-down menu grows as you add your own bookmarks). Later when you display help, you can quickly jump to any place you've marked by double-clicking that bookmark instead of having to search or wade through help screens to get to that topic again.
Help	Here's how helpful Visual Basic is: Visual Basic offers help on using the online help system! The Help menu describes the complete online help system. The Always on Top command ensures that a help screen window will remain open and visible when you return to work in Visual Basic. The About Help command displays a dialog box that describes the Windows online help system.

Fig. 4.15

Adding your own annotation to a help screen.

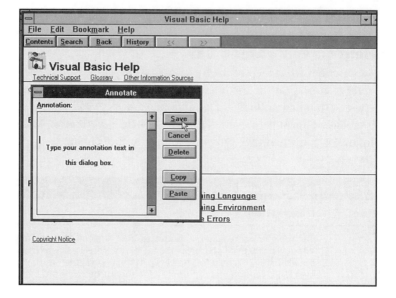

Conclusion

By now, you are much more familiar with Visual Basic's screen components than you were before this chapter. At this point, you are getting more comfortable with the windows and controls available to you as a Visual Basic programmer. More importantly, you know how to get help on any topic that you need further assistance with.

Now that you are familiar with the names and uses of the various screen items, you have enough tools in your belt to begin exploring Visual Basic program specifics. In the next chapter, you'll walk through an explanation of every major control on the toolbox. Before adding any of the controls to your own programs, you must understand how the controls work.

This chapter did not talk much about COBOL. There is a lot in the Visual Basic programming system that simply cannot be related directly to the programming environment with which you're currently familiar. Nevertheless, this book always remembers your roots! Whenever possible, and there will be many instances, this book uses your current COBOL knowledge to teach a Visual Basic concept.

Chapter 5

The Graphical Controls

You'll be coming back to this chapter as a reference throughout the rest of the book. This chapter explains the details of the most important toolbox controls you'll be using in Visual Basic applications. You'll see how each of the controls works and learn about properties of the controls.

In a way, this is a "try it before you use it" chapter. As you read about each new control, you can use that control and see how the control's properties might change depending on the control's current state.

Here are some of the topics that will be discussed in this chapter:

- Running the control demonstration

- Learning the way several major controls operate

- Learning about the properties of the controls and seeing how those properties can change from a user's action

- Understanding when using one type of control is more appropriate than another

This chapter gives you lots of hands-on practice in running a Visual Basic program. Although you don't start writing your own programs until Part II, "Point & Click Programming," this chapter teaches you how the toolbox controls work by giving you a chance to try each of them at your own pace. Only after seeing how the controls work can you be expected to know when and where to use them in your own programs.

> **Note**
>
> You might think I've forgotten your COBOL background when you read this chapter—but I haven't! This chapter covers Visual Basic exclusively because there is nothing close to the concept of visual controls in the COBOL language. More formal COBOL conversion will be discussed as this book progresses.

Loading the Control Program

This book comes with a sample application named CONTROLS.MAK. Loading CONTROLS.MAK will enable you to practice using the controls described in this chapter. You need to start Visual Basic, load CONTROLS.MAK, and run the program while following along in this chapter. To load the program, follow these steps:

1. Start Visual Basic if it isn't already running.

2. Load the control demonstration by opening the File menu and choosing Open Project (or pressing Alt+F, O). Visual Basic displays the Open Project dialog box.

3. Locate the disk drive and directory where you installed this book's disk.

4. Type the pathname followed by **controls.mak** at the File Name prompt. For example, if you installed the disk in a directory named BOOK on drive C:, you would type **C:\BOOK\CONTROLS.MAK**. Visual Basic loads the file from the disk and you see the busy screen shown in Figure 5.1. If you don't see the Form window, click the View Form command button on the Project window to see the form.

> **Note**
>
> Unlike UNIX and other operating systems, Windows is *case-insensitive,* meaning that it doesn't matter if you use uppercase or lowercase letters in file names and commands. When you enter file names in Windows, you can type the file name in any case.

Don't worry, you'll get rid of all that screen mess in just a moment. This program loads several controls on top of each other. Of course, during the program's execution, you won't see them piled on top of each other. This is not a compiled version of a Visual Basic program, so you see all the bad as well as the good just as though you were looking at source code.

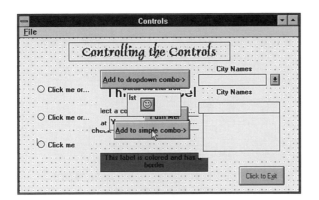

Fig. 5.1
CONTROLS.MAK
produces a screen
that looks com-
plicated and full.

Close the Project window to reduce some of the clutter and start the program. Remember how to do that? Open the Run menu and choose the Run command. Visual Basic begins the program's execution as shown in Figure 5.2.

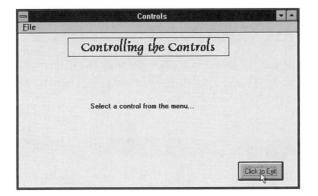

Fig. 5.2
Finally, a nice,
clean screen that's
ready for a user
control.

The Toolbox Controls

As you learned in Chapter 4, "The Visual Basic Screen," the toolbox contains all the controls you'll put in your applications. Before taking a look at each individual control, you need to know where all the tools are on the toolbox.

Figure 5.3 shows a toolbox with labels that identify several of the more commonly used controls. Your toolbox may look slightly different depending on your version of Visual Basic and the controls your installation loads. Chapter 6, "Presto, No Code Required!" explains how to eliminate some controls from your toolbox to make it smaller and more manageable. Familiarize yourself with these controls and their names. The remaining sections of this chapter describe how each of these controls operates.

> **Note**
>
> No matter what version of Visual Basic you use, the labelled controls in the toolbox will exist. These are the most common controls used in Windows programs.

Fig. 5.3
The location of common controls on the toolbox.

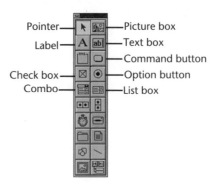

Your First Control: The Label

The first control you'll explore, the label, controls the placement and format of labels on your application. Anytime you want to display text on a window, such as a boxed title prompt or result of a calculation, you can use a label control.

> **Note**
>
> Labels are *read-only*, which means the user of the application can read the text in a label but can't change it.

Look at the screen of the CONTROLS.MAK program. The label control produced the title, Controlling the Controls. The text in the middle of the screen is also a label. You can see that the font style, size, and placement depends on how the programmer designs the control and sets up the properties of the control.

Properties make each control unique.

Properties determine how one control differs from another. When you design an application, you decide how you want each label to appear. Don't get too fancy with font styles and sizes. Don't you think the CONTROLS.MAK application's title label is a little too much? The italics and odd font style almost distract from the screen. The title is fine for now, however, because the strange font style does demonstrate that labels can take on different looks.

Table 5.1 lists several of the most important properties of the label control. As you read through the table, try to determine what properties are used in the CONTROLS.MAK window.

Table 5.1 Label Control Properties	
Property	**Description**
Alignment	Determines how you want the text in the label justified. You can center, left-justify, and right-justify text in a label. The label and its surrounding objects on the screen determine the best alignment.
BackColor	Indicates a *color hexadecimal value* (a strange base-16 Windows coding scheme that determines how colors appear) that represents a screen color. You determine what color appears behind a label's text with the BackColor property.
BackStyle	Sets one of two values, 0 (transparent) or 1 (opaque), that determines whether the form and background shows through the label or whether the label completely overwrites whatever is behind the label. If you want your label to have a background color that differs from the form's color, set the BackStyle to 1 (opaque).
BorderStyle	Adds a single-line border around the label (as done with the CONTROLS.MAK title) with the 1 (fixed single) property value or choose to use no border by specifying 0 (none).
Caption	Determines the text that appears in the label.
FontBold	Determines whether the label's text is boldfaced.
FontItalic	Determines whether the label's text is italicized.
FontName	Indicates the name of the font. Typically, you use one of the Windows TrueType fonts, such as those in Windows-based word processors.
FontSize	Indicates the size, in *points*, of the caption. A point is 1/72nd of an inch. To give you a point of reference, typical word-processed text is from 10 to 12 points high.
FontUnderline	Determines whether the label's text is underlined.
ForeColor	Indicates a color hexadecimal value that represents a screen color. You determine what color appears as the label's text with the ForeColor property.
Height	Specifies the label's (not the text's) height in *twips*. A twip is 1/1440th of an inch.

(continues)

Table 5.1 Continued	
Property	**Description**
Left	Specifies the number of twips from the window's left edge to the label's left edge.
Name	Assigns a name to the label. If you don't assign a name, Visual Basic assigns its own (Label1, Label2, and so on). You'll use the Name property to refer to the control in Visual Basic programs.
Top	Indicates the number of twips from the window's top edge to the label's top edge.
Visible	Holds a True or False value that determines whether the label can be seen by the user when the program executes. You can make the text appear and disappear by changing the Visible property.
Width	Indicates the width, in twips, of the label.

The CONTROLS.MAK File menu contains several commands for you to choose to demonstrate controls. For now, open the File menu and choose Label (or press Alt+F, L) to look at two more labels with properties that differ. Figure 5.4 shows the labels you'll see.

Fig. 5.4
Two labels that have different property settings.

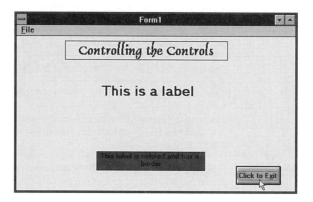

Each of these labels previously had Visible properties set to False but the program changed these label controls' Visible properties to True when you chose the Label command from the File menu.

What other properties do you think are set? Obviously, the top label's FontSize property is different from the bottom label's. The bottom label control has a BackColor property set to a red color. Also, the second label has a border around it so the BorderStyle is set to a single, fixed-line border.

You'll see how to set all of these control properties, both at application design time and with code as you progress through this book. For now, concentrate on becoming comfortable with each control and with the control properties.

Better than *DISPLAY*?

Visual Basic leaves COBOL's DISPLAY statement choking in a cloud of dust. DISPLAY can't come close to setting font size, color, and appearance of program output as can the label control and its properties. Even the formatting capability of WRITE is primitive when compared to label controls.

Many COBOL programmers use screen-generating tools, but such tools often do little more than determine color and placement of text. Although COBOL's screen output capability is more limited than Visual Basic's, you still have to get used to setting properties to take advantage of Visual Basic's label power. Also, you always use COBOL's DISPLAY and WRITE statements inside code, whereas, you set many of Visual Basic's control properties at the time you draw and design the application's output window. Knowing when to change property values at design time and when to change them through code will be one of the learning challenges you face throughout this book.

When you display a control using the File menu, you can get rid of that control by choosing File again. Anytime you open the File menu, the program sets all of the application's Visible control properties to False—so you begin with a clean window that's free of controls.

Go ahead and open the File menu again. When it appears, the two labels go away and you're ready to explore the next control.

The Text Box Control

Visual Basic supplies several ways to get user input, and one of the most common ways is with the text box control. The text box control is powerful because it works almost like a mini-word processor; it lets the user type, backspace, edit, insert, and delete text inside the control. Not only can the user enter text in a text box control, but you can specify a default text value that the user can keep or change. The user can choose to keep the default value, change the default value, or type a completely new value in the text box.

Text box controls accept user input.

You can control the way the text looks inside the control with the text box control's many properties. Table 5.2 lists several of the most common text box control properties.

Note

Many of the text box control properties are the same as the label control properties; both controls determine how text appears on a program's Form window.

Table 5.2 Text Box Control Properties

Property	Description
Alignment	Determines how the text in the text box control justifies. You can center, left-justify, and right-justify text in a text box. The text box and its surrounding objects on the screen determine the best alignment to use.
BackColor	Indicates a color hexadecimal value that represents a screen color. You determine what color appears behind a text box control's text with the BackColor property.
BorderStyle	Adds a single-line border around the text box or chooses to use no border. A border sometimes helps show the user how much input is desired.
FontBold	Determines whether the text in the text box is boldfaced.
FontItalic	Determines whether the text is italicized.
FontName	Indicates the name of the text font. Typically, you'll use one of the Windows TrueType fonts such as those in Windows word processors.
FontSize	Indicates the size, in points, of the text.
FontUnderline	Determines whether the text is underlined.
ForeColor	Indicates a color hexadecimal value that represents a screen color. You determine what color appears as the text box's text with the ForeColor property.
Height	Specifies the text box's (not the actual text's) height in twips.
Left	Specifies the number of twips from the window's left edge to the text box's left edge.
MaxLength	Sets the text box width. If you set the MaxLength property to 0, the user can enter as much text as she wants inside the text box. You can limit the number of characters that the user can type, however, by setting the MaxLength property to a value other than 0.

Property	Description
MultiLine	Determines if a text box can contain multiple lines. If set to True, the user can enter more than one line of text (each line separated when the user presses Enter) in the text box control. If set to False, the user can enter only a single line of text and finish by pressing Enter.
Name	Indicates the name you assign to the text box. If you don't assign a name, Visual Basic assigns its own (Text1, Text2, and so on) as you add text boxes. You use the Name property to refer to the control in Visual Basic programs.
ScrollBars	Specifies whether or not you want scroll bars to appear in the text box, vertical scroll bars only, horizontal scroll bars only, or both. The amount of text you allow in the text box determines whether you want to provide scroll bars.
Text	Indicates the initial default value of the text box. If you leave the Text property blank, the user sees an empty text box when the application executes. If you specify an initial default Text value, the user sees that value in the text box when the program runs, and the user can keep or change the value.
Top	Indicates the number of twips from the window's top edge to the text box's top edge.
Visible	Determines whether the text box can be seen by the user (if True) or not (if False) when the program executes. You can make the text box appear and disappear by changing the Visible property.
Width	Indicates the width, in twips, of the text box.

Look at the CONTROLS.MAK text box by opening the File menu and choosing Text Box. You see the text box shown in Figure 5.5. The default text, You can change this text..., appears in the text box. Unlike a label control, you as the user can change the text box's contents. Use the Delete, Insert, and arrow keys to move back and forth to change the text.

After you enter new text in a text box control, the text stays in the text box unless you write code that deletes it. For example, close the text box by opening the File menu again (or pressing Alt+F). As with all the controls, the File menu code sets all Visible properties to False. From the File menu, choose the Text Box command again. You see the text box with the changes you made to the text still in effect.

As you now know, the COBOL output statements DISPLAY and WRITE are limited compared to the Visual Basic label control. In a like manner, COBOL's ACCEPT input statement does not provide the graphical user-input power that

Visual Basic's text box controls provide. The text box property values let the text box behave just the way you want it to behave.

Fig. 5.5
A text box control that the user can change.

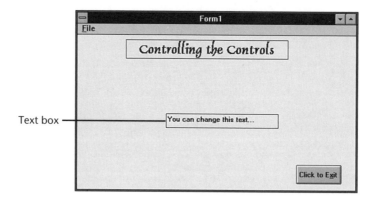

Text box ——

Command Button Controls

Command buttons are probably the most popular Windows control in use. Command buttons mimic real-world pushbuttons. When "pressed" (with the mouse or keyboard), the user sees the command button graphically press inward on the screen and a corresponding action then occurs.

You can supply command buttons so your users can trigger events when they're ready. For example, you might place a command button on a program's form window, labeled Print, that the user can press when ready for a printed listing of some kind.

As with every Visual Basic control, command buttons take on several different kinds of property values. Table 5.3 lists the most common command button control property values.

Table 5.3 Command Button Properties	
Property	**Description**
BackColor	Indicates a color hexadecimal value that represents the color that appears as a dotted line inside the command button when the user clicks the button. The actual color of the command button does not change from its typical Windows-gray color.
Caption	Determines the label that appears on the command button.

Property	Description
Default	Sets the command button's default state. If True, the command button is the form's default button. Only one command button can have a True Default property at the same time. If more than one command button appears on the form, the command button that has the *focus* is the one with a True Default property. (The command button with the focus is the one that is activated next unless the user presses Tab to send the focus to another command button or control.) Unless the user selects another command button, the Default command button will be pressed when the user presses the Enter key.
FontBold	Determines whether the command button's text is boldfaced.
FontItalic	Determines whether the command button's text is italicized.
FontName	Indicates the name of the command button's text font. Typically, you use one of the Windows TrueType fonts such as those in Windows word processors.
FontSize	Indicates the size, in points, of the command button's text.
FontUnderline	Determines whether the command button's text is underlined.
Height	Specifies the command button's height in twips.
Left	Specifies the number of twips from the window's left edge to the command button's left edge.
Name	Assigns a name to the command button. If you don't assign a name, Visual Basic assigns its own (Command1, Command2, and so on) as you add command buttons. You use the Name property to refer to the control in Visual Basic programs.
Top	Indicates the number of twips from the window's top edge to the command button's top edge.
Visible	Determines whether the command button can be seen by the user (if True) or not (if False) when the program executes. You can make the command button appear and disappear by changing the Visible property.
Width	Indicates the width, in twips, of the command button control.

To see a good example of how you can program command buttons, in the CONTROLS.MAK menu, open the File menu and choose Command Button. Figure 5.6 shows the command button that appears.

Fig. 5.6

Press the command button to see a message.

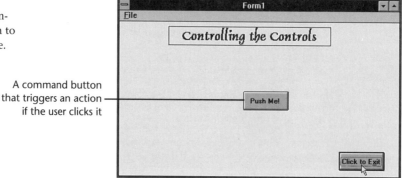

A command button that triggers an action if the user clicks it

When you click the command button, the following two things occur:

■ The command button's caption changes to Thanks!.

and

■ A beep sounds.

As you'll see in this book, you can change command button properties, such as the Caption property, through code. Command buttons are extremely useful for applications that need the user's response before continuing. Visual Basic also enables you to provide access key shortcuts to command buttons that let your users access a command button by pressing an Alt keyboard combination.

Tip

Always include a command button that mimics the operation of opening the File menu and choosing Exit. In other words, give the user a quick exit to the application through the use of a command button. The Click to Exit command button in the lower-right corner immediately terminates the program if the user clicks it.

Get rid of the command button by opening the File menu now. The next section explains another control called check boxes.

Multiple Selections with Check Boxes

Check boxes offer a simple way for users to select more than one option from a list of options. For example, if you wrote an application to find out the user's top three favorite foods from a choice of ten that you display on the screen, you could represent the user's three selections with check box controls.

Open the <u>F</u>ile menu and choose <u>C</u>heck Boxes. You see the list of three check boxes shown in Figure 5.7. Move the arrow cursor over one of the check boxes and click the mouse. An X appears in the box next to the check box description (called *selecting* the check box). Click again on the check box and the X disappears (called *deselecting* the check box). You can click one, two, or all three check boxes. The Value property becomes True when the user selects the check box and False when the user deselects the check box. Table 5.4 explains several check box control properties including Value.

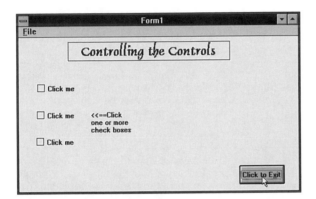

Fig. 5.7
Check box controls let the user pick and choose.

Table 5.4 Check Box Control Properties

Property	Description
Alignment	Determines if the box containing an X is to the left (with the property value of 0—Left Justify) or to the right (with the value 1—Right Justify) of the check box caption text.
BackColor	Indicates a color hexadecimal value that represents a screen color. You determine what color appears behind a check box control's caption with the BackColor property.
Caption	Determines the label that appears next to the check box.
FontBold	Determines whether the check box caption is boldfaced.
FontItalic	Determines whether the check box caption is italicized.
FontName	Indicates the name of the check box caption font. Typically, you use one of the Windows TrueType fonts such as those in Windows word processors.
FontSize	Indicates the size, in points, of the check box caption.
FontUnderline	Determines whether the check box caption is underlined.

(continues)

Table 5.4   Continued

Property	Description
Height	Specifies the check box's height in twips.
Left	Specifies the number of twips from the window's left edge to the check box's left edge.
Name	Assigns the name to the check box. If you don't assign a name, Visual Basic assigns its own (Check1, Check2, and so on) as you add check boxes. You use the Name property to refer to the control in Visual Basic programs.
Top	Indicates the number of twips from the window's top edge to the check box's top edge.
Value	Holds the value of the check box's checked state. 0 (Unchecked) if the check box is not selected. 1 (Checked) if the check box is selected. You can also assign 2 (Grayed) if you want the check box to be grayed out—for when a check box becomes ineligible for selecting due to a data problem.
Visible	Determines whether the check box can be seen by the user (if True) or not (if False) when the program executes. You can make the check box appear and disappear by changing the Visible property.
Width	Indicates the width, in twips, of the check box control.

Re-Focus

Earlier in this chapter, in the section "Command Button Controls," the term focus was defined. The focus is the most active control. Only one control can have the focus at any one time. For example, when you first start CONTROLS.MAK, the Click to Exit command button in the lower-right corner has the focus. If, while that command button had the focus, the user pressed Enter, the program would terminate. The control with the focus is the one executed by pressing Enter.

Display the three check box controls once again if they no longer appear on your screen. Instead of clicking one or more of the check boxes, press Tab several times. As you press Tab, the focus moves from the command button to each of the three check boxes in turn. If you press Enter while one of the check boxes has the focus, you select that check box. If the check box is already selected, pressing Enter deselects the check box.

You learn how to control the focus through the Visual Basic programming language as you progress through this book. You also learn how to control the focus order as the user presses Tab.

When you're done selecting and deselecting check boxes, open the File menu once again to make the check boxes disappear. You're now ready to tackle the next control.

Option Buttons: Mutually Exclusive

Option button controls behave almost exactly as check box controls. You can display one or more option buttons on a form window and the user can use the mouse (or the keyboard) to select or deselect option buttons.

Unlike check boxes, however, you can select only one option button control at a time. In other words, option buttons are *mutually exclusive*. Open the File menu and choose Option Buttons. Click the various option buttons you see (see Fig. 5.8). Select one of the three option buttons to make the option active. Select another and Visual Basic deselects the first one.

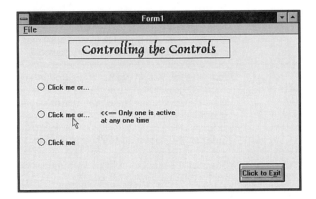

Fig. 5.8
Option button controls let the user pick one of the options.

> **Note**
>
> Have you ever seen a radio dial that has pushbutton station selections? Because only one button stays in at a time, you can only play one station at a time. Option button controls are just like those radio selection buttons.

Through advanced Visual Basic form design, there are ways to create groups of option buttons that appear at the same time on a form. Your users can select any option button in a group.

The option button control properties are similar to check box properties, as Table 5.5 shows.

Table 5.5 Option Button Control Properties	
Property	**Description**
Alignment	Determines if the circle containing the select dot is to the left (with the property value of 0—Left Justify) or to the right (with the value 1—Right Justify) of the option button caption.
BackColor	Indicates a color hexadecimal value that represents a screen color. You determine what color appears behind an option button control caption with the BackColor property.
Caption	Determines the label that appears next to the option button.
FontBold	Determines whether the option button caption is boldfaced.
FontItalic	Determines whether the option button caption is italicized.
FontName	Indicates the name of the option button caption font. Typically, you use one of the Windows TrueType fonts such as those in Windows word processors.
FontSize	Indicates the size, in points, of the option button caption.
FontUnderline	Determines whether the option button caption is underlined.
Height	Specifies the option button height in twips.
Left	Specifies the number of twips from the window's left edge to the option button's left edge.
Name	Assigns a name to the option button. If you don't assign a name, Visual Basic assigns its own (Option1, Option2, and so on) as you add option buttons. You use the Name property to refer to the control in Visual Basic programs.
Top	Indicates the number of twips from the window's top edge to the option button's top edge.
Value	Determines the option button's selected state. The state is True if the user deselects the option button.
Visible	Determines whether the option button can be seen by the user (if True) or not (if False) when the program executes. You can make the option button appear and disappear by changing the Visible property.
Width	Indicates the width, in twips, of the option button control.

Open the File menu to get rid of the option buttons and prepare for the next control, the list box control.

Providing List Controls for Data

Visual Basic offers the following three ways for you to present your user with a list of possible choices:

- List box controls

- Simple combo box controls

- Drop-down combo box controls

The list box control is the only one that does not enable the user to add items to the list. However, it's a convenient way to display a list of choices from which the user can choose; list box controls allow the user to scroll through the choices if needed.

Open the File menu and choose List Box Control. A list box appears (see Fig. 5.9). Scroll through the list and select one of the names. Visual Basic highlights the name. Through programming, your running application can tell when the user selects one of the values from the list, and your application can continue processing with the user's selection.

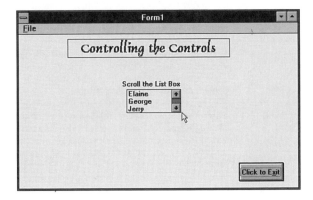

Fig. 5.9
The list box can contain many items because of the scroll bars.

You may fill list box control items through Visual Basic code only. The user, however, cannot directly add to the items in a list box control. Table 5.6 describes several of the list box control properties you can set and test for in your Visual Basic programs.

Table 5.6 List Box Control Properties

Property	Description
BackColor	Indicates a color hexadecimal value that represents a screen color. You determine what color appears in the background of a list box caption with the BackColor property.
FontBold	Determines whether the option list box items are boldfaced.
FontItalic	Determines whether the list box items are italicized.
FontName	Indicates the name of the font in the list box. Typically, you use one of the Windows TrueType fonts such as those in Windows word processors.
FontSize	Indicates the size, in points, of the list box's items.
FontUnderline	Determines whether the list box items are underlined.
Height	Specifies the list box's height in twips.
Left	Specifies the number of twips from the window's left edge to the list box's left edge.
MultiSelect	Sets a selection description to one of three possible values depending on how you want the user to select values. 0 (None) means the user cannot select values from the list; the contents are simply informative for the user. 1 (Simple) means the user can only select one item from the items in the list box. 2 (Extended) means the user can select more than one item from the list by using the Shift and Ctrl keys in conjunction with the mouse and Enter.
Name	Assigns a name to the list box. If you don't assign a name, Visual Basic assigns its own (List1, List2, and so on) as you add list boxes. You use the Name property to refer to the control in Visual Basic programs.
Sorted	Determines how Visual Basic keeps items in a list box sorted. If True, Visual Basic keeps the items in a list box sorted even if you add random values with code at runtime. If False, the items appear in the list box in the same order that you added the items to the list box.
Top	Indicates the number of twips from the window's top edge to the list box's top edge.
Visible	Determines whether the list box can be seen by the user (if True) or not (if False) when the program executes. You can make the list box appear and disappear by changing the Visible property.
Width	Indicates the width, in twips, of the list box control.

When you are done scrolling through the items in the list box, open the File menu to prepare for the next control.

> **Note**
>
> If the list box Height property is large enough to display all the list box values, Visual Basic does not display scroll bars at the side of the list box.

User-Generated List Boxes: Combos

There are two additional kinds of list boxes called *simple combo boxes* and *drop-down combo boxes*. Each control provides a different way for the user to add items to a list, or to select items from an existing list. In a way, both of these new kinds of combo controls are similar to the list box control in the previous section. The user, however, can enter values directly into the list using a combo box.

Open the File menu and choose Simple Combo Box. You see a simple combo box control appear. Nothing is in the simple combo box at first, but you can add items. Type **Dallas** to enter a city name in the simple combo box. Click the Add to Simple Combo button (or press Alt+A). Visual Basic immediately adds Dallas to the list. Type **New York City** and then click the Add to Simple Combo button. Continue by adding Miami to the list. Your screen should look like Figure 5.10.

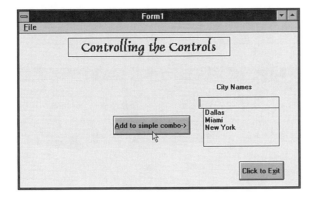

Fig. 5.10
The simple combo control contains the added items.

Note

If you keep adding city names, Visual Basic eventually adds scroll bars to the simple combo box so the user can scroll through the items in the list. Note also the names are in alphabetical order because the Sorted property is set to True.

When you want to give the user a chance to choose from a list of items, or add *another* item to the list, the simple combo is the perfect control. Notice that the city names appear in sorted order. The Sorted property determines whether Visual Basic keeps simple combo items alphabetized.

After adding items to the simple combo box, open the File menu and choose Dropdown Combo. A drop-down combo box takes less space on the screen than the simple combo box; the drop-down combo usually consumes only a single line of screen (unless the user wants to display the entire list of items in the drop-down combo). As before, type **Dallas**, then choose the Add to Dropdown Combo button (or press Alt+A). Continue by adding **New York City** and **Miami** in the same manner.

Tip

The drop-down combo does not expand to show all items in the list. The user can click the down arrow (located to the right of the data-entry field) to see the list of items in the combo, as shown in Figure 5.11. Therefore, you use the drop-down as well as the simple combo when you want to give the user a chance to select an item from a list or add another item to the list. Use the drop-down combo when screen space is limited and use the simple combo when you can afford the space to display one or more items from the list.

Fig. 5.11
An open drop-down combo control.

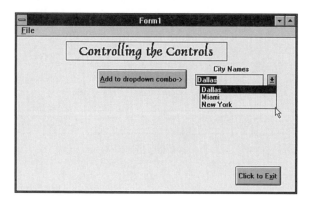

You use the same control on the toolbox to add both the simple combo and the drop-down combo to your form. The Style property determines whether the resulting combo box looks like a simple combo or a drop-down combo. Table 5.7 explains several other combo properties in addition to the Style property.

Table 5.7	Combo Control Properties
Property	**Description**
BackColor	Indicates a color hexadecimal value that represents a screen color. You determine what color appears in the background of a combo's item list with the BackColor property.
FontBold	Determines whether the combo box items are boldfaced.
FontItalic	Determines whether the combo box items are italicized.
FontName	Indicates the name of the combo content's font. Typically, you use one of the Windows TrueType fonts such as those in Windows word processors.
FontSize	Indicates the size, in points, of the combo box items.
FontUnderline	Determines whether the combo box text is underlined.
Height	Specifies the combo box height in twips.
Left	Specifies the number of twips from the window's left edge to the combo box left edge.
Name	Assigns a name to the combo box. If you don't assign a name, Visual Basic assigns its own (Combo1, Combo2, and so on) as you add combos. You use the Name property to refer to the control in Visual Basic programs.
Sorted	Determines how Visual Basic keeps items in a combo box sorted. If True, Visual Basic keeps the items in a combo list sorted even if the user adds random values at runtime. If False, the items appear in the combo box list in the same order that you added the items to the list box.
Style	Describes the type of combo box. If 0 (Dropdown Combo), the combo becomes a drop-down list of items that is normally closed. If 1 (Simple Combo), the combo becomes a simple combo box. The user can select from either kind of combo or enter a new item into the combo's list. If 3 (Dropdown List), that makes the drop-down combo act like a list box—the user can select but not add items to the list that drops down (opens) when requested by the user.
Text	Assigns a single initial default value that first appears in the combo box list.

(continues)

Table 5.7 Continued	
Property	**Description**
Top	Indicates the number of twips from the window's top edge to the combo box's top edge.
Visible	Determines whether the combo box can be seen by the user (if True) or not (if False) when the program executes. You can make the combo list appear and disappear by changing the Visible property.
Width	Indicates the width, in twips, of the combo list control.

After trying the drop-down combo control for a while, open the File menu once more to get ready for the next section's control.

Adding Pictures to Applications

Visual Basic is graphical so you can display pictures on your applications. The *picture box control* is one control that lets you show images on your form. The images must be a Windows-compatible bitmap, icon, or metafile (these are three kinds of Windows image files).

Tip

Several bitmaps, icons, and metafiles come with Visual Basic—stored in the BITMAP, ICONS, and METAFILE subdirectories. Scanned images and drawings work also, as long as they are in one of the mentioned formats. Feel free to use these image files in your own applications or add your own.

Open the File menu and choose Picture Box. When you do, Visual Basic displays a happy face in the middle of the window (see Fig. 5.12).

Table 5.8 describes several property values available for picture box controls.

Table 5.8 Picture Box Control Properties	
Property	**Description**
Align	Aligns the picture box with the top of the Form window (for toolbars) with 1 (Align Top) or with 2 (Align Bottom). If you use 0 (None), Visual Basic does not align the picture box with either edge and lets you place the picture box anywhere on the form.

Property	Description
AutoSize	Determines how the picture box control sizes to fit its contents. If True, the picture box control resizes to fit its contents no matter how large or small you designed the picture box when you placed it on the Form window. Often, you'll want to retain the original size for picture images, so you'll set the AutoSize property to True. The image is chopped off if AutoSize is False and if the image is too large to fit in the area you designed for it.
Height	Specifies the picture box height in twips.
Left	Specifies the number of twips from the window's left edge to the picture box's left edge.
Name	Assigns a name to the picture box. If you don't assign a name, Visual Basic assigns its own (Picture1, Picture2, and so on) as you add items. You use the Name property to refer to the control in Visual Basic programs.
Picture	Sets the full path and file name of the image you want to display inside the picture box control area.
Top	Indicates the number of twips from the window's top edge to the picture box's top edge.
Visible	Determines whether the picture box can be seen by the user (if True) or not (if False) when the program executes. You can make the picture box appear and disappear by changing the Visible property.
Width	Indicates the width, in twips, of the picture box control.

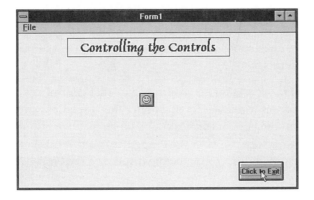

Fig. 5.12
Smile, a picture box control is on the screen.

Now that you've seen all the controls in the CONTROLS.MAK application, open the File menu and choose Exit—or choose the Click to Exit button—to close the application.

The Properties Window

Anytime you want to see all the properties available for any control, select that control and press F4. For example, on your busy CONTROLS.MAK application screen, you can easily find the Click to E_xit button in the lower-right corner of the window. Click this button—even though the application is not running. Eight black squares appear around the command button to indicate that you selected it (in a way, you highlighted it). These black squares are called *resizing handles*. As long as the eight resizing handles appear around the command button, all of your subsequent commands apply to that command button.

Press F4 to see the Properties window. You see a list of scrollable properties. The properties apply to all command buttons, and the properties currently set apply to the selected command button. For example, the Caption property is Click to E&xit. The ampersand (&) determines where the underline appears for the access keystroke, in this case, Alt+X. If you change the Caption property, the caption on the command button changes also.

Caution

If you change any of the command button properties, be sure you *don't* save the program's project file when you exit Visual Basic or load another project. If you happen to change this project and save those changes, you'll need to restore the project and all associated files using this book's original disk.

As you can see, the Properties window not only lists the current properties for each control but also gives you the ability to change property values. You'll use the Properties window a lot during your development of Visual Basic programs with this book.

To see a list of properties for any control, click that control and press F4 to open the Properties window. The title under the Properties window title bar always tells you the kind of control you're looking at. For example, the word CommandButton appears under the Properties window title bar when you select a command button control before displaying the Properties window.

The Form Window's Properties

The Form window itself has specific properties. For example, when you first start Visual Basic, the Form window background is white. The background color is a property of the form. The form acts as the backdrop for all the other controls, so it's often easy to forget to set the form's properties to needed values.

Click anywhere in the Form window and press F4 to see its properties. The word Form appears beneath the form title bar to let you know that you're looking at a form's properties and not a control's properties. Table 5.9 describes several property values available for your application's forms.

Table 5.9 Form Properties	
Property	**Description**
BackColor	Indicates a color hexadecimal value that represents a screen color. You determine what color appears in the background of a form with the BackColor property.
BorderStyle	Determines how and when the user can resize the form and how the form's borders look. If the BorderStyle is 0 (None), the form has no control buttons or resizing buttons. If the BorderStyle is 1 (Fixed Single), the form can contain the Control menu, title bar, and Maximize and Minimize buttons. By default, the BorderStyle contains 2 (Sizable). The form can contain all the elements just listed for 1 (Fixed Single) and the user can resize the window by dragging a window edge. If the BorderStyle is 3 (Fixed Double), the user can't change the size of the form, but the form can include a Control menu and a title bar.
Caption	Determines the text that appears in the form title bar. CONTROLS.MAK's Caption property contains Form1, but Form1 is a lousy title for this program. Change the Caption by clicking the Caption Property window row and typing **Controls**. Instantly, the form title changes.
ControlBox	Determines whether or not the Control menu appears. If True, the form contains a Control menu. If False, no control menu appears.
Height	Specifies the form height in twips.
Icon	Specifies the icon the user sees when the user minimizes the form.
Left	Specifies the number of twips from the screen's left edge to the form's left edge.
MaxButton	Determines whether or not the Maximize button appears. If True, the form contains a Maximize button. If False, no Maximize button appears.
MinButton	Determines whether or not the Minimize button appears. If True, the form contains a Minimize button. If False, no Minimize button appears.

(continues)

Table 5.9 Continued

Property	Description
Name	Assigns a name to the form. If you don't assign a name, Visual Basic assigns its own (Form1, Form2, and so on) as you add new forms. You use the Name property to refer to the form in Visual Basic programs.
Top	Indicates the number of twips from the screen's top edge to the form's top edge.
Visible	Determines whether the form can be seen by the user (if True) or not (if False) when the program executes. You can make the form appear and disappear by changing the Visible property.
Width	Indicates the width, in twips, of the form.

Now that you've seen lots of property values, it's time to clear your head! Exit Visual Basic by opening the File menu and choosing Exit. If asked if you want to save your changes, click No.

Conclusion

This chapter was a hands-on tutorial that walked you through several major Visual Basic controls. As mentioned throughout earlier chapters, one of the most important steps in creating a Visual Basic application is adding controls to your application forms. The controls let the user graphically interact with the program.

Before Visual Basic, programmers couldn't tap into such powerful I/O mechanisms. The traditional text-based I/O statements in languages such as COBOL simply don't let you easily design GUI programs. Even advanced COBOL screen-generators let you do little more than place and color text on the screen.

One of the most important things to remember about controls is that they contain properties. The property value settings determine how the control looks and behaves. You will be setting these important property values in the Properties window as well as with Visual Basic code.

Your patience with these introductory chapters will pay great dividends when you get to the second part of the book—where you'll actually create your first Visual Basic program. You deserve a rest now! You just completed Part I of this book. In Part II, "Point & Click Programming," you'll begin creating your own applications from scratch.

Part II

Point & Click Programming

Chapter 6

Presto, No Code Required!

Do you want to create your first truly interactive, GUI, Windows-based, Visual Basic application? You can do so in this chapter. Not only that, but you'll make sure this fully working Windows application comes equipped with controls, a resizable application window, a Control menu, a Minimize button, and a Maximize button. The amazing news is that you'll be able to create this application using a minimum of mouse movements, a few clicks here and there, and by typing just a few words on the screen.

Simple Visual Basic applications are extremely easy to write as this chapter demonstrates. Powerful and advanced applications aren't always difficult to produce either. The program-creation tools that Visual Basic provides make the most of the Windows environment. Microsoft designed Visual Basic to increase your productivity dramatically over the traditional text-based programming approach.

Here are some of the topics that will be discussed in this chapter:

- Preparing the Visual Basic development work area for a new application

- Learning the new Visual Basic development routine

- Clearing your Project window of extra files

- Developing a Visual Basic application from scratch

This chapter is fairly short on purpose. With this chapter, you see that the entire Visual Basic design and production process takes little time. A quick application can be just as impressive as a long, detailed application when you use a GUI environment and development tool such as Visual Basic.

Note

You type some Visual Basic code in this chapter but not much. Again, most Visual Basic development consists of screen design and placement of controls such as the ones you've learned about in the previous chapter.

Although you may not fully understand the code you type here, focus on the complete development process and don't worry so much about understanding the small details. Visual Basic is a tool whose forest is more important than its trees in many ways. Get the big picture first.

Approaching Application Development

Visual Basic program development differs greatly from the traditional programming paradigm, and you may find it difficult to compare the new and old development processes. The most important thing to remember as you approach Visual Basic programming is that the user interface is as important as any code that you write. The user interface handles most of the tedious details that you once had to code explicitly.

This chapter walks you through the creation of a sample Visual Basic program. You begin with a blank Form window and end up with a running program. Don't blink because you'll miss everything! Creating simple Windows programs is a snap thanks to Visual Basic.

Proper Programming Is Still Vital

When you switch to Visual Basic, the traditional programming safety measures you've used in the past are still just as important. End-user testing, as well as clear, clean program code are still a must if you want maintainable applications.

For example, you can *prototype* while developing final production code. Prototyping gives users early peeks at screens and I/O interaction. As soon as you finish adding controls to a form, save a copy of the form and compile it despite the program's unfinished state; then let the user interact with the interface. The user can tell you early in the development process where I/O changes can be made.

Getting Ready To Design Your Application

When designing your application, use the Form window as if it is a blank piece of paper you are going to draw on. The Form window holds all the controls that you place in your application. In many ways, the Form window becomes the user's application. Here are some important points to remember about Visual Basic program development:

The Form window is the user's screen.

- When you begin writing a Visual Basic program, you'll begin with a blank Form window.

- The size of the Form window becomes the size of the end-user's Program window. Therefore, if you design a program with lot of controls on a single Program window, you may want to enlarge the Form window before placing controls on it.

- You can dynamically adjust the Form window's size at program runtime through Visual Basic code. For example, you can ensure that the user's program begins in a maximized state, or that it always appears in the center of the user's screen—no matter what size the user's monitor is.

- To build the user interface, you select controls (the "tools") from the toolbox to add to the Form window.

- Once you place controls, you optionally add code to manipulate those controls through control property values. You also add code to manipulate data as needed for certain calculations.

As you place controls, you'll want to consider the user's perspective. For example, you'll see in the next section that the size of the Form window determines how much of the form the user sees. Sometimes, you'll want to reduce the Form window's size just to make more room for the other windows. However, in reducing the size, you may be reducing the application's work area, unless you take precautions to ensure that the user's form enlarges when needed.

Preparing Your Workspace

Before creating your first Visual Basic application, you can greatly clean up your workspace by following these steps:

II

Point & Click Programming

1. Start Visual Basic. It's possible to make unwanted changes to AUTOLOAD.MAK, so you may want to use the Windows File Manager to copy AUTOLOAD.MAK to a backup file using a different name in case you need to restore the file later.

2. Choose the Open command from the File menu (or press Alt+F, O) to open the project named AUTOLOAD.MAK and type **AUTOLOAD.MAK**. Press Enter.

   The AUTOLOAD.MAK file tells Visual Basic how to start each time you run Visual Basic. Unless you or someone else has modified AUTOLOAD.MAK, the typical AUTOLOAD.MAK file causes extra files to load every time you begin a new program, which lowers your memory and consumes extra screen space by clogging up your toolbox and Project window. Remove all of the files (they are extra toolbox controls that you don't need here) from AUTOLOAD.MAK's Project window.

3. Highlight one of the files in the Project window and choose Remove File from the File menu (or press Alt+F, R). Visual Basic removes the highlighted file from the Project window. Continue removing the files until every file listed in the Project window is removed. The Project window will adjust in size to reflect the number of entries in the Project window.

4. Save the AUTOLOAD.MAK project by choosing File Save Project (Alt+F, V).

Whenever you begin a fresh Visual Basic application, you will add forms and other files to that application's Project window, and you won't have the other automatically loaded files in your way.

> **Caution**
>
> Your toolbox will probably shrink now that you have eliminated some of the extra tools that the Project window contained.

Create a brand-new application.

You're ready to begin your first application. Since you've cleaned out the Project window, the Project window will contain only those files needed by your application. Follow these steps to prepare for the new application:

1. Select the New Project command from the File menu (Alt+F, N) to begin creating a new project.

2. If you can see only a part of the Form window, click the window to
bring it completely into view.

> **Tip**
>
> If you cannot see the Form window anywhere, it may be closed. One of the
> problems with many versions of Visual Basic is that there is no way to access
> the Form window through the menu bar. Therefore, to make a Form window
> appear, you first have to display the Project window by choosing the Project
> command from the Window menu. Click the Project window's View Form
> command button to see the Form window.

Size your Form window so it appears to be approximately the same size
as the Form window in Figure 6.1.

Location measurement

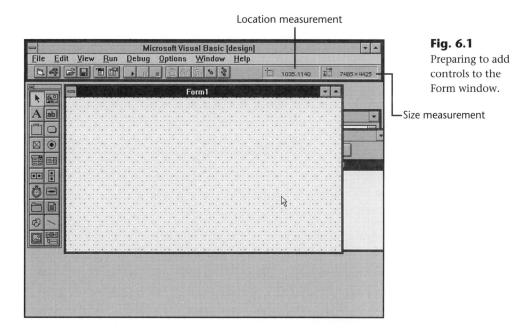

Fig. 6.1
Preparing to add
controls to the
Form window.

Size measurement

3. Just for grins, display the Project window. Notice there is only one file
in your new project, Form1. You may recall from the previous chapter
that Visual Basic names the first form Form1, although you can change
the name through the form's Properties window Name property. You
won't need to see the Project window for the rest of this chapter so
close it by double-clicking its control button.

Before going further, look to the right of the toolbar in Figure 6.1. You'll see two indented areas with two numbers next to each area. The left pair of numbers indicates the screen location, in twips, of the currently highlighted object, and the right pair of numbers indicates the size measurement.

In Figure 6.1, the form in the Form window (the form really *is* the Form window as you develop programs) is located exactly 1,035 twips from the left edge of the screen and exactly 1,140 twips from the top edge of the screen. The form is 7,485 twips wide and 4,425 twips high. Your form may differ slightly and you can adjust your form to closely match the location and size of the one in Figure 6.1. It's difficult to locate forms *exactly* at the twip you want (remember that a twip is 1/1440th of an inch, very small indeed!).

> **Note**
>
> When you place controls on the form, each of the control's location and size measurements will appear to the right of the toolbar when you highlight the control.

Creating the Application

Although it may seem as if you've already spent a great deal of time developing this chapter's application, you have done very little. Remember that you first edited AUTOLOAD.MAK so that your Visual Basic session begins cleaner than the default session normally begins. You won't have to modify AUTOLOAD.MAK ever again, unless you decide that you want a new file loaded with each new project you create in the future.

Other than modify AUTOLOAD.MAK, you have only started a new application, sized the Form window a bit, and closed the Project window to clear away some screen clutter. Figure 6.2 shows what your screen looks like at this point.

> **Note**
>
> The AUTOLOAD.MAK is to Visual Basic what AUTOEXEC.BAT is to DOS. You may or may not be familiar with AUTOEXEC.BAT, but AUTOEXEC.BAT is a batch file that executes every time you start your computer. Some operating systems, such as Windows NT, can bypass AUTOEXEC.BAT and ignore its contents. A batch file to a PC is like JCL to a mainframe. A batch file is a set of instructions that automatically executes at the operating system level. Because you are using Windows now, you won't be as concerned about AUTOEXEC.BAT as PC programmers were when DOS was the only operating system available.

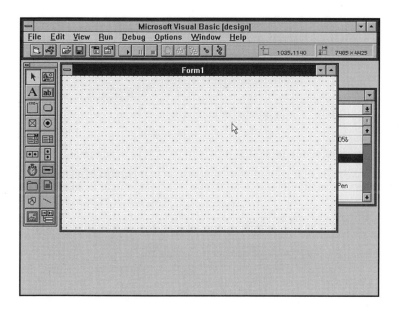

Fig. 6.2
You've now
cleaned up the
Project window
and resized the
form.

Adding Controls to the Application

You're ready to finish developing your first application by adding the controls and code. As you follow the step-by-step procedure listed here, consider how little effort you are spending.

1. Double-click the label control. (Remember that the label control contains the capital letter A.) As soon as you double-click the label control, Visual Basic displays a new label in the middle of the form.

2. Type **First App**. As you type, you'll see the letters appear in two places: on the label itself and in the Properties window Caption property as shown in Figure 6.3.

3. Notice that the text consumes only a small portion of the label. The label overwrites a rectangle of grid dots in the Form window. The label's Top, Left, Height, and Width properties control the size of the entire label, not the text on the label's caption. You can scroll through the Properties window and view the location (in the Top and Left properties) and the size (in the Width and Height properties) values to the right of the toolbar buttons.

II

Point & Click Programming

Fig. 6.3

Adding a new
label caption.

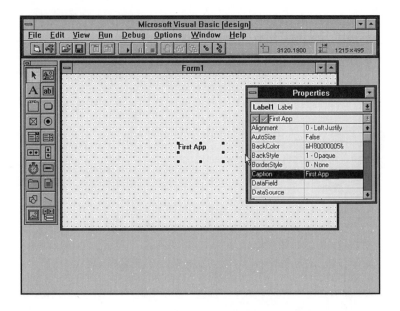

Caution

When viewing the location and size measurements of controls on the form,
the location measurements are relative to the form but *not* to your screen.
A Form window's location twip measurements will always appear as screen
measurements, which means that the Top property measures the number of
twips from the top of your screen to the top of the form, and the Left property
measures the number of twips from the left of your screen to the left of the
form. A control such as the label control always measures from its location
relative to the *form's* upper-left corner, not your screen's. Figure 6.3 indicates
that the label control appears 3,120 twips from the left of the form's left edge,
not from the screen's left edge, and 1,800 twips from the form's top edge.

4. You can make the font larger for the label. Changing the font size gives
   you practice in using the Properties window to change property values.
   Scroll the Properties window until you see the FontSize property. Click
   the FontSize property and Visual Basic also displays the current value in
   the box below the Properties window's title bar. (8.25 is the default
   point size for many Visual Basic installations although yours may differ
   depending on the installed fonts you have.) Click the down arrow that
   appears to the right of the number to see a drop-down list of available
   point sizes. Figure 6.4 shows your Properties window at this point.

When you want to change a property value, you can either type a new value or select from a drop-down list by clicking the down arrow as shown in Figure 6.4. Select 12 for the FontSize value by clicking the drop-down list or by typing **12**. As soon as you change the FontSize to 12, the text in the label is displayed in a point size of 12.

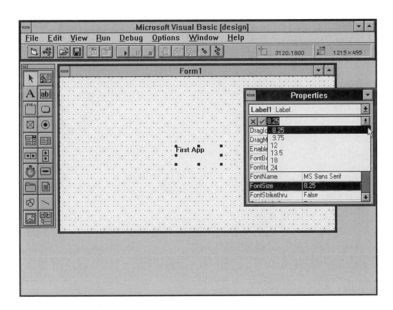

Fig. 6.4
Selecting a new font size for the label control.

Some property values, such as Caption, do not have drop-down lists and you must enter a new value with the keyboard to change the Caption property. The reason the Caption property changes as soon as you type **First App** is that Visual Basic always makes the Caption property the default selected property when you start Visual Basic. In other words, you don't have to go to the Properties window to change a Caption property. Instead, you can change a caption by entering text just as soon as you place the label control.

5. When you double-clicked the label control on your toolbox, Visual Basic placed the control in the middle of the form. Rarely will you want controls placed in the middle of the form. You can move controls by dragging them with your mouse. Drag the label control by clicking (and holding) the mouse button while the mouse cursor rests anywhere on the label. Drag the label towards the upper-middle portion of the Form window. As you drag the mouse, the toolbar location measurements change. Drag the label until it rests approximately in the label area as shown in Figure 6.5.

Fig. 6.5

The label is placed at the top of the form.

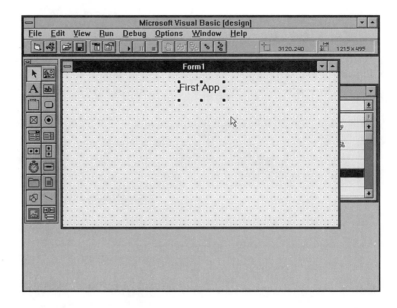

Of course, you can spend much more time on the label—changing the font style and the label's color—but this chapter's focus is demonstrating how little you need to do to create a fully working application, so let's move on without honing the label any further.

> **Note**
>
> In a COBOL program, how do you display a label? You use DISPLAY or WRITE, but how do you easily place the label at the top of the screen? Whether or not you use a screen generator, dragging a label with the mouse is much more efficient and easier (and more fun) than placing a label with code or with screen-generating commands.

6. Double-click the command button control from the toolbox. (Figure 5.3 in Chapter 5 showed you where the command button is located. You'll know how to find all the major controls in no time at all.) Visual Basic displays the command button in the middle of the screen.

7. Click the Caption property in the Properties window. Type **Push Me**. The command button's Caption property changes and your screen looks like Figure 6.6.

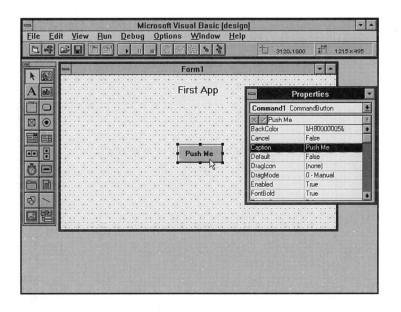

Fig. 6.6
Adding a com-
mand button.

8. Move the command button to the left side of the form (try to maintain the same vertical placement) to make room for a second command button.

9. Double-click the command button control on the toolbox to place a second command button on the form. As Chapter 5, "The Graphical Controls," explained, this second command button will have the name Command2 unless you change the command button's Name property.

10. Type **&Quit**. Visual Basic adds the new caption to the command button and underlines the first letter, Q.

An ampersand before a caption's letter makes that letter an access key. Therefore, you can see from the second command button's caption that you select this button by clicking the button with the mouse, pressing Enter while the button has the focus, or by pressing the button's Alt+Q access key. (You may have to click the Form window to hide the Properties window so you can see the second command button.)

Move the second command button to the right of the form so your screen looks like Figure 6.7.

This first application is extremely simple and does not contain a fancy form relative to many other Windows programs on the market. Nevertheless, you really are building an application that would have impressed anyone in computers less than a decade ago, and you're building this application without any real effort.

Fig. 6.7
After placing the
second command
button.

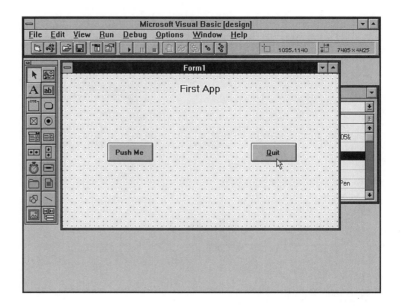

11. Save your work in the project file by choosing the Save Project As command from the File menu and typing **INSTANT** (Visual Basic adds the
.MAK filename extension) for the project name. Save the form by
choosing the Save File As command from the File menu and typing
INSTANT (Visual Basic adds the .FRM filename extension) again for
the form name.

Adding Code to the Application

Add a little code
to tie the controls
together.

Even this simple application needs some Visual Basic code to put the pieces
together. The following steps may not make a lot of sense to you because
you're going to be adding code that is triggered by the command button
clicking events. Chapter 7, "Capturing Events," explains where code that
handles events is inserted and where you write that code. For now, follow
these steps to add code that ties functionality to the two command buttons:

1. Double-click the first command button. Visual Basic always supplies
some code for you as you can see in the Code window.

The code that Visual Basic supplies is sometimes called *wrapper code*
because the code will wrap around any code that you add. Here is the
code that Visual Basic added to your Code window:

```
Sub Command1_Click ()

End Sub
```

Visual Basic puts the cursor between the two lines. These two state-ments enclose the beginning and end of a Visual Basic *procedure*. A pro-cedure is a section of code that operates like a COBOL paragraph.

2. Insert the following lines of code between the two lines supplied by Visual Basic (press Tab before each line to indent the middle two lines):

```
Beep
Command1.Caption = "Thanks!"
```

Your screen should look like the one in Figure 6.8. By indenting your code, you can easily separate your code from that supplied by Visual Basic. More important, you will be able to tell from the indention where long procedures begin and end when you read through a printed listing of them.

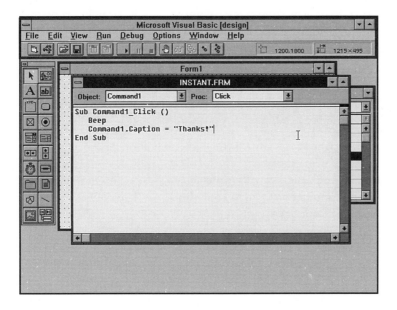

Fig. 6.8
Adding code to a command button procedure.

II

Point & Click Programming

3. Close the Code window by double-clicking the control button.

4. Double-click the second command button to display another Code window. Press Tab and type **End**. The second command button's event code should now look like this:

```
Sub Command2_Click ()
    End
End Sub
```

> **Note**
>
> Sometimes, Visual Basic procedures are called *subroutines* or *subprograms*. That's why Visual Basic begins each procedure with Sub and ends each procedure with End Sub.

5. Close the Code window.

You are now finished! You have clicked a few mouse clicks, dragged three controls around a form, and typed a total of five words on the screen! What do you have to show for your work? Well, you cannot see the results of any program, neither a COBOL nor a Visual Basic program, without running the program. With COBOL, you'd have to compile, link, and load the program. With Visual Basic, you simply click a button, or select from a menu, or press an access key to run a program! All three of the following actions will execute the program you just ran:

■ Choose the Run command from the Run menu.

■ Click the Run icon on the toolbar (the arrow directly beneath the D in the menu bar's Debug).

■ Press F5 (the access key for the Run command).

Pressing F5 is the easiest way to run your program, so do that now. Voila! A form window appears just like the one shown in Figure 6.9. You are running your program! Notice the following:

■ The second command button has the focus because it was the last control on which you worked. If you pressed Enter now (don't do so yet), you would click the Quit command button.

■ You can also activate the second command button by pressing Alt+Q. Again, don't do this just yet or you'll terminate the application too soon.

■ Click the label and nothing happens. Remember that labels are not active, but are read-only and exist just to display characters on a form.

■ The Form window during the application's design and creation becomes the Program window when you run the program.

■ Click the first command button and listen closely. Did you hear the beep? Also, the caption changes from Push Me to Thanks!. Once you press the button once, the caption remains but the button keeps beeping every time you press it.

■ When you are ready to quit, select the second command button. Visual Basic terminates the application and returns you to the program-editing area.

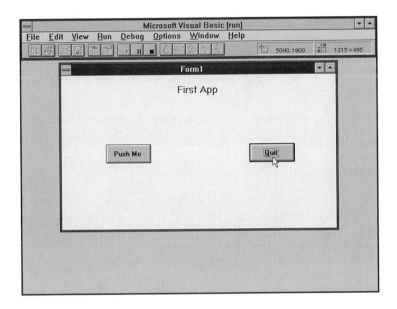

Fig. 6.9
Running your first program!

Save the program by choosing the Save Project As command from the File menu (Alt+F, V). Saving the project saves all files within the project. In this case, the form file (INSTANT.FRM) is the only file in the project. Visual Basic saves the project under the name INSTANT.MAK because that's the name you gave the project earlier.

Note

If you want to run a Visual Basic program as a stand-alone Windows program without the Visual Basic environment surrounding the output, compile the program just as you compile COBOL programs by choosing Make EXE File from the File menu (Alt+F, K) and typing an executable file name that ends with the .EXE extension.

There is more to this program than three simple controls (a label and two command buttons). When you run this program, you can minimize and maximize the window and select from the Control menu as well.

The INSTANT.MAK program is a true Windows application. In the next chapter, you'll add to this program, so don't exit Visual Basic if you plan to go directly to the next chapter.

Conclusion

You're now a Visual Basic programmer! Sure, you have a lot of understanding left to develop but you've already tackled the most important step: using the toolbox to place controls on the form. Subsequent chapters go into much more detail. This chapter introduced you to the keyboard and gave you an idea of what program creation is all about.

As a review, here are the steps you take to create the INSTANT.MAK program:

1. Start Visual Basic.

2. Size the program's Form window.

3. You add three controls to the form. As you add each control, change the caption of each and drag the control to where you want it to go.

4. Write two code procedures using Code windows to tie actions to the two command button click events.

5. Run the program.

Even if you were using Visual Basic to write the next multi-million software success story, you would perform this same sequence of events.

Chapter 7, "Capturing Events," explains the process of adding code to events. As you see sections of code in the next few chapters in this part of the book, realize that you don't have to understand every nook and cranny of every word to get a general understanding of what's taking place. Part III, "Primary Differences," and Part IV, "Advanced VB Programming," will use COBOL to teach you the details of Visual Basic's language. Until then, keep paying close attention to the overall design process because that process is what you have to get used to most of all.

Chapter 7

Capturing Events

This chapter explains the event-capturing process. By reading how the event processes work, you'll gain a deeper understanding of how Visual Basic code interacts with the user's interface. You will better understand the INSTANT.MAK program in Chapter 6, and you will make the program do more by adding to it.

There is no way to jump directly to the Visual Basic language until you've mastered the way the language works with Windows events. Therefore, if you were to see now what Visual Basic's equivalent statement to COBOL's PERFORM VARYING is, you would not have a context in which to understand when and where to use that equivalent statement. The *event* is the fundamental trigger for all Visual Basic code with the exception of some preliminary data-definition statements.

Here are some of the topics that will be discussed in this chapter:

- Learning when events occur
- Distinguishing between events and properties
- Determining what kinds of events are available for the controls
- Improving the INSTANT.MAK project by capturing additional events
- Seeing how Visual Basic tracks objects as you add objects to the form
- Learning how to compose proper Visual Basic names

Events Revisited

Keep in mind that events are not properties. Some people often confuse the two. The distinction is so obvious to the teacher (or author), that we often forgot how much of an "information overload" we faced when we originally made the transition from a procedural, top-down, text-based programming mode to the event-driven GUI programming.

An event is almost always triggered by the user. There are some internal Windows events that can take place, such as an internal timer reaching a preset time. Specific Visual Basic code executes because an event takes place. Your code itself can trigger events. Therefore, through code, one event might be the catalyst for several more events taking place.

Set properties both at design and runtime. As you learned in Chapter 5, "The Graphical Controls," controls have certain properties. When you design a user interface, you specify property values for the controls you place on the form. Therefore, you specify properties at design time. In the previous chapter, you wrote a program (although the verb *wrote* seems strange when you develop programs using a point-and-click GUI environment!) and assigned the Push Me caption to the left command button whose name was Command1. Remember that Visual Basic names controls for you unless you change the names to something else, and you did not change the command button's name from Command1.

During the execution of the program, certain actions may take place that require control properties to change. Therefore, you can, through code, change property values. Properties can be changed at both design time and at runtime because part of the Visual Basic programmer's responsibility is to specify property values and change those values when needed. Although you haven't yet seen an explanation of Visual Basic code, you changed INSTANT.MAK's Command1 command button with the following assignment statement (which you typed when creating the program):

```
Command1.Caption = "Thanks!"
```

This statement is a preview of what you'll learn as we go along. It tells Visual Basic to assign the value Thanks! to the Caption property of Command1, the first command button. In a way, the equal sign works just as COBOL's MOVE statement does. Although COBOL does not have property values, here is the way you'd write this property-changing statement if COBOL supported GUI properties:

```
MOVE "Thanks!" TO Command1.Caption
```

Why does the previous statement change the Caption property? You might want to run INSTANT.MAK again to review the first command button's purpose. When the user (you in this case) clicks the first command button, the command button's caption changes to Thanks!. The assignment statement you just saw assigned the new caption to the command button's Caption property when an event occurred. That event was the user's pressing of the command button, accomplished by either clicking the mouse or by pressing the Enter key.

> **Tip**
>
> Here's the difference between properties and events in a nutshell: properties deter-
> mine how controls look and behave. The user usually causes events to happen, often
> by using a control such as clicking a button. A command button has Caption and
> Width properties. When the user clicks a command button, Windows generates an
> event. The event is the clicking of the command button and if you tie code to that
> click, then that code will then execute.

Using the Code Window's Lists

The Code window contains code (you used the Code window in Chapter 6 to
write two lines of code). Figure 7.1 shows a Code window that displays part of
INSTANT.MAK's code which contains the Caption property-changing code
mentioned in the previous chapter.

Fig. 7.1
The Code window
displays event-
changing Visual
Basic code.

II

Point & Click Programming

> **Caution**
>
> Visual Basic statements *do not* end with a period as COBOL statements do. Adding a
> period at the end of Visual Basic statements generates a quick error!

There are two very important drop-down lists inside every Code window.
You'll recall from Chapter 5, "The Graphical Controls," that a drop-down list
is a list of items from which the user can select. A click of the drop-down list's
arrow enables the user to see the full list.

Note

In Visual Basic terminology, the word *object* is often used generically for controls and forms.

The two drop-down list controls are labeled Object and Proc. The next few sections explain both of these drop-down lists.

The Object Drop-down List

The Object drop-down list contains a list of every object in the current program. The INSTANT.MAK project form (named INSTANT.FRM) contains these four objects:

- The Push Me command button named Command1
- The Quit command button named Command2
- The form named INSTANT.FRM (you named the form when you saved the project)
- The title at the top of the form displayed with a label control

Click the INSTANT.MAK Code window's Object drop-down list now to see the list shown in Figure 7.2.

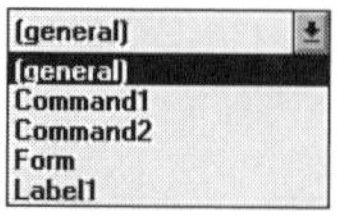

Fig. 7.2
View all the objects in the program.

Note

Don't be alarmed by the list of five objects when you thought there were only four. The first item in the Object drop-down list, (general), does not describe an object but a general purpose procedure that sets up data values and contains code that handles the routine startup processing some programs need. This (general) procedure is a Visual Basic routine, similar to a COBOL HOUSEKEEPING-SECTION paragraph, where you add code that's not tied to a particular event on the form.

Practice with One Additional Object

You now see how Visual Basic dynamically changes to accommodate your design, and to make programming as easy as possible. In this section, you will

add a control to the INSTANT.MAK program and immediately jump to the
Code window to see how Visual Basic updated the Object drop-down list with
the new control. In other words, Visual Basic watches what you're doing and
updates your workplace as you work. You do not have to wait for a compile
every time you change the user interface.

> **Note**
>
> One of the most time-consuming parts of traditional programming is waiting for
> compiles. When you want to change one character of output, you must recompile
> your program and every other program down the line that depends on the first
> program. Only after your entire application is rebuilt can you see whether the change
> you made in the output is correct.
>
> Visual Basic streamlines output design. When you must make a change to the output,
> even if that change involves removing or adding a new control to the user's window,
> Visual Basic recognizes that change immediately and updates the environment to
> reflect the changed screen.

Be sure you have project INSTANT.MAK loaded. Add a label control to
INSTANT.MAK's form by following these steps:

1. Double-click the label control (the control with a capital A). Visual Basic
   displays a label in the center of the form with the name Label2.

   Visual Basic always displays controls that you select in the center of the
   screen. Rarely will you want these new controls in the middle of the
   screen and rarely will you prefer the default size that Visual Basic
   starts with. You can drag the control with the mouse to a new location.
   Drag the label control to the bottom of the screen at approximately the
   $2,640 \times 2,880$ location (the location measurement is in the left of two
   boxes in the upper-right corner of your screen near the right end of the
   toolbar. This reminds you where your selected control begins). If you
   have Align To Grid set to Yes in the Option, Environment (Alt+O, E)
   dialog box, you can easily get to the $2,640 \times 2,880$ location. If not,
   adjust the control as close as you can to this measurement.

2. The eight resizing handles around a selected control let you resize
   the control. Move the mouse cursor to the center black square in the
   middle of the label's right side. The mouse cursor changes to a double-
   pointer. Drag the right edge, by dragging this handle, until the label
   control is 2,295 twips wide. As you drag the side, the control's size measurement to the right of the toolbar buttons changes. When the width

is 2,295, release the mouse button. Your screen should look like the one in Figure 7.3.

Fig. 7.3
The label control
after you resize it.

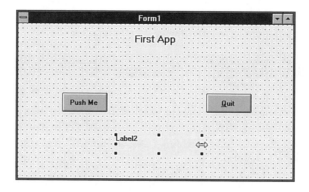

Visual Basic sets the label's Caption property to the same value as the Name property. The name of this new label is Label2. Label1 is the name for the first label you placed on the form in the previous chapter (the label holds the title at the top of the screen).

Change the Caption property to **Adding Controls Is A Snap!** by pressing F4 to see the Property window, clicking the Caption property, and entering the new caption. As you type the caption, Visual Basic displays the new label caption in the Form window.

Don't worry about the font style or size now. When you expand the size of the label, you ensure that the entire message fits on the label using the default font information.

3. Display the Code window once again by pressing F7. When you display the Code window, display the Object drop-down list by clicking the down arrow next to the list. The new label control, Label2, appears in the list. Visual Basic already added the control to the Code window list.

Tip

The Object drop-down list lets you jump directly to a specific object's related code. For example, when you want to see code related to the first command button, click Command1 and Visual Basic displays related code.

If it's not already open, open the Object drop-down list again and then select the Command1 entry. Visual Basic once again displays the code that relates to the Command1 command button.

Names Are Important!

One of the reasons COBOL programmers spend a lot of time thinking up long DATA DIVISION names, such as DEPT-GROSS-PAY, is that long data names provide self-documentation for the program. It's fairly easy to figure out that the name DEPT-GROSS-PAY is probably a department's gross payroll amount.

Just as names offer clues about what data values contain, control names can provide a good clue about their use as well. For example, the second command button's Name property, Command2, does not tell you a lot about the purpose of the command button. The second command button lets the user terminate the program; therefore, it is better to change that program-terminating control's name to Exit.

Good control names are self-documenting.

Just as with COBOL data-naming rules, Visual Basic requires that you follow certain rules for naming values, including control and data holder names:

- Names must begin with an alphabetic letter.

- Names may contain letters, numbers, and the underscore (_) character. The underscore is sometimes used for separating parts of a name. Depending upon the control there are other special characters which may be used like the & (ampersand) described in Chapter 5.

- Names can contain from one to 40 characters.

- A name cannot be a reserved word such as a Visual Basic command.

Here are a few valid names:

```
gross_sales   GrossSales   mktg1995
```

Names can have uppercase characters, lowercase characters, or a mixture of both.

When an application is as small as INSTANT.MAK, taking the time to change the names doesn't always improve the program's maintenance. However, you don't always know how large a program will become or how many people will eventually work on the program. Therefore, take the time to add meaningful names to all your controls at the time you place the controls on the user's form.

Caution

One of the most important things to remember as a former COBOL programmer is that the dash is *not allowed* in Visual Basic names. In other words, GROSS‑SALES is a proper COBOL name, but it will not work as a Visual Basic name. More important, GROSS‑SALES will almost always produce a Visual Basic syntax or logic error. If you want to include separate words in a data name, use the underscore, as in GROSS_SALES. In Visual Basic, GROSS‑SALES means GROSS minus SALES.

A name can do more than describe the data that the label holds. A control name can also indicate the type of control you're working with. Table 7.1 lists three-letter, control prefix names to use when adding names to controls. As you can see from the table, a better name for the second command button would be cmdQuit instead of Command2, which is what Visual Basic originally named the command button. From the name, you not only know what kind of control the name describes, but also what the purpose of the control is (exiting the program).

Table 7.1   Three-Letter Prefix Names for Controls

Prefix	Control
frm	Form
chk	Check box
cbo	Combo box
cmd	Command button
lbl	Label
lst	List
mnu	Menu
opt	Option box
pic	Picture box
txt	Text box

There are additional controls, and therefore additional prefixes available for them. Table 7.1 lists only the objects we're concerned with here. The Visual Basic reference manuals list suggestions for other controls.

When you begin writing longer programs, some of the controls will hold data. The control name prefix you add provides useful documentation while you program. You know that you can't accidentally treat cmdNames as a text box that can capture user input, but the name txtNames does indicate a text box control name that can enable the user to input text.

Caution

If you don't name a control using a three-letter prefix, and you need to find out what kind of control you're working with, you have to select the control on the Form window and press F4 to see the Properties window for the control. The prefix saves a lot of time later, so be sure to name the control as soon as you get a chance.

Every control has a Name property. When you place a label on the form, take a moment to change the default name to a more descriptive name. Be sure to use the three-letter prefix so you always know the kind of control you're working with.

Note

Sadly, despite this section's promotion of good naming conventions for objects and data, *do not* rename INSTANT.MAK's objects at this time! If you do, the code you already entered for Command1 and Command2 is no longer connected to the two command buttons. The code attaches to controls named Command1 and Command2, and there are no controls *named* Command1 and Command2 if you rename them to something else.

This book will always suggest names when requiring that you add controls and before you write code for the controls. Therefore, you won't have this naming problem again.

The Proc Drop-down List

The second drop-down list, labeled Proc, lists all events for each particular object. At this time, you should have the Command1 command button selected in the Object drop-down list. Open the Proc drop-down list to see a list of events for the Command1 object. Your screen should look like the screen in Figure 7.4.

Fig. 7.4

Viewing events related to Command1.

The Proc drop-down list is somewhat mislabeled. Perhaps, especially for new-comers to Visual Basic, this drop-down list would be better labeled with the title Event. The Proc stands for *procedure,* and is a list of every event belonging to the selected object for which you can write Visual Basic procedures. At this point, think of the Proc drop-down list as an exhaustive list of all events that the object selected in the Object drop-down list can trigger.

Every command button you select in the Object drop-down list contains this same set of events in the Proc drop-down list. However, if you select a label in the Object list, the list of items in the Proc list differs and applies only to label controls.

From the drop-down list, you can see that all command buttons trigger the events in Table 7.2, and that you can write code for each of these events.

Table 7.2	**Event Procedure Names**
Event	**Control**
Click	The user clicks the command button, either with the mouse or keyboard
DragDrop	The user drags and places the control
DragOver	The user drags a control over this control
GotFocus	This control just got the focus, due to either the user at the keyboard or by default
KeyDown	The user presses a key and possibly holds down the key
KeyPress	The user presses a key (this action also triggers a KeyDown event)
KeyUp	The user releases a key that he pressed earlier

Event	Control
LostFocus	This control, which previously had focus, just lost the focus
MouseDown	The user presses the mouse button and may or may not have released the button
MouseMove	The user just moved the mouse
MouseUp	The user just released the mouse button

From the object list, select one of the labels (such as Label2, the new label you added to INSTANT.MAK earlier in this chapter) and view the list of Proc events for labels. In the list, you don't see any of the key- or focus-related events; labels have a read-only status. In addition, you see events that are not part of command button events such as LinkClose.

Keep in mind that all similar controls have the same list of Proc event properties. When you add subsequent controls, all similar controls share the same list of Proc events. That's because all controls work the same way. Controls may behave differently from each other depending on their properties, however. For example, one command button might be wider than another and contain a different Caption property, but all command buttons will work the same way and trigger the same kinds of events.

If you don't write code for a specific control's event, nothing happens when that event occurs. If you want to respond to a certain control event, you write code for that event.

Suppose you want to write code for the first command button, Command1, that responds to a user's click. First choose Command1 from the Object drop-down list. Then, choose Click from the Proc drop-down list, if Click is not already selected. By making these two selections, you instruct Visual Basic to display a code procedure (remember, procedures are like paragraphs) that automatically executes whenever this control event takes place.

The Code window displays your now-familiar code, shown below:

```
Sub Command1_Click ()
    Beep
    Command1.Caption = "Thanks!"
End Sub
```

You already know from running INSTANT.MAK that when the user clicks the first command button, something happens (because you typed code here in the previous chapter). You did not know at the time that you were writing code for the `Command1` object's `Click` event, but your Code window proves that there is code for this event. If you select a different event for `Command1`, such as `DragDrop`, you won't see any code except for the two wrapper lines that Visual Basic always supplies for every event. If you selected `DragDrop` just to see there was no code, select the `Click` event to look at the code for `Click` once again.

Learn to name event procedures.

Now for an interesting part of Visual Basic coding that will set up all future Visual Basic programming you do: all procedures are named. The name of every procedure tells you *exactly* what control and event that procedure handles. An underscore is required, and separates the control name from the event name. Here is the format of all event procedure names:

```
ControlName_Event ()
```

> **Note**
>
> When you see italicized parts of code in this book, remember that the italics are placeholders for other text. Therefore, you never use ControlName as the first part of an event name or Event as the second part. In their places, you use an actual control name such as Command1 and an actual event name after the underscore, such as Click.

The parentheses are not really part of the name, but all procedures end in them. You learn the purpose of the parentheses in Chapter 21, "Modular Visual Basic Programming." Therefore, if you click the first command button, the code in `Command1_Click()` executes. If you click the second command button, the code in `Command2_Click()` executes. If you press the mouse button, the code in `Label2_MouseDown()` executes. There happens to be no code in a `MouseDown` event procedure for the second label, so this program ignores such an event until you add code.

All event procedures begin with Sub.

An event procedure's code always begins with a `Sub` statement. Visual Basic keeps track of where event procedures begin and end. The format of every event's first statement, sometimes called the *procedure definition statement,* is

```
Sub ControlName_EventName ()
```

Therefore, the first line of the `Command1` command button's `Click` event procedure must be

```
Sub Command1_Click ()
```

If you look at this procedure in your Code window by selecting `Command1` in the Object drop-down list and `Click` in the Proc drop-down list, you see the first line of this event.

All event procedures must terminate with an `End Sub` statement. Look at the last line in `Command1_Click ()` and you see `End Sub`. As with the `Sub` statement, Visual Basic adds the `End Sub` for you when you open the Code window for any new procedure.

All event procedures end with `End Sub`.

> **Caution**
>
> Just in case you look ahead or study other Visual Basic programs while you study this book, some special procedures begin with `Function` and `End Function` statements. Don't be alarmed. The distinction between `Sub` and `Function` is not critical at this point. Until you learn the difference, use `Sub` in your procedure wrappers.

This is a good time to add code to the second label. Doing so can help bring all this chapter's material into the focus you need for the rest of the book. Suppose you wanted to change the second label's color whenever the user presses a mouse button, but only when the mouse cursor rests in the label area. You have to put the code in an event procedure named `Label2_MouseDown()`.

The following steps enable you to change the label's background color from white to cyan whenever the user presses a mouse button over the label. As always, until you read about language specifics in Part V, "Your Next Step with VB," you don't have to understand the individual commands you type here. Instead, concentrate on the procedure name, how to open the procedure's Code window, and how the event procedure will execute. These steps describe how to add code to the label's mouse click event:

1. Choose Label2 in the Object drop-down list.

2. Choose MouseDown in the Proc drop-down list.

3. Visual Basic opens the Code window and writes the first and last line of `Label2_MouseDown ()` for you.

4. Add the following line of code to the middle of the two statements:

   ```
   Label2.BackColor = QBColor(3)
   ```

5. Press Tab to indent the new statement so you won't have trouble finding the body of the event procedure. Your Code window should look like Figure 7.5.

Fig. 7.5
Adding code to
a new event
procedure.

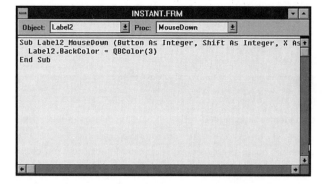

```
┌──────────────────────────────────────────────────────────┐
│ ─                        INSTANT.FRM                   ▼ ▲ │
├──────────────────────────────────────────────────────────┤
│ Object: │Label2          │±│ Proc: │MouseDown         │±│   │
├──────────────────────────────────────────────────────────┤
│ Sub Label2_MouseDown (Button As Integer, Shift As Integer, X As▲│
│     Label2.BackColor = QBColor(3)                          ▓│
│ End Sub                                                    ▓│
│                                                            ▓│
│                                                            ▓│
│                                                            ▓│
│                                                            ▼│
│ ←│                                                       │→ │
└──────────────────────────────────────────────────────────┘
```

As mentioned earlier in this chapter, the parentheses following an event procedure name sometimes hold something. As you see in Figure 7.5, the parentheses of the Label2_MouseDown () procedure contain named values. Although this procedure does not use those values, you can utilize them as you progress in your Visual Basic programming. For now, don't worry about the parentheses because the values there are not useful for this application.

6. Run the program (press F5). You see the new label at the bottom of the screen. Now, move the mouse cursor directly over the bottom label's text and press the mouse button. As soon as you do, the label's background changes to a cyan color.

If you click the label with the mouse button again, nothing happens. That's because you only added code for the MouseDown event. Now, add the following event procedure code to Label2_MouseUp () using the same steps as you just performed for the MouseDown event:

```
Sub Label2_MouseUp (Button As Integer, Shift As Integer,
➥ X As Single, Y As Single)
    Label2.BackColor = OBColor(3)
End Sub
```

Again, you don't have to type the first and last statement, and don't worry about the contents of the parentheses at this time.

Run your program by pressing F5. Now, when you press the mouse on the bottom label, the label's background turns cyan. When you release the mouse button, the label becomes green. You've captured these two events. Now, move the mouse cursor over the label (without pressing the mouse button) and nothing special happens. The only way that anything could happen by moving the mouse over the label is if you filled the `Label2_MouseMove ()` procedure with code. Visual Basic ignores all events except those events for which you write code.

Working in the Code Window

When you're in the Code window, you really don't have to select from the two drop-down boxes to see all the code. After viewing any event procedure, you can press the PageUp and PageDown buttons to scroll through all code. Visual Basic only displays the code you've written when you scroll through the Code window.

You can also print a listing of your Code window by opening the File menu and choosing Print. When you choose the Print command, Visual Basic displays the Print dialog box (see Fig. 7.6).

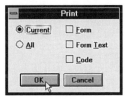

Fig. 7.6
Getting ready to print.

You can print either a camera-ready copy of the form, a text-based description of the form, or all the code from the Code window—depending on the check box(es) you select. If you choose the Current option, Visual Basic prints only the current form or code listing. If you select All, Visual Basic prints all forms and code listings related to the current project. For your first several applications, you can select either Current or All with the same printed results.

Note

Long code listings for more powerful programs make indenting of the body of code most important: you can scan through the listing and easily find where event procedures begin and end.

II

Point & Click Programming

Additional Types of Procedures

Although you've been reading about Event procedures, there are actually three kinds of procedures:

- *Event procedures.* Described in this chapter, these are the most common procedures they run when their associated events activate.

- *General procedures.* General procedures are not tied to particular events but are called from other procedures. Often, general procedures contain code that performs application-specific calculations and data-manipulation routines that are not associated directly with any event.

- *Declaration procedures.* These appear in all Visual Basic programs (although sometimes left empty). At the most, there is one declaration event for each form's Code window. You define and initialize certain data values in the declaration procedure.

A characteristic that distinguishes Visual Basic from COBOL is Visual Basic's modular approach. A Visual Basic program is really just made up of many small procedures, most of them being event procedures. Programmers often view COBOL programs, although broken into paragraphs, as long listings of one single program and not distinct code fragments, as is the case with Visual Basic.

Conclusion

You are now ready to hit the ground running with code! As this chapter pointed out, the way a programmer approaches Visual Basic programs differs greatly from the way COBOL programmers approach their code. When a COBOL programmer writes code, the programmer goes to the text editor and begins typing. When Visual Basic programmers begin a program, they design the user interface screen and then use the Code window to enter code for one or more event procedures.

Each kind of control has the same list of events as other similar controls. When coding event procedures, you now know that you must link the control name to the event name (separated with an underscore), and use that newly formed name as the event name. From the event definition line (the first line in the event), you can determine exactly what control and event will trigger the code's execution.

The next chapter explores more mechanics of Visual Basic program development. You'll learn how to compile stand-alone Visual Basic programs and explore Visual Basic coding in more depth. Before moving to the next chapter, save the INSTANT.MAK program because you made several changes in this chapter. Although this book's disk contains the code for INSTANT.MAK, you might want to save your own version so you can add to your copy as you learn more about Visual Basic.

II

Point & Click Programming

Chapter 8

VB's *IDENTIFICATION* and *ENVIRONMENT* Equivalents

Visual Basic really has no program areas that are equivalent to COBOL's IDENTIFICATION and ENVIRONMENT divisions. The Visual Basic programming environment is too dramatically different from a typical COBOL environment for there to be any one-to-one comparison. However, this chapter explores many aspects of the Visual Basic environment that you can control both through programming and through the Visual Basic menus. Therefore this chapter is about as close as you can come to the familiar IDENTIFICATION and ENVIRONMENT COBOL divisions.

This chapter further explores Visual Basic's environment by discussing the compilation of Visual Basic programs. As a COBOL programmer, you probably work in a production environment, and this chapter offers clues for you to improve your productivity while working with Visual Basic. Although you already have a fundamental grasp of how project files work, this chapter explains advanced project file usage.

You have an advantage over many Visual Basic programmers because you've worked in groups and understand the importance of maintenance and support through documentation and standards. Only until you've worked on someone else's code can you really appreciate the standards that data processing shops around the world promote. One standard promoted by Microsoft involves using a file of defined constants throughout all Visual Basic programming. You learn about that file in this chapter.

Here are some of the topics that will be discussed in this chapter:

■ Managing project files like a pro

■ Using the compiler to create stand-alone applications

■ Adding items to a new Windows program group

■ Including the CONSTANT.TXT file in your projects to standardize common data items

■ Using remarks to document Visual Basic code

■ Changing environment settings to increase programming productivity

The Project File

So far, the only application you've developed from scratch is INSTANT.MAK. The INSTANT.MAK application is very simple. INSTANT.MAK contains a single form named INSTANT.FRM. Due to the fact that there's only one file associated with INSTANT.MAK, a project file containing that one form file is probably overkill for such a small application.

As you write more and more powerful programs, you'll better appreciate the need for the project file. Often, you will create several files for your applications. An application might have one or more of the following kinds of files:

■ *Form files* hold the user's interface screens. All form file names have the extension .FRM.

■ *Code module files* contain Visual Basic code not directly related to specific events. As you know, you store form code inside the form itself using the Code window. In addition, you can write general-purpose routines that aren't related to events but are called by event code. You also write this general-purpose code in the Code window and store the code in files called *code module files*. All code module file names have the extension .BAS.

■ *Custom control files* contain new controls that you can add to your toolbox. In Chapter 6, "Presto, No Code Required!" you removed several custom control files from your AUTOLOAD.MAK project so that your toolbox became smaller and less cluttered. Often, you'll purchase custom controls from third-party sources instead of writing your own. Custom control files have the file name extension .VBX.

■ The *project file* keeps track of everything else. Each application can have at most one project file. Project files have the file name extension .MAK.

One of the neat ways that Visual Basic increases productivity is by enabling you to create forms and then use those forms in more than one application. For example, suppose that your company requires a user password to execute data in several places. You can create a password form such as the one shown in Figure 8.1. The form gets and stores the password in a common data area that subsequent routines can check for validity.

You may reuse forms and other files.

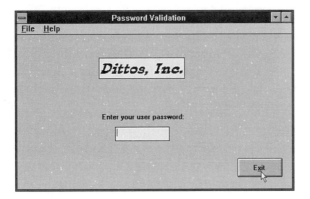

Fig. 8.1
Collecting the password in a universal form file.

Suppose that you created such a password form and stored the form in a file named PASSWORD.FRM. The File, Save command lets you save the form file, unlike the File, Save Project command, which saves the current project file described in the Project window.

After saving the password form file, any application that you write can use that form. You won't have to re-create the form file ever again. Therefore, you create building block applications over time. As you create form files (as well as the other kinds of files mentioned earlier, such as code module files), you create potential pieces of future applications at the same time.

Tip

When designing forms and other kinds of files, keep the future in mind. If you can make your forms as generic as possible, you'll be able to reuse them later.

This book's disk contains the PASSWORD.FRM file. For practice, follow these steps to create a new project file that inserts PASSWORD.FRM in the new file by loading the PASSWORD.FRM file into the new application's Project window:

1. Start Visual Basic if you do not currently have it running.

2. If you already have a file or project loaded, save any changes you want to keep and generate a brand new project by selecting File, New Project to open a new Form and Project window.

3. Display the Project window or bring the window into complete view if you cannot see it.

4. A new project always begins with a new form file (unless your AUTOLOAD.MAK startup project file does something else) named FORM1.FRM. Be sure FORM1.FRM is highlighted. Remove this form by choosing the File, Remove File command from the menu bar. The form should disappear from your screen.

5. Add the PASSWORD.FRM file by choosing the File, Add File command. Visual Basic displays the Add File dialog box. From this dialog box you can type or select a form, code module, or custom control file name. When you click OK, Visual Basic adds that new file to the Project window. When you type the PASSWORD.FRM file (be sure to include the full pathname to this book's diskette files), Visual Basic adds PASSWORD.FRM to the Project window as shown in Figure 8.2. You then can click the View Form command button to see the form, or you can select the File, New Form command to work on a new form.

6. Now that you've seen how to add new files to projects, start with a fresh work area by selecting File, New Project (don't save the former project that included the PASSWORD.FRM file).

Fig. 8.2
The Project window now includes the PASSWORD.FRM file.

Tip

Consider creating a separate directory for all your forms, a separate directory for all your code modules, and a separate directory for all your custom controls, to make locating these files easier when you build new applications.

Need Passwords?

If you need to add a text box control for passwords in your own forms, check out the text box control's PasswordChar property. When you type a character such as * for this property's value, Visual Basic displays only asterisks when the user enters text in the text box at runtime. The text box's Text property will hold the value actually typed by the user, but the asterisks keep other users from looking over another user's shoulder and stealing the password.

Your Code window will be able to access the actual value of the Text property for password verification. Read Visual Basic's online help (search for PasswordChar) if you want more detailed information. Although this book cannot describe every property for every control in detail, it explains the most useful properties when they apply to the current subject.

Compiling Applications

Your users should not have to run Visual Basic applications from within the Visual Basic environment. Although throughout this book you'll often be running your programs from within Visual Basic, your users should run stand-alone applications from the Windows Program Manager. The Visual Basic environment gets in the way of the user. Requiring that the user start Visual Basic before running a Visual Basic application would be somewhat like requiring the user to understand source code before running a program. The user should not be able to change forms easily or accidentally. The application is bulletproof only if you compile the application and distribute the compiled code.

When you compile a Visual Basic application, Visual Basic compiles all the forms, modules, and custom controls into a single file. The file name extension will be .EXE because .EXE files are executable from within Windows.

You may distribute compiled applications.

> **Caution**
>
> A compiled Visual Basic application is not a true, 100 percent compiled program. A compiled Visual Basic application does not contain complete stand-alone runtime information needed by a Windows program. Your version of Visual Basic comes with a file named VBRUN300.DLL (the *300* indicates version 3.0—your application may require VBRUN200.DLL or VBRUN400.DLL depending on the version) that you'll have to distribute along with all .EXE files you compile.
>
> This VBRUN file must reside in the user's path set by their AUTOEXEC.BAT batch file. If you are unfamiliar with paths and the AUTOEXEC.BAT batch file, you may want to read *Using DOS* (Que) for an excellent review of PCs and the DOS environment. The compiled application uses routines stored in the VBRUN file. Visual Basic .EXE applications cannot run without access to the VBRUN file. Microsoft enables you to freely distribute the VBRUN file along with your applications.

Create a very simple application from scratch and compile the application now. In doing so, you'll gain further understanding of the Visual Basic compilation command. Follow these steps to create the file named COMPILE.EXE, which you can run from the Windows Program Manager:

1. Double-click the command button in the toolbox to send a new command button to the form.

2. Type **E&xit** (when you first place the command button, its Caption property is the default property) to add a new caption. As soon as you begin typing the new caption, you'll see the new caption appear both on the command button itself and in the Properties window.

3. Scroll to the Name property. Click the Name property and type **cmdExit**.

> **Note**
>
> This application is going to be extremely simple because the primary focus is teaching you about the compilation process. However, good habits are best learned early, and you should get in the habit of properly naming controls as soon as possible.

4. Double-click the cmdExit command button. Visual Basic displays the Code window. Double-clicking a form's control always opens that control's Code window and positions the Code window at the most common procedure for that control. A command button's most

common procedure is `Click` because the most common command button action is clicking the command button with the mouse or keyboard.

5. Press Tab and type **End**. The `End` statement works just as COBOL's `STOP RUN` statement works. When the user clicks the cmdExit command button, the running program terminates. Your screen should look something like the screen in Figure 8.3, although your window sizes may differ slightly from the figure's.

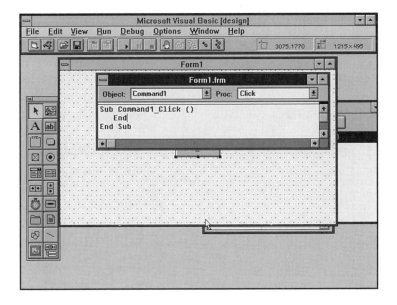

Fig. 8.3
Writing the command button's code.

II

Point & Click Programming

6. Close the Code window.

7. Click anywhere in the Form window's white background and press F4 to display the Form window's properties. Click the Caption property and type **Compiled Application** to change the form's title. Change the form's Name to **frmCompile**.

Caution

Don't confuse the form's Name property with the form's file name. You'll reference the form with its Name property from within the application's code. The individual forms go in a disk-saved file with .FRM file names. The PC file-naming convention (1 to 8 characters with the .FRM extension) differs from Visual Basic's property-naming convention (as described in Chapter 7). The form's Name property properly begins with the `frm` prefix and always differs from the form's file name, which has the .FRM file name extension.

> ## Tip
>
> Here's an easy way for COBOL programmers to recognize the difference between a form's Name property and the form's file name: a COBOL's IDEN-TIFICATION DIVISION's PROGRAM-ID value never matches the program's file name (or the *dataset* name, as some installations call the file). Likewise, a program internally uses the form's Name property, whereas you access the form externally using the form's file name.

8. Test the application by pressing F5. The form simply displays a command button. Click the command button to stop the program's execution.

9. Compile the application now by selecting File, Make EXE from the menu bar. Visual Basic displays a Make EXE File dialog box such as the one shown in Figure 8.4.

Fig. 8.4
Getting ready to compile the application.

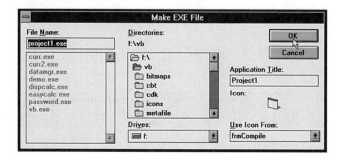

10. Visual Basic uses PROJECT1.EXE as the default .EXE file name. Change the file name to COMPILED.EXE. If you don't type the .EXE extension, Visual Basic adds .EXE for you when you close the dialog box.

11. Change the directory and drive to the location where you want to store the compiled file. Don't save the file to the same location where this book's files are located or you'll overwrite the original file.

12. The Application Title text box contains the text that appears in the Windows Program Manager screen for this application. Change the default text box value to **My Compiled VB Program**.

13. The Use Icon From text box needs a little explanation. Remember that your project may contain one or more forms. Each form has an Icon property that contains a file name for an icon image. When the user minimizes the form at runtime, the Icon property determines which icon appears as the minimized icon. Unless you specify a different icon, Visual Basic uses the same icon for all minimized forms. That default icon appears on the Make EXE File dialog box directly under the Icon label.

You can specify any form's icon image for the application's Program Manager icon. For example, if your application contained three forms, named frmOpening, frmClosing, and frmUser, and each of these forms contained a different Icon property value, you could select any of these forms' Icon values for the application's Program Manager icon image.

Since this project contains only a single form named frmCompile, that's the form name you see in the Use Icon From text box.

14. Click OK and Visual Basic compiles the program. The larger your project is, the longer Visual Basic takes to compile the project. Typically, however, the compilation takes only a moment, and you are quickly returned to the Visual Basic environment.

15. Exit Visual Basic to try the new program. Select File, Exit from the menu bar and save the form and project under the names COMPILE2.FRM and COMPILE2D.MAK so you don't overwrite the book's COMPILED.FRM and COMPILED.MAK files

Compiling Visual Basic programs is easier than compiling COBOL programs. No more JCL, no more lengthy make files, no more waiting on other jobs to complete before yours gets its turn at the compiler!

You're now sitting at the Program Manager ready to run your program. There are two ways to run a Windows program from the Program Manager:

■ Choose the File, Run command from the Program Manager menu bar and type the full pathname and file name of the program you want to run.

or

■ Add a new program item to one of your Program Manager program groups. When you add the new item, you'll see that the program's icon as well as the title appear in the program group, just as they do for the other Windows programs on your system.

Running the program from the Control menu is simple, so do that now. Display the Program Manager's Control menu and select File, Run. Type the full pathname and file name for your compiled application (such as C:\VB\COMPILED.EXE if you stored the program in the C:\VB directory) and press Enter. You should see the running application appear on top of the Program Manager, as shown in Figure 8.5. Once you run the program, click the Exit button and return to the Windows Program Manager.

Fig. 8.5

The program's opening screen after running the program from the Program Manager's Control menu.

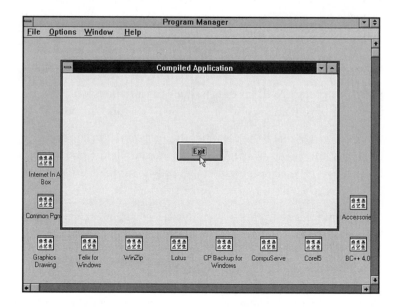

Creating a new program group is easy.

If you want to create a separate program group for your Visual Basic programs (and this is good practice if you're fairly new to Windows, even if you don't plan to keep your Visual Basic programs in one program group), follow these steps:

1. Choose File, New from the Program Manager's Control menu. Visual Basic displays a dialog box with option buttons that let you specify whether you're creating a new program group or item within a program group. Click the Program Group option button and press Enter.

2. A program Group Properties dialog box opens so that you can specify the new program group's title. Type **My Visual Basic Programs** for the title. (There is no group file, so leave Group File blank.) Press Enter and Windows opens a new and empty program group. Now you must fill the group with the program icon.

3. Again, choose File, New from the Program Manager's Control menu. Windows selects the Program Item option button for you, so press Enter. Windows opens the Program Item Properties dialog box shown in Figure 8.6.

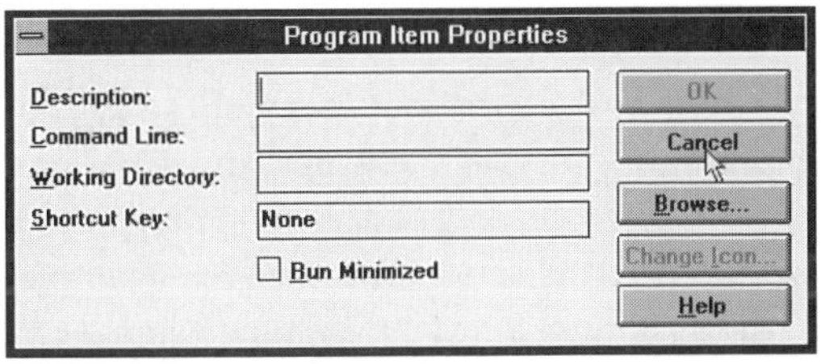

Program Item Properties

Description: ▢
Command Line: ▢
Working Directory: ▢
Shortcut Key: None
☐ Run Minimized

OK · Cancel · Browse... · Change Icon... · Help

Fig. 8.6
Specifying the program group information.

4. For Description, type **Compiled Program**. Press the Tab key to get to the next prompt area. In the Command Line prompt, type the full path and file name for the COMPILED.EXE program (such as C:\VB\COMPILED.EXE). You need not enter a value for the Working Directory or Shortcut Key prompts.

5. Press Enter and Windows adds the program to the program group and uses the program's icon and description for the program item inside the group.

6. To execute the program, double-click the icon just as you execute any other Windows program. When you are finished running the program, close the program group by double-clicking its command button.

Often, applications contain several related but separately compiled programs. You can create different program items for all an application's related programs and store the program items in a single program group.

Tip

Although its use is slightly beyond the scope of this book, you'll find the Application Setup Wizard icon in the Visual Basic program group that helps you create a complete installation package for end users. When you subsequently distribute your application, the users will run an automatic installation routine containing a simple interface that installs your application on their computers. Check the online help for more information on the Application Setup Wizard.

Following the Standards

Visual Basic comes supplied with a special text file named CONSTANT.TXT that you can use in your own applications. CONSTANT.TXT contains defined data for all common elements of Visual Basic programs. You'll find defined values for colors, keyboard values, error codes, and many other common values.

Throughout this book, you'll learn about many of the constants in this file because using a named constant such as BLUE is much easier than using a strange numeric equivalent such as &HFF0000 (you may have heard of hexadecimal values, and &HFF0000 is one such value). For example, suppose you want to turn the background color of a form blue when a certain event takes place. Instead of having to assign a form's background color number such as this:

```
frmDataEntry.BackColor = &HFF0000
```

you can use the defined constant named BLUE like this:

```
frmDataEntry.BackColor = BLUE
```

because BLUE is one of the named constants in CONSTANT.TXT.

Whenever possible, this book uses values from CONSTANT.TXT, to familiarize you with the contents of the file.

Tip

Print a listing of CONSTANT.TXT and keep the listing handy. You can load CONSTANT.TXT into your word processor (CONSTANT.TXT is a simple text file) and print the listing with the word processor's printing command.

When you and your co-programmers use the defined constants in CONSTANT.TXT, all of you will be staying with standard common data values and your programs will be easier to maintain. To load CONSTANT.TXT into your Project window, add the file to your project as described in the section, "The Project File" at the beginning of this chapter. Better still, if you plan to use the constants a lot (and you *should* for better documentation in your code), open your AUTOLOAD.MAK project file and add CONSTANT.TXT to AUTOLOAD.MAK's Project window. When you save the project, all subsequent applications that you create will include CONSTANT.TXT. All of the rest of this book's projects will include CONSTANT.TXT automatically. Add CONSTANT.TXT to your AUTOLOAD.MAK file now.

When CONSTANT.TXT appears in an application's Project window, the file's defined constants appear as code inside the application's Code window. The code appears in the (general) object's (declarations) procedure section. (Chapter 7, "Capturing Events," describes (general) and (declarations).) If you open a project's Code window and select the (declarations) procedure, you can scroll through the CONSTANT.TXT file and view its contents. Figure 8.7 shows the Code window with CONSTANT.TXT displayed.

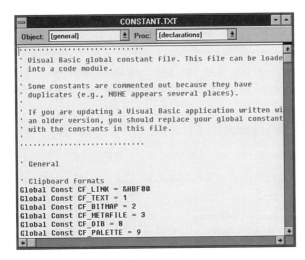

Fig. 8.7
Viewing the contents of CONSTANT.TXT.

Caution

You can use CONSTANT.TXT values only inside the Code window. Unfortunately, the Properties window does not recognize CONSTANT.TXT's defined values. Therefore, you could not use BLUE as the BackColor property in any Properties window, but you can assign BLUE to properties in event code.

Documenting Code

Perhaps the most important statement in any programming language is not an executable statement at all. As a COBOL programmer, you are familiar with comments. Comments let you document your code. Here are just a few advantages of comments:

- Comments describe the purpose of a particular procedure

- Comments help describe complex code

■ Comments explain who wrote the program and when

■ Comments provide a change log of all source code modifications

The first few lines in Figure 8.7's Code window contain comments that describe the purpose of CONSTANT.TXT. As you can see if you load CONSTANT.TXT into a Code window, comments appear in green. Visual Basic applies certain colors to source code to help you distinguish among comments, keywords, and data.

Visual Basic comments are called *remarks*.

Visual Basic comments are called *remarks*. Unlike COBOL, a Visual Basic remark can begin in any column. (*Any* Visual Basic statement can begin in any column of code.) You typically indicate a comment line in COBOL with an asterisk in column 7. Therefore, the following three lines contain two comments:

```
*  Keep reading a file until the file's end.
*  Once finished, display the data-entry screen.
   READ IN-DATA-FILE AT END MOVE 1 TO EOF.
```

Visual Basic remarks always begin with the keyword Rem or an apostrophe (sometimes called a single quote mark), '. The Rem keyword is still supported for compatibility with older versions of BASIC, but the apostrophe is used by more programmers today due to its brevity. Visual Basic treats any statement beginning with Rem or ' as a remark. Here is a Visual Basic remark that is identical to the earlier COBOL comment:

```
Rem  Keep reading a file until the file's end.
Rem  Once finished, display the data-entry screen.
```

Use apostrophes in place of Rem and you get this:

```
'  Keep reading a file until the file's end.
'  Once finished, display the data-entry screen.
```

An additional advantage of the apostrophe over the Rem keyword is that you can place remarks at the end of executable statements. For example, here is a Visual Basic statement with a remark at the end of the statement:

```
MsgBox UsrMsg, MB_Ok, Title  ' Display user's message
```

You cannot append a remark to the end of such a statement with Rem. Therefore, the following is illegal and produces an error:

```
MsgBox UsrMsg, MB_Ok, Title  Rem Display user's message
```

Note

Technically, there is a way to place Rem remarks at the end of statements. If you first terminate a Visual Basic statement with a colon, you can use Rem to begin a remark as in this statement:

```
MsgBox UsrMsg, MB_Ok, Title : Rem Display user's message
```

If you use the colon so that you can use Rem to start the remark, you simply convolute the code more than needed. An apostrophe remark is much simpler and less cumbersome. And the purpose of remarks is to clarify, not to add complexity. Stick to the apostrophe and your remarks will be as unobtrusive as possible while still providing program documentation.

Changing the Environment

If you don't like the colors that Visual Basic assigns to text within the Code window, you can change the colors. The colors are just part of the Visual Basic environment that you can control.

In Chapter 4, "The Visual Basic Screen," you used the Option, Environment command from the menu bar to display and hide grid dots on the Form window. The Environment command contains several other options that you can change, including colors used for the Code window.

Table 8.1 describes every option that you can control using the Environment command. Some programmers like to color remark lines yellow to mimic the yellow sticky notes that we use for real-world comments. Scan Table 8.1's options now so that you'll know what you can modify when and if the need arises. Once you master Visual Basic, you'll know better which environment options you may want to change.

Table 8.1   Environment Option Settings that You Can Change

Setting	Description
Tab Stop Width	The number of spaces the Code window skips when you press Tab
Require Variable Declaration	Requires that you declare all data values before you use them. COBOL requires that all data values be declared in the DATA DIVISION, but Visual Basic does not require that you declare all data unless you set this option's value to Yes.

(continues)

Table 8.1   Continued

Setting	Description
Syntax Checking	Visual Basic can check for syntax errors as you enter code instead of waiting for you to compile or run the program.
Default Save As Format	If set to Binary, Visual Basic compresses your saved forms and modules in a binary file. Otherwise, Visual Basic saves your forms and modules in text files (where forms and their controls are described).
Save Project Before Run	If Yes, Visual Basic ensures that you save your project before running the project.
Selection Text	The color of selected text in data-entry windows.
Selection Background	The background color of selected text in data-entry windows.
Next Statement Text	A debug option that determines the color of the next statement to execute.
Next Statement Background	A debug option that determines the background color of the next statement to execute.
Breakpoint Text	The color of debug breakpoints.
Breakpoint Background	The background color of debug breakpoints.
Comment Text	The color of remarks.
Comment Background	The background color of remarks.
Keyword Text	The color of Visual Basic statements.
Keyword Background	The background color of Visual Basic statements.
Identifier Text	The color of data values in the Code window. *Identifiers* are Visual Basic named data values, procedure names, and labels.
Identifier Background	The background color of data values in the Code window.
Code window Text	The color of miscellaneous text in the Code window.
Code window Background	The background color of miscellaneous text in the Code window.
Debug window Text	The color of miscellaneous debug text in the Code window.

Setting	Description
Debug window Background	The background color of miscellaneous debug text in the Code window.
Grid Width	The number of twips between grid dots.
Grid Height	The number of vertical twips between rows of grid dots.
Show Grid	Determines whether the grid appears in the Form window.
Align To Grid	Determines whether controls automatically align to grid dots.

Tip

If you change any of the text colors in the Environment Options dialog box, Visual Basic immediately displays your change to the right of the color-indicator rows. Figure 8.8 shows such an example. When the user changes the selection background color, Visual Basic displays your chosen colors so that you'll know exactly what your color change will look like. Some color and background color combinations don't look good together. By showing you the colors when you change them, Visual Basic keeps you from having to return to the Environment Options dialog box later.

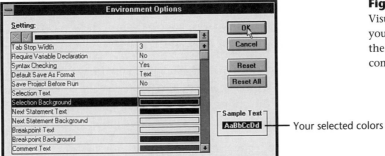

Fig. 8.8
Visual Basic helps you determine the best color combinations.

— Your selected colors

II

Point & Click Programming

At any time, you can reset one or all of the Environment values to their original values by clicking the Reset or Reset All command button. For now, you'll probably leave the Environment values alone until you are comfortable with Visual Basic.

Conclusion

This chapter showed you Visual Basic's equivalents to COBOL's IDENTIFICA-TION and ENVIRONMENT divisions. Although you cannot make a direct comparison because of the tremendous language differences, you can manage Visual Basic's environment through the use of the Options menu, and you can control how Visual Basic executes programs.

This chapter explored the Project window and showed you how to add and remove files from your application's Project window. By adding the CONSTANT.TXT file to all your Project files, you ensure that your applications use common declared data names, and you help future maintenance. Maintenance is especially important for programming departments where several programmers work on portions of the same application.

Maintenance is virtually impossible without comments. Visual Basic offers free-form remarks, which you can start in any column. COBOL's comment requirements are much more rigid, requiring that you begin all comments with an asterisk in column 7. Use the Visual Basic apostrophe to preface your Visual Basic remarks.

This chapter also explained how to compile your Visual Basic programs. By compiling programs before you distribute them, you'll give your users programs that they can run directly from the Program Manager. If you do not distribute compiled programs, your users must have a copy of Visual Basic before they can run your programs.

As you program more with Visual Basic, you'll want to change values in the Environment Options dialog box to improve your efficiency as a programmer. Not all of the options will be meaningful at this time, but you'll be more familiar with them as you use Visual Basic more.

Speaking of debugging, the next chapter ends your tour of the Visual Basic environment by explaining and demonstrating Visual Basic's online debugging aids. You won't believe how easy and powerful Visual Basic's debugger can be. Many COBOL programmers have never used debuggers. If you have not, you're in for a treat.

Chapter 9

Debugging the Visual Basic Way

Effective debugging is often considered a fine art. Complete books have been written on debugging techniques as well as *anti-bugging* techniques (keeping bugs out of your programs). Some people view debugging as though they were solving a puzzle, looking for the stumbling block (the bug) that keeps them from reaching their goal (a working program).

Of course, many people—perhaps most people—approach debugging in a much less spirited way. As programmers, we rarely want to admit that the bug is *ours*. End users might even believe the old data processing joke: "If it compiles cleanly, put it in production and start the next project."

Visual Basic often keeps programmers from dreading the debugging process. First, you have fewer errors because the program I/O is already debugged; you perform all program I/O using pre-written Visual Basic controls. Visual Basic also makes debugging relatively fun and easy as you'll see in this chapter.

Here are some of the topics that are discussed in this chapter:

- Seeing the importance of learning Visual Basic's simple but effective debugger

- Learning how Visual Basic finds syntax errors immediately *as you type code*

- Understanding Visual Basic's *break mode*

- Studying the <u>T</u>oggle Breakpoint command (on the <u>D</u>ebug menu) that pinpoints trouble areas in your code

- Learning how the Add Watch window watches for specific values as your program runs

- Stepping a program through its execution one line at a time.

Why Learn about Debugging Now?

You might wonder why this chapter explains Visual Basic program debugging even though you know very little about the Visual Basic language at this point. It's true that a complete coverage of the Visual Basic language does not commence until the next chapter. Chapter 10 begins Part III, "Primary Differences," of this book. Finally (you've been patient!) you will get to explore the technical differences between the languages—of which there are many.

The Visual Basic environment consumes almost one-third of this book. There is simply no way for you to follow language comparisons without a thorough coverage of Visual Basic's environment first. Until you saw how event-driven programs work and how the user's interface to programs works through controls that you place on the form, you would have no reference for the kind of code needed in Visual Basic programs.

Visual Basic code is not traditional in any sense.

Now that you're about to begin exploring the language differences in the next part of the book, there's no better time to learn how to debug that code than before you begin learning the language syntax. A Visual Basic program does not execute in a top-down, sequential procedural order. Traditional programs execute in a much more predictable fashion than Visual Basic programs.

As you begin to write Visual Basic programs, you must understand the debug tools provided by Visual Basic to help you trace code and analyze data values. You certainly won't understand all the code presented in this chapter. You also may not completely understand why certain debug options work well in Visual Basic. Nevertheless, as you learn programming in subsequent chapters, you'll feel more comfortable in trying various language statements and options. If something goes wrong, you'll be able to analyze the bugs and eliminate them as soon as you locate them.

Finding Syntax Errors Easily

Syntax errors are the easiest kinds of errors to find. As you already know from your years as a COBOL programmer, the compiler finds syntax errors *for you* so you don't have to find them yourself. If you misspell a keyword, the compiler is more than happy to let you know about the mistake.

At the end of the previous chapter, Table 8.1 listed the Options Environment dialog box values. By opening the Options menu and choosing Environment, you can modify the way that Visual Basic behaves. One of the options, Syntax Checking, contains the value Yes or No. If Yes (the default value), Visual Basic checks your syntax *as you write code*; you don't have to wait for a long compile to finish, only to discover that you misspelled a command. Even if you forget an opening or closing parenthesis you'll know as soon as your cursor leaves the code line.

The programs you have seen and written in the earlier chapters of this book have been very small programs. Nevertheless, depending on the speed of your computer and the size of the Visual Basic programs you write, compiling programs does consume time.

As you know, however, you don't have to compile a program to run and test the program. Visual Basic runs a program interactively if you press F5 from the Visual Basic environment. If the executing program finds a syntax error, the program stops and refuses to continue until you fix the error. As mentioned in the previous chapter, the good news is that with Visual Basic, you don't even have to run a program to find syntax errors. As you enter code in the Code window, Visual Basic checks your syntax (as long as you set the Syntax Checking option to Yes). A value of No keeps Visual Basic from checking your code until you run or compile the application.

Start Visual Basic and open a new project now. Follow these steps to see Visual Basic's online syntax checker in progress:

1. Double-click the form in the Form window. The Code window opens, letting you write code for the form's Load event. When the form loads (the primary form always loads when the user first runs an application—so you'll often put startup code in the Form_Load() procedure), this procedure executes.

2. Type the following exactly as you see it, pressing Tab before typing the line:

```
Dim First, Next, Last As String
```

Press Enter when you finish typing this line.

> **Note**
>
> As you'll see in Part III, Dim works a lot like COBOL's DATA DIVISION. Dim declares named data values and reserves storage for those values. Dim is also used to set aside memory for arrays, which are called TABLES in COBOL.

II

Point & Click Programming

3. As soon as you press Enter, Visual Basic displays the error message shown in Figure 9.1.

Fig. 9.1
Visual Basic
immediately finds
an error.

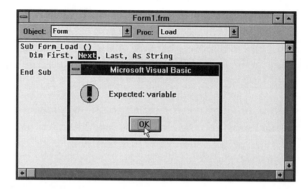

There is a keyword in Visual Basic called Next. The previous code treats Next like a named data value. The error message tells you that Visual Basic expected a variable but you typed something else. In this case, the *something else* is the keyword, Next, that's reserved for use as a command and not a data value.

4. Press Enter or click OK to get rid of the error message box.

5. After Visual Basic displays a syntax error message, such as the one in Figure 9.1, you can do one of two things: you can fix the problem by correcting the syntax error, or you can change Next to NextValue or something else that isn't a reserved keyword. If you fix the problem properly, you won't hear from Visual Basic again about the error.

Or if you want to, you can completely ignore the error message. If you close the message box and type more of the program, without correcting the error, Visual Basic won't tell you about the error again unless you change the line, run, or compile the program. Be assured that Visual Basic always lets you know about the problem eventually, but not while you're in the Code window (unless you edit the line again).

Most of the time, you'll avoid long-range problems by correcting the error as soon as Visual Basic tells you about it.

Now that you've seen the online syntax checking, the next section describes a way to explore the error message in more detail.

Using Online Help for Errors

You may not always know why you get an error message such as the one in Figure 9.1. Visual Basic's online help may be able to rescue you, however. While viewing an error message, if you press the F1 key (the Help key), Visual Basic displays a detailed help screen for the error.

If you press F1 while viewing the previous section's error message, Visual Basic displays the help screen shown in Figure 9.2. The succinct help message may not be a lot better than the original error message, but sometimes the online help gives you insight into the problem. So check out the online help for further details if you don't understand an error message.

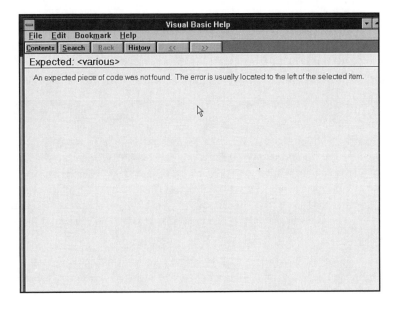

Fig. 9.2
Getting help with an error message.

II

Point & Click Programming

Exterminate Pesky Bugs

Logic errors are not as easy to find as syntax errors because it's *your* job to find the logic errors. Visual Basic includes several tools to help you locate problems when they occur. The following section offers insights into Visual Basic's debugging tools. After you master the language, these tools will greatly increase the speed of your program development time.

Logic errors can be troublesome.

To help with debugging practice, you need to load a program that contains lots of code. Start Visual Basic—if you don't have it running—and load the project file named CALC.MAK from the \VB\SAMPLES\CALC\ directory. This is a calculator program. Run the program to get a feel for how the calculator works. You must click the number buttons on the screen just as you press a real world's calculator buttons to compute results.

After you calculate a few values, terminate the program by clicking the End button on the toolbar, the sixth button from the right that contains a square box. Press F7 to view the Code window. Keep the Code window displayed for the next few sections of the chapter.

Entering Break Mode

You can temporarily halt a Visual Basic program's execution at any time. When you do this, you force the program to enter *break mode*. The break mode is neither a runtime nor a designtime state. The break mode lets you examine data values and control program execution one line at a time.

Tedium: Debugging the Old Way

When you couldn't find the cause of a COBOL program's problem, how did you go about tracing the error? Perhaps you inserted several DISPLAY statements throughout the problem area of the code, compiled the code, and ran the program. The DISPLAYs provided an output trace that you could follow while examining the source code. Maybe you used READY TRACE, or if you were lucky you may have had access to a PC-based COBOL that had a debugger or animator allowing you to step through the code.

Visual Basic moves you into the 1990s by letting you forego adding output statements throughout a program. When you have a problem, you can enter the break mode and look at any value you want without having to insert output statements, and without having to *remove* those same output statements after you find the problem. More important, after you enter the break mode, you can execute the rest of the program or portions of the program one statement at a time. After each statement's execution, you can change and examine data values to get a handle on the problem. You can even change data values at runtime if needed.

After you begin executing a program, there are the several ways to enter break mode:

1. Press Ctrl+Break when the program reaches the point where you want to break.

2. Click the Break command button on the toolbar when the program reaches the point where you want to break.

3. Open the <u>R</u>un menu and choose <u>B</u>reak. Visual Basic enters the break mode. The <u>B</u>reak option does not appear until you run a program.

4. When the program reaches a `Stop` statement, Visual Basic enters the break mode. `Stop`, unlike the `End` statement you've already used, does not terminate a program's execution, but breaks the program so you can examine data at that point in the execution. Programmers rarely use `Stop` because of the power offered by breakpoints (described in the next section, "Setting Breakpoints"). The big problem with `Stop` is that you must remove every occurrence of `Stop` when you finish debugging the program.

> **Caution**
>
> Visual Basic's `Stop` statement is *not* equivalent to COBOL's `STOP RUN` statement. `Stop` enters break mode where you can continue the program's execution if you want. `STOP RUN` and Visual Basic's `End` statement, which do the equivalent actions, completely terminate programs.

5. When execution reaches a preset *breakpoint,* Visual Basic enters the break mode. A breakpoint is simply a place in the program where you want Visual Basic to stop execution and enter the break mode.

6. When execution reaches a preset *break expression,* which you set up in the Add Watch dialog box, Visual Basic enters the break mode. When you designate a break expression, you instruct Visual Basic to stop when a certain data element contains a specific value, either as a result of the user's input or a calculation.

7. When the program reaches an error condition, Visual Basic enters the break mode. For example, if the program asks the user for a disk drive letter and that drive does not exist, the program displays an error message and enters the break mode when the program attempts to access the invalid drive.

> **Note**
>
> You can only enter break mode if you execute the Visual Basic program from within the Visual Basic environment. In break mode, you need the Visual Basic tools to help you examine data; therefore, executing a compiled program from the Program Manager means you have to forego the break mode and deal with error messages that occur.

II

Point & Click Programming

Often, it's not possible to force a program to break in the middle of execution. The program execution runs too rapidly and the section of the program where you want to break flies by too quickly for you to request the break mode. Therefore, you'll often set a breakpoint on a statement where you want the break mode to take over. The program runs, as usual, until execution reaches the breakpoint line and then Visual Basic enters the break mode.

Tip

You know when you're in the break mode because the form title displays [break] to the right of the program title. When you're not in break mode, the title contains either a [design] or [run] message to indicate the current mode of operation.

Setting Breakpoints

The best way to learn about setting breakpoints is by example. Follow these steps to set a breakpoint:

1. Select `Operator()` from the Object drop-down list.

2. Open the Proc drop-down list and choose `Click`.

3. Scroll down in the Code window until you see this code:

```
Select Case OpFlag
    Case "+"
        Op1 = Val(Op1) + Val(Op2)
    Case "-"
        Op1 = Op1 - Op2
    Case "X"
        Op1 = Op1 * Op2
    Case "/"
        If Op2 = 0 Then
```

4. Move the mouse cursor over the line following `Case "-"` and click the mouse button. The insertion cursor moves to the line. Be sure the line you click looks just like this:

```
Op1 = Op1 - Op2
```

5. Open the Debug menu and choose Toggle Breakpoint (or press F9). The toolbar button with the hand icon serves the same purpose.

This sets a breakpoint on the current line. Visual Basic changes the color of the line so you know there is a breakpoint on the line. Figure 9.3 shows how your screen should look now.

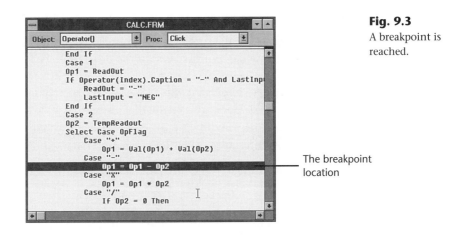

Fig. 9.3
A breakpoint is reached.

The breakpoint location

If you choose Toggle Breakpoint again, the color goes away indicating that the breakpoint is no longer on the line. The reason this command sequence is called the *toggle breakpoint* command is because the breakpoint toggles on and off as you press F9 or choose Toggle Breakpoint from the Debug menu.

6. Close the Code window by double-clicking the document Control menu button (in the upper-left corner of the window).

Don't worry about what the code actually means. After you learn to use the debugger, you'll have powerful tools to help you learn the Visual Basic language.

You can set as many breakpoints as you need in a program.

Now that you've set a breakpoint, you can run the program and the program enters break mode as soon as execution reaches that breakpoint. After the breakpoint is reached (as in the example, by performing a subtract operation and selecting the equal button), you can do one of several things:

■ You can look at and change data values.

■ Depending on the severity of the change, you can sometimes change the breakpoint's code line or change code in lines that follow the breakpoint and then resume execution.

■ You can *single-step* the execution of the program. When you single-step through a program, you control the subsequent execution by executing the code one line at a time, reviewing data values along the way.

II

Point & Click Programming

■ You can execute the rest of the program at normal speed. Execution continues at normal speed until another breakpoint is reached or until execution reaches a normal end of the program.

Breakpoints are very important when debugging Visual Basic programs. Remember that code does not execute in a procedural style as in traditional languages. Therefore, you'll be setting one or more breakpoints to halt a program when certain events trigger the procedures that include the breakpoints.

To see the breakpoint stop the program flow, follow these steps:

1. Run the CALC.MAK program by pressing F5.

2. Click the 4 to *press* the 4 key and see the on-screen 4 command button depress. Click the + to *press* the + key and see the on-screen + command button depress.

3. Click the = to *press* the = key. The calculator window displays the resulting 12. So far, execution has gone along at a normal rate because the breakpoint has not been reached.

4. Click the 9 to *press* the 9 key and click the C to clear the display.

5. Click the – to *press* the – key on the calculator.

6. Click the 5 to *press* the 5 key.

7. Click the = to *press* the = key. As soon as you do, the Code window opens and you're at the same breakpoint you set earlier.

   Although you may not understand the code, it should be fairly obvious what the statement is going to do. Visual Basic is going to subtract a value named Op2 from a value named Op1 and store the result in a value named Op1 (thereby overwriting the original contents of Op1).

   Before executing the statement, look at the contents of Op1. Notice that the cursor is resting on Op1, so you don't have to select Op1 before going further. Click the toolbar button that contains the glasses icon (or open the Debug menu and choose Instant Watch or press Shift+F9). The Instant Watch dialog box appears (refer to Fig. 9.4).

   You can see from the Instant Watch dialog box that the value of Op1 is 9. Good! 9 is the key you pressed first when you began this subtraction series.

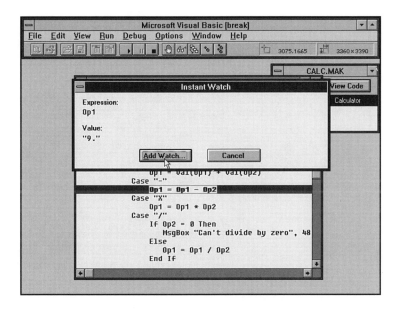

Fig. 9.4
Viewing contents
of values in the
Instant Watch
dialog box.

8. Choose Cancel to close the Instant Watch dialog box. Click the Op2 value on the breakpoint line and click the Glasses button on the toolbar again. The Instant Watch dialog box now displays the value for Op2 (which is 5).

As you see, you can look at individual data values very easily while at a breakpoint. The data values don't have to be on the breakpoint line, either. You can scroll back through the code and click any data value name to see its contents. For now, because Visual Basic is very unfamiliar to you, please don't look at other data values at this time. You could inadvertently change the execution and you would have to repeat these steps.

Tip

If you choose the Add Watch command button in the Instant Watch dialog box, Visual Basic displays the Add Watch dialog box shown in Figure 9.5. Don't display the Add Watch dialog box yourself (or if you do, cancel the dialog box when you see it). After you better understand the way Visual Basic's data values (called *variables*) interact with programs, you'll better understand how and when to use the Add Watch dialog box. For now, you should know that inside the Add Watch dialog box, you can specify specific data values and contents for Visual Basic to break on. If, during subsequent program execution, that data value contains those exact contents, Visual Basic immediately enters the break mode.

Fig. 9.5

Adding a value to
the Add Watch
list.

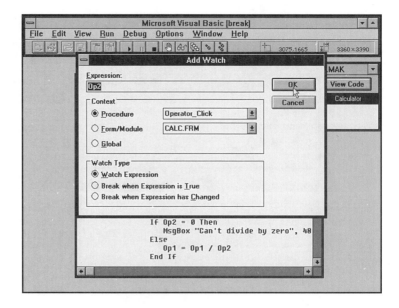

9. Single-step through some more code by clicking the single step button
in the toolbar or by pressing F8. As you click this button with the footstep icon, Visual Basic highlights each subsequent statement as the
execution continues. At any point you can analyze other data values.

The toolbar buttons with the single and double footstep icons work
almost the same way by single-stepping through all of the code except
for procedure calls that execute in their entirety. Again, you'll be able to
understand the rest of the debugging, such as the need for the double
footsteps, as you learn more about Visual Basic.

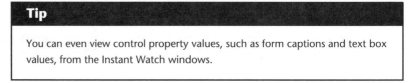

Tip

You can even view control property values, such as form captions and text box
values, from the Instant Watch windows.

10. To finish the program's execution at normal speed, press F5. You can
terminate the program by double-clicking the calculator's control
button.

Now that you've seen some of Visual Basic's powerful debugging tools, are
you ready to really use them? It's time to dive into the Visual Basic code
itself.

Conclusion

This chapter taught you how Visual Basic recognizes syntax errors. Unlike many languages, Visual Basic finds syntax errors as you type them; you don't have to recompile just because you find a typo. If the syntax checking distracts you too much, you can turn it off by opening the Options menu and choosing Environment. Deselect the Syntax Checking option.

The real debugging power comes into play when you learn about the break mode. Visual Basic offers several ways to halt a program's execution at any point in the program. You can view data values and control the subsequent execution once you enter the break mode. When you practice with the Add Watch window (master the Visual Basic language a little first), you'll soon see how value watches you preset can help you trace hard-to-find errors during program execution. Visual Basic watches for a certain value to be reached and enters a break on that value where you then can watch other values, change values, and continue the execution at your own pace.

II

Point & Click Programming

Part III

Primary Differences

Chapter 10

Visual Basic's Version of the *DATA DIVISION*

As you may have already guessed, Visual Basic does not have COBOL-like divisions. Therefore, the title of this chapter is misleading in that there *is no* Visual Basic DATA DIVISION. Visual Basic does, however, work with data effectively and defines that data using statements that work a lot like COBOL's DATA DIVISION. Before targeting specific Visual Basic keywords and statements, you must understand the kinds of data that Visual Basic can manage.

Visual Basic programs work with more kinds of data than COBOL does. This may surprise you because you may think that COBOL supports every kind of data type imaginable. It's true that you can represent any kind of data in COBOL programs, but COBOL does not break down data into as many different types as Visual Basic does. By letting you work with a wider range of data, you have more programming power when you need to deal with unique data such as dates and highly scientific numbers.

In this chapter, you'll learn how to declare data and how to assign values to data storage. Data values form the underlying base on which all your programs operate. After all, without data, what good would *data processing* be?

Here are some of the topics that will be discussed in this chapter:

- Learning the different kinds of Visual Basic data

- Using variables of all types and sizes to hold data

- Understanding the importance of explicit declaration in Visual Basic

- Using type-declaration characters as an alternative declare data approach

- Assigning values to variables

- Managing the scope of your data

- Learning how to define your own record data types

Visual Basic's Data Types

COBOL supports these three types of data:

Alphabetic

Alphanumeric

Numeric

Before you can use a data value, such as a field in a record or a working storage value, you must first define the data in the DATA DIVISION. When you define data, you tell the COBOL compiler exactly what types of data the value will hold, the name of the value, and the size of the value. Often, the incoming record format dictates the size and type of data. The name of the data is a reference that your program uses to access and manipulate the data.

Most of this chapter sticks to working storage data values. Visual Basic's data is more easily explained when sticking to the working data you are used to. Consider the COBOL WORKING-STORAGE SECTION shown in Listing 10.1. Listing 10.1 declares four data values. The first data value is 25 alphabetic characters wide, the second consists of two unsigned numeric digits, the third is a signed value with an implied decimal point, and the fourth is a 4-character alphanumeric location.

Listing 10.1 A Sample *WORKING-STORAGE SECTION* in COBOL

```
WORKING-STORAGE SECTION.
01 WORK-AREAS.
    02 NAME          PIC A(25).
    02 AGE           PIC 99.
    02 AMT           PIC S9999V99.
    02 CODE          PIC XXXX.
```

All numeric Visual Basic data types are automatically signed. Therefore, you won't have to worry about specifying signed or unsigned as you do in COBOL. Most COBOL programmers learn early that using signed numeric values is often more efficient than using unsigned values; therefore, most programmers use only signed values when possible.

> **Caution**
>
> There is no Visual Basic equivalent to COBOL's PICTURE clause P character (the zero-fill) or 88-level (condition name) data. Also, unless you work with record data, you can think of all Visual Basic data as being 77-level data. Although 77-level data is rare in COBOL, using stand-alone data values for Visual Basic programs makes more sense than in COBOL, which is a record-based language.

Data values that you declare, name, and use in Visual Basic programs are called *variables*. Visual Basic holds all kinds of data values, both field data and working storage values, in variables. The data habits that you learned in COBOL will pay off with Visual Basic. You should declare all variables before you ever use them. By declaring all variables, you'll explicitly tell Visual Basic what names to assign to the variables, what the data types should be, and the size of the data.

Variables hold data.

> **Note**
>
> You might think that declaring variables before using them is the *only* way to approach data. You'll learn later in this chapter that Visual Basic provides an option that lets you use a variable without declaring that variable ahead of time. Although you can use undeclared variables, doing so can easily add bugs to your code. Stick with your COBOL training and declare all variables before using them.

Can you remember way back when you learned COBOL? Your first few weeks were spent learning about the DATA DIVISION. Knowing how to declare data is important, but the different kinds of Visual Basic data make learning about this data difficult. The next few sections walk you through Visual Basic's data declarations.

Data Types

Table 10.1 lists all of Visual Basic's different kinds of data types. There are a lot of data types and some of them overlap others. Study the table to familiarize yourself with the data types.

Table 10.1 The Visual Basic Data Types	
Data Type	**Description**
Integer	Whole numeric values that have no decimal places and range from -32,768 to 32,767.
Long	Whole numeric values that have no decimal places that range from -2,147,483,648 to 2,147,483,647. Long data types can hold more extreme values than Integer data types but are less efficient during runtime.
Single	Numeric values that range from -3.402823E38 to 3.402823E38. Sometimes, the Single data type is called *single precision*.
Double	Numeric values that range from -1.79769313486232E308 to 1.79769313486232E308. Sometimes, the Double data type is called *double precision*.
Currency	Holds dollar amounts from -922,337,203,685,477.5808 to 922,337,203,685,477.5807.
String	Holds from 0 to 65,500 characters of alphanumeric data.
Variant	Holds any kind of data. You'll often store time and date values in Variant variables.

In COBOL, values that had no V in their PIC clauses were integers. In Visual Basic, variables that you define using the Integer and Long keyword are integers. Notice that instead of the simplified 9 PIC clause character that COBOL has, Visual Basic supports five different kinds of numeric data. When you first declare a variable, you'll tell Visual Basic which of these data types the variable is to be.

Never give a data value a larger data type than needed. For instance, it would be inefficient to store a person's age in a variable declared as a Long variable. The Long variable will take much more space than Integer, and someone's age is always well within the range of possible values that an Integer can hold. You would use the Single data type for most decimal values, reserving the larger range of Double data types for highly scientific and engineering applications where high decimal accuracy is required.

Visual Basic forces you to think about your data before you declare variables. If you will be working with extremely large integers, you'll have to declare those variables with the Long data type. Declare all money variables with the Currency data type. Even though the range of the Currency data type in

Table 10.1 includes four decimal places, Visual Basic keeps all `Currency` accurate to two decimal places so your money calculations will always come out to the correct penny.

Note

Not every COBOL programmer has a scientific background. If you don't, that's okay and you don't have to have a scientific mind to understand Visual Basic fully. However, you may not be familiar with the *scientific notation* used in Table 10.1. Scientific notation is a shortcut method for describing extremely small and extremely large numeric values. Table 10.1 expresses all ranges containing the letter E in scientific notation. The E stands for *exponent*.

To convert from scientific notation to a regular number, here's all you do: multiply the number to the left of the E by 10 raised to the number to the right of the E. Therefore, 3.402823E38 means to multiply 3.402823 by 10 raised to the 38th power, or 10^{38}. 10^{38} is a very large number (it is 10 followed by 38 zeroes). The bottom line is that 3.402823E38 means 3402823 followed by 32 zeroes. (Six of the 38 places are consumed by the digits to the right of the 3.)

Scientific notation is often used to show extreme values in a range of numbers and it keeps the numbers manageable. Table 10.1 would look ridiculous listing the non-scientific notational value of 3.402823E38 because of the number of zeroes necessary to reflect the actual number.

Use the `String` data type for all alphabetic and alphanumeric data variables. Rarely do COBOL programmers use `A` declarations in `PIC` clauses, so you're probably already used to working with alphanumeric values that hold all kinds of data.

Variant is too flexible to use for all data.

The `Variant` data type can hold *any* of the other kinds of data. In other words, if you declare a variable to be a `Variant` variable, you can store `Currency`, `Long`, or `Double` data values in the `Variant` variable without a problem. Despite the flexibility of `Variant`, resist the temptation to overuse it. Storing date values in `Variant` data types is discussed in Chapter 22, "Using Dates and Times," and storing control property values with `Variant` is discussed in Chapter 11, "Controls also Contain Data."

Caution

The `Variant` data type is more inefficient than the other data types. To keep your programs as efficient as possible, use `Variant` only when the application requires it.

III

Primary Differences

Visual Basic is flexible enough to let you use variables that you have not declared. If you use an undeclared variable, Visual Basic treats that variable as if you had declared it as a `Variant` variable.

> **Note**
>
> All Visual Basic keywords, such as commands and data types, begin with an initial uppercase letter and end with lowercase letters. If you don't follow this convention when typing code into the Code window, Visual Basic will change your case to match the requirement. In other words, if you type `INTEGER` when declaring a variable, Visual Basic will change `INTEGER` to `Integer`.
>
> You're used to typing all COBOL code in uppercase letters so turn that Caps Lock key off!

Naming Variables

Assign names to all variables.

Before you can use variables, you must understand how to assign names to variables. Just as you must make up names for all DATA DIVISION values, so must you make up names for variables. Be sure to use meaningful variable names so that the names can help document your code.

Variables follow the same naming rules as all Visual Basic *identifiers*, including control names. Here is a list of naming rules for Visual Basic variables (in Chapter 6, "Presto, No Code Required!" you learned these same rules for control names):

- Variable names must begin with a letter.

- Variable names must contain letters, numbers, and the underscore (_) character. The underscore is sometimes used for separating parts of a name.

- Variable names can contain from one to 40 characters.

- A variable name cannot be a reserved word such as a Visual Basic command.

Declaring Variables

Dim stands for dimension.

There are several ways to declare variables in Visual Basic. The best way is to use the `Dim` command. There are several extended formats of the `Dim` command but here is the simplest format for declaring variables:

```
Dim VarName As DataType
```

Using this format, you'll substitute a new variable name in place of the *VarName* and one of the variable data types (from Table 10.1) in place of *DataType*. The following are four `Dim` statements that declare the variables that take on the same qualities that you saw earlier in Listing 10.1's COBOL DATA DIVISION:

```
Dim Name As String * 25
Dim Age As Integer
Dim Amt As Currency
Dim Code As String *4 4
```

Instead of using all uppercase letters for the variable names, Visual Basic programmers often follow the same initial capital letter format that Visual Basic requires for all keyword commands. You don't have to type variable names by using a mixture of uppercase and lowercase letters, but you should stick to the standards set forth by others who came before you. You want to write code that's as maintainable by as many people as possible.

Visual Basic does not consider variable case significant. In other words, all of the following variable names are equivalent and all reference the same variable:

```
Sales    SALES    sales    sALES
```

Caution

If you declare a variable using a combination of uppercase and lowercase letters, then change the case later in the program, Visual Basic has a nasty habit of converting the previous variables to the most recent case. Therefore, if you declare a variable like this:

```
Dim Sales As Currency
```

then later in the program, access the variable by typing **SALES**, Visual Basic immediately converts the `Dim` statement you typed to this:

```
Dim SALES As Currency
```

Be careful and consistent in how you specify the case. If you notice that a variable has a different case from what you intended, you probably typed the name incorrectly the most recent time you used it. All you have to do is change the variable name back to the format you intended, and Visual Basic restores all the other occurrences for you.

If you wish, you can consolidate variable declarations. You can combine the four variable declarations into a single line of code like this:

```
Dim Name As String * 25, Age As Integer, Amt As Currency,
➡ Code As String * 4
```

Don't declare too many variables on the same line, however, because long line lengths often scroll off the Code window's right edge and make subsequent maintenance difficult. Perhaps a better declaration would be this:

```
Dim Name As String * 25, Code As String * 4
Dim Age As Integer
Dim Amt As Currency
```

This code declares each data type on a separate line.

Fixed-Length Strings

As a COBOL programmer, you're used to specifying data lengths for values. Visual Basic lets you limit the number of characters that a string can hold. You cannot limit other data type lengths, however.

Strings can hold a maximum of 65,500 alphanumeric characters unless you declare the string variable to be a *fixed-length string*. You declare a fixed-length string in the same way as you declare other string variables except that you add an asterisk and a size value to the right of the definition. The following statement declares Name to be a string variable that can hold at most 25 characters:

```
Dim Name As String * 25
```

By declaring fixed-length strings, you determine in advance exactly how long each string value can be that will appear in that variable. Fixed-length strings, such as Name defined here, more accurately represent the COBOL character data equivalent shown here:

```
02 NAME           PIC A(25).
```

Fixed-length strings can hold a maximum of their fixed-length size. The Name variable can hold a maximum of 25 characters. If you attempt to store a longer string in Name, Visual Basic truncates the string after the first 25 characters.

Note

If you don't declare string variables as fixed-length strings, Visual Basic automatically makes the strings *variable-length strings*. You're unfamiliar with variable-length data values because COBOL does not support variable-length data.

When you declare a string to be variable-length, you can store any string of any length inside the variable (up to the 65,500-character maximum). For example, if you assign a 10-character literal to the string, the variable will hold 10 characters. If, later in the program, you want to store a 75-character literal, Visual Basic expands the string variable to hold the 75 characters. If you then store a smaller string literal, Visual Basic shrinks the size of the variable to hold the smaller string.

Variable-length strings are flexible but require slightly more runtime efficiency than fixed-length strings. Also, when dealing with fixed-length records, you'll want to declare fixed-length strings to maintain a stable record length.

Declaring Variables by Default

When you choose the Environment command from the Options menu, you find the Explicit Declaration option. You can set the Explicit Declaration option to either No (the default) or Yes. When set to Yes, Visual Basic requires that you declare all variables, with Dim, before you ever use those variables in your programs.

If you change Explicit Declaration from Yes value, to No, you can start using variable names anywhere in the program without first declaring them. All variables will be the Variant data type. Such undeclared variables are *implicitly declared* by Visual Basic, meaning that Visual Basic automatically assumes the Variant data type.

Explicitly declaring variables often prevents bugs from creeping into your code. By keeping the Explicit Declaration set to Yes, you ensure that you cannot accidentally misspell a variable name. Suppose you didn't want to explicitly declare variables so you started using a variable named MySalary. Later in the program, you typed MySallary instead of MySalary. Visual Basic will not issue an error message because Visual Basic assumes that you're using a brand new variable name. How could Visual Basic know that you meant to type MySalary? The value of MySallary will be zero (all numeric variables are zero until you set them to some other value) so you'll get an incorrect result in the code. Such incorrect results can be tricky to find, even with the debugger.

Leaving the Explicit Declaration set to Yes ensures that Visual Basic checks all spellings of all variables and immediately issues an error if you incorrectly misspell a variable's name.

III

Primary Differences

Alternative Variable Definitions

Visual Basic offers additional ways to declare variables but using Dim is the preferred method. There are two specific methods that you should learn about now because you may run across them in Visual Basic programs that you maintain. Don't use these type-declarations in your own programming work, however. Visual Basic retains these outdated methods for compatibility with older versions of BASIC.

Using Type-Declaration Suffix Characters

Type-declaration suffix characters describe data types.

There are six special characters that you can place at the end of variable names that indicate what data type the variable contains. Table 10.2 lists these *type-declaration suffix characters*. (There is no suffix character for Variant data types.)

Table 10.2 The Type-Declaration Suffix Characters	
Suffix Character	**Data Type**
%	Integer
&	Long
!	Single
#	Double
@	Currency
$	String

The suffix character indicates what type of data the variable can hold. Therefore, you don't have to declare variables with Dim if you use the type-declaration suffix characters.

For example, suppose you needed to define a variable that holds a city name. Instead of first using Dim to declare a string variable named CityName, you could use CityName$ without first declaring the variable. Visual Basic knows from the $ suffix that the variable is a string variable.

The suffix characters, at first glance, seem to be easier to use than taking the time to declare them. After all, you don't have to waste time with a Dim statement. There are two drawbacks to using the suffix characters, however, and they are:

1. You must always type the suffix character every time you use the variable name in the program.

2. You face the same problem as you do if you set the Explicit Declaration option to No. That is, you might begin using a variable named `CityName$` and misspell the variable as `CityNam$` later in the program. Visual Basic will not recognize or warn you that you're using an undefined variable (`CityNam$`). This bug can be difficult to trace because you might think that you stored a value in a variable that did not really get the value.

The `Dim` statement offers several additional options that this chapter cannot describe. You learn the entire format of the `Dim` statement in Chapter 16, "Table-Handling and Control Arrays," when you learn how to process table data. Nevertheless, you'll keep more bugs out of your code if you get in the habit of using `Dim` now; you'll be ready for the more advanced `Dim` options when this book discusses them.

Using Def*type* To Declare Variables

Table 10.3 lists seven new Visual Basic statements that you can use, in place of `Dim`, to declare variables. Notice that the syntax of these statements includes letter ranges. When you declare a variable with one of the `Def*type*` statements, you're informing Visual Basic that all variables whose names begin with a letter in the letter range will be a specific data type.

Table 10.3 Using DEF*type* To Declare Variables	
Syntax	**Data Type Declared**
`DefInt letterrange [, letterrange]...`	Integer
`DefLng letterrange [, letterrange]...`	Long
`DefSng letterrange [, letterrange]...`	Single
`DefDbl letterrange [, letterrange]...`	Double
`DefCur letterrange [, letterrange]...`	Currency
`DefStr letterrange [, letterrange]...`	String
`DefVar letterrange [, letterrange]...`	Variant

III

Primary Differences

The following variable declaration:

```
DefInt I-N
```

tells Visual Basic that any variable beginning with the letters I, J, K, L, M, or N (or their lowercase equivalents) in the rest of the code will all be integer variables. The data type suffix characters can override DEF*type* though. If you were to use a variable named Length#, Visual Basic knows the variable is a double-precision variable due to the #.

As with type-declaration suffix characters, the Dim statement is safer to use than the Def*type* statement and suffix characters, so use Dim whenever you can.

Putting Values in Variables

Now that you can declare variables, you must see how to store data in the variables. COBOL uses the MOVE command to assign values to data such as this:

```
MOVE 'Smith' TO NAME.
MOVE 'X34A' TO CODE.
MOVE 34 TO AGE.
MOVE 3234.56 TO AMT.
```

Visual Basic uses the *assignment* statement to put values into variables. The assignment statement assigns, or stores, values to variables that you have defined. Here is the format of assignment:

```
[Let] VarName = ExpressionValue
```

The assignment used to be called LET because older versions of BASIC required LET at the beginning of the statement. LET has been optional in BASIC incarnations for years and today's programmers rarely use LET. The *VarName* must be a valid variable name, hopefully one that you have declared before. The *ExpressionValue* can be any of these kinds of values:

A literal

A variable name that has an equivalent data type

A control property value (Chapter 11, "Controls also Contain Data," explores controls used with variables)

An expression made up of mathematical or string operations, including combinations of literals and variables

As you progress through this book, you'll learn about the many combinations of items that you can assign to variables. The most important thing to know at this point is that the assignment stores values in variables.

To represent a Visual Basic numeric literal, just as in COBOL, you only need to type the number. All of the following are numeric literals:

```
30    5.642    -9    0.0434    1234.5676
```

If you are working with extremely large or small numbers, you can type a numeric literal in scientific notation.

To represent a string literal, you must enclose the string in quotation marks. All of the following are string literals:

```
"PC"    "a quick brown fox"    "Conservative"    ""
```

The last string literal is a special literal called a *null string*. Sometimes, you'll assign null strings (empty quotation marks) when values are missing or when strings have yet to be assigned values. There are also some Visual Basic language extensions that deal with null and missing data that you'll learn about as you progress with the language.

> **Caution**
>
> Notice that Visual Basic supports regular (double) quotation marks for string delimiters as opposed to COBOL's single apostrophe marks. 'A string' is a COBOL string, but to represent the same literal in Visual Basic requires this: "A string".

The following is the Visual Basic code that both declares four variables and then assigns values to all four variables:

```
Dim Name As String * 25, Code As String * 4
Dim Age As Integer
Dim Amt As Currency
'
' Now, put values in the variables
'
Name = "Smith"
Code = "X34A"
Let Age = 34
Amt = 3234.56
```

Notice how the three-line remark helps separate the declaration area from the assignment area. The more you can clarify your code with remarks and extra spacing, the more readable and maintainable your code will be.

III

Primary Differences

The third assignment used the optional Let keyword. The rest of this book follows current trends, however, and avoids using Let. Figure 10.1 shows how these variables reside in memory after the assignments occur. The Name variable has lots of unused space right now, but perhaps the 25 characters of storage can be used later in the program.

Fig. 10.1

These four variables hold four values after assignment statements.

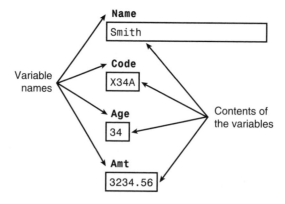

Variable names

Name
Smith

Code
X34A

Age
34

Amt
3234.56

Contents of the variables

Caution

Remember that fixed-length strings truncate their data values. In other words, if you assigned a string that is too long to the Code variable:

```
Code = "A344FE52"
```

Visual Basic only stores the first four characters of the literal, A344, in Code because the Dim statement declared Code to be a 4-character fixed-length string.

Chapter 12, "The Math Operations," describes all of Visual Basic's math capabilities. However, it's not too difficult to get a glimpse into simple mathematical expressions. The following statements declare three variables, then assign values to each of them. Notice that you can assign literals and expressions to variables.

```
Dim GrossPay As Currency, Taxes As Currency
Dim Rate As Single
Dim Hours As Integer
'
' Calculate the pay amounts
'
GrossPay = Rate * Hours
Taxes = GrossPay * .35
```

> **Note**
>
> The asterisk is Visual Basic's multiplication sign. Therefore, this statement:
>
>   GrossPay = Rate * Hours
>
> is equivalent to COBOL's
>
>   MULTIPLY RATE * HOURS GIVING GROSSPAY.
>
> or
>
>   COMPUTE GROSSPAY = RATE * HOURS.

The assignment's equal sign tells Visual Basic to take whatever is on the right side of the equal sign, calculate the expression (if there is a calculation), and store that result in the variable on the left side of the equal sign. Figure 10.2 helps show what happens when the two expressions are assigned to variables. The equal sign acts as a left-pointing arrow, sending the right side of the equal sign over to fill the variable on the left side.

GrossPay = Rate * Hours

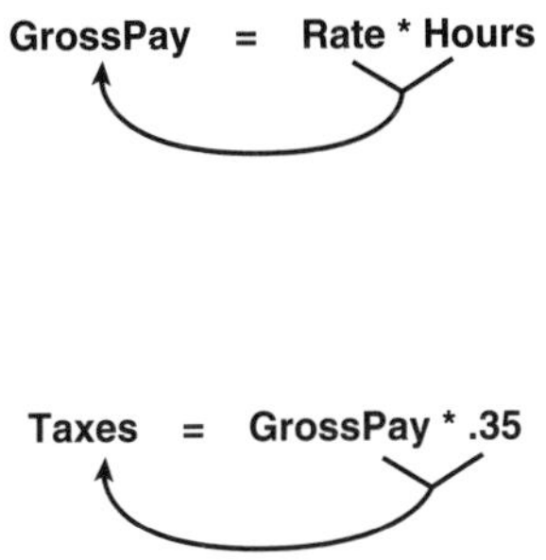

Fig. 10.2
Storing computed results in variables.

Taxes = GrossPay * .35

Even a statement such as this:

    NumCusts = NumCusts + 1   ' Adds 1 to NumCusts

works without issuing an error. The + acts like a plus sign. You may study this assignment statement and think that nothing can be equal to itself plus one more. Your math logic is correct, but the assignment, remember, works as if it's a left-pointing arrow storing the right-hand result into the left-hand variable. Therefore, Visual Basic first adds 1 to NumCusts and then stores that resulting value in NumCusts overwriting NumCusts original value. The equivalent COBOL statement would look like this:

    ADD 1 TO NUMCUSTS.

III

Primary Differences

Declaring Variables before Using Them

Unlike COBOL, which requires that you declare all named data values in the DATA DIVISION, you can declare variables in these three places within a Visual Basic program:

- Within an event procedure. These variables are called *local variables*.

- Within the (declarations) procedure of the object named (general). You might recall from Chapter 7 that the Code window contains an object named (general) and a procedure named (declarations). When you add the CONSTANT.TXT file to your Project window, Chapter 8 explained that named variables from CONSTANT.TXT load into the (declarations) procedure of the object named (general).

  Actually, these named locations are misleading. There really is not an object named (general) (hence the parentheses) or a procedure named (declarations). This section of your code, however, contains general-purpose data definitions that *all* the rest of the procedures can access. These variables are called *module variables*.

- Within a BAS code module that you create by choosing the New Module command in the File menu. You must substitute Global for Dim when declaring these variables. These variables are called *global variables*.

These three kinds of variables, local, module, and global, have different scoping rules. The *scope* of a variable (the location of the variable's definition) determines how far away in the current program other code can recognize the data values.

COBOL programs contain only global variables. Once you define a data value in the DATA DIVISION, any code in the rest of the program can use that value. However, such global variables are rarely used by Visual Basic programmers. Visual Basic programmers prefer to declare variables on a need-to-know basis. In other words, if only one event needs access to a certain variable, then that event should declare the variable. If two or more events within the same file need to access the same variable's value, that variable should be a module variable. If two or more modules within the same application (such as two or more BAS code modules) need to use the same variable's value, that variable should be a global variable.

Each of the following sections describes local, global, and module variable scopes and shows an example of how you declare them.

Declaring Local Event-Level Variables

When you declare a variable at the top of an event procedure, you declare a local variable that Visual Basic only recognizes for the life of that event. The following is the complete code for a command button's `Click` event:

```
Sub cmdInvFactor_Click()
' Adds an inventory factor to a module-level
' inventory total when the user clicks the
' inventory command button
   Dim FactAdd As Single
   FactAdd = 25
   InventoryAmt = InventoryTotal + FactAdd
End Sub
```

Notice how the three-line remark describes the purpose of the procedure. In this procedure, the variable named `FactAdd` is a local variable. No other procedure can use `FactAdd` (unless another event procedure declares a new local `FactAdd` used only in that procedure). Visual Basic creates the variable in this procedure's fifth line and Visual Basic destroys `FactAdd` at the `End Sub` statement. Other procedures, therefore, cannot use `FactAdd`. Think of `FactAdd` as if it were a temporary variable because `FactAdd` really *is* temporary and lasts only as long as this procedure executes.

You must assume that the other two variables, `InventoryAmt` and `InventoryTotal`, are either module or global variables. These two variables are already declared when this procedure begins and they may already have values in them.

Declaring Module Variables

When you declare variables in the `(declarations)` procedure list of the `(general)` object, you declare module variables. All events within the form's scope can use module variables.

You'll declare major variables used throughout your form's scope in the `(declarations)` procedure list of the `(general)` object. Figure 10.3 shows a Code window open to the `(declarations)` procedure and five variables are declared there. Any subsequent event in the form can access or change these variable values.

> **Note**
>
> The only procedure available in the Proc drop-down list of the `(general)` object is the `(declarations)` procedure. `(declarations)` is not really a procedure, because it does not contain the Sub and End Sub statements. Instead, it is a section of code available to all other event procedures in the file.

Fig. 10.3

These variables are module variables.

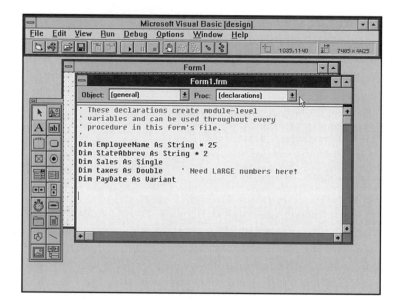

Declaring Global Variables

Avoid declaring too many global variables.

When you declare global variables, every procedure in every form of your application can use and change these variables. This advantage can also be a disadvantage, however, because debugging is difficult when all variables are available to all locations in the program.

Consider what happens when you write a COBOL program that displays an incorrect value. You must search through the entire program looking for the incorrect calculation. However, if that variable were a module or a local variable, you could narrow the focus and better target the offending code.

You must open or create a module code file before declaring global variables. Recall that module files end with the .BAS extension. One of the most important reasons for opening module files is to declare global variables for those times when you need globals. To open a module code file, choose New Module from the File menu. A new Code window opens and Visual Basic names your first module file MODULE1.BAS. If you open a second module file, Visual Basic names it MODULE2.BAS, and so on.

> **Tip**
>
> The New Module toolbar button, the second toolbar button from the left, opens a new module.

The only event and procedure available in a module file are (general) and (declarations). If you want to move to the form's Code window, press the F7 access key. Once you exit a module's Code window, you will have to use the Project window to edit the module once again. Once you open a new module, use Global in place of Dim to declare the variables. Global is identical to Dim only Global declares global variables whereas Dim is reserved for local and module variable declarations.

You can declare variables in a module by using Dim, but those variables are only module-level variables. These variables are available only to the code within the module, not to other modules and forms in the application. You must use Global if you want to declare global variables that are available throughout all files and modules in the application.

After opening a new module, the following code declares three global variables:

```
Global MyName As String
Global MyWeight As Single
Global MyBirthDate As Variant
```

If you choose the Save command from the File menu, Visual Basic gives you a chance to store the file in a module file. Module files usually end with the .BAS or .TXT file name extension.

Figure 10.4 shows the three types of variables and how they relate to each other.

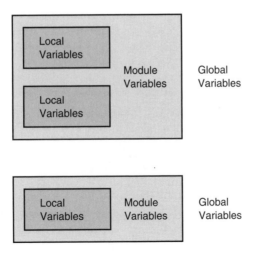

Fig. 10.4
The relationship between Visual Basic's three types of variables.

Constant **Variables**

If your program works with values that don't change, you write much more maintainable code than if you store those fixed values in variables. For example, suppose that your company uses a minimum age value of 19 for part-time help. Every place in the code that tests for the minimum age can use the *hard-coded* value of 19. However, if the minimum age that your company uses changes to another value, you will have to change that value every place in the program where it appears.

You will be better off storing such variable values in the global or module scoping level. If the company's minimum age changes, you'll only have to change the value in one location.

The CONSTANT.TXT file is an excellent example of such values. For example, the Windows color value for green is the hexadecimal number &HFF00. Although it's not likely that the Windows color value for green will change anytime soon, Microsoft might decide to change this value somewhere down the road. If you've used the CONSTANT.TXT file and referenced the color green with the GREEN variable stored in CONSTANT.TXT, you'll only need to update the value in CONSTANT.TXT and recompile your applications using the new CONSTANT.TXT file.

If you were to look through CONSTANT.TXT, you would see a new keyword, Const. For example, here is a section from CONSTANT.TXT's code:

```
' DrawStyle
Global Const SOLID = 0         ' 0 - Solid
Global Const DASH = 1          ' 1 - Dash
Global Const DOT = 2           ' 2 - Dot
Global Const DASH_DOT = 3      ' 3 - Dash-Dot
Global Const DASH_DOT_DOT = 4  ' 4 - Dash-Dot-Dot
Global Const INVISIBLE = 5     ' 5 - Invisible
Global Const INSIDE_SOLID = 6  ' 6 - Inside Solid
```

You'll notice that these statements not only declare seven global variables, but also assign values to the variables as well. The Const keyword indicates that the assigned value can *never change*. Therefore, you can not accidentally change the value for DOT with an assignment elsewhere in your application.

You can define your own constants by using Const and you can declare local, module, or global constants. If you use Const to the right of a Global statement, the constant will be a global constant available to all other code in the application. If you don't use Global, the constant will be either a local or module constant, depending on where you declare the constant. (Don't ever use `Const` with a `Dim` statement or Visual Basic issues an error.)

Suppose you were working with a sales reporting program that offered sales discounts to all sales over $100,000. You could declare a global constant in a code module like this:

```
Global Const SalesBreak = 100000.00
```

Visual Basic looks at the value with which you initialize the constant and determines the appropriate data type. For example, Visual Basic would declare `SalesBreak` as a single-precision value because of the `100000.00` constant value.

> **Tip**
>
> Often, programmers type their constant names in all uppercase letters, as done in the CONSTANT.TXT file. The full uppercase constants help remind you that you're working with data that cannot be changed.

User-Defined Types

Although most newcomers to Visual Basic have to wait until later in their study to learn about records, you have a big advantage with a COBOL background. The data that you work with most often in COBOL is record-based data. Visual Basic calls record data *user-defined types*. In other words, a record is not an integer, a single-precision, or a double-precision, but a user-defined type that is a collection of all those other types combined into a single unit.

Records are called *user-defined types*.

> **Note**
>
> Don't let the word *user* in *user-defined type* throw you. You, the programmer, define records, so as far as the program code is concerned, you are the *user* of records. *User-defined type* has nothing to do with the end user.

Whenever you want Visual Basic to treat a collection of data values as a single record unit, use the `Type` and `End Type` statements to enclose the new data type definition. You'll best learn how user-defined types work by example. Consider the following user-defined type declaration:

```
Type CustomerRecType
  LastName As String * 15
  FirstName As String * 15
  Address1 As String * 25
  Address2 As String * 25
  CityName As String * 10
  StateName As String * 2
  Zipcode As String * 9
  CustBalance As Single
  CustRepeat As Integer
End Type
```

Here is how you might define this data type in COBOL:

```
01 CUSTOMERRECTYPE.
   02 LASTNAME      PIC A(15).
   02 FIRSTNAME     PIC A(15).
   02 ADDRESS1      PIC A(25).
   02 ADDRESS2      PIC A(25).
   02 CITYNAME      PIC A(10).
   02 STATENAME     PIC A(2).
   02 ZIPCODE       PIC A(9).
   02 CUSTBALANCE   PIC 99999V99.
   02 CUSTREPEAT    PIC 99.
```

CustomerRecType is *not* a record yet! CustomerRecType is a new data type that you've just added to the program. To declare a record variable, you must use CustomerRecType:

```
Dim Customer1 As CustomerRecType
```

Use the dot operator to access fields.

When it comes time to assign values to the record's fields, you must qualify the field names with the dot operator. Consider this: more than one record type, such as an employee record, and a vendor record, may contain fields that have the very same name as one or more of the CustomerRec's fields (such as Address1, CityName, and ZipCode). Therefore, to assign an address to the customer's first address line, you would have to tell Visual Basic that you want to assign the value like this:

```
Customer1.Address1 = "4394 E. Maple Dr."
```

Remember that Customer1 is the name of the record variable (due to the Dim statement that created Customer1). You would never do the following:

```
CustomerRecType.Address1 = "4394 E. Maple Dr."
```

because CustomerRecType is not a variable but is a description of a data type that you've defined. To attempt the preceding would be like saying Integer = 5.

> **Tip**
>
> The Visual Basic dot operator works just like COBOL's OF or IN *qualified names* option.

Conclusion

In this chapter, you learned about Visual Basic's data types. Visual Basic supports more data types than COBOL, so you get more flexibility with your data as you'll see throughout this book. After you understand the data types, you'll be ready to declare variables that hold data.

The Dim statement declares variables, as does the Global statement. The scope of variable that you declare can be local, module, or global. The scope determines exactly how other parts of your application can use the variables.

Remember to initialize all variables before you use them. If you forget, Visual Basic initializes variables for you but you won't always like the result. If you declare a variable but never store a value in that variable, Visual Basic stores either a null string or a zero in the variable. Therefore, if you use a variable on the right of an equal sign, but you've not stored any value in the variable, Visual Basic uses zero for the variable's value. Even if you want to have a zero in the variable, good programming practice dictates that you explicitly assign zero to the variable to show your intent and purpose.

The next chapter explains how Visual Basic's control properties interact with data variables. Using variables, you can access and set control properties while the program runs. You'll be able to grab the user's text box input and know how the user responded to multiple-choice controls such as option buttons and check boxes.

III

Primary Differences

Chapter 11

Controls also Contain Data

This chapter explains how you use controls to work with the user's response and how to set up controls that display results of calculations. Controls and variables work closely together and pass information to each other. Just as you can assign literal values and calculations to variables, you can also assign control values to variables as well as initialize control values using code assignments.

Here are some of the topics that will be discussed in this chapter:

- Using the dot operator to set specific control properties

- Capturing the values of text boxes and labels

- Initializing text boxes and labels through Visual Basic code

- Selecting and deselecting check box and option button control values

- Using code to access the user's combo and list box selection

- Learning why the list box's MultiSelect property determines how many values you can access from the list box at one time

- Using the AddItem method to initialize combo boxes and list boxes

We'll be somewhat limited in the examples for this chapter. You have yet to master Visual Basic's control statements such as If. Chapter 13, "Conditional Operations," discusses Visual Basic's If statement. Although Visual Basic's If works a lot like COBOL's IF, an explanation of the differences is discussed later in this book. This chapter explains how to read control values, but not how to check which values are set when the user selects from multiple-choice controls.

Accessing Control Properties

In the previous chapter, you used the dot operator to access field values within records. The dot operator also works to access property values within controls on the form. Remember that text box controls have a Text property. If a text box control is named txtUserName, txtUserName.Text refers to the Text property of that text box. Therefore, if you want to store the value of the text box in a string variable named Uname, here is how you do so:

```
Uname = txtUserName.Text
```

After Visual Basic executes this assignment, the string variable named Uname holds the name that the user entered in the form's text box control. You can display a data-entry form on the screen, and as soon as the user enters values in all the text boxes and clicks a command button, you can save all the text box values in variables. Subsequently, you can save those variables to a disk file.

You can set control properties also.

Perhaps more importantly, the assignment statement lets you assign values to controls on your forms. As soon as you assign a value to a text box's Text property, the user sees that value in the text box on the form. For example, the following assignment statement sends the text Now you see me! to the text box named txtMessage:

```
txtMessage.Text = "Now you see me!"
```

Now you see me! appears on the form inside the text box control right after Visual Basic executes this assignment. You can change and display labels as well.

You can access any property on any control using the dot operator. If you want to change a command button's caption, you can do so. If you put the following statement inside a command button's Click event procedure,

```
cmdAnnounce.Caption = "You clicked me"
```

the caption changes from its original runtime value to the new message.

Now would be a good time to create a simple application so that you can see the assignment of control properties in action. The following steps walk you through the creation of an application named PROP1.MAK. This application will be one of several small applications that you create for this chapter. This book's disk contains the completed PROP1.MAK application, but you'll get better practice if you walk through these steps yourself.

1. Start Visual Basic if Visual Basic is not currently running.

2. Press F4 to view the form's Properties window.

3. Change the form's Name property to **frmTextAssign**.

4. Change the form's title (stored in the Caption property) to **Text Box Assignment**. The form's title bar instantly changes to reflect the new caption as you type the title.

5. Double-click the toolbox's text box control to place a new text box on the screen.

6. Press F4 to see the Properties window for the text box control. Change the following properties to the indicated values:

> Alignment: **2 - Center**
>
> Height: **360**
>
> Left: **2400**
>
> Name: **txtMovie**
>
> Text: (blank)
>
> Top: **2265**
>
> Width: **2250**

All the other property defaults work without change.

7. Double-click the toolbox's label control to place a new label on the screen.

8. Press F4 to see the Properties window for the label control. Change the following properties to these values:

> Caption: **Type a favorite movie:**
>
> Height: **255**
>
> Left: **2640**
>
> Name: **lblPrompt**
>
> Top: **1920**
>
> Width: **1995**

All the other label property defaults work without change.

III

Primary Differences

Your screen should look like Figure 11.1 at this point.

Fig. 11.1
Your application's
form should look
like this.

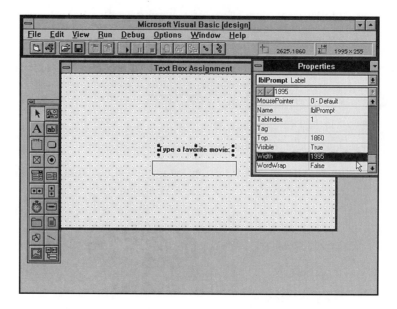

9. Double-click the toolbox's command button control to place a command button in the center of the screen. Move the command button to the lower-right corner of the form.

Press F4 to see the Properties window for the command button. Change the following properties to these values:

Caption: **E&xit**

Left: **5970**

Name: **cmdExit**

Top: **3090**

All the other property defaults work without change.

10. Double-click the toolbox's command button control once again to place a second command button in the center of the screen. Move the command button to the lower-left corner of the form.

Press F4 to see the Properties window for the command button. Change the following properties to these values:

Caption: **&Click to see mine...**

Height: **495**

Left: **240**

Name: **cmdLook**

Top: **3120**

Width: **1935**

All the other property defaults work without change.

11. Double-click the cmdExit command button to open up the
cmdExit_Click() event procedure. Type **End** as the sole statement
inside the opening and closing Sub statements to ensure that the
program terminates when the user clicks the Exit command button.

12. Display the Object drop-down list in the Code window and show
the cmdLook_Click() event procedure. This event executes as soon as
the user clicks on the screen's cmdLook command button. Type the
following assignment statement between the opening and closing
Sub statements:

```
txtMovie.Text = "The Wall Street Wizards"
```

Remember to press Tab before typing the statement.

This assignment statement executes only if the user clicks the left command button. If the Click event never occurs, the Text property of the
text box in the middle of the screen never changes from the user's
entered response.

13. Run the program. Type a movie title in the text box. Then click the left
command button. The text box changes to The Wall Street Wizards
because the command button's Click event executed. Your screen
should look like Figure 11.2.

14. Click the Exit command button to terminate the program.

15. Save the application's form as PROP1.FRM and the project file as
PROP1.MAK.

See if you can change the program so that the left command button's caption
changes when the user clicks the button. (Hint: You'll need to reference
cmdLook's Caption property inside cmdLook's Click event procedure.)

III

Primary Differences

Fig. 11.2
The code sent a
movie title to the
text box.

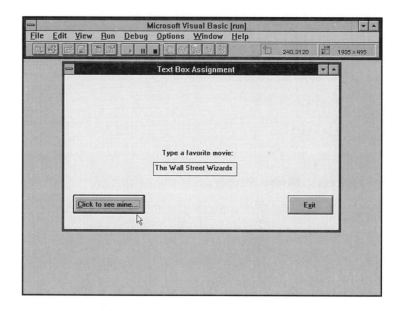

If There Is More Than One Form...

If your application contains more than one form, you'll have to qualify your
property values by appending the form's name to the front of the property
and separating the form name from the property with an exclamation point.
Prefacing the form name is easier than it sounds.

Suppose that your application contains two data-entry forms, one named
frmCustData and one named frmVendorData. If both forms contain a text box
control named txtAddress and you want to assign the customer's address to a
variable named CustAddr, you do so in the following way:

```
CustAddr = frmCustData!txtAddress.Text
```

Read such convoluted statements from right to left to more easily interpret
them. This statement assigns the Text property from the text box control
named txtAddress located on the form named frmCustData to a variable
named CustAddr.

You always have the option of specifying the form name before all control
names, but when there is only one form, adding the form name takes a lot of
extra typing. If you create an application, however, and plan to add more
forms to the application eventually, you might want to preface the form
name to all control references from the start so you won't have to add the
form name later.

> **Note**
>
> If you are accessing any form properties, such as a form's `BackColor` property, you must use the form name in front of the dot operator, as in `frmApp1.BackColor`.

Chapter 18, "Adding Menus and Extra Forms," describes how to add and manage more than one form inside an application.

Declining Property Values

As you read in Chapter 5, "The Graphical Controls," a property often contains a value selected from a list of several possibilities, such as the label control's `BackStyle` property that can hold either of the following:

```
0 - Transparent

1 - Opaque
```

When you assign values to such a control, you only assign the prefix number to the control, not the entire value. In other words, the following statement changes the background style of the label, assuming the label's name is `lblSort`:

```
lblSort.BackStyle = 0
```

You could not change the `BackStyle` property with either of these statements:

```
lblSort.BackStyle = 0 - Transparent      ' INVALID!
lblSort.BackStyle = "0 - Transparent"     ' Also wrong!
```

Working with Check Boxes

When working with check boxes, remember that one or more of the boxes can be checked and that each of the check box Value properties can contain one of these three values:

```
0 - Unchecked

1 - Checked

2 - Grayed
```

Although the user often selects from check boxes, there will be times when your application needs to set certain check box values. For example, your application might need to gray a check box, making that check box unavailable, until a certain data condition becomes true.

This book's PROP2.MAK application demonstrates how you can access check box controls from Visual Basic code. Instead of simply loading the application, you'll get good form development practice by following these steps:

1. Open a new project. Change the form's name from form1 to **frmCheck**.

2. Change the form's Caption property to **Check Box Form**.

3. Double-click the check box control on the toolbox to send a new check box control to the form. Change the check box properties to these values:

   Caption: **Apples**

   Left: **1200**

   Name: **chkBox1**

   Top: **720**

4. Double-click the check box control on the toolbox to send another check box control to the form. Change the check box properties to these values:

   Caption: **Oranges**

   Left: **1200**

   Name: **chkBox2**

   Top: **1320**

5. Double-click the check box control on the toolbox to send the third check box control to the form. Change the check box properties to these values:

   Caption: **Pears**

   Left: **1200**

   Name: **chkBox3**

   Top: **1920**

6. Double-click the check box control on the toolbox to send the fourth check box control to the form. Change the check box properties to these values:

    Caption: **Peaches**

    Left: **1200**

    Name: **chkBox4**

    Top: **2520**

Your screen should now look like the screen in Figure 11.3.

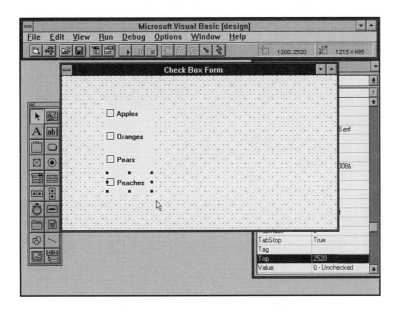

Fig. 11.3
The four check box controls let the user select choices.

These are four check boxes that the user can check on and off. However, code that you add in later steps controls how the check boxes appear to the user.

7. Double-click the command button control to add a command button to the form. Set the command button's properties to these values:

    Caption: **All in stock**

    Left: **4080**

    Name: **cmdAll**

    Top: **840**

Primary Differences

You'll later add code for this command button's `Click` event that selects every check box (placing an X in each box).

8. Double-click the command button control to add another command button to the form. Set the command button's properties to these values:

Caption: **Sold out**

Left: **4080**

Name: **cmdOut**

Top: **1680**

You'll later add code for this command button's `Click` event that deselects every check box (clearing all Xs from each box).

9. Double-click the command button control to add a third command button to the form. Set the command button's properties to these values:

Caption: **Never citrus**

Left: **4080**

Name: **cmdNeverCitrus**

Top: **2520**

You'll later add code for this command button's `Click` event that grays out the second check box (the one with the `Oranges Caption` property), preventing the user from being able to select the second check box.

10. Double-click the command button control to add a fourth command button to the form. Set the command button's properties to these values:

Caption: **E&xit**

Left: **5880**

Name: **cmdExit**

Top: **3240**

As always, this button controls the user's exit from the program. If you don't add a way to exit, the user has to select the <u>E</u>nd command on the <u>R</u>un menu.

11. Insert the End command inside cmdExit's Click procedure by double-clicking the command button and typing **End** in the body of the procedure's Code window named cmdExit_Click().

12. You must now add code to the other three command buttons. Open the first command button's Code window by double-clicking the command button labeled: All in stock. The purpose of this command button is to select all check box controls. A check box control is selected if its Value property is set to 1 - Checked. Add statements to the body of the procedure so that cmdAll_Click()'s procedure looks like this:

```
Sub cmdAll_Click ()
' Selects all check boxes
  chkBox1.Value = 1
  chkBox2.Value = 1
  chkBox3.Value = 1
  chkBox4.Value = 1
End Sub
```

13. Open the second command button's Code window by double-clicking the command button labeled: Sold out. The purpose of this command button is to deselect all check box controls. A check box control is deselected if its Value property is set to 0 - Unchecked. Add statements to the body of the procedure so that cmdOut_Click()'s procedure looks like this:

```
Sub cmdOut_Click ()
' Deselects all the check boxes
  chkBox1.Value = 0
  chkBox2.Value = 0
  chkBox3.Value = 0
  chkBox4.Value = 0
End Sub
```

14. Open the third command button's Code window by double-clicking the command button labeled: Never Citrus. The purpose of this command button is to gray out the Orange check box control. A check box control is grayed and unavailable to the user if its Value property is set to 2 - Grayed. Add statements to the body of the procedure so that cmdNeverCitrus_Click()'s procedure looks like this:

```
Sub cmdNeverCitrus_Click ()
' Gray out the citrus check box
  chkBox2.Value = 2
End Sub
```

15. Save the form file as PROP2.FRM and the project file as PROP2.MAK.

III

Primary Differences

Run the program to see your new creation. Before clicking any command buttons, click one or more check boxes on and off to see the Xs appear and disappear. Clicking the first command button selects all the check boxes. Clicking the second command button deselects all the check boxes.

Now, click the third command button to gray out the Oranges check box. Try to select the Oranges check box. What happens? Even though you grayed out the box, the user can still select the box. The reason is not clear at first glance. There is a property available for almost all kinds of controls called Enabled. When Enabled is set to True, the control works as expected. When the Enabled property is set to False, the control remains unavailable to the user. The 2 - Grayed option only grays out the check box but does not disable the check box from future clicking by the user.

To make the Oranges property both grayed out and unusable to the user, insert the following line before the End Sub statement in the cmdNeverCitrus_Click() procedure:

```
chkBox2.Enabled = False
```

Save the form and project file and run the program once again. When you click the third command button, the Oranges check box becomes gray and unavailable until you click one of the other command buttons. Once you learn how to test for selected values using If, you'll be able to keep the Oranges check box unavailable for the entire program once the user clicks the third command button.

You're beginning to see now how the assignment statement can control the form at runtime just as you can control the form's design and initial behavior at designtime through the properties.

Putting CONSTANT.TXT To Work

Do you have a hard time remembering if the 0 means unchecked, checked, or grayed? Every preset value for every property has a corresponding named constant in the CONSTANT.TXT file. If you highlight CONSTANT.TXT in the Project window and click the View Code button, you can scroll down in the code until you find this section:

```
' Check Value
Global Const UNCHECKED = 0   ' 0 - Unchecked
Global Const CHECKED = 1     ' 1 - Checked
Global Const GRAYED = 2      ' 2 - Grayed
```

Microsoft provides you with easy-to-remember named constants for the check box values. Therefore, instead of assigning 0, 1, or 2 to check box properties inside your code, you can assign UNCHECKED, CHECKED, or GRAYED. Here is an example of the cmdAll_Click() event procedure that uses the defined constant names instead of the hardcoded value of 1:

```
Sub cmdAll_Click ()
' Selects all check boxes
  chkBox1.Value = CHECKED
  chkBox2.Value = CHECKED
  chkBox3.Value = CHECKED
  chkBox4.Value = CHECKED
End Sub
```

Note

This book's disk contains the completed PROP2.MAK project. Therefore, if you're not creating this project from scratch, but instead loading this book's disk, the program does not contain the intermediate steps that you took here that displayed incorrect Oranges property assignments.

Also, the book's PROP2.MAK disk project uses the named constants in the CONSTANT.TXT file. Be sure to add CONSTANT.TXT to your AUTOLOAD.MAK project file (as described in Chapter 8, "VB's *IDENTIFICATION* and *ENVIRONMENT* Equivalents") before loading this book's disk, or you'll have trouble running the programs.

In a way, the named constants CHECKED, UNCHECKED, and GRAYED act somewhat like 88-level COBOL DATA DIVISION values.

Using the Option Buttons

Once you master check boxes, option buttons are simple to manipulate through Visual Basic code. Here are a few option button considerations that you must remember:

- The option button Value property contains True if the option button is selected or False if the option button is not selected.

- Only one option button in a series can be True. Therefore, if the user selects an option button, then that option button's Value property

III

Primary Differences

becomes `True`. If the user then selects another option button, the first option button's `Value` property immediately changes to `False` and the newly selected button's `Value` property becomes `True`.

- `True` and `False` are Visual Basic keywords, not strings. You can assign the `True` and `False` values to property settings when appropriate. To assign an option button's `Value` property the `True` value, you only need to assign the value of `True` as done here:

  ```
  optChoice1.Value = True
  ```

- If a user clicks an option button twice in succession, the button changes to its original selected or deselected state.

Working with Combo Boxes

Despite the fact that combo box controls grow as the user adds values to them, only one of the combo's values is selected at any one time. Whether the combo box is a simple combo box or a drop-down combo box does not matter.

Figure 11.4 shows the CONTROLS.MAK application running after the user enters several values into the simple combo box control. The value at the top of the combo box is always the combo's active value. This value, whether the user types the value or selects the value from the combo's list, always resides in the combo's `Text` property. Therefore, if the combo box is named `cboCity`, you can store the user's selected city (Peoria in Figure 11.4) in a variable with this simple assignment:

```
SelectedCity = cboCity.Text
```

Adding items to combo boxes using code is not quite as straightforward as storing the selected combo box item. You must use something called the `AddItem` method to add items to a combo box or a list box. The next section describes the `AddItem` method after discussing list boxes and code assignments.

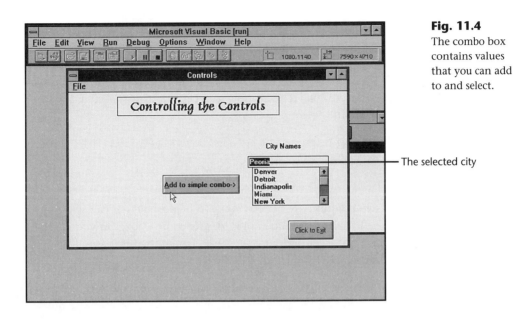

Fig. 11.4
The combo box contains values that you can add to and select.

The selected city

Introducing List Boxes and Code

The MultiSelect property of the list box determines how easy or difficult capturing list box values can be. Figure 11.5 illustrates how the MultiSelect property works. The left list box has its MultiSelect property set to 0 - None, which means that the user can select at most one item from the list box at any one time. The list box on the right has its MultiSelect property set to 1 - Simple, meaning that the user can select one or more items from the list box by clicking the mouse or pressing the spacebar over selected items. A value of 2 - Extended means that the user must press the Shift+mouse click, Shift+arrow key, or Ctrl+mouse click to select and deselect multiple items from the list.

MultiSelect describes how items are selected.

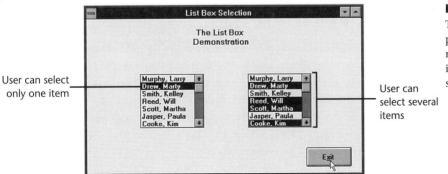

User can select only one item

User can select several items

Fig. 11.5
The MultiSelect property determines how many items the user can select at one time.

III

Primary Differences

When you want to access the user's selected list value, you can use the list box control's Text property to find the user's selection from the list. However, the Text property only works correctly when the list box's MultiSelect property is set to 0 - None. You'll have to wait until Chapter 16, "Table-Handling and Control Arrays," to learn how to access multiple-selected items from a list box whose MultiSelect property is set to 1 or 2.

The following assignment stores a list box's selected item in a variable named `Selected`:

```
Selected = lstBox.Text
```

You'll need to initialize list box controls before the user can select any items from the list box. The same holds for any combo boxes in your application that you want to put initial values in to which the user can select or add more items.

To add items to a list box or combo box with code, you must use the `AddItem` method. A method is really just a command, but it's a special command that you can only apply to certain controls. The dot operator plays a part with methods, so the dot operator performs triple-duty in Visual Basic as

A record and field separator

A control and property separator

A control and method separator

Here is the format of the `AddItem` method:

```
ControlName.AddItem "String to add"
```

The following section of code adds five colors to a list box named `lstColors`:

```
lstColors.AddItem "Blue"
lstColors.AddItem "Red"
lstColors.AddItem "Green"
lstColors.AddItem "Yellow"
lstColors.AddItem "Black"
```

You can add either string literals, as shown here, or the contents of string variables, as long as you've initialized the string variables with values first. A good place to add items is in the `Load` procedure of the form. Visual Basic loads the Form window before doing anything else in the application. Therefore, if you add items to your application's list and combo boxes in the `Form_Load()` procedure, the items are initialized before the first form is loaded and the list and combo boxes displayed.

The following code initializes the two list boxes, named `lstOneSelect` and `lstMultSelect`, with the values shown in Figure 11.5:

```
Sub Form_Load ()
  lstOneSelect.AddItem "Murphy, Larry"
  lstOneSelect.AddItem "Drew, Marty"
  lstOneSelect.AddItem "Smith, Kelley"
  lstOneSelect.AddItem "Reed, Will"
  lstOneSelect.AddItem "Scott, Martha"
  lstOneSelect.AddItem "Jasper, Paula"
  lstOneSelect.AddItem "Cooke, Kim"
  lstOneSelect.AddItem "Turner, Peter"
  lstMultSelect.AddItem "Murphy, Larry"
  lstMultSelect.AddItem "Drew, Marty"
  lstMultSelect.AddItem "Smith, Kelley"
  lstMultSelect.AddItem "Reed, Will"
  lstMultSelect.AddItem "Scott, Martha"
  lstMultSelect.AddItem "Jasper, Paula"
  lstMultSelect.AddItem "Cooke, Kim"
  lstMultSelect.AddItem "Turner, Peter"
End Sub
```

Tip

You can set a default item to be highlighted when the user first sees a combo box by typing the default value into the Text property of the combo box at design time. The first item in a list box is always the default selected item, and you cannot change the default for list box controls.

Note

You can find this short list box application in this book's PROP3.MAK disk file.

Conclusion

You're now well on your way to understanding the interaction with Visual Basic's forms and code. Your COBOL programming background has helped you more than you probably realize. You have no trouble understanding variables because you already understand named data values from COBOL's DATA DIVISION. You understand the movement of data values from one variable or control to another due to your background with MOVE (MOVE and Visual Basic's assignment statements are virtually equivalent to each other).

III

Primary Differences

Most of this chapter is a review of what you already know, however, you did learn how to access control property values using the dot operator. Once you use the dot operator, the simple assignment operator transfers control values back and forth between controls and variables.

To initialize combo lists and list boxes, however, you must use the AddItem method before the form loads on the screen. AddItem fills lists with initial items. The user can then select from the list or (in the case of combo boxes) add to the list.

So far, you can only access the selected item from a list box whose MultiSelect property is set to 0. Retrieving multiply selected list items requires an understanding of Visual Basic's table processing found in Chapter 16, "Table-Handling and Control Arrays."

The next chapter, "The Math Operations," teaches you how Visual Basic's mathematical operations work in very much the same manner as COBOL's math operations, except for slight syntax differences. Once you learn the math operations, you'll be able to display mathematical results (such as pay and balance amounts) in the form's labels and text box controls.

Chapter 12

The Math Operations

You need to know how Visual Basic calculates math even if you don't write scientific applications. Visual Basic provides stronger support for mathematical calculations than COBOL does. However, with Visual Basic, you don't have to tap into its detailed math capabilities unless you either want to or need to.

Many of Visual Basic's fundamental mathematical operations work a lot like their COBOL counterparts. Therefore, you should have little trouble understanding how to compute Visual Basic results. Once you master this chapter's math operations, Chapter 13, "Conditional Operations," continues the discussion of operators by explaining Visual Basic's comparison and logical operations. When combined with the math operations, the comparison operations prepare you for testing powerful data conditions.

One operator, the plus sign (+), works on both numbers as well as string data. This chapter explains when to use the plus sign for adding numbers and when to use the plus sign on string data.

Here are some of the topics that will be discussed in this chapter:

- Learning the primary Visual Basic math operators
- Seeing how COBOL's COMPUTE statement converts to Visual Basic better than COBOL's other mathematical statements
- Using the Val() function to convert strings to numbers when needed
- Concatenating string values with the & concatenation operator
- Learning how Visual Basic's mathematical hierarchy matches that of COBOL's
- Using Visual Basic's exponential operator to compute roots of values

> **Tip**
>
> You'll find that Visual Basic's math syntax closely matches that of COBOL's COMPUTE statement. Therefore, if you are used to using COBOL's ADD, SUBTRACT, MULTIPLY, and DIVIDE statements, you may want to review the COBOL COMPUTE statement before reading this chapter.

The Operators

An *operator* is a symbol or word that works on data values.

The Visual Basic language includes several calculator-style operators. Often, there is a one-to-one correlation between COBOL operators (and some math-related keywords) and Visual Basic operators. In COBOL, you can perform calculations in two ways:

- Using keywords such as ADD, SUBTRACT, MULTIPLY, and DIVIDE.

- Using the COMPUTE statement along with operators such as +, -, *, and /. COMPUTE statements are generally shorter than their other COBOL counterparts such as ADD and SUBTRACT.

Visual Basic uses only operators for its mathematical calculations. Luckily, Visual Basic's operators look just like many of COBOL's, so you'll have little trouble making the transition.

In addition, Visual Basic's mathematical hierarchy computes in the same precedence order as COBOL's. Just as COBOL computes multiplication before addition, so too does Visual Basic. The last section in this chapter, "Mastering the Math Hierarchy," reviews Visual Basic's operator precedence rules.

The Primary Math Operators

Table 12.1 lists Visual Basic's primary math operators and gives an example of each. Notice that there are three kinds of division operators. The operator that you use for division depends on the resulting division that you want Visual Basic to perform.

Table 12.1	The Fundamental Visual Basic Math Operators	
Operator	**Example**	**Description**
+	Net + Disc	Adds two values
-	Price - 4.00	Subtracts one value from another
*	Total * Fact	Multiplies two values
/	Tax / Adjust	Divides two values
\	Money \ Num	Calculates integer division and discards the remainder
Mod	Amt Mod Tot	Divides and returns only the whole number remainder

Note

The Mod operator does not look like an operator. Mod looks like a keyword command. Visual Basic has a handful of operators that look like keywords.

The values that you use within Visual Basic calculations can include literals, variables, control properties, and combinations of all three. You'll be storing the results of mathematical calculations in variables or properties, so your formulas usually appear on the right side of the equal sign. The following section shows how Visual Basic's operators correspond to COBOL's equivalent operators.

Addition with +

Suppose that you needed to add three salespeople's regional sales. In COBOL, you could use either of the following two statements to store the sum of the sales in a data value named TOTAL-SALES:

```
ADD SALESPER1, SALESPER2, SALESPER3, GIVING TOTAL-SALES.
```

or

```
COMPUTE TOTAL-SALES = SALESPER1 + SALESPER2 + SALESPER3.
```

III

Primary Differences

> **Caution**
>
> In this part of the book, you must remain especially aware that Visual Basic does *not* allow a dash, -, in variable names. Visual Basic thinks that the dash is a subtraction sign and not part of the variable's name. Unlike COBOL, however, Visual Basic does let you code an operator and a keyword next to each other without an intervening space.

Here is how you would code the same addition statement in Visual Basic:

```
TotalSales = SalesPer1 + SalesPer2 + SalesPer3
```

Visual Basic adds the three regional sales values, then stores the computed result in `TotalSales`.

Special Consideration for Control Values

When computing with control values, such as text box `Text` values that the user enters, you must make allowances because the controls contain non-numeric data. In other words, text boxes are designed to let the user enter any type of value at all, including names, special characters, and numbers.

Therefore, if the user enters a number in a text box, Visual Basic does *not* consider that value to be a number. Instead, Visual Basic considers the value to be a string that happens to contain numeric digits. You cannot compute with string values. Consequently, before doing math with control values, you'll have to tell Visual Basic to convert those values to numbers. For example, `"43.4"` is a string, and you cannot do math with the string.

Part IV of this book, "Advanced VB Programming," explains the concept of Visual Basic's built-in functions. A *function* is a routine supplied by Visual Basic that does work for you and eliminates unnecessary code on your part when you want common tasks performed such as data conversions. Although a full discussion of functions is reserved for Part IV, you need to see a few functions before then to be productive with this material and the material in the next few chapters.

Here is the typical format of a built-in function:

```
FunctionName(Argument [, Argument2...])
```

To execute the function, you have to supply the `FunctionName` as well as one or more arguments. Most functions take only one argument. If the function requires two or more arguments, you separate the arguments with a comma between each.

The purpose of a function is to take the argument (or arguments) that you put in parentheses and return a result based on the argument list. Figure 12.1 shows a high-level overview of how functions work. A function works like a machine into which you put one or more values (arguments) and the machine spits out a new value fabricated from the argument list.

> ### Note
>
> It is said that you *pass arguments* to functions and that functions *return values*.

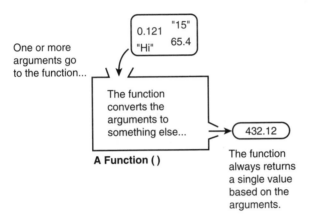

One or more arguments go to the function...

The function converts the arguments to something else...

A Function ( )

The function always returns a single value based on the arguments.

Fig. 12.1
Functions return values based on the arguments that you pass to them.

Functions are easy to use. There is a function named Val() that converts string values to numeric values. Of course, the string must contain valid numbers such as the following:

```
"42"      "-1233.432"      "9.343E+19"      "0"
```

> ### Tip
>
> This book will always place parentheses after function names, such as Val(), to remind you that you are learning about a built-in function and not a keyword.

Here's how you can use the Val() function: suppose that the user enters three text values into three text box controls named txtSales1, txtSales2, and txtSales3. You can add the sales and store the summed result in a numeric variable named TotalSales like this:

```
TotalSales = Val(txtSales1.Text) + Val(txtSales2.Text) +
➥Val(txtSales3.Text)
```

Neither `Val()` nor any other Visual Basic function changes arguments. Therefore, if you pass a string to `Val()`, `Val()` returns a converted number, but the argument remains unchanged and stays a string. In the previous assignment, `txtSales1.Text` is a string value before, during, and after the assignment, but Visual Basic adds a converted `txtSales1.Text` to the other converted values and uses that converted value only for the calculation.

What If You Don't Use *Val()*?

If you try to add string values, without first converting those values to numeric quantities with `Val()`, Visual Basic thinks that you want to concatenate the strings. *Concatenate* means merge. Therefore, Visual Basic will merge the strings you are trying to add into one long string. The following statement

```
Amt = "12" + "34" + "56"
```

stores the string `"123456"` in the variable named `Amt` (the quotation marks don't get stored, only the string's digits). That is, Visual Basic concatenates the strings if `Amt` is a string variable or a `Variant` variable. If you've defined `Amt` to be a numeric variable, Visual Basic issues an error because you cannot assign strings to numeric variables. Of course, you'd probably never attempt to add string constants together, but sometimes it's easy to forget that numbers stored in text boxes are strings until you convert those values to numbers by using `Val()`.

Microsoft does not recommend that you use + if you want to concatenate string values. Microsoft recommends that you use the & operator because + performs double-duty as an addition and concatenate operator, and you may possibly get confused using + for both. The only purpose that & serves is to concatenate strings. Both of the following statements are identical but the one that uses & is preferred:

```
FullName = FirstName + LastName
```

and

```
FullName = FirstName & LastName
```

The ADDSALES.MAK project that comes with this book demonstrates a simple application that accepts three sales values from the user and displays the resulting summed total sales. Figure 12.2 shows what happens after the user enters three sales values and clicks the Compute Total command button.

The Compute Total command button contains the following `Click()` event code:

```
Sub cmdCompute_Click ()
' Convert the three regional sales values
' to numeric quantities before adding them
```

```
        lblSales.Caption = Val(txtSales1.Text) + Val(txtSales2.Text) +
        ➥Val(txtSales3.Text)
    End Sub
```

Sometimes, lines of Visual Basic code can get lengthy, as is the case in the fourth line of the preceding procedure. Remember that the horizontal scroll bars at the bottom of the Code window let you scroll left and right across the Code window when you need to see the outer edges.

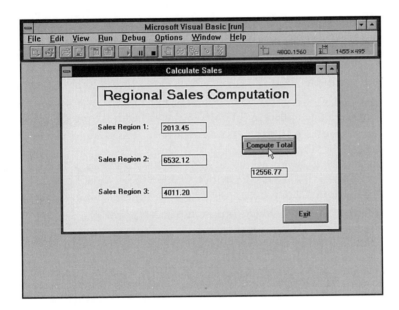

Fig. 12.2
Calculating sales totals using the math operators.

You'll learn about several more numeric functions as you progress through this book. You'll even be able to write your own functions. In effect, when you write your own functions, you extend the Visual Basic language to include features or functions that did not exist before.

Don't worry about formatting your output yet. Chapter 14, "Formatting Data," explains how to get the dollar sign and decimal places that your output requires.

Extra *Val()* Considerations

Most of the time, you'll never have to worry about the nuances of Val(), but you should know something about the nuances for those rare times when Val() does not return a result that you might expect.

If the string argument that you pass to Val() contains any data that is not a string, such as "221 East Oak Road, #4", Val() converts that string to the numeric value of 221 by converting only the first digits in the string to a valid number.

Also, Val() converts its string argument to a Double data type. In other words, both of the following statements store a Double data type in Result1 and Result2:

```
Result1 = Val("2")    ' "2" converts to a numeric Double
```

or

```
Result2 = Val("34.92934501")
```

If the variable receiving the result of Val() is not a Double data type but is an integer or single-precision value, everything works fine as long as the converted number will fit in the receiving variable. Therefore, if Result1 and Result2 are declared as Double variables in the preceding expressions, Result1 gets a 2 and Result2 gets a 34.92934501 because Double variables can hold both values.

However, if Result1 and Result2 are declared as Single variables, Result1 holds the 2 just fine, but Result2 gets a slightly truncated 34.92934 because of the limited precision that single-precision data supports.

You never have to use Val() to convert Variant data types. If you store a string of numeric digits in a Variant variable, then calculate with the variable, Visual Basic properly converts the Variant data type to a numeric data type for the purpose of the calculation. Nevertheless, the automatic type-conversion for Variant data types is inefficient and does not provide a good reason to declare all variables as Variant. You often need the various data types for operations and file I/O techniques.

Using Subtraction and Multiplication with - and *

Subtraction and multiplication are as easy to perform as addition. Suppose that you were computing the difference in gross sales and net sales by using COBOL. Here are two ways you can perform the subtraction:

```
SUBTRACT NET-SALES FROM GROSS-SALES GIVING DIFF.
```

or

```
COMPUTE DIFF  = GROSS-SALES - NET-SALES.
```

Visual Basic's subtraction works as you would probably expect. Here is an equivalent subtraction in Visual Basic:

```
Diff = GrossSales - NetSales
```

Both `GrossSales` and `NetSales` must be numeric values or you will have to convert them to numeric values with `Val()` before using them, as shown in the following example:

```
Diff = Val(GrossSales) - Val(NetSales)
```

The subtraction operator, -, can also negate values. Therefore, if you want to store a negative value (such as a payment), you can do so by prefacing the payment with a minus sign like this:

```
NewPayment = -Payment
```

The multiplication operator goes between two values as do the addition and subtraction operators. If you want to multiply an inventory amount by a factor using COBOL, here are two different statements that do just that:

```
MULTIPLY INV-AMT BY FACTOR GIVING ADJ-INV.
```

or

```
COMPUTE ADJ-INV = INV-AMT * FACTOR.
```

Here is how you compute the multiplication in Visual Basic:

```
AdjInv = IntAmt * Factor
```

As always, Visual Basic is more succinct than COBOL.

Visual Basic Provides Several Divide Operators

There are three kinds of divide operators in Visual Basic and this section describes all three. The most common divide is a regular decimal divide that mirrors COBOL's `DIVIDE` statement. Suppose that you were dividing the total number of students by a total class score to compute the class average. Here are two approaches using COBOL:

VB's / works like COBOL's /.

```
DIVIDE NUM-STUDENTS INTO TOTAL-SCORE GIVING AVERAGE.
```

or

```
COMPUTE AVERAGE = TOTAL-SCORE / NUM-STUDENTS.
```

Here is an equivalent Visual Basic division statement:

```
Average = TotalScore / NumStudents
```

Visual Basic keeps full decimal precision, so you don't need a `ROUNDED` option as you do with COBOL when performing COBOL calculations that work with fixed-length numeric fields.

If you reverse the divide operator and use the backslash, \, instead of the forward slash, /, Visual Basic computes an integer division. Visual Basic

\ computes integer division.

III

Primary Differences

divides the results and discards any remainder. Therefore, the following statement stores the whole-number division result in `Average`:

```
Average = Total \ 25
```

Mod **computes the remainder.**

The `Mod` operator computes division's whole number remainder. The following statement stores the remainder of the previous division in `LeftOver`:

```
LeftOver = Total Mod 25
```

COBOL's equivalent statement to both the integer divide and remainder statements can be the following (depending on how many decimal places you've reserved for the data values):

```
DIVIDE 25 INTO TOTAL GIVING AVERAGE ROUNDED REMAINDER LEFT-OVER.
```

> **Note**
>
> There is no Visual Basic equivalent to COBOL's `ON SIZE ERROR` division option. You can trap Visual Basic errors, including division domain errors, by using Visual Basic's `On Error` statement. Search Visual Basic's online help for `On Error` if you want additional details.

The Exponential Operator: ^

Visual Basic's exponential (`^`) operator raises a number to a specific power just as COBOL's `**` operator does. The following COBOL statement raises `NUM` to the power of four:

```
COMPUTE POWER = NUM ** 4.
```

Visual Basic's equivalent statement is this:

```
Power = Num ^ 4
```

Visual Basic multiplies `Num` by itself four times and then stores the results in `Power`. Using `^` is much less work than typing the multiplication like this:

```
Power = Num * Num * Num * Num
```

As with COBOL, you can compute the root of a number with some fancy exponential footwork. To find the square root of a number, you can raise the number to the one-half power like this:

```
Sq = Num ^ .5
```

or

```
Sq = Num ^ (1/2)
```

If you want to find the cube (third) root and fourth root, you would write these statements:

```
Cube = Num ^ (1/3)
Fourth = Num ^ (1/4)
```

Mastering the Math Hierarchy

Follow the standard mathematical hierarchy that COBOL uses when computing mixed expressions with Visual Basic. Table 12.2 lists Visual Basic's order of operators for the primary mathematical operators.

Table 12.2 The Visual Basic Mathematical Computation Hierarchy	
Level	Operator
1	( )
2	^
3	- (negation)
4	*, /
5	+, -

If more than one kind of expression resides in the same statement, Table 12.2 dictates the order of the calculation. Therefore, multiplication takes place before subtraction in the following statement:

```
Result = A - B * C
```

The negation sign has a higher priority than both multiplication and subtraction. Therefore, the following statement negates C before multiplying that negated result by B and finally subtracting from A:

```
Result = A - B * -C    ' Negate C before multiplying
```

You may use parentheses to override the order of operators. Therefore, the following statement performs the addition before the multiplication because the parentheses tell Visual Basic to perform the addition first:

```
Result = (A + B) * C    ' Add first
```

As with COBOL, if two operators from the same level in Table 12.2 appear within the same expression, Visual Basic calculates the operators in

III

Primary Differences

left-to-right order. In the following statement, Visual Basic computes the division before the multiplication because the division appears to the left of the multiplication operator and both operators reside on the same level in Table 12.2:

```
Result = A / B * C
```

Tip

Use as many parentheses as you need to clarify math calculation ordering of your expressions.

The following statement is clearer

```
NetPay = GrossPay - (GrossPay * taxRate)
```

than this one

```
NetPay = GrossPay - GrossPay * taxRate
```

even though the parentheses are redundant. The normal hierarchy ensures that the multiplication computes first, but the parentheses help clarify the code's intent to the programmer who must maintain the code.

Conclusion

This chapter had to be one of the easiest in the book for you so far. As I promised earlier, your COBOL background would come in handy. It took only 12 chapters to prove it!

This chapter explained how Visual Basic computes the results of mathematical expressions. Visual Basic's mathematical operators mimic their COBOL counterparts. Visual Basic's calculation statements closely follow the format of COBOL's COMPUTE statement, so if you've used COMPUTE, you'll feel at home here.

Visual Basic also supports the same mathematical operator hierarchy (sometimes called the *operator precedence*) that COBOL's expressions follow. Therefore, when an expression contains more than one kind of operator, the hierarchy determines which operator Visual Basic first computes.

When computing with string values, you first have to convert those values to numbers by using the Val() function. Functions accept one or more arguments and convert those arguments to resulting values. A function, however, does not change the arguments themselves. The Val() function converts any string or control value that contains a valid numeric representation into a number so you can compute with the value. There are several numeric and string functions, and you'll learn many of them during your study of this book.

Chapter 13, "Conditional Operations," continues exploring Visual Basic's operators by explaining how the comparison and logical operators work. You will continue to apply your knowledge of COBOL to Visual Basic in the next chapter by discovering that COBOL performs relational and logical comparisons in the same way Visual Basic does.

Chapter 13

Conditional Operations

This chapter describes the difference between Visual Basic and COBOL's conditional tests. As with the math operators that you learned about in Chapter 12, there is a fairly direct one-to-one correspondence in the way that Visual Basic handles conditional testing and the way that COBOL handles them. Therefore, you will sail through this chapter's material.

Visual Basic supports all the conditional operations that COBOL supports, as well as provides an If statement that virtually mirrors that of COBOL's. With If, Visual Basic also includes an Else option so that you can test for any data condition needed.

Combo and check box controls often require conditional logic processing. You'll need to use If and If...Else to check the user's response to the choices that your program offers.

Here are some of the topics that will be discussed in this chapter:

- Mastering the If and If...End If statements

- Studying the ASCII table and learning how it corresponds to the EBCDIC table

- Using the Chr$() for accessing the ASCII table

- Learning how to write compound conditional tests in Visual Basic

- Adding the Else option to If to improve Visual Basic's comparison power

- Performing sign and class testing

- Using Select Case to clarify multiple-level nested If statements

- Increasing the power of Select Case with the Is and To options

The Fundamental *If* Statements

Visual Basic supports these two kinds of If statements:

- Single-line If statements

- Multiple-line If statements

Multiple-line Ifs are preferred.

Both formats are almost identical, but the single-line If is more limited, and most current Visual Basic programmers use the multiple-line If even when the single-line If would work. If you stick to the multiple-line If format, you'll find that the code is easier to add to later if you have to maintain subsequent programs.

Here is the format of the single-line If:

```
If Condition Then VBStatement
```

Here is the format of the multiple-line If:

```
If Condition Then
    One or more VBstatements
End If
```

If the Condition that the If tests triggers only one action, you may use the single-line If. For example, if the user clicks an option button that requires a single calculation, you can use the single-line If. However, if the user clicks an option button that requires several calculations, you need to list those calculations in the body of a multiple-line If statement.

Note that you must terminate the multiple-line If with the End If statement so that Visual Basic knows where the body of the If ends and the rest of the code starts. The End If does for Visual Basic what the terminating period does for COBOL's multiple-line IF statement. The End If tells Visual Basic where the conditional code ends and the rest of the program begins.

> **Tip**
>
> Get in the habit of using the multiple-line If because if you subsequently add statements to a single-line If, you may forget to also add the required End If.

Visual Basic's condition tests are almost identical to COBOL's as explained in the next section.

> **Note**
>
> Both the single-line and multiple-line If statements support an Else option. This chapter explains Visual Basic's Else statement in a later section entitled "Adding the *Else* Option."

The Condition Test

The If statement's *Condition* tests for equality, inequality, and data comparisons. You can test for both numeric and string comparisons. Table 13.1 lists the six Visual Basic comparison operators (sometimes called *relational operators*) and their COBOL counterparts. Some COBOL comparison operators have two versions while others do not.

Table 13.1   The Comparison Operators for *Condition* Tests

Operator	Description	COBOL Equivalents
=	Equal	IS EQUAL TO, =
>	Greater than	IS GREATER THAN, >
<	Less than	IS LESS THAN, <
<>	Not equal	IS NOT EQUAL TO
>=	Greater than or equal to	IS GREATER THAN... OR EQUAL TO
<=	Less than or equal to	IS LESS THAN... OR EQUAL TO

> **Tip**
>
> There are no COBOL >= or <= equivalent operators. In Visual Basic, you don't need to resort to extra logical OR operators to perform simple greater than or equal to and less than or equal to operations.

You must place the same data type on each side of the comparison operator. Therefore, you cannot compare a string to a number unless the string contains numeric digits and you first convert that string to a number Val(). Also, you can compare variables against literals and control properties.

III

Primary Differences

The following comparison determines if the Age variable is greater than or equal to 18:

```
If Age >= 18 Then
```

The body of the multiple-line If follows the Then. For now, let's concentrate on the comparison and then analyze the full If statement in the next section. Here is the COBOL equivalent of this If:

```
IF AGE IS EQUAL TO 18 OR AGE IS GREATER THAN 18
```

Using COBOL's support of operator symbols, you can shorten the comparison a bit by typing this:

```
IF AGE = 18 OR AGE > 18
```

> **Caution**
>
> Be sure to type the required keyword Then when writing Visual Basic If statements, or Visual Basic issues an error message. Several languages require Then but COBOL isn't one of them. Remembering Then is almost as tough as remembering not to put a period at the end of every Visual Basic statement.

The following If compares as true only if the string variable named UserName contains the value of Newt:

```
If UserName = "Newt" Then
```

The equivalent COBOL code looks like this:

```
IF USER-NAME = 'Newt'
```

The following If statement compares as true only if the string variable named Addr contains the numeric value 1234:

```
If Val(Addr) = 1234 Then
```

There is no preset order needed when coding the comparison. The following is identical to the previous statement:

```
If 1234 = Val(Addr) Then
```

Many Visual Basic programmers like to put parentheses around comparisons to make the comparisons stand out. The following If is identical to the previous one:

```
If (1234 = Val(Addr)) Then
```

The following statement checks to see if a text box control's font name is MS
Sans Serif:

```
If txtTitle.FontName = "MS Sans Serif" Then
```

Both of the following statements check to see if the same text box contains a
BorderStyle property value of 1 - Fixed Single:

```
If Text1.BorderStyle = 1 Then
If Text1.BorderStyle = "1" Then
```

Why do both of these comparisons work? The property values are all defined
as Variant data types. Therefore, you can test against a number or a string
when comparing certain property values. The only real limitation is that you
cannot compare against a predefined lengthy constant like

```
If Text1.BorderStyle = "1 - Fixed Single" Then
```

because Visual Basic requires that you either compare such values against
the number at the beginning of the value or against the corresponding
value in CONSTANT.TXT. In the text control's BorderStyle property's
case, CONSTANT.TXT contains FIXED_SINGLE and compares like this:

```
If Text1.BorderStyle = FIXED_SINGLE Then
```

True and False Results

In Visual Basic, all non-zero values are evaluated as true and all zero values are false.
Therefore, the following If statements both compare as true, even though their
usage is questionable:

```
If 1 Then
```

```
If -23 Then
```

The following If statement always compares as false:

```
If 0 Then        ' Always false
```

There's some trivia you probably think you'll never use. Later in this chapter, the
section named "COBOL-like Condition Names in Visual Basic," describes how to
utilize this If shortcut.

Visual Basic compares string values based on the *ASCII table*. You'll find a
complete ASCII table in Appendix A of this book. Many values in the ASCII
table correspond to EBCDIC. The PC uses the ASCII table to code characters
exactly the way larger computers use EBCDIC, so you should have no problem understanding the ASCII table and its purpose.

ASCII is the PC
version of EBCDIC.

III

Primary Differences

The following If is true because, in the ASCII table, "Smith" appears before "Smythe" since i is lower than y in the ASCII table:

```
If "Smith" < "Smythe" Then
```

The following If is false because, in the ASCII table, lowercase letters are *higher* than uppercase letters:

```
If "XYZ" > "xyz" Then
```

Refer to the ASCII table in Appendix A when comparing string data so that you'll know how to set up If statements properly.

Completing the *If* Statement

Now that you understand comparisons, the complete If statement is easy. Here is an If statement that computes a sales bonus only if the sales are over $5,000:

```
If (Sales > 5000.00) Then
   Bonus = 50.00
End If
```

Here is the corresponding COBOL IF:

```
IF (SALES IS GREATER THAN 5000.00)
   MOVE 50.00 TO BONUS.
```

If you wanted to use Visual Basic's shortened form of If, you can here because the body of the If statement is only one statement long. Here is the corresponding single-line If:

```
If (Sales > 5000.00) Then Bonus = 50.00
```

The body of the If can contain more than one statement in either Visual Basic or COBOL as shown here:

```
If (Sales > 5000.00) Then
   Bonus = 50.00
   Points = Points + 5
End If
```

or

```
IF (SALES IS GREATER THAN 5000.00)
   MOVE 50.00 TO BONUS
   ADD 5 TO POINTS.
```

Figure 13.1 shows the opening screen of the CHKIF.MAK application that prints one, two, or three messages in the gray center label. The program determines which message to print based on the check boxes that the user checks before clicking the Press Me command button.

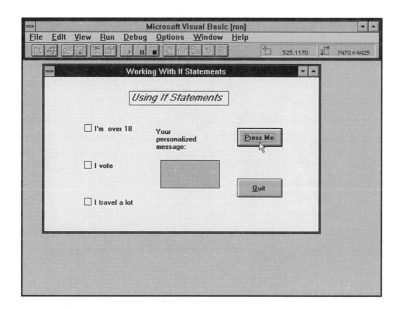

Fig. 13.1
If will test the
check boxes.

Load CHKIF.MAK from this book's disk and check some boxes before clicking the Press Me command button to read the gray label box. Change the check boxes by unchecking one and click Press Me again. Try various combinations to see the messages appear.

Although you may approach this application's code a little differently once you learn more about Visual Basic, CHKIF.MAK does demonstrate some interesting capabilities and the application centers around the If statements located in this cmdPress_Click() event procedure:

```
Sub cmdPress_Click ()
' Builds a short or long user message
' depending on the user's selected statistics.
' The message appears in a label on the screen
'
' First, empty the message string
  lblUserMsg.Caption = ""          ' Assign a null string

  If (chkOver18.Value = 1) Then
    lblUserMsg.Caption = "You're an adult!"
  End If

  If (chkVote.Value = 1) Then      ' Append a string
    lblUserMsg.Caption = lblUserMsg.Caption & Chr$(13) & Chr$(10)
    lblUserMsg.Caption = lblUserMsg.Caption & "You get involved!"
  End If

  If (chkTravel.Value = 1) Then    ' Append a string
    lblUserMsg.Caption = lblUserMsg.Caption & Chr$(13) & Chr$(10)
```

```
        lblUserMsg.Caption = lblUserMsg.Caption & "You're lucky!"
    End If

End Sub
```

The procedure begins by assigning a null string, `""`, to the gray label's Caption property. As you know, a label's Caption property determines what the user sees on the screen inside the label. The null string ensures that nothing initially appears in the label when the procedure first begins.

The code then checks each check box's Value property. Here are the three names of the check boxes:

```
chkOver18
```

```
chkVote
```

```
chkTravel
```

If a check box is checked, its Value property is set to 1. The first If is easy to understand. If the user has selected the first check box, the gray label's Caption property gets the message, `You're an adult!`. Figure 13.2 shows how the message appears.

Fig. 13.2

The user selected only the first check box.

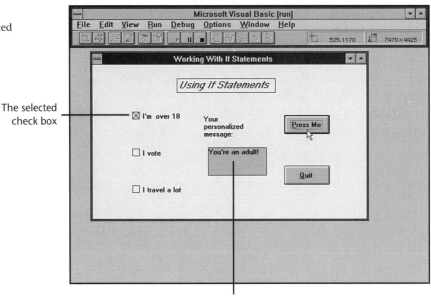

The selected check box

The resultant message

The next two `If` statement bodies aren't quite as straightforward. The second `If` tests to see if the user selected the second check box. If so, you'll notice that some data values are concatenated to the gray label's Caption with this statement:

```
lblUserMsg.Caption = lblUserMsg.Caption & Chr$(13) & Chr$(10)
```

The concatenation isn't such a difficult operation to understand, but the `Chr$()` stuff is at this point.

Before discussing `Chr$()`, what is the value of `lblUserMsg.Caption` before this statement? The value is either a null string or a string containing the message `You're an adult!`. In other words, the first `If` statement either did or did not replace the null string with the message `You're an adult!`.

No matter what the content of the label is, null or not, another string will be concatenated with the body of this second `If` statement. However, the second message, `You get involved!` should start on a line by itself. In other words, you don't want `You're an adult!You get involved!` to appear crunched together. The gray label isn't wide enough to hold that squeezed message in the first place. Even though only a little of the second message would appear at the end of the first string (assuming the first `If` is true), you don't want the first few letters of the second string to appear at the end of the first message.

Therefore, the code ensures that the second string begins on a fresh line within the label. To start the string on the next line, use the built-in function named `Chr$()`. Unlike the `Val()` function that you now know so well, `Chr$()` is a string function and returns a string value. The dollar sign, the string-variable suffix type-declaration character as you learned in Chapter 10, "Visual Basic's Version of the *DATA DIVISION*," indicates that `Chr$()` returns a string value. As a matter of fact, programmers call the `Chr$()` function the *character string function*.

`Chr$()` is a built-in string function.

When `Chr$()` executes, Visual Basic looks at the numeric argument inside `Chr$()`'s parentheses. Visual Basic then goes to the ASCII table (refer to Appendix A to see this table) and finds the character associated with that number. You'll see that the *line-feed character* is associated with the ASCII value of 10. Therefore, `Chr$(10)` returns the line-feed character, which automatically sends the cursor to the next line on the screen. Sometimes the line-feed character is called the *vertical tab character*.

III

Primary Differences

Before the code first appends the line-feed character string, the code then appends Chr$(13), which, as you'll find in the ASCII table, is the *carriage-return character*. The bottom line is that the two values, Chr$(13) and Chr$(10), when concatenated together, send the cursor to the beginning of the next line on the screen. When sending text to a label's Caption property, the line-feed/carriage-return sequence sends the cursor to the beginning of the next line in the label.

The second If then continues to append another string to the gray label's Caption property. Therefore, the string You get involved! appears at the end of the null string. The string makes You get involved! appear to be the first string in the label, or at the end of You're an adult! if that string were placed in the label by the first If. Figure 13.3 shows your screen after selecting the first two check boxes.

Fig. 13.3

The user selected the first two check boxes.

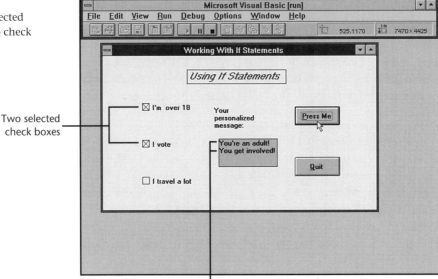

Two selected check boxes

Two messages appear

If the user selected only the second check box, you would not see You're an adult! in the gray label.

Once you understand the entire second If, the third If is relatively easy. The third If statement takes care of sending text to the gray label if and only if the user selects the third check box. You can see the results of all three check box controls being selected in Figure 13.4.

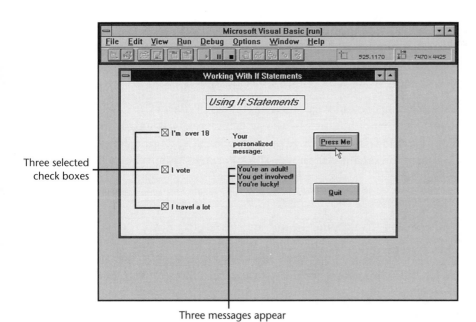

Fig. 13.4
The user selected all check boxes.

Three selected check boxes

Three messages appear

The next couple of sections explain how you can improve the application's code by implementing some minor changes.

COBOL-like Condition Names in Visual Basic

In a limited sense, Visual Basic supports condition names in a way similar to COBOL's 88-level condition names. The drawback to Visual Basic's version of condition names is that you can only use condition names for true and false conditions.

The following *If* statement taken from the CHKIF.MAK project:

```
If (chkVote.Value = 1) Then    ' Append a string
   lblUserMsg.Caption = lblUserMsg.Caption & Chr$(13) & Chr$(10)
   lblUserMsg.Caption = lblUserMsg.Caption & "You get involved!"
End If
```

is not quite as efficient as it could be. Although the change is minor, remember that if the chkVote.Value is 1, its value *means* true. Therefore, the test for the 1's equality is redundant, and you can rewrite the first line of the *If* like this:

```
If chkVote.Value Then          ' Append a string
   lblUserMsg.Caption = lblUserMsg.Caption & Chr$(13) & Chr$(10)
   lblUserMsg.Caption = lblUserMsg.Caption & "You get involved!"
End If
```

III

Primary Differences

I'm stretching this a bit by comparing the shortcut to COBOL's 88-level condition names; however, if you declare integer variables that will hold true and false results, such as check box values, be sure to name those variables a name that makes sense when comparing for specific conditions.

For example, suppose an integer variable contains a true or false value indicating whether or not the user was an employee of a company (non-employees would be handled by a customer processing routine, for example). If you named the variable IsEmployed, the following If is virtually self-documenting:

```
If IsEmployed Then
```

It is much clearer than coding the full equality test like this:

```
If IsEmployed = 1 Then        ' Redundant
```

Visual Basic also supports the Not keyword, so the following tests for the alternate condition:

```
If Not IsEmployed Then
```

Now that you see the two ways to test, a better name might simply be Employed. Consider how much better each of these If statements is compared to the others mentioned so far:

```
If Employed Then
```

and

```
If Not Employed Then
```

The bottom line is that you can somewhat improve your code's readability by thinking ahead when you create variable names. When naming true or false variables (declared with the Integer data type), think about the kinds of If tests that your code will make with the data and use meaningful variable names. You can almost always improve the readability by eliminating the redundant = 1 and = 0 conditions.

Streamlining Your Code with *Newline* Variables

There is another way to streamline the CHKIF.MAK project's code. If you look through the cmdPress_Click() event procedure, you'll see some redundancy. For this small project, the redundancy isn't great, but the two sets of Chr$() add bulk to the code without adding a lot of flexibility.

Suppose that you define a string variable at the top of the procedure like this:

```
Const NewLine As String
```

On the next line, concatenate the carriage-return and line-feed sequence to the NewLine variable like this:

```
NewLine = Chr$(13) & Chr$(10)
```

Instead of remembering the ASCII codes for carriage-return and line-feed, you only have to use the NewLine variable.

The event procedure becomes easier to follow as you can see here:

```
Sub cmdPress_Click ()
' Builds a short or long user message
' depending on the user's selected statistics.
' The message appears in a label on the screen
'
' Create a line feed/carriage return variable
  Dim NewLine As String
  NewLine = Chr$(13) & Chr$(10)

' Empty the message string
  lblUserMsg.Caption = ""              ' Assign a null string

  If (chkOver18.Value = 1) Then
    lblUserMsg.Caption = "You're an adult!"
  End If

  If (chkVote.Value = 1) Then      ' Append a string
    lblUserMsg.Caption = lblUserMsg.Caption & NewLine
    lblUserMsg.Caption = lblUserMsg.Caption & "You get involved!"
  End If

  If (chkTravel.Value = 1) Then    ' Append a string
    lblUserMsg.Caption = lblUserMsg.Caption & NewLine
    lblUserMsg.Caption = lblUserMsg.Caption & "You're lucky!"
  End If

End Sub
```

Caution

You cannot define a constant with an expression. In other words, you cannot define NewLine as a constant like this

```
Const NewLine = Chr$(13) & Chr$(10)     ' Invalid!
```

because you can only assign literal values and not expressions to constants when you define constants.

Tip

You can define the NewLine variable in the (declarations) object to make NewLine accessible to all the form's event procedures.

III

Primary Differences

You can find a version of the check box application that uses the `NewLine` variable and the shortcutting of the `If` tests (discussed in the previous section, "COBOL-like Condition Names in Visual Basic") in the CHKIF2.MAK project on this book's disk.

Compound Conditionals

Visual Basic contains an `Or` and `And` that you can use to separate relational tests. Visual Basic's `Or` and `And` work exactly like COBOL's `OR` and `AND`. You can use `Or` and `And` to combine relational tests into a compound relational test (often called *compound conditionals* in the COBOL world).

Suppose that you want to see if a value falls between a range of two numbers. For instance, you want to test to see if a total is more than $1,000 and less than $5,000. Without compound operators, you need to code a nested `If` like this:

```
If (Total > 1000) Then
  If (Total < 5000) Then
     MidRangeSales = True        ' 1000 <= Total <= 5000
  End If
End If
```

Nested `If` statements detract from the code's readability. By using `And`, you have a much cleaner way of coding this test:

```
If (Total > 1000) And (Total < 5000) Then
     MidRangeSales = True        ' 1000 < Total < 5000
End If
```

Such a test might look like this in COBOL:

```
IF TOTAL > 1000 AND TOTAL < 5000
     MID-RANGE-SALES = TRUE.
```

Visual Basic's `<=` and `>=` operators offer tremendous coding advantages over COBOL when you must test for similar conditions to see if they fall within a range of two values *inclusively*. The previous code tested to see if a total value fell between 1000 and 5000. However, if you want to test to see if the total value falls *from* 1000 to 5000 (meaning the test is true if the total is 1000 or 5000 as well as anything between), Visual Basic is almost just as easy as you can see here:

```
If (Total >= 1000) And (Total <= 5000) Then
     MidRangeSales = True        ' 1000 <= Total <= 5000
End If
```

COBOL, however, requires some extra work because traditional COBOL does not support >= and <= operators. COBOL requires this:

```
IF (TOTAL > 1000 OR TOTAL = 1000)
➡AND (TOTAL < 5000 OR TOTAL = 5000)
    MID-RANGE-SALES = TRUE.
```

If the user leaves all three check boxes unselected, the following `If` appears at the end of the IFCHK2.MAK's `cmdPress_Click()` event procedure code to issue a default message:

```
' Last If in procedure that executes if
' all check boxes are still unchecked
If (chkOver18.Value = 0) And (chkVote.Value = 0) And
➡(chkTravel.Value = 0) Then
  lblUserMsg.Caption = "Not interested?"
End If
```

Finally, the logical operators `And` and `Or` eliminate the need for `If` within `If` statements such as the following that otherwise replace the earlier combined `If`:

```
If (Total >= 1000) Then
  If (Total <= 5000) Then     ' NO - Combine 2 Ifs with And
    MidRangeSales = True      ' 1000 <= Total <= 5000
End If
```

Adding the *Else* Option

As with the compound conditionals, Visual Basic's `Else` option works similarly to COBOL's `ELSE` option. The optional `Else` leg of an `If` statement determines what code executes if the relational test is false. Here is the format of the `If...Else...End If`:

Visual Basic's `Else` performs like COBOL's ELSE.

```
If Condition Then
    One or more VBstatements
Else
    One or more VBstatements
End If
```

The following `If...Else...End If` assigns a message to a label control depending on the user's dependent claim:

```
If (DependentClaim >= 14) Then
  lblMssg.Caption = "Call the IRS first."
Else
  lblMssg.Caption = "You can have the claim."
End If
```

Here is COBOL's equivalent code:

```
IF (DEPENDENT-CLAIM > 14) OR (DEPENDENT-CLAIM = 14)
   MOVE 'Call the IRS first.' TO MSSG-CAPTION
ELSE
   MOVE 'You can have the claim.' TO MSSG-CAPTION.
```

You'll notice very little difference other than language style between the two examples except for COBOL's more limited greater than or equal operation.

Note

If you routinely code ELSE NEXT SENTENCE in your COBOL programs, you are coding redundantly because ELSE NEXT SENTENCE is redundant. After all, if the condition is false, control falls into the next sentence anyway.

Visual Basic has no ELSE NEXT SENTENCE equivalent because none is required. If you are in the habit of coding ELSE NEXT SENTENCE clauses, simply code a Visual Basic End If statement in its place to shorten your coding time and to improve the readability of your programs.

Tip

Okay, I'll give in, some COBOL programmers have *ingrained* the ELSE NEXT SENTENCE into their programming repertoire, and you may be one of those programmers who feels that their programs are more complete by coding the ELSE clause. If you want to continue the habit because you are used to coding such clauses, go ahead and code a Visual Basic remark after the Else like this:

```
Else ' Next statement
```

You can also use this remark trick to code the NEXT STATEMENT clause for the If code such as this:

```
If (GoalReached) Then
   ' Next Statement
Else
   SalesDiff = ActualSales - PredictedSales
End If
```

What Would Visual Basic Be Without *ElseIf*?

In COBOL, any statement can go inside the ELSE clause, even another IF statement. Here is an example of such a COBOL statement:

```
IF SALES < QUOTA
  MOVE 'Yes' TO CATCH-UP
ELSE
  IF SALES = QUOTA
    MOVE 'Yes' TO AT-PAR.
```

In Visual Basic, if you want to code an `If` within an `If`, you can do so using the `ElseIf` statement. Here is a statement in Visual Basic that uses `ElseIf`:

```
If (Sales < Quota) Then
  CatchUp = "Yes"
ElseIf (Sales = Quota) Then
  AtPar = "Yes"
End If
```

You can nest several `ElseIf` statements, such as when you need to check for an option button selection, like this:

```
If (optBut1.Value) Then         ' 1st Button is Checked
  Call LowTotalProc
ElseIf (optBut2.Value) Then     ' 2nd Button is Checked
  Call MedTotalProc
ElseIf (optBut3.Value) Then     ' 3rd Button is Checked
  Call OverTotalProc
Else
  Call SendUserErrProc
End If
```

> **Note**
>
> Visual Basic's `Call` statement works exactly like COBOL's `PERFORM` statement. `Call` executes other procedures that you've written. You'll learn more about `Call` in Part IV, "Advanced VB Programming."

If you begin to nest several `If` statements within other `If` statements, your code can become extremely confusing. The last section in this chapter, named "Eliminating Nesting with *Select Case*," explains how to use the `Select Case` statement to eliminate nested `If...ElseIf` statements and to improve your code's readability.

Sign and Class Testing

Despite the claim that the original BASIC language got its roots from FORTRAN, modern-day Visual Basic *must* get some of its commands from COBOL. Visual Basic includes two add-on options for the `If` statement that virtually mimic COBOL's sign and class tests.

III

Primary Differences

Sgn() tests for numeric signs.

Use Visual Basic's built-in Sgn() function to determine the sign of a number. Sgn() returns one of three values based on the sign of the argument you pass to Sgn(). Here are the possible return values of Sgn():

Sgn() returns -1 if its argument is negative.

Sgn() returns 0 if its argument is zero.

Sgn() returns +1 if its argument is positive.

The following Visual Basic comparison is true if Amt is negative:

```
If (Sgn(Amt) = -1) Then
```

Here is the same statement in COBOL:

```
IF AMT IS NEGATIVE
```

The following Visual Basic comparison is true if Amt is equal to zero:

```
If (Sgn(Amt) = 0) Then
```

Here is the same statement in COBOL:

```
IF AMT IS ZERO
```

The following Visual Basic comparison is true if Amt is positive:

```
If (Sgn(Amt) = 1) Then
```

Here is the same statement in COBOL:

```
IF AMT IS POSITIVE
```

As with all If statements, you can add the Else option to the end of these sign tests.

COBOL's class tests are more limited than Visual Basic's simply because COBOL supports fewer individual data types. The following COBOL IF is true if the STORE-CODE is numeric:

```
IF STORE-CODE IS NUMERIC
  THEN GOOD-CODE = 1.
```

The following COBOL IF is true if the STORE-CODE is alphabetic:

```
IF STORE-CODE IS ALPHABETIC
  THEN GOOD-CODE = 0.
```

Visual Basic includes a class checker that determines the control types. You'll sometimes need to find out what kind of control you're working with. Part IV, "Advanced VB Programming," explains how to send controls to procedures. Those procedures need a way to know what kind of control they receive.

To find out the kind of control a procedure is working with, use the TypeOf...Is option for If. Here is the format of If when used with TypeOf...Is:

TypeOf...Is **tests for control types.**

```
If TypeOf object Is objectType Then
```

Here is an example of how Visual Basic tests to see if a StoreCode control is a list box:

```
If TypeOf StoreCode Is ListBox Then
   GoodCode = 1
```

You can only test controls, not properties or variables, with TypeOf...Is. Therefore, StoreCode must be a control of some kind and this If returns true if StoreCode is a list box control. (This code assumes that StoreCode was sent to the current procedure using tools found in Part IV of this book.) TypeOf...Is checks for any of the objects in Table 13.2. Notice that the object keywords must be all one word; TypeOf...Is checks against ListBox, not List Box.

Table 13.2	The Data Types that *TypeOf...Is* Supports
Object	**Example**
CheckBox	If TypeOf PassedControl Is CheckBox Then
ComboBox	If TypeOf PassedControl Is ComboBox Then
CommandButton	If TypeOf PassedControl Is Command Button Then
Image	If TypeOf PassedControl Is Image Then
Label	If TypeOf PassedControl Is Label Then
ListBox	If TypeOf PassedControl Is ListBox Then
OptionButton	If TypeOf PassedControl Is OptionButton Then
TextBox	If TypeOf PassedControl Is TextBox Then

Eliminating Nesting with *Select Case*

Here's a little secret among Visual Basic programmers: Select Case is one of the most flexible and powerful statements in any language. Visual Basic supports any kind of data test, whether that test be a relational test, a range, a single value comparison, or a mixture of all kinds of data tests, within a Case branch. The only kind of data comparison that Select Case does not support is a compound relational test using the And and Or operators.

Visual Basic's Select statement is not an equivalent to COBOL's FILE SECTION's SELECT statement. By using Select, you can eliminate a common overuse of multiple-level nested If statements.

> **Tip**
>
> The COBOL statement that comes the closest to working the same as Visual Basic's Select Case is the GO TO *PARA1*, *PARA2*, ...DEPENDING ON *DATA-NAME* statement.

There are three versions of the Select Case statement that make Select Case mimic any nested If statement. Here is the format of the first of those three Select Case statements (the other versions are described later in the sections named "Comparing Case Values" and "Using a Range of Case Values"):

```
Select Case Expression
  Case Value1
    One or more Visual Basic statements
  Case Value2
    One or more Visual Basic statements
  Case Value3
    One or more Visual Basic statements
  Case Else
    One or more Visual Basic statements
End Select
```

This format suggests an indention method that you may want to follow. Here is the way Select Case works: if the *Expression* equals the first Case value, that Case's code executes. If, however, the *Expression* equals the second Case value, that Case's code executes, and so on. If none of the Case values equal the *Expression*, the body of the Case Else executes. The *Value* can be a numeric or string expression.

Displaying Messages

Suppose that an employee is requesting the morning status for his or her department. The employee's department resides in a variable named Department. If there are five departments in the company, numbered 10, 20, 30, 40, and 50, Listing 13.1 initializes a label's Caption control with the employee's department status.

Listing 13.1 Using *Select Case* To Display a Status Message

```
' Initialize a label caption with a message
' that is based on the user's department code
Select Case Department
  Case 10
    lblMsg.Caption = "Report to Room 1431"
  Case 20
    lblMsg.Caption = "Send your payroll to Accounting"
  Case 30
    lblMsg.Caption = "Nothing to report"
    ResetVar = True
  Case 40
    lblMsg.Caption = "Charity donations due Tuesday"
  Case 50
    lblMsg.Caption = "Call the boss at home"
  Case Else
    lblMsg.Caption = "You have an invalid department code"
End Select
```

Each Case section call includes one or more Visual Basic statements. Notice that if the user's department code is 50, two assignments occur, whereas the other Case values trigger only single assignments. Any kind of statement can go in the Case sections, not just assignment statements. Often, Case code calls other procedures.

The Case Else handles any unmatched Case value. If the user's department code is not 10, 20, 30, 40, or 50, the invalid message appears in the label's Caption property.

The Select Case is easy to read and maintain. Listing 13.2 shows an equivalent but less readable nested If...ElseIf...End If statement. If you compare the two listings, you'll see that Select Case demonstrates a much clearer approach to handling such logic.

Listing 13.2 Using Nested *If...ElseIf...End* To Display a Status Message

```
' Initialize a label caption with a message
' that is based on the user's department code
If (Department = 10) Then
    lblMsg.Caption = "Report to Room 1431"
ElseIf (Department = 20) Then
    lblMsg.Caption = "Send your payroll to Accounting"
ElseIf (Department = 30) Then
    lblMsg.Caption = "Nothing to report"
    ResetVar = True
    End
```

(continues)

III

Primary Differences

Listing 13.2   Continued

```
ElseIf (Department = 40) Then
    lblMsg.Caption = "Charity donations due Tuesday"
ElseIf (Department = 50) Then
    lblMsg.Caption = "Call the boss at home"
Else
    lblMsg.Caption = "You have an invalid department code"
End If
```

Comparing Case Values

The only problem with Select Case is that the Select Case format that you've seen only compares single values. Consider the following nested If:

```
If (Sales < 2000) Then
  UnderQuota = True
ElseIf (Sales < 3000) Then
  AtQuota = True
Else
  OverQuota = True
End If
```

Although this is a fairly simple nested If, additional sales quota comparison levels can add to the If statement's complexity. By using the Case Is option of the Select Case statement, you can use Select Case for data comparisons. Here is the format of the Select Case with the Case Is option:

```
Select Case Expression
  Case Is Condition1
    One or more Visual Basic statements
  Case Is Condition2
    One or more Visual Basic statements
  Case Is Condition3
    One or more Visual Basic statements
  Case Else
    One or more Visual Basic statements
End Select
```

The Condition can be any data comparison that uses a relational operator. Here is a Select Case that uses the Case Is option to mimic the previous nested If:

```
Select Case Sales
  Case Is < 2000
    UnderQuota = True
  Case Is < 3000
    AtQuota = True
  Case Else
    OverQuota = True
End If
```

If you need to make a comparison based on string data, you can. The following `Select Case` prints a message depending on how the user's last name falls alphabetically:

```
Select Case LastName
  Case Is < "J"   ' Name begins with A - I
    lblMsg.Caption = "Go to line #1"
  Case Is < "R"   ' Name begins with J - Q
    lblMsg.Caption = "Go to line #2"
  Case Else       ' Name begins with R - Z
    lblMsg.Caption = "Go to line #3"
End Select
```

Caution

Visual Basic does not support compound relational testing in `Select Case` statements, as attempted in the following line:

```
    Case Is < 20 And < 40    ' Invalid
```

If you want to use And and Or, you'll have to use If statements instead of `Select Case`.

Using a Range of Case Values

Visual Basic supports an additional `Select Case` option called the `Select Case` range option. Using the range option, you can use `Select Case` to test for ranges of values. Here is the format of the `Select Case` that uses the range option:

```
Select Case Expression
  Case Range1
    One or more Visual Basic statements
  Case Range2
    One or more Visual Basic statements
  Case Range3
    One or more Visual Basic statements
  Case Else
    One or more Visual Basic statements
End Select
```

The *Range* requires the To keyword. Here are some sample ranges that are possible:

```
Case 1 To 25              ' Ranges from 1 to 25 inclusive

Case "Sanders" To "Smith"   ' Inclusive of these strings

Case 4.25 to 4.99         ' Any number from 4.25 to 4.99
```

Perhaps the most powerful aspect of the Select Case statement is that you can combine *all three options* if your data checking requires that you use combined selection. Therefore, the following Select Case is valid, although its readability may be somewhat questionable during maintenance. Notice how each Case statement checks for a range of values, a relational value, and single values.

```
Select Case MonthNum
   Case 1 To 3, 7          ' For months 1, 2, 3, 7
      Call AcctReport
   Case 4, 9, 10 To 11     ' For months 4, 9, 10, 11
      Call MktgReport
   Case Is <= 12           ' For months 5, 6, 7, 8, 12
      Call ExecReport
   Case Else
      Call ErrReportProc
End Select
```

Conclusion

You can now write programs that conditionally operate on data values. The nice thing about Visual Basic is that Visual Basic supports virtually the same data-testing statement, If, that COBOL supports. Actually, Visual Basic's If statement is more flexible than the traditional COBOL's IF because COBOL does not support the <= and >= relational operators.

When a nested If...Else includes another If statement, you must use ElseIf options to code the internal If branches. However, if you find yourself nesting several layers of If...ElseIf...End If code, use the Select Case statement.

The Select Case statement often offers a simple way to code complex If...Then logic. When your code must choose from among several multiple-choice values, the Select Case statement is easier to read and maintain than a complex If statement. There are three different Case options that let you check against exact matches, ranges, and relational conditions using the Select Case.

Your Visual Basic programming toolkit is growing by leaps and bounds. Your inventory of the Visual Basic language is getting fuller each chapter, and you've already mastered some major constructs of the language. You need a break, so the next chapter is a short one that explains how you can format output data so that the output looks just the way you want it to.

Chapter 14

Formatting Data

As a COBOL programmer, you understand how important the format of data is. You've seen that Visual Basic is more free with declared data types than COBOL. When you declare Visual Basic variables, you don't have to specify lengths as you do in the PIC clauses of COBOL. The only data type that you can indicate a specific length for is the fixed-length string data type using Dim's * *n* option.

Although you don't have to be as picky when declaring data, you'll certainly want to be picky about how you output that data for the user. When displaying precision values, such as currency, you need complete control over the output's format. Also, if you print checks and reports, you'll want to control how the numeric spacing appears as well as how dollar values and negatives appear on the reports.

This chapter explains how you format data using Visual Basic. There are many different kinds of Visual Basic formats to choose from. You may be surprised at how much control you have over data within Visual Basic programs.

Here are some of the topics that will be discussed in this chapter:

- Learning how the two format functions work to modify data output
- Using predefined numeric formats for easy numeric formatting
- Using format characters to build your own numeric formats
- Using predefined date and time formats for easy date and time formatting
- Using format characters to build your own date and time formats
- Using format characters to build your own string formats

Using Visual Basic's extensive list of formatting capabilities, you'll never have to worry about properly filling COBOL PIC clauses again. Also, you can forget the struggle that you went through when learning how COBOL's implied decimal place moved left and right depending on the data you move to certain fields. With Visual Basic, you can design output so that your data appears on the form, in labels and text boxes, with the exact format you need no matter how the data resides internally.

The Format Functions

Format data with built-in Visual Basic functions.

Once again, it's time to learn about built-in Visual Basic functions that are tremendously helpful when you want to convert data values to specific formats for outputting or storing to disk. The two functions and their syntax are

```
Format$(expression [, format])
```

and

```
Format(expression [, format])
```

The *expression* may be either a string or numeric expression, depending on the kind of data you need to format. The *format* argument is a string argument that specifies how you want the function to change the look of the first argument. For example, if you want to display a date on the form, you'll need to format that date so that it appears in the format you need, such as spelling out the day of the week, using only the month number, using just the month and year but not the day, or all the other date combinations that Visual Basic supports.

The only difference between these two functions' syntax is the inclusion of the dollar sign in the first one. If you use Format$(), the function returns a string value. If you use Format() (without the $), the function returns a Variant data type. Other than the dollar sign, the functions require the same kinds of arguments.

> ## Note
>
> Even though the second argument, *format*, is optional, Visual Basic programmers rarely, if ever, use the function without the important second argument. Without the second argument, the functions return their first argument as a string (using Format$()) or as a Variant (using Format()) data type.
>
> As you read this chapter, keep in mind that you'll use the format functions to change the appearance of output data values. These functions never change their own argument data, but they do produce new values that are modified versions of the first argument's expression.

The format functions allow considerable flexibility, but in doing so they can also be complex. As you read about these functions in the sections that follow, remember that you don't have to memorize every possible form of the functions. The format functions accept numerous values defined in this chapter's table. When you need to format data, such as a string, numeric, or date value, you can use this chapter as a reference guide to find the format you need to use at the time.

Formatting Numbers

Visual Basic provides two methods that you can use to format numbers. You can use a built-in, predefined format or define your own format. The next two sections explain how to format numbers using either method.

Predefined Numeric Formats

If possible, use the predefined format values in your format functions when you format numeric values. Visual Basic does not include every possible format; hence, you have the ability to define your own. Nevertheless, you'll find all of Visual Basic's predefined formats in Table 14.1, and there is probably a predefined format available that takes care of most of your needs. Each of the predefined formats describe how the format functions can change the look of their first argument.

Table 14.1   The Predefined-Numeric Formats

Format	Description
Currency	Displays the expression with two decimal points and a comma between every three digits to the left of the decimal point. Negative values are enclosed in parentheses. The Currency format follows the country standard you specified when you set up Windows.
Fixed	Displays at least one digit to the left and always two digits to the right of the decimal. Ensures that the user sees at least 0.00 (would be similar to a variable-width PIC 9.99 clause if COBOL supported variable-width PIC clauses).
General Number	Displays the number without modifying its format.
On/Off	Displays Off, if the value is 0; otherwise, displays On. This mimics the True/False and Yes/No formats.
Percent	Displays the value as a percentage. To do so, Visual Basic multiplies the value by 100 and adds a percent sign, %.

(continues)

III

Primary Differences

Table 14.1 Continued	
Format	**Description**
Scientific	Displays the number in scientific notation.
Standard	Always displays the number with comma-separators every three places and with two digits at the right of the decimal point.
True/False	Displays True if the value is 0; otherwise, displays False. This mimics the On/Off and Yes/No formats.
Yes/No	Displays Yes if the value is 0; otherwise, displays No. This mimics the On/Off and True/False formats.

The remaining chapters in this book use the format functions when needed for displaying output. Listing 14.1 helps you get a feel for how these various predefined formats work. The comments to the right tell you what the label's Caption property looks like after the formatting takes place.

Listing 14.1 Using Predefined-Numeric Formats

```
' Using Currency:
Label.Caption = Format(1234.5678, "Currency")
' The Caption gets $1,234.57
' Notice the rounding for cents
' Using Fixed:
Label.Caption = Format(1234.5678, "Fixed")
' The Caption gets 1234.57
' Using General Number:
Label.Caption = Format(1234.5678, "General Number")
' The Caption gets 1234.5678
' If you use a single-precision variable in place of
' the numeric literal (Visual Basic always interprets
' numeric literals as if they were double-precision),
' Visual Basic would lose some accuracy starting with
' the fourth decimal place due to rounding
' Using On/Off:
Label.Caption = Format(1234.5678, "On/Off")
' The Caption gets On
' If you formatted a value that evaluated to
' zero, Caption would be assigned Off
Using Percent:
Label.Caption = Format(1234.5678, "Percent")
' The Caption gets 123456.78%
' Using Scientific:
Label.Caption = Format(1234.5678, "Scientific")
```

```
' The Caption gets 1.23E+03
' You lose a little precision when you format
' with scientific precision
' Using Standard:
Label.Caption = Format(1234.5678, "Standard")
' The Caption gets 1,234.57
' Notice the rounding to two decimal places
' Using True/False:
Label.Caption = Format(1234.5678, "True/False")
' The Caption gets True
' If you formatted a value that evaluated to
' zero, Caption would be assigned False
' Using Yes/No:
Label.Caption = Format(1234.5678, "Yes/No")
' The Caption gets Yes
' If you formatted a value that evaluated to
' zero, Caption would be assigned No
```

Defining Your Own Numeric Formats

Although Visual Basic supplies the nine predefined formats that you saw in the last section, you may want your data to appear differently. For example, none of the predefined formats let you output data with three decimal places.

Table 14.2 contains format characters that you can build your own formats with. You may never use all of these format characters, but you will use many of them over your course of programming.

Sadly, there is no direct one-to-one correspondence between all these formats and COBOL's PIC clauses that you are so accustomed to. Nevertheless, you can see from this chapter's tables that Visual Basic takes seriously the formatting of output and provides many more formatting opportunities than you had with COBOL's DATA DIVISION clauses.

Table 14.2 The Numeric-Format Characters

Format	Description
0	A digit appears in the output at the 0 position if a digit appears in the number being formatted. If no non-zero digit is at the 0's position in the number being formatted, a 0 appears. If there are not as many zeros in the number being formatted as there are zeros in the format field, leading or trailing zeros print. If the number contains more numeric positions, the 0 forces all digits to the right of the decimal point to round to the format's pattern and all digits to the left print as is. You mostly use this format character to print leading or trailing zeros when you want to see such zeros.

(continues)

III

Primary Differences

Table 14.2 Continued	
Format	**Description**
#	The pound-sign character works like the 0 placeholder, except blanks appear if the number being formatted does not have as many digits as the format has #s.
.	The period character specifies how many digits (by its placement within 0 or #s) are to appear to the left and right of a decimal point.
%	The number being formatted is multiplied by 100, and the percent sign, %, prints at its position inside the displayed string.
,	If a comma appears in the midst of 0s or #s, the thousands are easier to read because the comma groups every three places in the number (unless the number is below 1,000, in which case no comma appears). If you put two commas together, you request that the number be divided by 1,000 to scale down the number.
E-,E+,e-,e+	The number is formatted into scientific notation if the format also contains at least one 0 or #.
\	Whatever character follows the backslash appears at its position in the formatted string.

Note

Any characters that do not appear in Table 14.2 but appear in the format string show as-is in the formatted value.

Listing 14.2 contains several examples of how you can build your own format strings. Although Table 14.2 may seem confusing when you first read it, you can see from the examples that building your own format is fairly easy to do.

Listing 14.2 Using Your Own Numeric Formats

```
    Label1.Caption = Format(  9146, "######")
 ' Caption gets   9146 with two leading spaces
    Label2.Caption = Format(9146, "000000")
 ' Caption gets 009146
    Label3.Caption = Format(2652.2, "00000.00")
 ' Caption gets 02652.20
    Label4.Caption = Format(2652.2, "#####.##")
 ' Caption gets 2652.2
```

```
    Label5.Caption = Format(2652.212, "#####.##")
' Caption gets 2652.21 (VB rounds when needed)
    Label6.Caption = Format(2652.216, "#####.##")
' Caption gets 2652.22
    Label7.Caption = Format(45, "+###")
' Caption gets +45
    Label8.Caption = Format(-45, "-###-")
' Caption gets -45-
    Label9.Caption = Format(-45, "###-")
' Caption gets 45-
    Label10.Caption = Format(2445, "$####.##")
' Caption gets $2445.
    Label11.Caption = Format(2445, "$####.00")
' Caption gets $2445.00
    Label12.Caption = Format(2445, "a#b###.##c#d#")
' Caption gets a2b445.cd
' Non-format characters print as-is
    Label13.Caption = Format(2445, "00Hi00")
' Caption gets 24Hi45
```

Formatting Dates and Times

You can't work with dates and times until you learn how to display them
properly. Therefore, despite the importance of date and time values for business programming, this book has not focused on date and time values because you had no way to properly output those values until you learned the
format functions.

You'll recall that you must declare Variant data typed variables for date and
time values. In a single Variant data typed variable, Visual Basic stores both
the date and time of any particular time period. Through the date and time
format codes described in Tables 14.3 and 14.4, you control whether you
want the output to contain the date portion, the time portion, or both portions of Variant data.

As with the numeric formats, Visual Basic supplies predefined date and time
formats as well as date and time formatting characters so you can build your
own formats. The next two sections explain the date and time formats.

Predefined Date and Time Formats

Visual Basic supports various kinds of date and time formats because different
applications demand different formats. As with the numeric format codes,
the designers of Visual Basic strived to make formatting date and time values
as simple as possible. Table 14.3 contains the date and time formats.

III

Primary Differences

Table 14.3	The Predefined Date and Time Formats
Format	**Description**
General Date	Displays the date and time in MM/DD/YY HH:MM PM format. This format may differ slightly if your international country code setting requires a different format. You can store a date and time value in a single- or double-precision variable if you want to display only the date or the time. If you format a precision value with the General Date, only the date appears in the MM/DD/YY format if there is no fractional part, and only the time appears in the HH:MM PM format if the whole number portion to the left of the decimal is zero.
Long Date	Searches for your Windows international Long Date setting and formats the date accordingly.
Long Time	Searches for your Windows international Long Time setting and formats the date accordingly.
Medium Date	Same as the Short Date setting in your Windows international setting except the month's short abbreviation (for example, Jan) is spelled out.
Medium Time	Displays the time in a 12-hour format in the HH:MM setting with either AM or PM.
Short Date	Searches for your Windows international Short Date setting and formats the date accordingly.
Short Time	Searches for your Windows international Short Time setting and formats the time accordingly.

The Now function returns the current date and time.

Before showing you code that uses these predefined date and time format strings, you must understand the Now function. Now is one of the few functions that does not take parentheses. Now is discussed more fully in Chapter 22, "Using Dates and Times."

Now stores the current date and time as indicated by the values set in your computer's internal clock and calendar. Listing 14.3 demonstrates the predefined date and time format strings. The data comes from a Variant variable that holds Now's return value.

Listing 14.3	Using the Predefined Date and Time Formats

```
' First, declare the date/time variable
Dim Today As Variant
' Store today's date and time
Today = Now
```

```
Label1.Caption = Format(Today, "General Date")
' Caption gets 1/12/98 7:43:16 PM
Label2.Caption = Format(Today, "Long Date")
' Caption gets Thursday, January 12, 1998
Label3.Caption = Format(Today, "Long Time")
' Caption gets 7:43:16 PM
Label4.Caption = Format(Today, "Medium Date")
' Caption gets 12-Jan-98
Label5.Caption = Format(Today, "Medium Time")
' Caption gets 07:43 PM
Label6.Caption = Format(Today, "Short Date")
' Caption gets 1/12/98
Label7.Caption = Format(Today, "Short Time")
' Caption gets 19:43
```

Defining Your Own Date Formats

Table 14.4 lists the date format characters that you can use to build your own date format conversion strings. As with the numeric format characters, you can use the date format characters to customize your own date appearances.

Table 14.4   The Date and Time Format Characters

Format	Description
c	Displays either the date (just like the ddddd symbol if only a date is present in the value being formatted) or the time (just like the ttttt symbol if only a time is present in the value being formatted); displays both the date (ddddd) and time (ttttt) if both values are present.
d	Displays the day number from 1 to 31.
dd	Displays the day number with a leading zero from 01 to 31.
ddd	Displays an abbreviated three-character day from Sun to Sat.
dddd	Displays the full day name from Sunday to Saturday.
ddddd	Displays the date (month, day, year) according to your international Short Date format settings of your Windows installation.
dddddd	Displays the date (month, day, year) according to your international Long Date format settings of your Windows installation.
w	Displays the day of the week number (1 for Sunday, 2 for Monday, and so on)

(continues)

Table 14.4 Continued

Format	Description
ww	Displays the year's week number from 1 to 54.
m	Displays the month number from 1 to 12. The m also means minute if it follows an h or hh.
mm	Displays the month number with a leading zero from 01 to 12. The mm also means minute if it follows an h or hh.
mmm	Displays the abbreviated month name from Jan to Dec.
mmmm	Displays the full month name from January to December.
q	Displays the quarter of the year.
y	Displays the number of the day of the year from 1 to 365.
yy	Displays the two-digit year from 00 to 99.
yyyy	Displays the full year number from 100 to 9999.
h	Displays the hour number from 0 to 23.
hh	Displays the hour as a two-digit number from 00 to 23.
n	Displays the minute number from 0 to 59.
nn	Displays the minute number with a leading zero from 00 to 59.
s	Displays the second number from 0 to 59.
ss	Displays the second number with a leading zero from 00 to 59.
ttttt	Displays the time (hour, minute, second) according to your international Time format settings of your Windows installation.
AM/PM	Uses the 12-hour clock time and displays either AM or PM as needed.
am/pm	Uses the 12-hour clock time and displays either am or pm as needed.
A/P	Uses the 12-hour clock time and displays either A or P as needed.
a/p	Uses the 12-hour clock time and displays either a or p as needed.

Format	Description
AMPM	Uses the 12-hour clock to display the string assigned to the s1159 and s2359 variables (usually these strings are assigned AM or PM unless they are changed) in your Windows installation file.

The code in Listing 14.4 shows examples of these date format characters. The comments explain what each label's Caption date looks like after each assignment.

Listing 14.4   Using the Date Format Characters

```
' First, declare the date/time variable
Dim Today As Variant
' Store today's date and time
Today = Now
Label1.Caption = Format(Today, "c")
' Caption gets 1/14/98 7:43:16 PM
Label2.Caption = Format(Today, "w")        ' day
' Caption gets 4
Label3.Caption = Format(Today, "ww")       ' week
' Caption gets 2
Label4.Caption = Format(Today, "dddd")     ' Alpha day
' Caption gets Wednesday
Label5.Caption = Format(Today, "q")        ' quarter
' Caption gets 1
Label6.Caption = Format(Today, "hh")       ' hour
' Caption gets 19
Label7.Caption = Format(Today, "h AM/PM")
' Caption gets 7 PM
Label8.Caption = Format(Today, "hh AM/PM")
' Caption gets 07 PM
Label9.Caption = Format(Today, "d-mmmm h:nn:ss")
' Caption gets 14-January 19:43:16
```

Formatting Strings

If you want to modify the appearance of string output, you must define your own format strings. Table 14.5 lists the format characters available to format strings. One reason there are not many formatting characters is that Visual Basic supports a wide variety of string functions. Many of the string functions modify strings and change strings more drastically than formatting characters can accomplish. You'll learn all about the string functions in Chapter 20, "Built-in String Functions."

Visual Basic supplies no pre-defined string formats.

III

Primary Differences

Table 14.5 The String Format Characters	
Format	**Description**
@	The next character from the string you are formatting appears in the output at the @ position. If there is no character at the @'s position in the string, a blank appears. The @'s are filled if there are more than one from right to left.
&	This character is just like @, except nothing (a null) appears (instead of a blank) if no character at the &'s position appears in the string being printed.
!	The exclamation point forces all placeholder characters (the @ and &) to fill from left to right instead of from right to left.
<	The less-than character forces all characters being formatted in the string to appear in lowercase.
>	The greater-than character forces all characters being formatted in the string to appear in uppercase.

The code in Listing 14.5 shows examples of these string format characters. The comments explain what each label's Caption string looks like after each assignment.

Listing 14.5 Using the String Format Characters

```
Label1.Caption = Format("AbcDef", ">")
' Caption gets ABCDEF
Label2.Caption = Format("AbcDef", "<")
' Caption gets abcdef
Label3.Caption = Format("A", "@@@")
' Caption gets   A (two spaces precede A)
Label4.Caption = Format("A", "!!!")
' Caption gets A   (two spaces follow A)
Label5.Caption = Format("2325551212", "(@@@) @@@-@@@@")
' Caption gets (232) 555-1212
```

Tip

As you can see from the final format string, you can put string data into any format you prefer such as a phone number. Use string formats to format such data as social security numbers and nine-digit zip codes.

Conclusion

This chapter explored the many formatting capabilities of Visual Basic. Microsoft did a great job of offering the flexibility to format your numeric, string, date, and time output so that the output appears exactly the way you want it to look.

Visual Basic's data-formatting capabilities go so far beyond COBOL's `PIC` clauses that it's difficult to compare the two languages. You never have to worry about implied decimal places in Visual Basic. By building format strings, you create the exact look of the output that you want to appear on your screen.

III

Primary Differences

Chapter 15

Controlling Program Flow

This chapter explains how to convert your thinking from COBOL's PERFORM loops to Visual Basic's loops. You'll learn the Visual Basic equivalents for these standard COBOL control statements:

```
PERFORM...TIMES

PERFORM...UNTIL

PERFORM...VARYING
```

Well, you'll learn *almost all* the equivalents. You're not quite ready to tackle Visual Basic's calling of procedures from within procedures. That is, not until Chapter 21, "Modular Visual Basic Programming." There you'll master the Call statement that calls procedures in the identical way that PERFORM calls paragraphs. Nevertheless, you don't need Call to learn how Visual Basic approaches program control statements that loop.

Loops are vital to data processing, and Visual Basic requires looping statements just as any programming language does. Once you learn how to code Visual Basic loops in this chapter, you'll have all the tools you need to tackle table handling in the next chapter.

Here are some of the topics that will be discussed in this chapter:

■ Comparing COBOL's PERFORM...UNTIL statements to Visual Basic's Do Until and Do...Loop Until statements

■ Learning how to distinguish between loops that test their condition at the top and bottom of the loop

III

Primary Differences

■ Understanding how the While loop gives your program more flexibility than the Until loop can do by itself

■ Mastering Visual Basic's major looping statement, the For loop

■ Coding For loops to count down as well as up

■ Nesting For loops properly

■ Adding early termination to loops by using the two versions of the Exit statement

Although Visual Basic's two versions of the Do Until loop aren't necessarily the most often-used looping statements in the language, these statements do mirror COBOL's PERFORM...UNTIL statement and you'll start with them.

The *Do Until* Loops

The two Visual Basic Do Until loops repeat a section of code until a condition becomes true. In other words, they loop as long as a condition remains false, stopping the loop when the condition becomes true.

There are two versions of the Do Until loop. They differ only slightly in syntax and the version you use depends on whether you want to test the condition at the top or bottom of the loop.

The *Do Until* Looping Statement

Do Until **closely matches COBOL's** PERFORM...UNTIL **loop.**

Before getting more into the Visual Basic loops, you need to know that Visual Basic allows a little more looping flexibility than COBOL. The COBOL PERFORM...UNTIL statement executes a loop, but the body of that loop must be a paragraph. In other words, the following COBOL statement

```
PERFORM ADD-EMP-PAY UNTIL EOF = 1.
```

triggers a loop and the body of that loop is the execution of the ADD-EMP-PAY paragraph. Figure 15.1 shows the flowchart for such a loop.

Notice where the condition test occurs. The name of the loop, PERFORM...UNTIL, is somewhat misleading because it tends to make one think that the body of the loop executes at least once, when in reality, the body of a PERFORM...UNTIL loop may not execute at all if the condition is true to begin with.

COBOL's PERFORM...UNTIL statement *first* tests its condition. Only if that condition is false does the paragraph execute and the condition test occurs once again. Both COBOL and Visual Basic operate the same way with true and false; it's the location where they check for those values that differs at times.

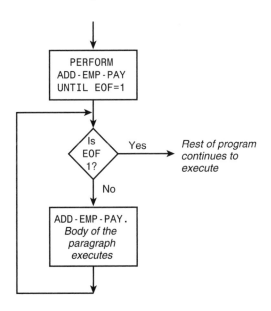

Fig. 15.1
COBOL's PERFORM...UNTIL loop tests relational conditions at the top of the loop.

With this review in mind, consider the format of Visual Basic's Do Loop shown here:

```
Do Until Condition
   One or more Visual
   Basic statements
Loop
```

The following Visual Basic Do Until loop is the equivalent of the COBOL PERFORM...UNTIL loop you saw earlier:

```
Do Until EOF = 1
   Call AddEmpPay
Loop
```

Unlike COBOL's PERFORM...UNTIL loop, Visual Basic's Do Until often spans several lines. The Loop statement must appear at the bottom of the loop to tell Visual Basic where the loop finishes and the rest of the program code begins.

The nicest aspect of Visual Basic's looping statements, as opposed to COBOL's, is that you don't have to perform only procedures inside the loop. You can put one or more Visual Basic statements in the body of the loop that do anything. Consider the routine shown in Listing 15.1. The body of the Do Until loop calculates the final compound investment total assuming an annual compounded interest rate.

Listing 15.1   Using a *Do Until* To Calculate Compound Interest

```
' Use a loop to calculate a final total
' investment using compound interest.
' N is a loop control variable
' IRate is the annual rate
' Term is the number of years in the investment
' InitInv is the investor's initial investment
' Interest is the total interest paid
N = 1
IRate = .08
Term = 5
InitInv = 1000#
Interest = 1    ' Begin at one for first compound

' Use loop to calculate total compound amount
Do Until N > Term
  Interest = Interest * (1 + IRate)
  N = N + 1    ' Next term's calculation
Loop

' Now we have total interest,
' calculate the total investment
' at the end of N years
CompTotal = InitInv * Interest
lblFinalInv.Caption = Format$(CompTotal, "Currency")
```

Given the values assigned at the start of the program, the `Caption` property for the `lblFinalInv` label will contain `$1,469.33`. Notice how the `Format$()` function modifies the look of the output value to a formatted dollar amount result.

The code inside the body of this loop continues looping until `N` equals the `Term` of the loan. Basically, the loop executes five times and continues until `N` equals the `Term`, which means that the loop has executed `Term` times (5 in this program's case).

Caution

It's vital that you change the loop's conditional test within the body of the loop. For example, if Listing 15.1 didn't add one to `N` in the body of the loop, the loop would never terminate and would be endless, which would require the user to press Ctrl+Break or choose the Run, End menu command.

Normally, the work values that this code uses come from the user or a data file instead of being directly assigned as in Listing 15.1's short routine.

Keep Structured

Proper structured programming practices dictate that code be as modular as possible. COBOL helps enforce the modular approach by requiring that you execute paragraphs (modules) from within UNTIL loops, whereas Visual Basic is more lax about what you do in the body of the loop. Sometimes, the body of a loop is so short—that is, you only want to repeat a couple of statements in the loop—that the overhead of putting those two statements in their own procedure does not justify the expense of runtime speed or coding time just to create a separate module.

If, in Visual Basic programs, the body of your loops contains several statements, you are much better off putting those statements in their own procedure and executing that loop as you would a PERFORM...UNTIL loop. Chapter 21, "Modular Visual Basic Programming," discusses modular programming in more detail.

Unlike COBOL, Visual Basic supports the testing of the loop's condition at the *end* of the loop instead of at the beginning. The Do...Loop Until loop tests at the end of the loop and has a syntax that is almost identical to that of the Do Loop.

Alas, one of the nicest COBOL statements, the PERFORM...THRU...UNTIL statement, has no Visual Basic equivalent. You can only execute a single body of code within a Visual Basic loop. If you want to execute more than one procedure (simulating the *PARA1* THRU *PARA2* option), you'll have to group those procedure calls in a single high-level procedure and call that high-level procedure within the body of your loop. Again, you'll read more about calling procedures in Chapter 21, "Modular Visual Basic Programming."

The *Do...Loop Until* Looping Statement

Here is the format of the Do...Loop Until loop. Notice the slight syntax difference between this loop and the Do Loop syntax:

```
Do
   One or more Visual
   Basic statements
Loop Until Condition
```

Tip

If you want the body of the loop to execute at least once, you'll need the test at the end of the loop.

The only difference is the placement of the Until `Condition` relational test. The placement at the end of the loop's body indicates that the relational test takes place *after* the body of the loop executes at least once. Figure 15.2 shows a flowchart of the Do...Loop Until.

Fig. 15.2

Visual Basic's
Do...Loop Until.

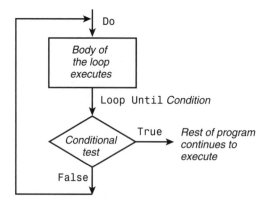

The illustrative code in Listings 15.2 and 15.3 shows the difference between the two Do loops using a very simple loop and conditional test. The body of Listing 15.2 never executes because the condition is true before the loop body ever gets a chance to execute. The body of Listing 15.3 executes exactly one time. Even though the condition is true before the body of the loop begins, the use of Do...Loop Until forces Visual Basic to execute the loop once and then to test the condition after that first execution.

Listing 15.2   The Body of the Loop Never Executes

```
amt = 25
Do Until amt = 25
  txtScrn.Text = "*** Body of the loop ***"
  ' Does this body execute?
Loop
```

Listing 15.3   The Body of the Loop Executes One Time

```
amt = 25
Do
  txtScrn.Text = "*** Body of the loop ***"
  ' Does this body execute?
Loop Until amt = 25
```

Sometimes, using the `Do Until` loops can cause confusion because of the negative condition that triggers the loops. In other words, these loops keep looping as long as some conditional test is *false*. Often, you'll want to code a loop so that the loop's body executes as long as a condition remains *true*. The next section describes the `Do While` loops that do just that.

The *Do While* Loops

The `Do While` looping statement loops as long as an expression is true. You don't have an equivalent in COBOL. Here are possible conditions for such loops to execute:

The `Do While` **loops continue to loop for true conditions.**

■ Loops as long as the user answers `Yes` to a question

■ Loops as long as there are more records to process

■ Loops as long as the input value is above a certain value

■ Loops as long as the day of the week is a weekday

You can always write any kind of loop using `Do Until` loops. For example, you can execute the loop as long as the end of file has yet to be reached or as long as the day of the week is *not* a weekend day. However, you want your code to contain as much readability as possible. Sometimes, the positive looping condition offered by the `Do While` loops provides better coding documentation than the looping condition of the `Do Until` loops.

As with `Do Until`, there are two formats for `Do While`: a `Do While` loop and a `Do...Loop While` loop. The only difference between the two is the placement of their conditional test. Here is the format of the `Do While`:

```
Do While Condition
  One or more Visual
  Basic statements
Loop
```

The body of the loop can be a procedure call or any other Visual Basic statement or set of statements. As long as the `Condition` is true, the body of the loop continues to execute.

> **Caution**
>
> As with any loop, you must ensure that the `Condition` changes at some point within the body of the loop or you'll wind up with an infinite loop.

The Do While loop may never execute because its test appears at the top of the loop and before the first statement of the loop's body. Figure 15.3 illustrates the action of the Do While.

Fig. 15.3

Visual Basic's Do...While loops while the relation is true.

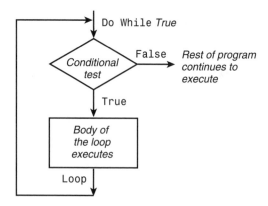

You could write Listing 15.1's interest calculating routine by using a Do While loop instead of the Do Until loop. Listing 15.4 contains a rewritten version of the interest routine that loops *while* the calculation has gone less than the full length of the investment term. As with the previous interest-calculating listing, concentrate on the way the loop behaves and don't worry about the specifics of the interest calculation.

Listing 15.4   Calculating Interest with a *Do While*

```
' Use a Do While loop to calculate a final total
' investment using compound interest.
' N is a loop control variable
' IRate is the annual rate
' Term is the number of years in the investment
' InitInv is the investor's initial investment
' Interest is the total interest paid
N = 1
IRate = .08
Term = 5
InitInv = 1000#
Interest = 1    ' Begin at one for first compound

' Use loop to calculate total compound amount
Do While N <= Term
  Interest = Interest * (1 + IRate)
  N = N + 1    ' Next term's calculation
Loop
```

```
' Now we have total interest,
' calculate the total investment
' at the end of N years
CompTotal = InitInv * Interest

lblFinalInv.Caption = Format$(CompTotal, "Currency")
```

If you want the body of the loop to execute at least once, use a Do...Loop While statement that places the conditional test after the body's first execution. Here is the format of the Do...Loop While:

```
Do
    One or more Visual
    Basic statements
Loop While Condition
```

Figure 15.4 shows how this loop differs from the Do While loop. The coding difference is small. The syntax difference between the loops varies only by where you code the While *Condition* portion of the statement.

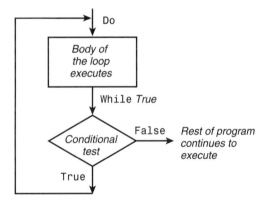

Fig. 15.4

Visual Basic's Do...Loop While tests the condition at the bottom of the loop.

Tip

Often, programmers use looping mechanisms to display error messages. The program keeps displaying the error until the user does what is expected in that particular case. Chapter 17, "Screen I/O: Message and Input Boxes," explains how to display errors and message boxes that pop up on the screen. The Do loops discussed in this chapter often control error handling by displaying an error message when a user incorrectly responds to a prompt from the program.

III

Primary Differences

The *For* Loop Controls Its Own Variables

Most beginning Visual Basic books have to spend at least an entire chapter discussing the ins and outs of the For loop. You certainly don't need deep coverage of the For loop because you've been using a similar statement for years: both the PERFORM...VARYING statement and even the PERFORM...TIMES statement mimic Visual Basic's For loop.

The For loop repeats a section of code—the body of the loop—over and over. Unlike the Do loops discussed in the previous sections, the For loop automatically increments or decrements a control variable in the same way that PERFORM...VARYING automatically increments counter variables.

Here is the format of the Visual Basic For statement:

```
For CounterVar = StartVal To EndVal [STEP Increment]
  One or more Visual Basic statements
Next [CounterVar]
```

The For loop's format looks a little confusing, but so does the PERFORM...VARYING to COBOL beginners. Remember that these two language statements are virtually identical.

Here is a COBOL PERFORM...VARYING statement that I'll translate to a Visual Basic For loop to show you the similarities:

```
PERFORM READ-VALS-RTN VARYING CTR FROM 1 BY 1 UNTIL CTR > 100.
```

As you should already know, this PERFORM...VARYING executes a loop, the calling of the READ-VALS-RTN paragraph, exactly 100 times. The loop controls the exact number of loop executions with the CTR variable. When the loop begins, CTR is 1. The loop then increments CTR by 1 and repeats the loop until CTR reaches 100.

Here is an identical Visual Basic loop. Notice how Visual Basic's support for multiple-line statements (the Next statement terminates the loop body) makes the code easier to read than COBOL's PERFORM...VARYING, which programmers often write on a single line:

```
For Ctr = 1 To 100
  Call ReadValsRtn
Next Ctr
```

The variable that follows Next is optional. Visual Basic can figure out, even when you nest For loops, exactly which For loop is terminating. Therefore, here is an identical Visual Basic loop without the explicitly placed counter variable following Next:

```
For Ctr = 1 To 100
   Call ReadValsRtn
Next
```

Visual Basic automatically increments the Ctr variable by one each time the loop executes. In a nutshell, the For loop executes until the variable is greater than the To parameter. At the end of the previous example, Ctr is actually equal to 101. If you want to specify the increment explicitly (as done with COBOL's PERFORM...VARYING), you can do so by specifying a Step value like this:

```
For Ctr = 1 To 100 Step 1
   Call ReadValsRtn
Next
```

> **Tip**
>
> Using For loops, you can also iterate a section of code an exact number of times. For example, the preceding For loop executes its body exactly 100 times. COBOL has a similar PERFORM statement: PERFORM...TIMES. Here is the equivalent COBOL PERFORM...TIMES statement:
>
> ```
> PERFORM READ-VALS-RTN 100 TIMES.
> ```

The Step value can be any number. You may want to increment a loop by 3's like this:

```
For Ctr = 10 To 50 Step 3
   Total = Total + Ctr
   Factor = Total / 2.5
   Amount = Factor + Total
Next
```

All three statements in this For loop body execute 14 times because Visual Basic begins the loop with 10 in the Ctr variable, adds 3 each time the body of the loop executes, and stops the loop when Ctr surpasses 50. (Ctr is actually equal to 52 at the loop's end.)

Note

You can use variables to control a For loop completely. Therefore, the starting value, ending value, and increment values can be variables. Also, you may use or modify these variables inside the loop. If, however, the loop changes one of the For controlling variables, you open yourself up to some maintenance headaches when you attempt to figure out the loop later. It's best to *not* change the control variables in the loop, but instead, let the loop control these variables. If you want to use the control variables in the loop's body, go ahead, but don't change them unless you're really sure about needing to do so.

You can code Listing 15.4's investment calculation code more cleanly by using a For loop than using any of the Do loops because of the iterative nature of the calculation. The interest rate calculation executes based on the time period, starting from time period one (a year from now) until the end of the term. Listing 15.5 shows the investment calculation routine with a For loop. The code does not have to use an assignment to initialize the control variable, and the body of the loop does not have to increments this variable either because For handles the initialization and increments automatically.

Listing 15.5 Computing an Investment with a *For* Loop

```
' Use a For loop to calculate a final total
' investment using compound interest.
' N is a loop control variable
' IRate is the annual rate
' Term is the number of years in the investment
' InitInv is the investor's initial investment
' Interest is the total interest paid
IRate = .08
Term = 5
InitInv = 1000#
Interest = 1    ' Begin at one for first compound

' Use loop to calculate total compound amount
For N = 1 To Term
   Interest = Interest * (1 + IRate)
Next

' Now we have total interest,
' calculate the total investment
' at the end of N years
CompTotal = InitInv * Interest

lblFinalInv.Caption = Format$(CompTotal, "Currency")
```

At the end of this code's execution, the `Caption` property of `lblFinalInv` holds
$1,469.33.

A similar COBOL loop looks something like this:

```
PERFORM CALC-INT-RTN VARYING N FROM 1 BY 1 UNTIL N = TERM.
```

The `CALC-INT-RTN` performs each individual period's interest calculation as
done inside the Visual Basic loop in Listing 15.5.

> **Note**
>
> You can write virtually any loop by using any of the four Do loops or the For loop.
> The kind of loop that you choose depends as much on style and personal preference
> as anything else. Nevertheless, you may find that For loops generally are easier to
> code when you need a loop that loops a certain number of times, instead of one that
> loops based on a condition's true or false value.

Negative *Step* Values

For loops don't have to count up. If you specify a negative `Step` value, the For
loop counts down (*decrements*) by the `Step` value. The code in Listing 15.6
produces a countdown in the label's `Caption` property by appending the numbers 10, 9, 8, and so on until the countdown reaches 1, to the label's caption.
The concatenation operator, &, works with string values, so the `Str$()` function is used to convert the loop's integer controlling variable to a string value.
`Str$()` is the mirror-image function to `Val()`, which you've used throughout
this book. (`Val()` converts strings to numeric values.)

The `Step` can be
negative.

Listing 15.6   Counting Down

```
' Set up a line feed and carriage return
NL = Chr$(13) + Chr$(10)

' Blank out the label's initial caption
lblOut.Caption = ""

' Store the numbers from 10 to 1 in the caption
' One number per line
For N = 10 To 1 Step -1
  lblOut.Caption = lblOut.Caption & NL & Str$(N)
Next N

' Add one final message
lblOut.Caption = lblOut.Caption & NL & "Blast Off!"
```

III

Primary Differences

When Listing 15.6 finishes, here is what you will see in the label's caption:

```
10
9
8
7
6
5
4
3
2
1
Blast Off!
```

You'll have to increase the size of the label so that you can see all eleven lines of output from Listing 15.6.

Nesting Loops

A nested loop is a loop within a loop.

Any Visual Basic statement can go inside the body of a For loop—even another For loop! When you put a loop inside a loop, you are creating *nested loops*. The clock in a sporting event works like a nested loop. You may think this example is stretching an analogy a little far, but it truly works. A clock in a football game counts down from 15 minutes to 0. It completely counts down four times. The first countdown is a loop going from 15 to 0 (for each minute), and that loop is nested within another loop counting from 1 to 4 (for each of the four quarters).

Any time your program needs to repeat a loop more than one time, use a nested loop. Figure 15.5 shows an outline of nested loops. You can think of the inner loop as looping "faster" than the outer loop. The For loop counting from 1 to 15 is the inner loop. It loops fastest because the variable Inside goes from 1 to 15 before the outer loop, the variable Outside, finishes its first iteration. Because the outer loop does not repeat until the Next Outside statement, the inner For loop has a chance to finish in its entirety. When the outer loop finally does iterate a second time, the inner loop starts all over again.

You can code nested loops in COBOL, but only if you insert the inner loop inside the paragraph that the outer PERFORM...VARYING performs. Such COBOL nested loops aren't as obvious as they are in Visual Basic code.

Note

The block of code inside the innermost loop of Figure 15.5 executes a total of 40 times. The outside loop iterates four times and the inner loop executes ten times for each of the outer loop's counts.

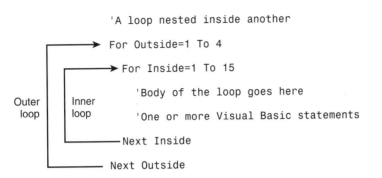

Fig. 15.5
An outline of nested loops.

Figure 15.6 shows two loops nested within a single outer loop. Both of these loops execute in their entirety before the outer loop finishes its first iteration. When the outer loop starts its second iteration, the two inner loops repeat all over again.

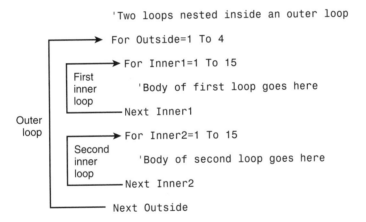

Fig. 15.6
An outline of two nested loops.

Notice the order of the Next variables explicitly stated in both Figures 15.5 and 15.6. The inner loop always finishes, and therefore its Next must come before the outer loop's Next variable. If no variables are listed after each Next, the loops still are correct and work properly.

> **Tip**
>
> To sum up nested loops, follow this rule of thumb: in nested loops, the order of the Next variables should be the opposite of the For variables. This arrangement gives the inner loop (or loops) a chance to complete before the outer loop's next iteration.

You can get into trouble if you forget that inner loops terminate completely before their outer loop gets another chance to iterate. Figure 15.7 shows an incorrect order of Next statements. The outer loop finishes before the inner loop (see the variable listed at the end of each Next statement). The loops in Figure 15.7 do not fit the correct description of nested loops, and you get an error if you attempt to terminate an outer loop before the inner loop finishes. If you explicitly code the statements as in Figure 15.7, Visual Basic issues a Next without For error as soon as you type the first Next statement.

Fig. 15.7

Two incorrectly nested loops.

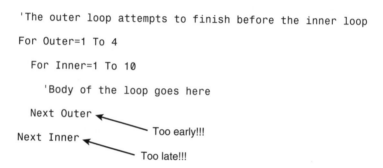

```
'The outer loop attempts to finish before the inner loop

For Outer=1 To 4

    For Inner=1 To 10

        'Body of the loop goes here

    Next Outer        Too early!!!

    Next Inner        Too late!!!
```

> **Caution**
>
> The indention of the Next statements has no effect on the order they execute. Indention serves only to make Visual Basic programs more readable to you and other programmers.

Exiting Early If Needed

Loops don't have to terminate on their own.

In some instances, you may not want a Do or For loop to terminate on its own. The Exit command lets you terminate loops early if certain conditions exist. There are two Exit statements available for you to terminate loops early:

```
Exit Do
```

and

```
Exit For
```

Exit Do terminates any of the Do loops described in the first part of this chapter. The Exit For statement terminates For loops. Generally, you'll use an

`Exit` in the body of an `If` statement. Therefore, you can write a loop that is controlled by the `Do` condition. However, if an extraordinary circumstance arises, such as the user enters an unexpected value inside the loop, the `Exit` statement forces Visual Basic to terminate the loop immediately and to continue with the rest of the procedure no matter how many additional iterations there are of the `Do` or `For` loop.

Listing 15.7 shows what can happen when Visual Basic encounters an unconditional `Exit For` statement, that is, one not preceded by an `If` statement.

Listing 15.7   An Early Exit

```
Dim N As Integer
Dim NL As String
' Set up a line feed and carriage return
NL = Chr$(13) + Chr$(10)

' Blank out the label's initial caption
lblOut.Caption = ""

' A For loop defeated by the Exit For
For N = 1 To 20
  ' Append the loop variable to the caption
  lblOut.Caption = lblOut.Caption & NL & Str$(N)
  Exit For        ' Exits the loop immediately
Next N            ' Next never executes

' Add one final message
lblOut.Caption = lblOut.Caption & NL & "That's all!"
```

The body of Listing 15.7's loop executes only one time. Here is what the user sees in the label's caption after this code finishes:

```
 1
That's all!
```

You can tell from this output that `Exit For` forced an early exit from the loop that normally loops 20 times. The `Exit For` immediately terminates the `For` loop before the `For` loop went through one complete cycle; the `For` loop may as well not be in this program.

Listing 15.7 is an extreme example that you should use `Exit` statements only if data or the user provides reasons to terminate a loop early. The `Exit For` inside an `If` statement is a great statement for missing data when you are processing a file. When you start processing a data file, you may expect 100 input numbers but only get 95 because of missing values. You can use `Exit`

For to terminate the For loop that was originally set up to iterate 100 times with a statement such as this:

```
For InputVal = 1 To 100     ' Plan to process 100 records
  ' File-reading code
  If (value = -99) Then      ' -99 indicates no more data
    Exit For
  End If
  '
  ' The rest of the loop would execute here
  ' and evaluates the file data just read
Next InputVal
```

Tip

Using Exit Do and Exit For means that you don't have to code GOTO statements when you have to leave a loop early. Many COBOL programmers use the EXIT statement as a *no-operation* statement where loops branch when they terminate early. Visual Basic's Exit statements are more functional than COBOL's EXIT statement because Visual Basic's Exit statements truly control looping execution and retain your non-GOTO structured programming approach.

Conclusion

The looping statements let you repeat sections of code. Often, you can code the looped code directly inside the Do or For statement's body, or you can call a procedure that executes just as you do with COBOL's PERFORM...UNTIL and PERFORM...VARYING statements.

There are several constructions of the Do loop. (Loops are often called *language constructs*.) The four Do loops center around the Until and While keywords. The Do...Until statement works almost exactly as COBOL's PERFORM...UNTIL statement. The body of the loop repeats until a certain condition is met. The Do...Until loop repeats as long as its condition is false, whereas, the Do...While repeats as long as its condition is true.

Not only must you be concerned with which true or false check (using While or Until) you use, but you also must be careful where you test for the condition. Both the Do...Until and Do...While loops provide a double syntax so you can check for the terminating loop condition at the top or bottom of the loop.

COBOL's PERFORM...VARYING statement has a Visual Basic cousin: the For loop. For is one of Visual Basic's most powerful statements because For initializes, tests, and increments its control variable for you. The For loop is a great loop to use when you want to execute a procedure a specific number of times (mirroring COBOL's PERFORM...TIMES looping statement as well).

Once you set up loops, there will be rare instances when data dictates that the loop terminates earlier than its Do condition or For control variables would otherwise allow. The Exit Do and Exit For statements are listed inside the body of an If statement so they remain conditional loop exits. These statements let you terminate loops before the loop's regular termination.

Now that you can write loops, you're ready to process larger amounts of data than was possible before you mastered looping. The next chapter, "Table-Handling and Control Arrays," introduces table handling by showing you how Visual Basic sets up tables of data and controls. Using loops, you then can step through the tables and process multiple values.

III

Primary Differences

Chapter 16

Table-Handling and Control Arrays

This chapter explains how Visual Basic supports the use of tables through data structures named *arrays*. An array is nothing more than a Visual Basic table. You are familiar with tables from your COBOL programming. COBOL's OCCURS clause sets up single-level and double-level COBOL tables.

Working with table data in Visual Basic is actually easier than working with COBOL tables. Nevertheless, table-processing in the two languages is extremely similar and you'll have no trouble switching from thinking in COBOL tables to thinking in Visual Basic tables. Visual Basic does not support the SEARCH or SET commands, but the For loop makes these statements unnecessary, anyway.

Here are some of the topics that will be discussed in this chapter:

- Declaring arrays and using subscripts

- Learning about the different kinds of arrays

- Initializing arrays

- Stepping through the array values

- Handling advanced arrays with multiple levels

- Controlling the form with control arrays

- Analyzing multiple-selection list boxes

Visual Basic even supports double-level, triple-level, and higher tables, whereas COBOL supports only up to three levels of table-handling. You'll rarely use more than two levels, however.

One of the most important array-related features of Visual Basic is a *control array* that you can set up. When you write applications with forms that contain several occurrences of the same control, you'll find that accessing those controls is easier through control arrays.

Caution

There is no direct INDEXED BY keyword in Visual Basic, so you cannot request that table data be sorted automatically by Visual Basic as you can in COBOL. Nevertheless, when you learn about database access in Part V, "Your Next Step with VB," you'll see that the database commands enable you to access file data in a sorted order.

Declaring Visual Basic Arrays

You use Dim, Static, and Global to declare array variables.

Three commands—Dim, Static, and Global—declare array variables. The command that you use depends on the kind of arrays you want to declare. Follow these rules to determine which statement to use:

- If you want to declare local (procedure-level) arrays, use Static.

- If you want to declare arrays that have module scope (all procedures in the form's file can access the arrays), use Dim.

- If you want to declare global arrays that are usable throughout every module in the entire application, use Global. Typically, you'll want to use the safer local and procedure arrays, however, because global arrays make for difficult maintenance.

As with OCCURS clauses, the Static, Dim, and Global statements must inform Visual Basic how many *elements* (table entries) the array will contain.

Here is the format of Dim when you use Dim to declare array variables:

```
Dim VarName(subMax) As VarType
```

The syntax for Static is the same, except you substitute Static for Dim:

```
Static VarName(subMax) As VarType
```

The syntax for Global is also the same, but you substitute Global for Dim:

```
Global VarName(subMax) As VarType
```

If you use Dim or Global inside a procedure to declare arrays, Visual Basic will issue an error message and remind you to use Static or ReDim.

Note

There is yet a fourth statement, ReDim, that you can use for special arrays. A section later in this chapter, "Dynamic Arrays," explains ReDim.

To declare a procedure's ten-element integer array named Weights, do this:

```
Static Weights(10) As Integer
```

Figure 16.1 shows how the Weights array looks in memory after Visual Basic declares the ten elements. Notice the subscripts, 1 through 10. As with COBOL, you'll access the individual table elements using the subscript.

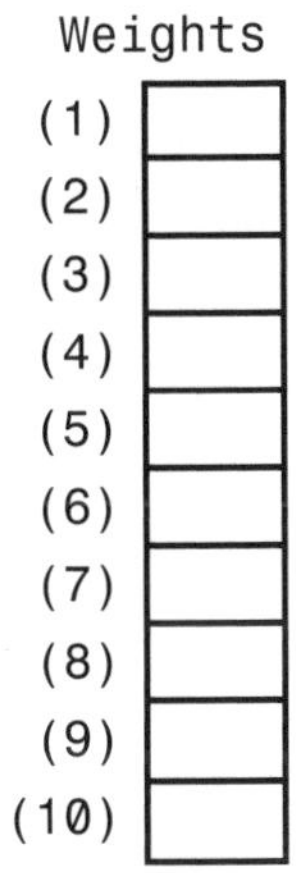

Weights

(1)
(2)
(3)
(4)
(5)
(6)
(7)
(8)
(9)
(10)

Fig. 16.1
Declaring a ten-element array.

Note

Technically, Visual Basic begins all arrays with a starting subscript of zero unless you code a special Option Base 1 statement in the (general) procedure. Most Visual Basic programmers ignore the zero subscript and so will this book. All array subscripts will be assumed to start at one. By ignoring the zero subscript, your code will match that of COBOL's subscripts, which makes the transition from COBOL even easier.

The Weights array has ten elements with subscripts that range from 1 to 10. Refer to each element using the array name followed by the subscript, just as in COBOL. The first array element is Weights(1) and the last is Weights(10). As in COBOL, the subscript designates which array element you want to work with.

III

Primary Differences

Here is a COBOL equivalent using OCCURS:

```
01  WORK-AREA.
    02  WEIGHTS OCCURS 10 TIMES, PICTURE 99999.
```

To declare a 50-element, module-level string array that holds state names, do this:

```
Dim States(50) As String * 2   ' Use only in (general)
```

Here is a COBOL equivalent using OCCURS:

```
01  WORK-AREA.
    02  STATES OCCURS 50 TIMES, PICTURE XX.
```

Of course, you can declare arrays of record data, as well. Way back in Chapter 10, "Visual Basic's Version of the *DATA DIVISION*," you learned how to declare Visual Basic record data using the Type keyword. Type first defines the record layout (not unlike the way that COBOL's DATA DIVISION defines the look of your COBOL data) and a subsequent Dim statement, then declares multiple occurrences of the record variable in an array. Given the following record definition:

```
Type CustomerRecType
   LastName As String * 15
   FirstName As String * 15
   Address1 As String * 25
   Address2 As String * 25
   CityName As String * 10
   StateName As String * 2
   Zipcode As String * 9
   CustBalance As Single
   CustRepeat As Integer
End Type
```

you can declare 200 variables of this user-defined data type (record) like this:

```
Static Customer(200) As CustomerRecType
```

Here is an equivalent data declaration in COBOL:

```
01 CUSTOMERRECTYPE.
   02 CUSTOMER OCCURS 200 TIMES.
      03 LASTNAME      PIC X(15).
      03 FIRSTNAME     PIC X(15).
      03 ADDRESS1      PIC X(25).
      03 ADDRESS2      PIC X(25).
      03 CITYNAME      PIC X(10).
      03 STATENAME     PIC X(2).
      03 ZIPCODE       PIC X(9).
      03 CUSTBALANCE   PIC S99999V99.
      03 CUSTREPEAT    PIC 99.
```

Later in this chapter, you'll see how to declare and work with arrays of multiple levels in "Multiple-Level Arrays." For now, let's keep it simple and stick with single-level or single dimension arrays.

Initializing Arrays

Now that you can declare arrays, you've got to put something in the arrays before the program can work with the table data. There are several ways to initialize arrays. Most of the time, array data will come from a file or from the user's data entry. You haven't yet learned how Visual Basic interacts with disk files, so we'll stick to assignment statements and some user input so that you can have some array data to work with.

Although such a lengthy assignment sequence doesn't necessarily provide a stellar programming example, here is one way to initialize the Weights array you saw initialized in the previous section:

```
Weights(1)  = 132
Weights(2)  = 210
Weights(3)  = 165
Weights(4)  = 112
Weights(5)  = 188
Weights(6)  = 192
Weights(7)  = 103
Weights(8)  = 139
Weights(9)  = 166
Weights(10) = 201
```

Suppose that you need to compute an average weight. The following code does that:

```
Total = 0      ' Total is defined as an integer
Avg = 0        ' Avg is defined as a single
For Ctr = 1 To 10
  Total = Total + Weights(Ctr)
Next Ctr
' Now that the total is computed, calculate the average
Avg = Total / 10
```

The For loop easily steps through the array and adds each value to the weight Total.

Arrays are no different than any other kind of variable except that you refer to array variables by their subscript and not just by an individual variable name. You can assign array values to control values and control values to array values. The following code assigns the first three weights to the label control Caption properties:

```
lblFirst.Caption = Weights(1)
lblSecond.Caption = Weights(2)
lblThird.Caption = Weights(3)
```

> **Caution**
>
> Don't attempt to reference an out-of-bounds subscript. If you refer to `Weights(-2)`
> or `Weights(46)`, Visual Basic will display an out-of-bounds subscript error unless you
> declare the arrays using the optional To keyword.

You can adjust the beginning and ending array subscripts.

For most programming, stick to the default array subscripts, from 1 to the ending subscript range number, for two reasons:

- COBOL supports only subscripts that begin with 1, so you'll be most comfortable sticking to traditional subscript ranges.

- Most Visual Basic programmers use the default subscripts, so you should too.

If your data happens to fit a different range of subscripts, you can request that Visual Basic declare the arrays with a starting subscript that is different than 1. Using the To option, your subscripts can range from -32768 to 32767.

Suppose that your company's 20 sales regions are numbered 101 through 120. The following array definition defines 20 sales region names with a starting subscript of 101 and an ending subscript of 120:

```
Dim Regions(101 To 120) As String
```

You can assign the first region name like this:

```
Regions(101) = "Washington/Maine"    ' 1st region name
```

You refer to the final region with the 120 subscript, as in

```
Regions(120) = "California/Nevada"    ' Last region name
```

If you ever referred to a region outside the 101 through 120 subscript range, such as `Regions(1)`, Visual Basic will issue an error message telling you that the subscript is out of bounds.

To Blank or Not To Blank?

Visual Basic never requires a space between the array name and the opening paren-thesis of the subscript. The space is optional, so you *can* use it like this:

```
Static Weights (10) As Integer
```

The problem with carrying this COBOL requirement into Visual Basic is that Visual Basic programmers rarely use the space. Therefore, if you use the space and others maintain your program, there is the real possibility of the maintenance programmer missing the fact that you're referring to an array element and not an individual variable.

Stay with the de facto standard and eliminate the space before the subscript to help your code maintain the Visual Basic-standard appearance, like this:

```
Static Weights(10) As Integer   ' No space before (10)
```

Multiple-Level Arrays

Due to the name of the Dim statement that often declares them, Visual Basic's multiple-level arrays are called *multidimensional arrays*. Unlike COBOL, which allows only double and triple levels, Visual Basic supports arrays of any di-mension. Rarely, however, will you be declaring arrays with more than two or three dimensions.

> Multiple-level arrays are called *multidimensional arrays.*

Array processing is yet another example of how the Visual Basic language works much like COBOL. Suppose you want to define a two-dimensional price array (or *double-level table,* as described by COBOL programmers) that has 12 rows for each of your product lines and four columns for the divisions within your company. The following declaration declares such a Prices array:

```
Dim Prices(12, 4) As Currency    ' 2-dimensional
```

You can also declare a local array (usable only within the procedure in which you define it) with Static. The following statement declares a four-dimensional array:

```
Static Scores(3, 22, 5, 2) As Integer    ' 4-dimensional
```

The far right (last) subscript always refers to the number of columns in the array, and the next-to-last subscript refers to the row count (as in COBOL). If there are additional dimensions, they represent additional occurrences of the columns and rows. More than two or three dimensions often makes for maintenance nightmares unless you're writing scientific and mathematical programs whose data inherently meets the multiple-dimension format.

Figure 16.2 illustrates what the two-dimensional Prices array declared earlier looks like. Inside each of the figure's elements is the dual subscript needed to access that array value. In other words, to store 16.74 in the third product line's second price, do this:

```
Prices(3, 2) = 16.74  ' Initialize 3rd row, 2nd column
```

Fig. 16.2

Declaring a two-dimensional array.

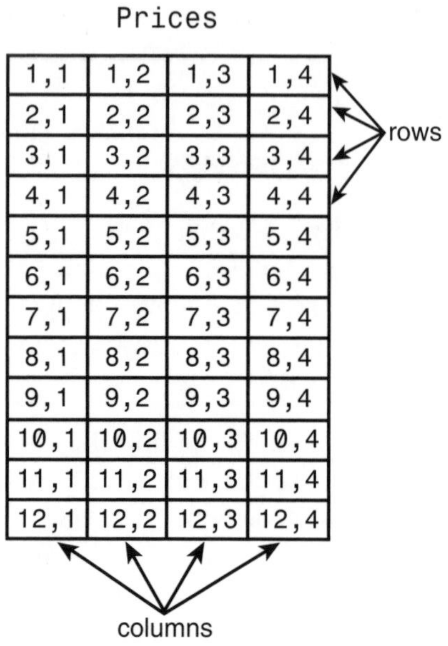

Prices

Here is how you would declare the two-dimensional array in COBOL:

```
01   PRICE-TABLE.
        02   LINE OCCURS 12 TIMES.
             03   DIVISION OCCURS 4 TIMES.
                  04 PRICE      PIC 99999V99.
```

To assign a price to the third row and second column in COBOL, you would do this:

```
MOVE 16.74 TO PRICE (3, 2).
```

Note

As with single-level arrays, don't put spaces before Visual Basic's two-dimensional subscript parentheses when you refer to the table elements.

The Visual Basic code in Listing 16.1 finds and reports the highest price in the entire table.

Listing 16.1   Finding the Highest Price in the Company

```
Static Prices(12, 4) As Currency
Dim HighPrice As Currency
Dim Row As Integer, Col As Integer

' Initialize highest price with an ultra-low
' initial value to trigger the first assignment
HighPrice = -99999.99

' Compare each table value against the current high
For Row = 1 To 12
  For Col = 1 To 4
    If (Prices(Row, Col) > HighPrice) Then
      HighPrice = Prices(Row, Col)
    End If
  Next Col
Next Row

' Found the highest price, send it to the label
lblHighPrice.Caption = Format$(HighPrice, "Currency")
```

Listing 16.2 refines the highest price search somewhat by displaying the highest price in *each* of the four divisions.

III

Listing 16.2   Finding the Highest Price in Each Division

```
Static Prices(12, 4) As Currency
' The following variables hold the highest
' price of each division
Dim High1, High2, High3, High4 As Currency
Dim Row As Integer, Col As Integer

' Initialize each division's highest price with an
' ultra-low initial value to trigger the first assignment
High1 = -99999.99
High2 = -99999.99
High3 = -99999.99
High4 = -99999.99
```

Primary Differences

(continues)

Listing 16.2   Continued

```
' Compare each table value against the current
' column's (division's) high price
For Row = 1 To 12
  If (Prices(Row, 1) > High1) Then
    High1 = Prices(Row, 1)
  End If
  If (Prices(Row, 2) > High2) Then
    High2 = Prices(Row, 2)
  End If
  If (Prices(Row, 3) > High3) Then
    High3 = Prices(Row, 3)
  End If
  If (Prices(Row, 4) > High4) Then
    High4 = Prices(Row, 4)
  End If
Next Row

' Send the four high prices to labels
lblHigh1.Caption = Format$(High1, "Currency")
lblHigh2.Caption = Format$(High2, "Currency")
lblHigh3.Caption = Format$(High3, "Currency")
lblHigh4.Caption = Format$(High4, "Currency")
```

If you have a true understanding of arrays, as you do already from your COBOL background, there is no reason why the four division-high variables should not be stored in a four-element array as well. If you were to add another division, you would need only to change the subscripts and not mess with adding additional variables. The code in Listing 16.3 uses an array to hold the division-high prices and also defines two constants to hold the number of product lines and divisions. If you add additional product lines and divisions, you'll need only to change the constant definitions.

Listing 16.3   A Better Division-High Price Locator

```
Const ProdLines = 12
Const Divs = 4
Static Prices(ProdLines, Divs) As Currency
Static High(Divs) As Currency
Dim Row As Integer, Col As Integer

' Initialize highest price with an ultra-low
' initial value to trigger the first assignment
For Col = 1 To 4
  High(Col) = -99999.99
Next Col
```

```
' Compare each table value against the current high
For Row = 1 To ProdLines
  For Col = 1 To Divs
    If (Prices(Row, Col) > High(Col)) Then
      High(Col) = Prices(Row, Col)
    End If
  Next Col
Next Row

' Once you master control arrays, you won't have
' to define four separately named labels
lblHigh1.Caption = Format$(High(1), "Currency")
lblHigh2.Caption = Format$(High(2), "Currency")
lblHigh3.Caption = Format$(High(3), "Currency")
lblHigh4.Caption = Format$(High(4), "Currency")
```

Note

The code in each of these listings assumes that you've already initialized the arrays with price values using assignment statements or I/O of some kind.

As you can see, other than some syntax differences, there is nothing really new when working with multidimensional subscript values in Visual Basic than you're already used to in COBOL.

Dynamic Arrays

The arrays you've declared so far have been *static* arrays. Even when you use Dim to declare arrays at the module level, the arrays are static. Static arrays are fixed in size. Once you define the array, you cannot change the array size later. COBOL supports only static arrays.

Dynamic arrays can change size.

Most of the time, static arrays fulfill all your array needs. Every once in a while, however, you may need to read a complete disk file of array data and you won't know in advance how many elements the disk file holds. You cannot hold such data in a static array because you cannot change the size of static arrays. If, however, you declare *dynamic arrays,* you can change the size of the arrays at runtime.

Initially, you declare a dynamic array just as you do static arrays. The difference, however, is that you don't specify initial subscripts. The following statement declares a dynamic array (an array whose size is initially undeclared) at the module level:

III

Primary Differences

```
        Dim DynArr() As Integer   ' Located in (general)
```

ReDim resizes arrays. Each procedure that uses this array can then size the array to whatever size is needed for the procedure's data. Once execution begins inside the procedure, the following statement resizes DynArr() to 30 elements:

```
        ReDim DynArr(30)    ' Resize to 30 integers
```

Use ReDim to change the number of elements you've dimensioned for a dynamic array. The following is the format of ReDim:

```
        ReDim VarName(subNewMax)
```

You can redimension an array within the same procedure. For example, after redimensioning DynArr to 30 elements and then using that array for various operations, the same procedure can redimension the array to 450 elements with another ReDim statement, like this:

```
        ReDim DynArr(450)    ' Resize to 450 integers
```

Any procedure in the module can access the array, as long as the procedure properly sizes the array first. The following statement declares a global dynamic array with three dimensions:

```
        Global DynVals( ) As Single
```

This subsequent ReDim statement dimensions the array size:

```
        ReDim DynVals(10, 20, 5)
```

Caution

You can change the number of dimensioned elements but *not* the number of dimensions using ReDim. This produces an error because you're attempting to change the number of dimensions, as in the following:

```
        ReDim DynVals(10, 20, 50, 6, 25, 15)    ' Invalid!
```

Array Declarations

Despite the redimensioning power offered by Visual Basic, you'll almost always work with static arrays. Rarely will you need to read an entire disk file into arrays. Even if you do, you'll be able to use functions to determine the file size ahead of time.

Static arrays are more efficient than dynamic arrays. Static array processing time is quicker and Visual Basic has to manage less overhead.

There is a special ReDim option named Preserve that preserves the data in an array before you redimension the array. In other words, you might want to increase the size of an array but not change the values that you've already stored locally in the array. The following statement tells Visual Basic to resize an array named `Values()`, preserving what values are already in the array:

```
ReDim Preserve Values(500)    ' Add size, save values
```

The `Preserve` option lets you redefine only the last subscript, so if you're redefining more than one dimension of a multiple-dimensioned array, you cannot preserve the values that originally resided in the array.

Introducing Control Arrays

Just as with array variables, you can declare an array of controls called a *control array*. A control array is nothing more than a table of controls. Each control has the same name and type. For example, your application may have five command buttons. The command buttons may be located in a control array named `cmdButtons`.

Control arrays **hold controls, not data.**

You use a subscript number to reference the individual controls in the array just as you use subscripts to reference elements in a data array. The only difference between control array subscripts and data array subscripts is that the first value in a control array has the subscript of 0 unless you change the starting subscript to a different value. Although each control in the array can be the same type of control, each control can contain different property values.

Control arrays let you write one event-handler for multiple controls. There can be as many as 254 controls in a control array. If several controls, such as numbers on a screen keypad, work in a similar manner and require similar event-handling code, you don't need a separate event procedure for each control. Instead, you can step through the control array using the same event procedure, thereby handling all of the controls in one procedure.

The place that each control falls within an array is determined by the control's `Index` property. So far, this book has not discussed the `Index` property because its use is unnecessary until you introduce control arrays into your applications. If the `Index` property of a control is 3, that control is the fourth element in the control array. Remember that the first control will have an `Index` property of 0, so the fourth control will have an `Index` property of 3.

A control's `Index` property determines its array location.

> **Tip**
>
> There is no reason to keep the zero-based subscript if you don't want to. Simply change the Index property of the first control to begin at 1.

Creating Controls

There are three ways to add a control array to your form. They are the following:

- Use the same name for more than one control. The names should apply only to controls of the same type. In other words, two or more command buttons can share the same name and be part of the same control array, but a command button cannot be part of an option button's control array.

- Use Visual Basic's copy and paste feature to make copies of existing controls.

- Usually a control's Index property is null unless you've specifically created a control array using one of the previous two methods. However, if you explicitly change the Index property of an existing control to a non-null value (the value must be a number from 1 to 254), that control becomes part of a control array and you then can add more controls to the array.

The third method makes sense for only the first control in a series that you place. However, it's usually easier to ignore the Index property when you begin and let Visual Basic figure out that you're creating a control array, as demonstrated in the next section.

Adding Control Arrays

Visual Basic recognizes that you're creating a control array.

Suppose you wanted to add a check box control array to a form. After placing the first check box that you named chkAns, you double-click the Check Box tool and move the new check box control under the first one to begin a column of check boxes. Visual Basic automatically named the second check box control Check1. As soon as you press F4 (to display the Properties window) and change the name of the second check box to chkAns, Visual Basic notices that the name matches the other check box control and displays the message box shown in Figure 16.3.

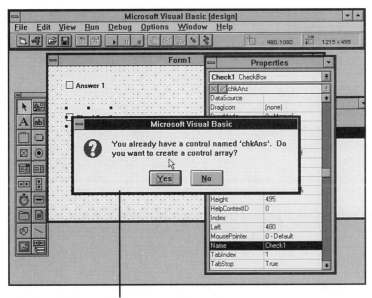

Fig. 16.3
Adding a second
control to the
control array.

Visual Basic asks if you really want to use the same name

To add the second check box to your application, click Yes to Visual Basic's
message box. After changing the Caption of the second check box, you can
add another check box by copying and pasting another check box instead of
going to the toolbox.

Move the mouse pointer to the form at a location just above and to the left
of the second check box's top left corner. Click the mouse button and drag
down to the lower-right corner to enclose the check box. Release the mouse
button. The resizing handles appear when you've enclosed the check box
within the mouse outline you created by dragging.

Press Ctrl+C. Ctrl+C is the access key for Edit, Copy and copies any selected
text or control (or multiple controls if you first select more than one) to the
Windows Clipboard. Once you've copied the control, press Ctrl+V (the access
key for Edit, Paste) to paste the contents of the Clipboard to the screen. You'll
see the new check box control in the upper-left part of the Form window, as
shown in Figure 16.4. You can now move the control down to its position
below the second check box and change its Caption property.

III

Primary Differences

Fig. 16.4
Adding a third
control to the
control array.

The pasted control
appears here

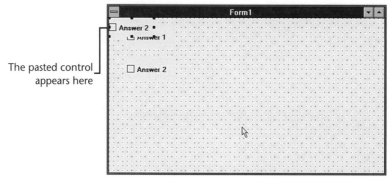

> **Tip**
>
> When you use the copy and paste feature, Visual Basic takes care of naming the Name property and adds the check box to the control array for you. Therefore, the copy and paste method for adding controls to a control array is generally the preferred method once you've added the first control using the toolbox.

If you were to display each check box's Properties window, you would see that Visual Basic automatically initialized the check box controls with Index properties of 0, 1, and 2, which are the subscripts for the individual controls. Therefore, your code can reference the first check box using `lblAns(0)`, the second with `lblAns(1)`, and the third with `lblAns(2)`.

The next section discusses a short application on this book's disk that uses a command button control array to print array price values based on earlier listings in this chapter.

Using a Control Array

Start Visual Basic and load the HIGHPRIC.MAK project. When you run the program, you see an opening form like the one shown in Figure 16.5.

Click any of the option buttons on the left to select a division, then click the See High Sales command button. That division's high sales price, from a list of 12 product lines, displays next to the High Sales: label. Select another division option button and click the command button again to see that division's high price.

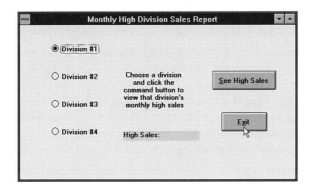

Fig. 16.5
Using a control
array to select a
division.

The bulk of the high price selection code comes from a modified version of Listing 16.2. Stop the program and display the Code window (press F7) to view some of the highlights described here:

■ The four division option buttons comprise a control array, the option button array, all named optDivision. The Index property of the control array is set from 1 to 4 for the four option controls.

■ The (general) procedure declares two constants that describe the number of products in the line (12) and the number of divisions (4). Also, both the Form_Load() and the cmdSeeHigh_Click() procedures need access to the same array, so you need a module-level array. Therefore, the (general) procedure uses Dim to declare the Prices() array.

■ The Form_Load() procedure initializes each of the 48 array elements with price data using a long sequence of assignment statements. There are more elegant ways for initializing tables as you know. Most often, such table data comes from a disk file.

■ The heart of the code lies in the cmdSeeHigh_Click() procedure shown in Listing 16.4. The first loop in the program scans the optDivision control array looking for the selected division number. The Index matches the number of each division (the column in the Prices() array). If the option buttons were all named with different names and if they were not part of a control array, you would have to check each option button using its unique name instead of looping through the option button array in a single loop.

> **Caution**
>
> Please don't be misled by this short example. It's true that, with only four divisions, the control array does not add a lot of efficiency to the code. However, what if there were a selection of *30* divisions? You would barely have to change this code. However, if the division option buttons all had unique names and were not part of an array, the code would become bloated because each option button on the form would have to be checked. You would have to check each button using a series of If-End If statements or a lengthy Select Case statement.

Listing 16.4 Using the Control Array To Search a Particular Division

```
Sub cmdSeeHigh_Click ()

    Dim Row As Integer, Col As Integer
    Dim Highest As Single
    Dim SelectCol As Integer

    ' Find the selected division number
    For Col = 1 To Divs
       If (optDivision(Col).Value = True) Then
          SelectCol = Col
          Exit For
       End If
    Next Col

    ' Initialize highest price with an ultra-low
    ' initial value to trigger the first assignment
    Highest = -99999.99

    ' Compare each table value against the current high
    For Row = 1 To ProdLines
       If (Prices(Row, SelectCol) > Highest) Then
          Highest = Prices(Row, SelectCol)
       End If
    Next Row

    lblHighHold.Caption = Format$(Highest, "Currency")

End Sub
```

Control arrays provide one final and huge advantage when you write event procedures for controls within the array. Suppose you wanted to write a Click() event procedure for the four option buttons in the HIGHPRIC.MAK application. If the option buttons are not part of a control array, you have to write *four separate* Click() event procedures. Because the option buttons are

part of a single control array, however, you have to write *only one* event procedure, and that one event procedure handles all of the option buttons!

Think of the advantage here, especially if you were to add more controls to
the array. No matter how many controls are in a control array, if the controls
need event procedures, you write only one set of event procedures for all
the controls. If you like, run the project named HIGHPRI2.MAK and click
the option buttons. You'll see something happen that differs from the
HIGHPRIC.MAK program you just finished running. When you click an
option button, the background changes to a different color.

If you analyze the code, you see that there is only one optDivision_Click()
procedure, which is shown in Listing 16.5. You have yet to master *argument*
passing, however, so the text inside the event's parentheses may throw you
off a bit. You'll learn all about arguments in Chapter 21, "Modular Visual
Basic Programming," and we'll come back to this application at that time.
For now, it's more important that you see that one event procedure handles
an entire array of controls. Without the array, you will need a different event
for each control.

Listing 16.5   Coloring Four Controls Using a Single Event Procedure

```
Sub optDivision_Click (Index As Integer)
' White the backgrounds of the controls
' Then color the single control that's selected
  Dim Ctr As Integer
  For Ctr = 1 To 4
    ' Make the background of each white to
    ' clear any color that's already set
    optDivision(Ctr).BackColor = QBColor(15)
  Next Ctr
  ' Set the background color using the Index
  ' property as a basis for the new color
  optDivision(Index).BackColor = QBColor(Index + 7)
End Sub
```

Multiple-Selection List Boxes

In Chapter 11, "Controls also Contain Data," you learned about list box and
combo box controls. At that time, you learned that you can use the AddItem
method to initialize list boxes. That chapter's coverage focused on list boxes
with single selection capabilities. In other words, the MultiSelect property
was set to 0. If, however, the MultiSelect property contains 1 or 2, the user

can select more than one item in the list, and you will have to process the list box somewhat as if it is an array. Due to its similarity to array processing, this is a better place for the complete discussion of multiple-selection list boxes.

Table 16.1 lists new methods that are extremely helpful when working with list boxes. Remember, as with the AddItem method, you trigger the execution of methods with the dot operator. The following code adds six names to a list box named lstNames:

```
lstNames.AddItem ("Frank")
lstNames.AddItem ("Luke")
lstNames.AddItem ("Kerry")
lstNames.AddItem ("Mary")
lstNames.AddItem ("Paula")
lstNames.AddItem ("Tonya")
```

Table 16.1 Methods for *MultiSelect* List Boxes

Method Name	Description
Clear	Clears all items from the list box or combo box.
List	Indicates a string array that holds each item within the list box.
ListCount	Indicates the total number of items in a list box.
RemoveItem	Removes a single item from a list box.
Selected	Determines whether the user has selected a particular item in the list box.

As you add items to a list box (or combo box) control, Visual Basic increases an index count called ListCount. Therefore, the value of lstNames.ListCount is 6 after the previous six AddItem methods finish. Those six list box items have an index from 0 to 5.

The following code calls a procedure named SelectItemProc() every time a name is found selected in the list. Therefore, if the user has selected four items (remember that if the MultiSelect property is not set to True, the user can select only one item), this routine calls the SelectItemProc() procedure four times. If no items are selected, the procedure is never called.

```
For Ctr = 0 To (lstNames.ListCount - 1)
    If lstNames.Selected(Ctr) = True Then
      Call SelectItemProc()
    End If
Next CtrItem
```

If you want to remove one of the items, use the `RemoveItem` method. The following statements remove the second and fifth items from the list box:

```
lstNames.RemoveItem (2)
lstNames.RemoveItem (4)    ' Careful!
```

Think about what happens when the first `RemoveItem` method executes. The `ListCount` automatically drops by 1 and all the index values reorder; the previous third item is now the second. Therefore, the second statement removes the fifth item (index number 4) from the current list, which is different from the list before the first `RemoveItem` executed. Every time you add or remove items from a list box, the index values reorder to range from 0 to one less than the total number of items in the list. What starts out as index number 4 will not necessarily *still* be number 4 after subsequent `AddItem` and `RemoveItem` methods.

> **Tip**
>
> To eliminate the renumbering problem that occurs as you remove list box items, remove the items from their highest item in the list to the lowest item.

The `Clear` method erases the entire list box. The following statement completely erases the contents of the list box:

```
lstNames.Clear    ' Removes everything
```

If you want a value from the list, use the `List` method. The following stores the third item, selected or not, from the list box and stores that item as a string in the variable named `AName`:

```
AName = lstNames.List(3)
```

Although list box and combo box controls don't behave exactly like arrays, they share many similarities.

Conclusion

You've now learned just about everything there is to know about Visual Basic's data support. You now can create arrays of any dimension and of any data type. Keep in mind that the location (procedure, module, or global) and declaration statement (`Dim`, `Static`, and `Global`) all affect how subsequent code can access the array. If you want to declare a local array to be used in a single procedure, use `Static`. Many times, unlike regular non-array variables, you'll declare module-level arrays using `Dim` in the (general) procedure and use those arrays in certain routines. Once you master Chapter 21, "Modular Visual Basic Programming," you'll be able to declare procedure arrays and pass them back and forth among the procedures that need access to them.

Visual Basic's arrays work very much like COBOL tables. Unlike in COBOL, however, you can declare arrays of several dimensions, and you may even redimension arrays for more or less storage room when needed.

The list box and combo box controls support the user's selection of more than one item. Therefore, there has to be a way for you to access any and all of the list box items, and to test to see whether the user has selected any of the items. Visual Basic supports several array-like command methods that count, list, add, and remove items inside a list box control.

The next chapter will be a nice change of pace for you! Chapter 17, "Screen I/O: Message and Input Boxes," explains how to send messages to the user and to receive responses from the user. Although you've been working with advanced controls that interact with the user, there are some kinds of messages that are simply better sent through a pop-up message box, as you'll see.

Chapter 17

Screen I/O: Message and Input Boxes

This chapter explains how to display *message boxes* and ask for the user's response with *input boxes*. Both message boxes and input boxes are pop-up windows that carry information to and from the user.

There are some messages that you need to issue to your users that you cannot adequately display using the controls from the toolbox. For example, you may need to issue an error message when the user enters unexpected data. If you use a form control for error messages, that control takes up room on the form and is not utilized in the majority of cases.

Also, there are times when you need to prompt the user for a keystroke or for a quick answer. Again, if you use a control such as a text box control to get such input, the control takes up room and is inappropriate the majority of the time.

Here are some of the topics that will be discussed in this chapter:

- Using the MsgBox statement to display messages

- Using the MsgBox() function to display messages and check the user's response

- Using the InputBox() function to get the user's answers

- Issuing the Print command when you need to display lines of text on the Form window

As a COBOL programmer, you often used ACCEPT and DISPLAY to accomplish the same goals as the statements and functions described in this chapter.

You'll forget about COBOL's ACCEPT and DISPLAY.

The best news for you as a Visual Basic programmer is that Visual Basic's MsgBox statement and InputBox() functions are *extremely* easy to use and let you interact professionally with your users.

Introducing the *MsgBox* Statement

MsgBox **displays your data in a dialog box.**

The MsgBox statement is simple. MsgBox displays data in a pop-up dialog box and optionally displays an appropriate icon and response buttons for the user. MsgBox is also capable of writing string data to the screen. The string contains the message you want to send. Figure 17.1 shows a sample dialog box generated with MsgBox. From the figure, you see that you control both the message and the title of the dialog box. You also determine the icon that is displayed and how many command buttons appear in the box.

Fig. 17.1
A dialog box
displayed with
MsgBox.

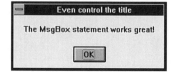

> ### Note
>
> The user may move or close the message box, but the user cannot resize the box.

Sometimes message boxes are called *dialog boxes*, although programmers often like to reserve the term *dialog box* for message boxes that include additional controls such as list boxes. You may want to display a message with MsgBox for several reasons. Message boxes are often used to display error messages.

The format of MsgBox is

```
MsgBox MessageString [, type] [, TitleString]
```

The *MessageString* is a string expression (either a literal, string variable, or text control value that evaluates to a string) that you want to display in the message box. If the string is long, the message box expands to hold the whole string, properly breaking each line between words.

Caution

The message string can be no longer than 1,024 characters. If the string is longer, the additional characters do not appear.

The last two arguments to the MsgBox statement are optional. The easiest kind of message box to display is one with only a message and an OK button as produced by this statement:

```
MsgBox "I am easy to display!"
```

Figure 17.2 shows what you see when you issue this MsgBox statement.

Fig. 17.2
Displaying the message.

Note

MsgBox automatically displays the OK command button so that the message does not flash on and then off the screen so quickly that the user doesn't have a chance to read the message.

Isn't that better than what you get in COBOL when you do something like this:

```
DISPLAY 'I am easy to display!'
```

The message box adds a professional look to user messages.

Controlling More of the Message

The *type* argument in the MsgBox format is a numeric value or expression that controls the number of buttons and the icon that appears in the message box. The *TitleString* is the string that appears at the top of the box in the title bar. If you don't specify a title string, Visual Basic displays the project name for the message box's title.

You control the buttons in the box.

III

Primary Differences

The value that you use for *type* consists of several indicators. Tables 17.1, 17.2, and 17.3 contain values that make up the *type* argument within MsgBox.

Table 17.1	Controlling the Buttons
Value	**Description**
0	Displays the OK button in the box
1	Displays the OK and Cancel buttons in the box
2	Displays the Abort, Retry, and Ignore buttons in the box
3	Displays the Yes, No, and Cancel buttons in the box
4	Displays the Yes and No buttons in the box
5	Displays the Retry and Cancel buttons in the box

If you want an icon to appear inside the message box, *add* one of the values from Table 17.2 to the *type* value from Table 17.1. In other words, if you want the OK and Cancel buttons to display (a *type* value of 1) and you want the Warning Query icon to display (a *type* value of 32), you specify 33 as the *type* (both table values added together).

Table 17.2	Controlling the Icons
Value	**Description**
0	Displays no icon in the box
16	Displays the Critical Message icon in the box
32	Displays the Warning Query icon in the box
48	Displays the Warning Message icon in the box
64	Displays the Information Message icon in the box

Figure 17.3 shows the icons that match the values from Table 17.2.

A message box always contains a default button. If the user presses Enter without clicking another button, the button defined as the default is selected. Therefore if you want the Cancel button to be the default button, add an additional 512 (from Table 17.3) to the 33 for a total of 545.

 The Critical Message Icon

Fig. 17.3
The MsgBox
icons and their
descriptions.

 The Warning Query Icon

 The Warning Message Icon

 The Information Message Icon

Table 17.3	Controlling the Default Button
Value	**Description**
0	The button on the left is the default
256	The button in the middle is the default
512	The button on the right is the default

Table 17.1 describes the layout of the buttons on the message box. The previous message box example did not specify a *type* value, so Visual Basic used 0 by default. The dialog box in Figure 17.2 contains only an OK button because it has 0 for the *type*. If you want a style of buttons different from the single OK button, use a different value from Table 17.1.

Caution

The MsgBox() function explained in "The *MsgBox()* Function" section in this chapter can use multiple-button boxes better than the MsgBox statement because the MsgBox() function sends a return value back to the calling code that indicates which button the user chose to end the message box.

Suppose that you want to display the message box shown in Figure 17.4. Notice that the center button is the default.

Fig. 17.4

A message box with a default center button.

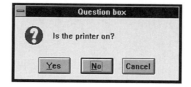

The following MsgBox statement creates the message box shown in Figure 17.4:

```
MsgBox "Is the printer on?", 291, "Question box"
```

Adding the *type* values together can be cumbersome but thanks to Visual Basic you don't have to add. The following MsgBox statement works just like the preceding example because the sum of the *type* numbers adds to 291:

```
MsgBox "Is the printer on?", 3 + 32 + 256, "Question box"
```

Have you any idea what's happening in the following statement?

```
MsgBox "Go for it", MB_ICONEXCLAMATION
```

If you've followed closely, you'll probably and correctly suspect that MB_ICONEXCLAMATION is a named constant defined as the value 48 in CONSTANT.TXT, so using the constant is the same as using 48 and an exclamation icon appears in the message box (see Fig. 17.5).

Fig. 17.5

An exclamation mark in the message box.

Instead of learning Tables 17.1 through 17.3, you can use the (supposedly) easier defined constants that appear in CONSTANT.TXT. Listing 17.1 shows the part of CONSTANT.TXT that relates to message boxes.

Listing 17.1 The Message Box Portion of CONSTANT.TXT

```
' Function Parameters
' MsgBox parameters
Global Const MB_OK = 0                ' OK button only
Global Const MB_OKCANCEL = 1          ' OK and Cancel buttons
Global Const MB_ABORTRETRYIGNORE = 2  ' Abort, Retry, and Ignore
                                      ' buttons
```

```
Global Const MB_YESNOCANCEL = 3        ' Yes, No, and Cancel
                                       ' buttons
Global Const MB_YESNO = 4              ' Yes and No buttons
Global Const MB_RETRYCANCEL = 5        ' Retry and Cancel buttons

Global Const MB_ICONSTOP = 16          ' Critical message
Global Const MB_ICONQUESTION = 32      ' Warning query
Global Const MB_ICONEXCLAMATION = 48   ' Warning message
Global Const MB_ICONINFORMATION = 64   ' Information message

Global Const MB_APPLMODAL = 0          ' Application Modal Message
                                       ' Box
Global Const MB_DEFBUTTON1 = 0         ' First button is default
Global Const MB_DEFBUTTON2 = 256       ' Second button is default
Global Const MB_DEFBUTTON3 = 512       ' Third button is default
Global Const MB_SYSTEMMODAL = 4096     ' System Modal

' MsgBox return values
Global Const IDOK = 1                  ' OK button pressed
Global Const IDCANCEL = 2              ' Cancel button pressed
Global Const IDABORT = 3               ' Abort button pressed
Global Const IDRETRY = 4               ' Retry button pressed
Global Const IDIGNORE = 5              ' Ignore button pressed
Global Const IDYES = 6                 ' Yes button pressed
Global Const IDNO = 7                  ' No button pressed
```

Are these defined constants easier to remember than their numeric equivalents? Some are and many really aren't. Once you've programmed with Visual Basic for a while, however, you'll learn the most common constant names. The last section in Listing 17.1 with the comment that begins MsgBox return values, is important once you begin using the MsgBox() function described in the next section.

The *MsgBox()* Function

The MsgBox statement is useful for displaying messages, but the MsgBox() function provides additional power that the MsgBox statement cannot attain. The function returns a value that indicates the button chosen by the user. Therefore, after the function displays multiple buttons, you know which button the user chose.

The MsgBox() function works just like the MsgBox statement by displaying a similar message box, and the MsgBox() function accepts the same three arguments as the MsgBox statement. Table 17.4 describes the return values that come from MsgBox().

III

Primary Differences

| Table 17.4 | The *MsgBox()* Return Values |
Value	Description
1	The user clicked the OK button
2	The user clicked the Cancel button
3	The user clicked the Abort button
4	The user clicked the Retry button
5	The user clicked the Ignore button
6	The user clicked the Yes button
7	The user clicked the No button

You'll have to use the value returned from MsgBox() to check for the user's message box response. Here is an example that stores the MsgBox() return value:

```
UserButton = MsgBox("Are you ready?", 35)
```

When Visual Basic reaches this function, the program waits for the user to answer the MsgBox() prompt by selecting one of the MsgBox buttons. The result of the button choice, a numeric value from Table 17.4, is then assigned to the variable named UserButton.

The 35 sends the Yes, No, and Cancel buttons to the message box and displays the Warning Query icon (3+32 equals the 35 argument). If the user selects Yes, the UserButton variable is assigned the value 6. UserButton gets a 7 if the user selects No, and UserButton gets 2 if the user selects Cancel.

Note

If the user presses Esc at any message box that contains a Cancel button, Visual Basic acts as though the user selected Cancel and returns the value 2 from the MsgBox() function.

Once the user selects a button, use the If or the Select Case statement to execute appropriate code based on that selection. For example, Listing 17.2 shows a cmdExit_Click() event procedure that, if tied to the Exit command button, makes sure the user wants to end the program.

Listing 17.2   Checking the *MsgBox()* Return Value

```
Sub cmdExit_Click ()
' The user clicked the Exit command button
  Dim MsgAns As Integer
  MsgAns = MsgBox("Are you sure you want to quit?", 35)
  If (MsgAns = 6) Then
    End
  End If
  ' The code returns to the form if
  ' nothing else is done in this procedure.
  ' Therefore, if the user clicks No or
  ' Cancel or presses Esc, this procedure
  ' returns to the form and the program
  ' continues its execution as before.
End Sub
```

Instead of exiting when the user clicks E<u>x</u>it, the code gives the user one final chance to stay with the program instead of terminating it.

The *InputBox()* Functions

The InputBox() and InputBox$() functions are the opposite of the MsgBox() function. Whereas, MsgBox() displays data for the user, the InputBox() and InputBox$() functions receive the user's input.

InputBox()
**functions get data
from the user.**

Note

The InputBox() and InputBox$() functions generally ask the user for data. Both functions display message boxes similar to those of MsgBox() (without the icons) that describe what data is being requested.

The InputBox() and InputBox$() functions do the same thing except that InputBox() inputs Variant data and InputBox$() inputs only string data. Here are the formats of these two functions:

```
InputBox(PromptString [, [TitleString] [, [DefaultString]
➥[, xpos, ypos]]])
```

and

```
InputBox$(PromptString [, [TitleString] [, [DefaultString]
➥[, xpos, ypos]]])
```

The functions' format brackets indicate that if you omit either the *TitleString* or the *DefaultString* (or both), the commas are still required as placeholders if you specify the final two arguments, *xpos* and *ypos*.

The *PromptString* is a string that you want to display so that the user knows what you're asking for. The *PromptString* can be as long as 255 characters. The *TitleString* is a string that becomes the input box's title. Unlike MsgBox(), with these functions no title displays if you do not specify a *TitleString*. The *DefaultString* is a default string that appears inside the typing area. The user can accept the string by pressing Enter if he or she doesn't want to enter a new value.

The *xpos* and *ypos* values specify the numeric value of the twips where you want the input box to appear on-screen. If you've displayed a message or table or form somewhere on-screen, you can position the input box wherever you want it to appear (as opposed to the middle of the screen if you specified no position). *xpos* is the x-coordinate (the horizontal position), and *ypos* is the y-coordinate (the vertical position) of the input box's upper-left corner.

> **Tip**
>
> Each twip, remember, represents 1/1440th of an inch.

Figure 17.6 shows an input box generated from the following InputBox$() function (assume that UserName is already declared to be a string variable):

```
UserName = InputBox$("What is your name?", "Ask a name", "J. Doe")
```

Fig. 17.6
Awaiting the user's
response.

The InputBox() functions always offer a typing area for the user to enter a value and an OK button so that the user can indicate when the input is completed. After the user enters a name (or presses Enter to choose OK and uses the default string, J. Doe), the variable UserName holds the user's answer.

Using *Print*

The Visual Basic `Print` command is a command that's a part of every BASIC incarnation. Whereas `Print` is one of the most common statements in most BASIC programs, Visual Basic makes `Print` a little less useful due to the powerful Windows controls and the message and input box functions offered by Visual Basic. Nevertheless, you sometimes need to display straight text directly on-screen or on the printer and `Print` is a good command to use for that.

`Print` **has been around since the first version of BASIC.**

> **Note**
>
> Chapter 24, "Controlling the Printer," discusses the use of `Print` and the printer. This chapter focuses on using `Print` to print on-screen, or more accurately, on the screen's form.

`Print`'s format is foreboding but there's really little to it. Here is the format of `Print`:

```
object.Print [Spc(n) ¦ Tab(n)] Expression [; ¦ ,]
```

In statement formats such as this one for `Print`, the ¦ symbol is an *or* symbol that means you can use either `Spc()` or `Tab()` but not both at the same time. The same holds for the semicolon and comma. Don't let the format lead you astray; `Print` is simple.

As you can see, `Print` is a method, but you'll use `Print` the majority of the time as if it were a stand-alone command, which doesn't require the dot operator. The reason you can treat `Print` as a command is because the `Print` method can apply to an *Object*, which is a form or printer in most cases. When you apply the form name to `Print`, `Print` routes all its output to the form. However, many applications contain a single form. If you don't specify a form when using `Print`, Visual Basic assumes that you want to apply the `Print` method to the current form. Therefore, assuming that your form's name is `frmMyForm`, both of the following lines are identical:

```
frmMyForm.Print "Hello"
```

and

```
Print "Hello"
```

III

Primary Differences

The second statement is much clearer and you now know that the Print applies to the current form, which is in many cases the only form in the application. If your application does contain two forms, you'll want to specify which form that each Print applies to.

If you print string expressions, such as Hello, the entire expression (less the quotation marks) appears on the form. Therefore, whenever a program executes Print "Hello", the word Hello immediately appears on the form. Printing always begins from the upper-left corner of the form.

Print eliminates the need to use a control when you want to send text to the form's background. Suppose that a Form_Paint() procedure (the procedure that executes as the form appears on-screen) looks like this:

```
Sub Form_Paint ()
  Print "This application does little more than print a message"
  Print "at the top of a blank form."
  Print
  Print "As you can see, specifying Print without any string"
  Print "produces a blank line."
End Sub
```

The printed strings appear, starting in the upper-left corner, as soon as the application paints the form on-screen (see Fig. 17.7).

Fig. 17.7
Reading the
printed strings.

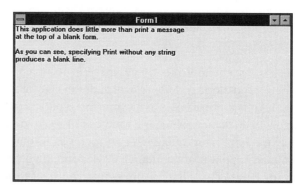

> **Note**
>
> When using Print, you won't have to mess with colors or font settings; however, you won't get all the output options that labels and the other controls provide.

Printing Variables

When you put a variable to the right of Print, Visual Basic displays the contents of that variable. Consider the following code:

```
Dim Hello As Integer
Hello = 18
Print "Hello"
Print Hello
Print "Hello"
Print 18
```

Here is the output of this section of code:

```
Hello
 18
Hello
 18
```

When you print literals, the literals print as is. Therefore, the string Hello prints when you print the string literal, but the value inside the variable named Hello prints when you print the variable. The 18 appears last simply because the Print statement prints the numeric literal of 18.

Caution

For some reason, the designers of Visual Basic decided to add a space before each positive number that you print using Print. The space is the reserved location where an implied plus sign appears. If the number is negative, the negative sign appears in place of the space.

Notice that each Print begins sending output onto the next line. If you want to print values on the same line, such as a literal and variable combination, separate the values with a semicolon or comma. The semicolon prints subsequent values right next to each other, while the comma prints subsequent values in the next *print zone*. A print zone appears every 14 spaces on your form.

The comma and semicolon combine output values.

The following Print

```
Print "I just turned"; 34
```

prints this

```
I just turned 34
```

Of course, you could have included the 34 inside the string. However, if the age were inside a variable named Age, you would need the semicolon to separate the output like this:

```
Print "I just turned"; Age
```

You can combine several values on the same line like this:

```
Print "I am"; Age; " years old."
```

If Age contains 34, The output looks like this:

```
I am 34 years old.
```

If you inserted commas instead of semicolons between the values, the output is spaced farther apart. Therefore, this statement:

```
Print "I am", Age, "years old."
```

produces this output:

```
I am            34            years old.
```

One of the nice things that the commas let you do is to print values in co-lumnar format. Suppose that you stored a table with five product lines worth of codes for each of your four salespeople; a two-dimensional string array would hold the data nicely. You can print the list of codes in columnar format, even if each code were a variable-length string, like this:

```
For Line = 1 To 5
  Print Prod(Line, 1), Prod(Line, 2), Prod(Line, 3), Prod(Line, 4)
Next Line
```

Such a table of product codes ensures that each column begins at the same location, creating an output such as this:

```
X1IU2         A3            ET44-1        PL900PI
C4            W333ERF       ET231         M390II-12
FSE344DSS2    QQ49E-2       OO2           KI01
LK890         CV7           UHGH77T       D7
WOP99         AS2E56        LP12A         MNWII9
```

Tip

Chapter 30, "Using the Grid Control," introduces a grid control that makes creating and displaying tables even easier than using Print.

If you want to control the output so that each subsequent column begins exactly where you want (such as every 10 spaces instead of every 14 as is the case for comma-separated output values), use the `Tab()` function inside the `Print`. The following code ensures that the previous table prints in columns 1, 10, 20, and 30 instead of groups of 14, 28, 32, and so on:

```
For Line = 1 To 5
  Print Prod(Line, 1); Tab(10); Prod(Line, 2); Tab(10);
  ➥Prod(Line, 3); Tab(10); Prod(Line, 4)
Next Line
```

The `Spc()` function works almost like `Tab()` except that `Spc()` adds a certain number of spaces to the output before printing the next character. The following three strings print exactly four spaces apart:

```
Print "Hi"; Spc(4); "there"; Spc(4); "you!"
```

Notice that you always use a semicolon on either side of a `Tab()` or `Spc()` function call.

There are some advanced formatting options available with a form of `Print` named `Print Using`, but the `Print Using` statement is rarely used with Visual Basic's controls.

Normally, you would learn even more about the `Print` command if Visual Basic were just another incarnation of BASIC. Visual Basic, however, is much more than a typical BASIC language, and you've learned in this chapter all you'll ever need to know about `Print`. When you want to display simple text on a form, such as on a message form that includes lengthy instructions to the user, a series of `Print` statements works better than label controls that you must size and adjust.

Conclusion

You can now display professional-looking message boxes from within Visual Basic. If you ever want to give the user a little extra message or get the user's attention in a way that a regular control cannot do, display a message box with `MsgBox`. `MsgBox` comes in two flavors: as a statement and function. If you need to test to see which buttons the user selects, you can call the `MsgBox()` function and test the return value.

You also learned how to write programs that accept input from the keyboard. Before this chapter, you had to assign variables specific values at the time you wrote the program. You now can write programs that prompt for variable data and the user then enters data when the procedure runs.

The MsgBox() and InputBox() functions are so much more powerful than COBOL's DISPLAY and ACCEPT commands but it may surprise you to see how much easier the Visual Basic I/O functions are to use and program. Often, you'll see a MsgBox statement and InputBox() function next to each other in code. The MsgBox statement displays information, and the InputBox() function asks questions of the user about that information.

Another way that you can print data on a form is to use the Print method. Print is closer to COBOL's DISPLAY than the MsgBox() function because Print is textual in nature. Print is useful for sending detailed instructions to the user directly on the form. However, in reality, you'll use Print more for controlling the printer than you ever will for displaying information on the screen's form. This chapter introduces Print and Chapter 24, "Controlling the Printer," picks up with Print once again by using the printer as the object to which you direct the Print method.

Chapter 18

Adding Menus and Extra Forms

This chapter explains how to add menus and additional forms to your applications. No set of controls or toolbar command buttons has been able to eliminate the use of menus in Windows programs. Menus give the user the ability to request actions such as printing and leaving the program. Menus began in the textual world of programming and the menu is one of the few carryovers from the user interaction of the text world to the GUI environment of Windows.

Some of your applications may require multiple forms. A single form simply does not always provide you with enough screen real estate at times to accomplish your task. This chapter introduces a second form to your applications by demonstrating how to add a Help About dialog box to your application.

This chapter completes your mastery of the basics of Visual Basic. Your next step will be to improve upon your Visual Basic programming skills and to finalize your thinking away from the text world into the GUI world.

Here are some of the topics that will be discussed in this chapter:

- Learning the Menu Design Editor and seeing how it relieves you of the tedious burden of menu design

- Learning how to add a menu bar to a new application

- Using the Menu Design Editor to add commands on the File and Help menus

- Learning to right-justify the <u>H</u>elp menu bar item by using the Windows Write word processor

- Discovering how About dialog boxes can inform the user of application-specific information

- Learning how to add a second form to your application

Other than a few statement comparisons, you've seen very little COBOL in the last few chapters. When you get to the point where you now are—you're comfortable with the Visual Basic paradigm and the Visual Basic development and user interaction—there isn't much left in the traditional programming environment to compare. We'll return to a full COBOL-to-Visual Basic discussion, however, when we get to Part V, "Your Next Step with VB," where you learn how Visual Basic handles file I/O in a manner that is quite unlike COBOL.

Menus Made Easy

Create menus like screens—*visually*.

As with all the other Visual Basic programming tools, designing menus takes more organizational and visual-placement ability than programming ability. Visual Basic supplies the Menu Design Editor, which is nothing more than an advanced Windows dialog box in which you design menus.

As with the controls, there will be code behind the menus that you design and you'll use Visual Basic language statements to supply that code. Menu code is nothing more than event-driven procedures that work like all the other event-driven procedures. That is, when the user selects a menu command, Visual Basic triggers an event procedure that you've written to handle that menu command.

Think about how you might approach a menu through programming. In Visual Basic terminology, the code behind a menu might, in more traditional environments, be one gigantic `Select Case` statement. If the user selects the first menu item, the first `Case` code executes. If the user selects the second menu item, the second `Case` code executes, and so on. Of course, a selected menu item often produces yet another menu, and menus often produce dialog boxes and message boxes. Therefore your menu code can get encumbered by lots of decisions.

Visual Basic ensures that each pull-down menu option that you add to your application—and each command on each menu option—triggers a unique event. As you build your application's menu and add commands to it, you're dynamically adding events to Visual Basic's repertoire of possible events.

The Menu Design Editor

Once you begin to build your application, you can begin working on the menu. You might want to build the menu as you add functionality to the program, you might want to add the entire menu before coding anything else, or you might wait until you've coded all the screen and controls before adding a single menu item. Whenever you are ready to build the menu, the Menu Design Editor gives you the tools that you need.

Before starting the Menu Design Editor, you must have a Form window open and active. Go to the Window menu and choose the Menu Design command (Ctrl+M is the access key) and the Menu Design Editor appears (see Fig. 18.1).

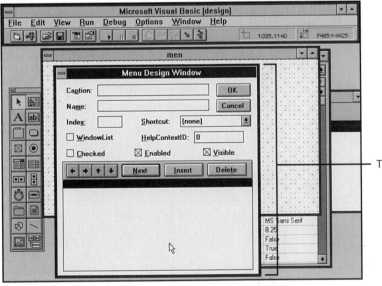

Fig. 18.1
The Menu Design Editor provides you with menu-building tools.

The Menu Design Editor

The Menu Design Editor consists of two primary windows. The top window contains the control properties that you'll set for each menu item. The lower window (which is blank in Fig. 18.1) displays the menu as you build it.

> **Note**
>
> The Menu Design Editor lets you add, change, delete, and even rearrange menu options with simple mouse clicks and movements.

Each form in your application can contain its own menu. You'll learn how to add a second form to your application in the section, "Adding a Second Form," later in this chapter.

Perhaps the best way to learn how to create a menu is to walk through the process yourself. In the following steps, we'll create a new application and add a complete menu bar and commands to that application. Not every menu command will do something here, however, because you should now focus on creating and designing the menu. Once you use the Menu Design Editor to create the menu, activating the menu's commands requires no new Visual Basic commands. Each menu command that you add will provide its own event procedure. Therefore if you want to add a menu item to exit the program, you'll put the End command inside the File, Exit menu item's event procedure—just as you've been doing for the Exit command button throughout the earlier chapters in this book.

The following sections create the menu bar shown in Figure 18.2. Although every Windows application that you write will differ, almost all of them will contain the same menu bar items shown in Figure 18.2. Many applications will require additional application-specific menu bar items as well.

Fig. 18.2
The menu bar that you'll create by following the steps in the next section.

The form's menu bar

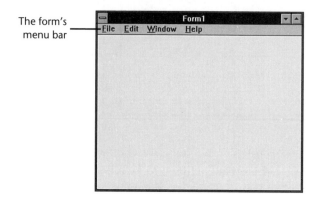

Creating the Menu Bar

Follow these steps to create a new menu bar:

1. Open a new project, click on the Form window, and display the Menu Design Editor (Ctrl+M) if you don't already have the Menu Design Editor showing.

2. The Caption text box holds the menu bar item's name that you are adding next. The first menu bar item to add is the File item. Therefore type **&File** in the Caption text box. (As with command buttons, & always appears before the letter you want Visual Basic to underline on the item's caption.) As you type, the caption appears in the Menu Design Editor's lower window.

3. Every menu item has a name. You'll specify that name in the Name text box. Naming conventions suggest that you begin each menu name with the 3-letter prefix mnu. Most programmers follow the prefix with the actual item name. Therefore press Tab to move to the Name panel and type **mnuFile** for the name of this item.

> ### Note
>
> The name you assign to each item forms the first half of the event procedure's name. Therefore if the File menu is named mnuFile, the event that the user triggers when selecting this item will be called mnuFile_Click().
>
> A menu is just another kind of Visual Basic control. When you add menu items, you're adding additional controls to the application that didn't exist before. As you add and name those control menu items, Visual Basic creates event procedures that respond to the user's control actions.

Instead of separately naming each menu item, you can include each item in a control array. If you create a menu control array, each item's Index text box will contain that item's position in the control array (the subscript in the menu array for that item). If you want to create a pull-down menu that grows dynamically—like one that displays a list of the user's open files—the control array makes adding menu items as simple as initializing the next item in the array. In this example, you're not creating a control array, so you'll assign each item a different name and you'll ignore the Index text box.

1. Once you've added the menu item's caption and name, you'll usually skip over several of the next few Menu Design Editor dialog box items. Tab past the Shortcut list box. Later, you'll add Ctrl key combinations to individual menu commands using the Shortcut list box, but you won't be adding shortcut keys for the menu bar's items.

> **Tip**
>
> Only commands on pull-down menus should have shortcut access keys. Don't add shortcut access keys to the menu items because you add their shortcut access keys through the underlined letter in the menu name.

Tab past the WindowList check box as well. When you create extremely advanced applications that contain additional windows called *child windows*, you'll be controlling individual windows from this check box.

2. You'll also need to tab past the next three check boxes. The Enabled and Visible check boxes should be selected already. Leave them selected. Your Menu Design Editor should look like the one shown in Figure 18.3.

Fig. 18.3
The Menu Design Editor's contents after you add the File menu bar item.

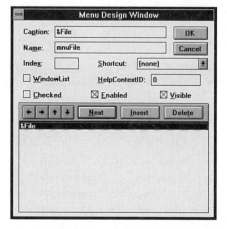

> **Tip**
>
> You can control the Checked, Enabled, and Visible check boxes from within your code. As the user responds to the application, you can control the check-marked, grayed, and visibility properties of individual menu commands. For example, if you're creating a data-entry application, you might want to hide or gray the File, Save menu option until the user adds the first data item. Your code then could make the Save command visible with this simple assignment statement:
>
> ```
> mnuFileSave.Visible = TRUE
> ```

3. Ignore the four arrows for now and click the Next command button. Of course, instead of tabbing through all the previous items, you can simply click Next. However, the previous paragraphs gave you a chance to learn about the other menu design options even though you won't be changing all of the options here.

4. It's now time to add the remaining three menu bar items. Although the previous steps spent a lot of time explaining every menu design editing option, you can add the remaining items very quickly.

   For the second Caption, type **&Edit**. As you type, the caption appears in the window's lower pane. Press Tab and type **mnuEdit** for the name. Leave all of the other items in the upper half of the Menu Design Editor as they are. Click Next to move to the next item. Visual Basic automatically highlights Next so you can either click it with the mouse, press Alt+N, or simply press Enter to move to the next menu item.

5. For the third Caption, type **&Window**. As you type, the caption appears in the window's lower pane. Press Tab and type **mnuWindow** for the name. Finally, type the fourth Caption, **&Help**, and then **mnuHelp** for the name.

6. Click OK to close the Menu Design Editor.

When you close the editor, Visual Basic updates the application's Form window to include the new menu bar. Your Form window should look like the one displayed in Figure 18.4. Across the top of the window are the four menu options with the appropriate underlined access keystrokes.

Your newly
added menu bar

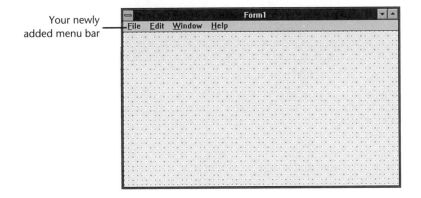

Fig. 18.4
The complete
menu bar appears.

III

Menu Standards

Almost every Windows application that you'll ever use contains these same menu bar commands. As already mentioned, the primary advantage of Windows programs is their consistency in the user interface, and the menu bar plays an important role in that consistency.

No matter how simple, elegant, powerful, or different your application is from other Windows applications, try to add these same four fundamental menu options to your application's menu bar. The user will always need a way to exit the application, and the File menu almost always contains the Exit command. You can also add a command button to allow the user an exit as well. Several shortcut access keystrokes will eliminate the need for the user to select from the menu, but you still need to include a common menu that users can resort to if all else fails when they want to exit.

Adding Commands to the File Menu

Now you can add commands to the File menu. Before you're done, your File menu will look like the one shown in Figure 18.5. As you can see, you're going to add several commands to the File menu. You will not be writing event procedures to handle all these commands, however, because you don't yet understand Visual Basic's file operations. Besides, once you learn how to hook up one menu command to an event procedure, all the rest work the same way.

Note

Notice that Figure 18.5 contains separator bars between some of the menu commands as well as shortcut access keys for some of the commands. The separator bars help group commands that perform similar tasks, and the shortcut access keystrokes (such as Ctrl+O) give your users the power to execute menu commands without first opening the pull-down menus.

Follow these steps to finish the File menu:

1. Press Ctrl+M again to open the Menu Design Editor.

2. Look in the window's lower pane. You'll need to insert some items between the &File and the &Edit options. Click the &Edit row to highlight it. Once highlighted, click the Insert command button to insert a blank row before &Edit. Clicking Insert always inserts a blank row above the highlighted line. Visual Basic automatically positions the cursor at the Caption text box so you can enter additional items.

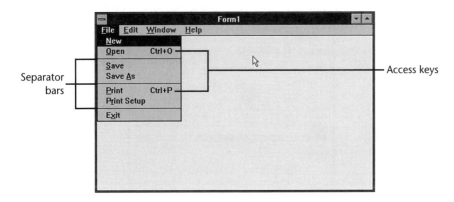

Fig. 18.5
The File menu's
commands.

3. Click the Caption text box and type **&New** for the caption. The New command will appear on the File pull-down menu. Name the New command **mnuFileNew**. Don't press Enter just yet. By naming the command in this manner, you'll know that the named event is a menu command, from the File menu, and it's the New command.

4. If you were to click Next now (don't do this yet), the New command would simply be another item on the menu bar. New shouldn't appear on the menu bar, however; it should appear on the File pull-down menu.

Therefore you must tell Visual Basic that New is to appear as a sub-menu item. Visual Basic utilizes a series of indentions that indicates which commands belong to which menu bar items. Click the right arrow (the second arrow of the four arrow command buttons) in the Menu Design Editor and Visual Basic shifts the New command over to the right a few places and four dots appear to show the shift. As you can see from the indention, Visual Basic now knows that New goes under the File menu and is not a stand-alone menu bar item.

Before continuing, make sure that your Menu Design Editor looks like the one in Figure 18.6.

1. Click Next and Insert to make room for File's second command, which you'll call Open. Click the right arrow to indent the new command within the File menu's commands.

Type **&Open** for the Caption and **mnuFileOpen** for the Name. Open will have a shortcut access keystroke, so open the Shortcut drop-down list box and select Ctrl+O from the list. As soon as you do, Ctrl+O appears to the right of the Open command in the lower pane of the window.

Fig. 18.6

<u>N</u>ew is now a part
of the <u>F</u>ile menu.

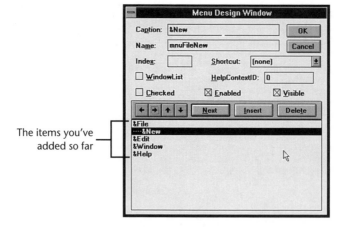

The items you've
added so far

2. Click <u>N</u>ext and <u>I</u>nsert to make room for <u>F</u>ile's third command, <u>C</u>lose. Click the right arrow to indent the new command within the <u>F</u>ile menu's commands and then click the Ca<u>p</u>tion prompt.

Type **&Close** for the Ca<u>p</u>tion and **mnuFileClose** for the Na<u>m</u>e. Click <u>N</u>ext to get ready for the next menu option.

**Separator bars are
menu items.**

3. The separator bars are nothing more than additional items on the pull-down menu. To add a separator bar, click <u>N</u>ext, be sure the &Edit line is highlighted, then press <u>I</u>nsert to make room for the bar. Click the right arrow to indent the bar and include it within <u>F</u>ile's menu commands.

For the Ca<u>p</u>tion, click the Ca<u>p</u>tion text box and press the dash key (-). When the Menu Design Editor sees the dash, it knows that you want a separator bar to appear at that position in the menu. Each separator bar needs its own name, however, so type **mnuFileBar1** for the Na<u>m</u>e of the bar. When the menu eventually appears for the user, the menu bar will not be an active command. Visual Basic will display the separator menu bars but it won't allow the user to select the separator bar. When the user selects from the <u>F</u>ile menu, the highlight will always skip over the separator bar as the user moves the bar throughout the commands.

4. Finish adding the remaining <u>F</u>ile menu commands. Table 18.1 lists the Ca<u>p</u>tion and Na<u>m</u>e values for each item as well as optional shortcut access keys when needed.

Table 18.1 The Remaining File Menu Commands		
Caption	**Name**	**Shortcut Access Key**
&Save	mnuFileSave	Shift+F12
Save &As	mnuFileSaveAs	
-	mnuFileBar2	
&Print	mnuFilePrint	Ctrl+P
P&rint Setup	mnuFilePrintSet	
-	mnuFileBar3	
E&xit	mnuFileExit	

After completely entering the captions and names from Table 18.1, your Menu Design Editor should look like the one shown in Figure 18.7. Before leaving the Menu Design Editor, add an About menu command to the Help menu bar item. In a later section entitled, "Adding a Second Form," you'll see how to attach the display of a dialog box to this command. Click OK to close the Editor and return to the Form window.

Fig. 18.7
The File menu design is complete.

Adding Menu Event Procedures

One of the easiest ways to hook up a menu command to an event procedure is through the Form window. Visual Basic keeps the menu that you create in a half-active state as you create your application. The menu bar's options pull down if you've added the commands for the pull-down menu.

It's easy to add menu event procedures.

The next few steps demonstrate how to activate the File, Exit command to terminate the application.

1. At the Form window, click File to display the pull-down menu.

2. Choose Exit. There isn't an additional menu option for Exit, so Visual Basic correctly assumes that you want to add an event procedure to the Exit command. Therefore Visual Basic opens a Code window for the mnuFileExit_Click() procedure.

3. Add the body of mnuFileExit_Click() so the complete procedure looks like the following:

```
Sub mnuFileExit_Click ()
' The File Exit menu option terminates the program
    End
End Sub
```

When the user chooses File, Exit, Visual Basic executes this event procedure and the End statement causes the program to terminate just as if you had added an End command to an Exit command button.

4. Close the Code window and run the program. Choose File, Exit and the program quits.

You continue adding event procedures to the rest of the menu commands to complete the application. To keep things simple at this point, the application that you've created here won't do any more than exit upon choosing File, Exit. Make sure that your changes are stored on the disk by saving your project before moving to the next section.

Getting Fancy

Many of today's applications add zest to the menu bar by right-justifying the Help menu option. Consider the menu shown in Figure 18.8. Although the menu bar contains the same items that yours currently contains, the Help option appears at the far right of the menu bar.

Tip

Separate Help from the other menu items. Help is more informative than active and the separation keeps the user's common tasks away from the Help item.

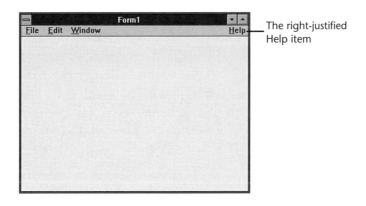

The right-justified
Help item

Fig. 18.8
The Help item is
right-justified on
the menu bar.

There is a trick involved in separating <u>H</u>elp from the other menu items. The trick requires that you add a backspace character to the beginning of the <u>H</u>elp item's name. It sounds crazy, but it works.

It's not exactly obvious how to add a backspace character to the <u>H</u>elp menu option. Doing so requires that you use another Windows program named *Write*. Windows Write is a simple word processor that comes with every version of Windows.

In Appendix A, you see that the backspace character occupies position 8 in the ASCII table. To prefix the <u>H</u>elp menu item with the backspace character, find some program that allows you to type the ASCII value of 8, save that value on the Windows Clipboard, and then return to Visual Basic to paste that ASCII 8 value before the <u>H</u>elp menu option. The following steps explain how to do just that:

**The backspace
character is ASCII 8.**

1. You have to start Write to right-justify the <u>H</u>elp menu item. You don't have to exit Visual Basic to start Write.

   Press Alt+Tab to return to the Program Manager. Open the Accessories program group. You find Write listed among the icons.

2. Double-click the Write icon to load and run Write.

3. If you were to press Backspace, Write would attempt to back the cursor up one space. You've got to trick Write into accepting the ASCII value of 8 as if the backspace character were just another character you typed. Hold down the Alt key and then press the 8 on your keyboard's numeric keypad. When you release Alt, Write displays a square box at the cursor's location.

III

Primary Differences

When Write receives a character that has no display equivalent, Write displays a square box to indicate the character's position. The square box at the top of Write's window contains the ASCII 8 backspace character.

4. Highlight the square box by selecting it with the mouse or by pressing Shift+Arrow. After highlighting the backspace, press Ctrl+C. Ctrl+C is the shortcut key for Edit, Copy. Ctrl+C sends a copy of the backspace character to the Windows Clipboard.

5. You can now close Write. Choose File, Exit to return to the Program Manager. Don't save the Write document when Write prompts you to do so. The backspace character remains on the Windows Clipboard even though you leave Write. Close the Accessories window group in the Program Manager to keep your screen uncluttered.

6. Return to Visual Basic by pressing Alt+Tab. Press Ctrl+M to reopen the Menu Design Editor. Scroll the lower part of the window to bring the Help item into view.

7. Highlight Help and press Alt+P to highlight the Caption text box. Press the Home key so that the insertion cursor rests at the start of the text box (before &). Paste the Clipboard's contents (the single backspace character) by pressing Shift+Insert at the cursor's location. Visual Basic uses a single boldfaced vertical character to represent the ASCII 8 character. Your Menu Design Editor should look like the one shown in Figure 18.9.

Fig. 18.9
After adding the backspace character.

An inserted ASCII 8

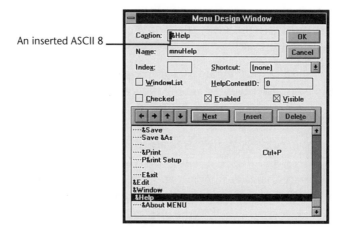

Keep this application open because you'll use it in the next section when you add a second form to the program. Save the application, however, by naming the form MENU.FRM and the project MENU.MAK. This chapter's completed MENU.MAK appears on this book's disk.

Adding a Second Form

When you add a second form to your project, that form contains its own set of controls, control names, and code. If you want the forms to share variable contents, you'll have to declare global variables. Otherwise, the forms will contain their own sets of variables.

There are many reasons why you may need a second form. A payroll application may contain a startup form that the user sees when the program first begins. If the user enters payroll data, perhaps an employee data-entry form will appear. If the user wants to look at payroll history data, another form can display a scrolling list of payroll history for selected employees and dates.

This section explains how to generate a second form that works as an About dialog box. Virtually every Windows application includes an About dialog box as a command on the Help menu. The About dialog box tells the user a little about the program being used. For example, if you choose Help About from Visual Basic's menu bar, you'll see an About dialog box similar to the one shown in Figure 18.10. About dialog boxes often display the program's version number and serial number in case the user needs technical support with the product.

Fig. 18.10
Displaying Visual Basic's About dialog box.

III

Primary Differences

Note

Depending on your version of Visual Basic and the system resources inside your computer, your About dialog box may differ from the one shown in Figure 18.10.

About dialog boxes are nothing more than a form window that an application displays. About dialog boxes always contain a command button so the user can return to the running application. When the user clicks the About dialog box's command button, the form holding the About dialog box must be unloaded.

> **Tip**
>
> Remember that you can reuse forms across more than one application. In other words, if you create a general-purpose form that more than one application needs to share, use the File, Add Visual Basic menu command to add the form to each subsequent application that needs to use the form.

The following sections walk you through the creation of an About dialog box for the MENU.MAK application that you created in the previous section.

Creating the Second Form

You should still have the MENU.MAK project loaded from the previous sections. If not, start Visual Basic and load MENU.MAK. There are two steps necessary in adding an About dialog box to the form:

1. Create the About box form.

2. Hook up the form's display to the Help, About menu command so the form appears when the user selects the command.

The following steps create the About box form. As you create the form, keep in mind that the About dialog box will appear on top of the application's main form, so the About dialog box is usually smaller than the application's primary form. Also, users can rarely—if ever—resize an About dialog box.

1. Choose New, Form from Visual Basic's menu bar. Visual Basic displays the new form in the middle of the screen.

2. Press F4 to see the second form's Properties window and make sure that the following properties are set:

   BorderStyle: **3 - Fixed Double**

   Caption: **About**

   ControlBox: **False**

   Height: **3825**

Left: **2055**

MaxButton: **False**

MinButton: **False**

Name: **frmAbout**

Top: **1845**

Width: **3915**

When the user sees the About dialog box, the user won't be able to resize the dialog box or display its control menu. The user can only press the About dialog box's command button that you'll now add.

3. Add the command button to the About dialog box form with the following properties:

Caption: **OK**

Height: **495**

Left: **1320**

Name: **cmdAboutOK**

Top: **2280**

Width: **1215**

4. Add a label to the About dialog box that has the following properties:

BorderStyle: **1 - Fixed Single**

Caption: **Menu Program Demonstration**

FontSize: **18**

Height: **975**

Left: **240**

Name: **lblAbout1**

Top: **360**

Width: **3135**

5. Add a second label to the About box that has the following properties:

Alignment: **2** - **Center**

Caption: **Version 1.0**

Height: **255**

Left: **1320**

Name: **lblAbout2**

Top: **1680**

Width: **1215**

Your About dialog box is now complete. Your screen should look something like the one shown in Figure 18.11.

Fig. 18.11
The About box form is now complete.

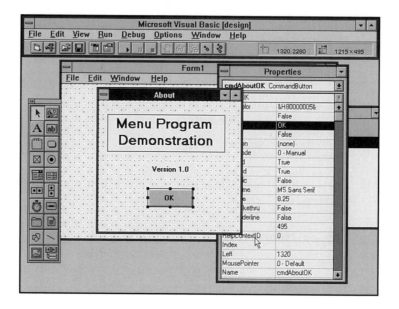

6. You've got to add the About dialog box's command button code so the user's command button click removes the dialog box from view. Double-click OK to open the Code window for the cmdAboutOK_Click () event procedure. Type the following statement in the body of cmdAboutOK_Click():

```
Unload frmAbout    ' Remove the form from view
```

The Unload command removes the form from the viewer's screen. Therefore when the user clicks the About box form window, this event procedure unloads the form, thereby removing the form from view. Close the Code window to return to the Form window.

7. Save the About dialog box under the name `ABOUT.FRM` using the File, Save menu command.

Now that you've created and saved the About box form, you can return to the MENU.FRM's Form window and connect the About box to the proper menu command.

Connecting the About Dialog Box

Before adding the About dialog box to the first form, you must add one command to the Help menu. To do so, follow these steps:

1. Choose the Menu Design command from the Window menu (or press Ctrl+M) to display the Menu Design Editor.

2. Scroll the lower pane until you highlight the blank *after* the &Help menu item then press Alt+P.

3. Type **&About_MENU** for the Caption.

4. Enter **mnuHelpAbout** for the menu name.

5. Click the right arrow to indent the item that places the About menu command within the Help menu.

6. Click OK to close the Menu Design Editor.

Add the code to the new menu item by following these steps:

1. Click Help About MENU to open the Code window.

2. Type the following code into the Code window:

```
' Display the About box form
    frmAbout.Show
```

Show is a method that you can apply to forms. Show performs the opposite of Unload. Whereas Unload removes a form from the screen, Show displays the form. Therefore Visual Basic displays the About box form when the user selects Help About MENU.

3. Close the Code window and save the project.

You have now completed the application. Run the MENU.MAK project (which now contains two forms) and choose Help, About MENU. You'll see the About dialog box, as shown in Figure 18.12.

III

Primary Differences

Fig. 18.12
Looking at the
About box.

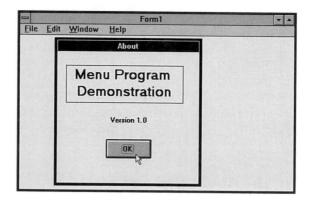

Conclusion

Your Visual Basic arsenal is improving every chapter. You can now add powerful pull-down menus without any coding whatsoever. The Menu Design Editor contains a comprehensive dialog box that includes every menu-building option your application may need.

With the Menu Design Editor, you can add menus, separator bars, check marks, and you can access shortcut keystrokes to menu commands. If you want to insert or delete menu items, you need only the mouse and a few keystrokes.

One of the most useful functions of the Menu Design Editor involves creating menu controls as you build the program. Your application responds to the user's menu commands by reacting to menu selections through a series of Click() event procedures. When the user chooses a menu command, that command's event executes.

Once you build menus, you can create an About dialog box. From the Help, About menu command, the user can request to see a second form (the About box) that shows application-specific information such as version and serial numbers. By adding more than one form to your application, you can increase the functionality of a program.

Part IV

Advanced VB Programming

Chapter 19

Built-in Numeric Functions

This chapter explains all about Visual Basic's built-in numeric functions. Although some of the functions are highly technical, many of them are used daily by Visual Basic programmers who don't use much math in their programs. Most of the built-in functions reduce your programming time. Instead of having to "reinvent the wheel" every time you need Visual Basic to perform a numeric operation, you can use one of the many built-in functions to do the job for you.

As a former COBOL programmer, you primarily programmed business applications. Unlike Visual Basic, COBOL doesn't support an extremely complex library of built-in math routines. In COBOL, if you wanted to compute a future value of cash flows, you'd have to write expressions that calculated the complete result. Visual Basic's numeric functions shorten the time needed to perform calculations because you won't have to write code that performs common routines.

Here are some of the topics that will be discussed in this chapter:

- The integer conversion functions: `Fix()` and `Int()`

- The data type conversion functions: `CCur()`, `CDble()`, `CInt()`, `CLng()`, `CSng()`, and `CVar()`

- The `Abs()` function

- The math functions: `Exp()`, `Log()`, and `Sqr()`

- The trigonometric functions: `Atn()`, `Cos()`, `Sin()`, and `Tan()`

- The randomizing tools: `Randomize` and `Rnd()`

- The Is() data type inspection functions

- The VarType() type determination function

- The IIf() selection function

- The Choose() function

You've used several functions, such as Sgn() and Tab(), throughout the first parts of this book. Remember that a function is just a built-in routine to which you pass one or more argument values. Visual Basic takes your argument value and uses that value to produce a result from the function.

Numeric functions return numeric values.

As with all built-in functions, the functions in this chapter return a value of some kind—usually a numeric value. Not all functions require arguments, but most do. Functions return one value at most. Therefore whether a function requires no arguments, one argument, or more than one argument, the function still returns only a single value.

In Chapter 21, "Modular Visual Basic Programming," you'll learn how to write your own functions. By writing your own functions, you're extending the Visual Basic language somewhat by teaching Visual Basic how to perform specific calculations and return the results.

The Integer Conversion Functions

The Int() and Fix() functions work with integers. Here are their formats:

```
Int(NumericValue)
Fix(NumericValue)
```

The *NumericValue* can be a numeric literal, expression, or variable of any data type. One of the most common integer functions is Int(), which returns the integer value of the number you pass in the parentheses. If you pass a single-precision or double-precision number to Int(), the function converts the argument to an integer.

Fix() truncates to integers.

Fix() returns the *truncated* whole number value of its argument. Truncation means that the fractional part of the argument is removed from the number. Therefore Fix() always returns an integer value.

The data type of these functions' values differs depending on the data type of their respective arguments. Int() and Fix() both return the same data type as their argument except in two cases:

■ If their argument is a string that can be converted to a number, the functions return double-precision.

■ If you pass null values to the functions (such as a null string), they return null values as well.

Caution

If you pass a nonnumeric argument (such as strings that cannot be converted to numbers by the functions) to either `Int()` or `Fix()`, you get a `Type mismatch` error.

For practical purposes, you can assume that `Int()` and `Fix()` return integer-like values (whole numbers) even though they may return those whole numbers in a higher precision format (such as single-precision or double-precision).

The following statement stores 8 (the `Int()` function's return value) in `Ans`:

```
Ans = Int(8.93)    ' Does not round!
```

Each of the following code's two function calls returns the value 8:

```
num = 8.94            ' Pass to Int() a variable
Ans = Int(num)        ' Stores 8 in Ans
num = 8
Ans = Int(num + 0.93)  ' Stores 8 in Ans
```

Note

For positive arguments, both `Int()` and `Fix()` return the same values.

The primary difference between `Int()` and `Fix()` appears when you pass them negative arguments, as shown here:

```
Ans1 = Fix(-8.93)    ' Stores -8 in Ans1
Ans2 = Int(-8.93)    ' Stores -9 in Ans2
Ans3 = Fix(-8.02)    ' Stores -8 in Ans3
Ans4 = Int(-8.02)    ' Stores -9 in Ans4
```

`Int()` doesn't truncate, but returns the closest integer less than or equal to its argument. `Fix()` simply drops the fractional part of the argument's number—whether the number is positive or negative.

The Data Type Conversion Functions

The data type conversion functions, denoted by their initial letter *C* for *convert*, are listed in Table 19.1 with their descriptions. Each function converts its argument from one data type to another.

Table 19.1 The Data Type Conversion Functions	
Function Name	**Description**
CCur()	Converts its argument to the Currency data type
CDbl()	Converts its argument to the Double data type
CInt()	Converts its argument to the Integer data type
CLng()	Converts its argument to the Long data type
CSng()	Converts its argument to the Single data type
CVar()	Converts its argument to the Variant data type

In the next chapter, "Built-in String Functions," you'll read about a conversion function that returns the String data type.

> **Caution**
>
> You must be able to convert the argument to the target data type. You cannot convert the number 123456789 to Integer with CInt(), for example, because the Integer data type cannot hold an integer that large.

Unlike Int() and Fix(), CInt() returns the closest *rounded* integer to the value of the argument. Look at the remarks to the right of each of the next statements to see what value is stored in each variable.

```
A1 = CInt(8.02)      ' Stores an 8
A2 = CInt(8.5)       ' Stores an 8
A3 = CInt(8.5001)    ' Stores a 9 in A3
A4 = CInt(9.5)       ' Stores a 10 in A4
```

CInt() does round.

Notice how CInt() (for *convert integer*) handles the rounding. For positive numbers, if the fractional portion of the argument is exactly equal to one-half (.5), CInt() rounds to the nearest integer.

For negative numbers, `CInt()` also rounds to the closest even integer.
For example:

```
A1 = CInt(-8.1)      ' Stores a -8
A2 = CInt(-8.5)      ' Stores a -8
A3 = CInt(-8.5001)   ' Stores a -9 in A3
A4 = CInt(-9.5)      ' Stores a -10 in A4
```

Use `CLng()` (for *convert long integer*) if you need to round numbers outside
`CInt()`'s limits. For example:

```
A1 = CLng(-44034.1)   ' Stores -44034 in A1
A2 = CLng(985465.6)   ' Stores 985466 in A2
```

> **Note**
>
> `CLng()` rounds integers within the range of –2,147,483,648 to 2,147,483,647.

The remaining conversion functions probably offer no real problems to you.
They convert their arguments to appropriate data types. The following code
declares a variable of four different data types and then converts each argument to those data types. Remember that you also can pass expressions to
these functions that produce numeric results so that you can control the data
types of your calculated results before storing them in a field or a variable.

```
Dim vCur As Currency
Dim vDbl As Double
Dim vSng As Single
Dim vVar As Variant

vCur = CCur(123)     ' Converts 123 to the Currency data type
vDbl = CDbl(123)     ' Converts 123 to the Double data type
vSng = CSng(123)     ' Converts 123 to the Single data type
vVar = CVar(123)     ' Converts 123 to the Variant data type
```

The *Abs()* Function

`Abs()` operates on the sign of its argument. `Abs()` returns the *absolute value* of
its argument. The absolute value always returns the positive value of its argument. At first glance, you may not see a real need for `Abs()`. The absolute
value of 10 is 10 and the absolute value of –10 is also 10. You may find some
good uses for absolute value, however, especially in distance and age/weight
difference calculations (the difference between two cities is always positive no
matter how you find the difference).

Suppose that you want to know how many years of difference there are between two employees' ages. The number of years between their ages is the absolute value of the difference between the ages. The following statement stores the difference in ages between Emp1Age and Emp2Age:

```
AgeDiff = Abs(Emp1Age - Emp2Age)
```

The Math Functions

You don't have to be an expert in math to use many of the mathematical functions that come with Visual Basic. Often, even in business applications, the following functions come in handy: Exp(), Log(), and Sqr().

Exp() returns the natural logarithm base, Log() returns the logarithm of a number, and Sqr() computes the square root of its argument.

If you don't understand the purpose of Exp() or Log(), that's okay. You may program in Visual Basic for years and never need them.

Exp() returns the base of natural logarithm (*e*) raised to a specified power. The argument to Exp() can be any constant, variable, or expression less than or equal to 709.782712893. *e* is the mathematical expression for the value 2.718282. The following code demonstrates Exp():

```
For num = 1 To 5
   Print Exp(num)
Next num
```

The code produces the following output on the current form:

```
2.718282
7.389056
20.08554
54.59815
148.4132
```

Notice that the first number—*e* raised to the first power—does indeed equal itself.

Log() returns the natural logarithm of its argument. The argument to Log() can be any positive constant, variable, or expression. The following code shows the Log() function in use:

```
For num = 1 To 5
   Print Log(num)
Next num
```

This code produces the following output on the current form:

```
0
.6931472
1.098612
1.386294
1.609438
```

Sqr()'s argument can be any positive numeric data type. Square root isn't defined for negative values. If you send a negative argument to Sqr(), you'll get an Illegal function call error message. This following section of code stores 2, 8, and 64 in the three respective variables:

Sqr()'s argument must be positive.

```
aVar1 = Sqr(4)
aVar2 = Sqr(64)
aVar3 = Sqr(4096)
```

The Trigonometric Functions

The trigonometric functions are probably the least used functions in Visual Basic. This isn't to belittle the work of scientific and mathematical programmers who need them; thank goodness that Visual Basic supplies these functions! Otherwise, programmers would have to write their own versions.

The Atn() function returns the arctangent of its argument in radians. The argument is assumed to be an expression representing an angle of a right triangle. The result of Atn() always falls between *-pi/2* and *+pi/2*. Cos() always returns the cosine of the angle, expressed in radians, of the argument. Sin() returns the sine of the angle, expressed in radians, of its argument. Tan() returns the tangent of the angle, expressed in radians, of the argument.

Tip

If you need to pass an angle expressed in degrees to these functions, convert the angle to radians by multiplying it by (pi/180). Pi is approximately 3.141592654.

The Randomizing Tools

Two randomizing tools are available in Visual Basic: the Randomize statement and the Rnd() function. You never use the Randomize statement by itself. If a procedure includes Randomize, you find the Rnd() function later in the procedure. Here is the format of the Randomize statement:

```
Randomize [number]
```

The format of the Rnd() function looks like this:

```
Rnd[(number)]
```

Notice that the Randomize statement and the Rnd() function don't require a value after them. The purpose of Rnd() is to generate a random number between 0 (inclusive) to 1 (non-inclusive; 1 is never generated by Rnd()). You can use the random number function for games, such as in the simulation of dice rolls or card draws.

If you run a procedure that prints four Rnd() numbers, each number will be different (hence, *random*) only if you don't include a *number* argument. If, however, you specify 0 as the argument to Rnd(), such as Print Rnd(0) four times, the four printed numbers are the *same*. If you specify a number greater than 0 as the argument to Rnd(), a different random number is produced (the same as leaving off the argument altogether). An argument less than zero, such as x = Rnd(-3), always produces the same random number *if* you specify the same negative argument, and it produces a different random number if the negative argument is always different.

All these Rnd() options become confusing. Here's the bottom line: if you want a different random number generated with Rnd() every time it executes within a procedure, don't specify an argument. If you want the same set of random numbers produced from a series of Rnd() function calls (such as a scientific simulation that you want to repeat several times), specify the same negative argument.

No matter which argument you use with Rnd(), it will always produce the *same* set of values between procedure runs unless you provide a Randomize statement before the first Rnd(). In other words, if you run a procedure 20 times, the *same* set of random numbers is guaranteed no matter what argument (or lack of argument) you use with the Rnd() function calls. The Randomize statement *reseeds* the random-number generator—a fancy term meaning that Randomize ensures that Rnd() produces a new set of random values each time you run a program.

If you don't specify a *number* after Randomize, the value of Timer is used (for more information, see Chapter 22, "Using Dates and Times). Timer returns the number of seconds since midnight. Because the value of Timer changes every second, the Randomize statement ensures that a new seed value is used for the next occurrence of Rnd().

> **Tip**
>
> If you want truly random values every time Rnd() appears—even between program runs—put the Randomize statement (with no arguments) at the top of the first procedure in the module and leave off all arguments to Rnd() in subsequent Rnd() calls.

The following procedure always produces the same three random numbers every time you run the procedure (assuming that no Randomize statement has executed yet within the module):

```
Sub RandIt()
  Print Rnd      ' A random number
  Print Rnd(0)   ' The same random number
  Print Rnd(0)   ' The same random number
End Sub
```

If you put a Randomize statement anywhere in the module so that it executes before the three Rnd() statements shown in the preceding example (as done in the following code), you still get the *same* three random numbers due to Rnd()'s zero argument. But at least these numbers differ from program run to program run.

```
Sub RandIt()
  Randomize      ' Ensures that the next Rnd() is random
  Print Rnd      ' A random number
  Print Rnd(0)   ' The same random number
  Print Rnd(0)   ' The same random number
End Sub
```

If you want three different random numbers always generated (as you usually do), don't specify an argument after Rnd(), as in the following:

```
Sub RandIt()
  Randomize      ' Ensures that the next Rnd() is random
  Print Rnd      ' A random number
  Print Rnd      ' A different random number
  Print Rnd      ' Another, still different random number
End Sub
```

You rarely want a random number from 0 to 1, as produced by Rnd(). Using the following simple formula, however, you can generate a random number from low to high (assuming those two variables have been initialized):

You can generate random numbers within a range.

```
Int((high - low + 1) * Rnd + low)
```

Suppose that you want to offer a special discount to a different customer each month. If your customer numbers fall between 1000 and 6456 (meaning that you have a total of 5,456 customers), you can do something like the following:

```
low = 1000        ' Lowest customer number
high = 6456       ' Highest customer number
SpecialCustNum = Int((high - low + 1) * Rnd + low)
```

You can even write games in Visual Basic!

The project named GUESS.MAK on this book's disk contains a number-guessing game written in Visual Basic that uses the random number generator. The computer generates a random number from 1 to 100 and then uses control statements to offer the user hints until the user correctly guesses the number.

The program consists of a series of message and input boxes that prompts the user for a number and displays the too-high, too-low, or correct result of the guess. Figure 19.1 shows the program's message box in progress. The form's Visible property is set to False so the form does not show through the message boxes because there is no reason to show a form in this program. Listing 19.1 contains the Form_Load() procedure that contains the entire program. Even though the form isn't visible, the Form_Load() procedure always executes (in effect, loading an invisible form on the screen).

Fig. 19.1
The opening screen when you run GUESS.MAK.

Listing 19.1   GUESS.MAK's Guessing Procedure

```
Sub Form_Load ()
' Number-guessing game
    Dim Num As Integer
    Dim UserNum As Variant
    Randomize     ' Ensure that the number is always different

    Num = Int(100 * Rnd + 1)    ' Generate a random #, 1-100

    ' Ask the user for the number
    UserNum = InputBox("Welcome to a game! Guess a number...")
    If (UserNum = "") Then      ' User pressed Cancel
        End
    End If
```

```
      ' Keep looping until the user correctly guesses
      Do While (Val(UserNum) <> Num)
        If (Val(UserNum) < Num) Then
          UserNum = InputBox("Too low, try again...", title)
        Else
          UserNum = InputBox("Too high, try again...", title)
        End If
        If (UserNum = "") Then    ' User pressed Cancel
          End
        End If
      Loop
      Beep    ' Ring the PC's bell
      MsgBox "Congratulations! You guessed my number!", 64
      End
   End Sub
```

Data Type Inspection

This part of the chapter extends your knowledge of conditional logic by describing the Is() data inspection functions and offering shortcuts for the If statement. So much programming in Visual Basic or any other language is devoted to looking at data and making decisions about what to do next based on that data.

The Is() and VarType() functions are called *data inspection functions*. These functions inspect the data *types*, not the contents, of variables. Your Visual Basic programs work with many different data types and you sometimes don't know in advance what kind of data you have to work with. Before you make a calculation, for instance, you want to make sure that the data is numeric.

The Is() functions analyze data.

Inspecting with *Is()* Functions

Table 19.2 lists the data inspection functions and offers a description of those functions. Each function receives one argument of the Variant data type. Therefore, if you receive Variant data from a control or another procedure, you can test the data type of the Variant's contents before performing an operation that requires a specific kind of data.

Table 19.2 The *Is()* Data Inspection Functions	
Function Name	**Description**
IsDate()	Determines if its argument is a data type (or if the data can be converted to a valid date)
IsEmpty()	Determines whether its argument has been initialized
IsNull()	Determines if its argument holds a Null value
IsNumeric()	Determines if its argument holds a number (or if the data can be converted to a valid number)

Note

Each Is() function accepts the Variant data type because it must be able to inspect any data and determine what type it is.

Caution

The Is() functions don't change their arguments to different data types. Is() functions only test their arguments for specific data types.

The following code makes sure that a valid date appears in the variable named ADate before calculating the century number:

```
If IsDate(ADate) Then
  Century = ((Year(ADate) - 1) \ 100) + 1
Else
  MsgBox "You entered an invalid date!"
end if
```

Chapter 22, "Using Dates and Times," explains the Year() function, but as you can easily guess, Year() returns the year number of its argument. You must pass Year() a value that contains a date and IsDate() ensures that Year() gets a valid date.

An empty variable is one that hasn't been initialized. Perhaps a procedure has declared a variable but has yet to store data in the variable. Newcomers to Visual Basic often wonder why an empty variable is different from a null value and a zero value. At times, you must have some way to tell whether the user has entered something into fields, and an empty variable signals that nothing has been entered.

The code in Listing 19.2 is rather simple, but it does demonstrate what happens when you apply the IsEmpty() function to variables that have and have not been initialized.

Listing 19.2   Finding Data Types with *Is()*

```
Dim V1 As Variant, V2 As Variant, V3 As Variant, V4 As Variant
V1 = 0      ' Zero value
V2 = Null  ' Null value
V3 = ""     ' Null string
If IsEmpty(V1) Then
  MsgBox "V1 is empty"
End If

If IsEmpty(V2) Then
  MsgBox "V2 is empty"
End If

If IsEmpty(V3) Then
  MsgBox "V3 is empty"
End If
If IsEmpty(V4) Then
  MsgBox "V4 is empty"
End If
```

The only output from Listing 19.2's execution is a message box that displays the following message:

```
V4 is empty
```

You receive this response because all other variables have some kind of data (they were initialized).

Tip

Use IsNull() to see if a control or field on a form contains data. Use IsEmpty() just for variables.

The IsNull() function checks its argument and returns true if the argument contains a Null value. Null is a special value that you can assign to variables to indicate that either no data exists or there's an error (the way that your program interprets a Null value depends on how you code the program). On form controls, a field is considered null if the user enters no data in the field.

Caution

Given that you can assign a `Null` value to a variable like this:

```
AVar = Null
```

you may be tempted to test for a `Null` value like this:

```
If (AVar = Null) Then
```

Be warned, however, that such an `If` always fails. Using `IsNull()` is the only way to check for a `Null` value in a variable.

If your Visual Basic procedure needs to know whether a window's control named `txtHoursWorked` has data, the procedure can check it with an `If` statement as follows:

```
If IsNull(txtHoursWorked) Then
  MsgBox "You didn't enter hours worked!"
Else
  MsgBox "Thanks for entering the hours worked!"
End If
```

The `IsNumeric()` function checks its argument for a number. Any `Variant` value that can be converted to a number returns a true result in the `IsNumeric()` function and a false result otherwise. The following data types can be converted to numbers:

- `Empty`

- `Integer`

- `Long`

- `Single`

- `Double`

- `Currency`

- `Date`

- `String` if the string "looks" like a valid number

The following code asks the user for his or her age using a `Variant` variable. The program displays an error message if the number entered by the user isn't numeric:

```
Dim Age As Variant
Age = InputBox("How old are you?", "Get Your Age")
If IsNumeric(Age) Then
  MsgBox "Thanks!"
Else
  MsgBox "What are you trying to hide?"
End If
```

IsNumeric() is the only function in the class of Is() functions that has a COBOL equivalent. The following COBOL statement mirrors the Visual Basic code that tested Age:

```
IF AGE IS NUMERIC
```

The Is() functions offer a way to test for the data conversion capabilities of a variable or control. Before storing a user's answer in a numeric variable, for example, you can test that variable with the IsNumeric() function before converting the value.

The Multitalented *VarType()* Function

If you need to know a variable's data type, use the VarType() function. Table 19.3 lists the return values from VarType(), and VarType() returns only the nine listed in the table.

Table 19.3 The *VarType()* Return Values

Returned Value	If the Variant Argument Contains This Type
0	Empty
1	Null
2	Integer
3	Long
4	Single
5	Double
6	Currency
7	Date
8	String

The following code contains a Select statement that prints the data type of the AVar variable:

```
Select Case VarType(AVar)
  Case 0: MsgBox "The argument is empty"
  Case 1: MsgBox "The argument is Null"
  Case 2: MsgBox "The argument is Integer"
  Case 3: MsgBox "The argument is Long"
  Case 4: MsgBox "The argument is Single"
  Case 5: MsgBox "The argument is Double"
  Case 6: MsgBox "The argument is Currency"
  Case 7: MsgBox "The argument is Date"
  Case 8: MsgBox "The argument is String"
End Select
```

There is no reason to specify a `Case Else` option because `VarType()` always returns a value from 0 to 8.

An *If* Shortcut: *IIf()*

The `IIf()` function performs a succinct version of a simple `If...Else...End If` statement. Because `IIf()` is a function, `IIf()` returns a value, and the value returned depends on a true or false test that you put at the beginning of `IIf()`. The format of `IIf()` is as follows:

```
IIf(Expression, TrueResult, FalseResult)
```

If the *Expression* is true, the *TrueResult* is returned and if the *Expression* is false, the *FalseResult* is returned. Here is an example of a statement that uses `IIf()`:

```
Ans = IIf(n < 0, "Cannot be negative", "Good data")
```

This statement does the following: if whatever is stored in n is less than 0, the string variable named `Ans` is assigned the string `"Cannot be negative"`. But if n contains any number equal to or greater than 0, the string `"Good data"` is stored in `Ans`. Figure 19.2 illustrates how this `IIf()` works.

Fig. 19.2
Dissecting the
`IIf()` function.

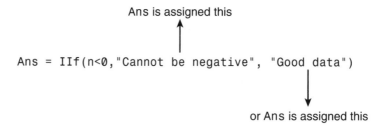

Ans is assigned this

```
Ans = IIf(n<0,"Cannot be negative", "Good data")
```

or Ans is assigned this

To rewrite the previous `IIf()` function as an `If` statement, do the following:

```
If (n < 0) Then
   Ans = "Cannot be negative"
Else
   Ans = "Good data"
End If
```

`IIf()` is more efficient and easier to write than a multiline `If` statement. However, `IIf()` replaces only simple `If` statements, and `If` statements with several lines of code in their bodies must remain regular `If` statements.

> **Note**
>
> The `IIf()` function is similar to Lotus 1-2-3's `@If()` function. If you've ever programmed in C, `IIf()` works a lot like the conditional operator `?:`.

You cannot divide by zero; therefore, the following `IIf()` function returns an average sale price or a `Null` value:

```
AvgSales = IIf(Qty > 0, TotalSales / Qty, Null)
```

You can assume there will be no negative quantities and that `Qty` will always be zero or greater. Remembering that a zero value produces a false result, you can rewrite the previous statement as follows:

```
AvgSales = IIf(Qty, TotalSales / Qty, Null)
```

If you were to rewrite this statement using an `If`, here is how you do it:

```
If (Qty) Then    ' Same as If (Qty > 0)
   AvgSales = TotalSales / Qty
Else
   AvgSales = Null
End If
```

Choosing with *Choose()*

The `Choose()` function can have as many as 14 arguments—more arguments than any other built-in function. Depending on the value of the first argument, `Choose()` returns only one of the remaining arguments. Here is the format of `Choose()`:

```
Choose(IndexNum, Expression [, Expression] ...)
```

Choose()
performs a list
lookup.

After the second argument (*Expression*), you can have as many as 12 more *Expression*s just like the second. The *IndexNum* must be a variable or control that equates to a number from 1 to the number of *Expression*s that are in the function argument list.

If, for example, you need to generate a small table of price codes, abbreviations, or product codes, using Choose() is more succinct than using an If statement. Choose(), however, is more limited in scope than If because Choose() can only select a match based on a single value that has to be equal to 1 through 12.

Caution

Choose() returns Null if *IndexNum* isn't between 1 and the number of *Expression*s.

The first argument of Choose() can be an expression. Therefore you have to adjust the first argument so that it falls within the range of 1 to 13. If the range of values goes from 0 to 4, for example, add 1 to the first argument so that the range goes from 1 to 5.

Suppose that a data-entry screen contains a price code text box control. When the user enters a new product, the user should also enter a price code from 1 to 5, which corresponds to the following codes:

1 Full markup

2 5% discount

3 10% discount

4 Special order

5 Mail order

The following Choose() function assigns to a description label the correct description based on the price code (type this code all on one line):

```
lblDescrip = Choose(txtPriceCode, "Full Markup", "5% discount",
➥"10% discount", "Special order", "Mail order")
```

Conclusion

As you have seen in this chapter, Visual Basic supplies many built-in functions. These functions save you work. You don't have to take the time to write the code yourself; instead, you can call on these functions to do the work for you. You may not use all these functions, but some prove useful as you program with Visual Basic.

Most of the functions described in this chapter are numerically based. Several numeric functions work with integers. These functions primarily round noninteger data to integer results. Other numeric functions exist to convert data from one numeric type to another for you. Several math and trigonometric functions are available in Visual Basic if you ever need them.

This chapter also showed several functions that tested for data values and data types. Using the Is() inspection functions, you can determine if a data value is a date, empty, null, or a number so that your code can operate accordingly. The IIf() function is a shortcut form of the If statement. Although IIf() will never replace the more readable If statement, IIf() is useful (and efficient) for coding simple decision statements that have a true part and a false part. The VarType() function is extremely useful for functions that can work with more than one data type. By first determining the data type, a subsequent If can then select the appropriate code to execute. Finally, the Choose() function returns a value based on an index, simulating the effect of a lookup table. Choose() is more limited, though, to the number of lookup items it can handle.

Whereas this chapter taught you many of the built-in numeric and data-testing functions, the next chapter, "Built-in String Functions," explains how to use Visual Basic's string functions. String data isn't always in the format that you need. The string functions manipulate and change strings according to your needs.

Chapter 20

Built-in String Functions

In the preceding chapter, you learned about the numeric and inspection functions. In this chapter, you learn the built-in functions that work with string data. Some functions described here convert between strings and numbers.

Visual Basic (as well as most of the dialects of the BASIC language) provides better string-handling capabilities than COBOL and other programming languages—including those languages considered to be more powerful than BASIC. The string functions described here are the primary reason for the Visual Basic string power. The user's data-entry text boxes are often comprised of string data. You may need to test and change string values, and you'll find those tasks easy after you learn the string functions.

Here are some of the topics that will be discussed in this chapter:

- Using the Len() length function to find string lengths

- Understanding how CStr(), Str$(), and Val() convert string values

- Learning the ASCII string functions: Chr$(), Asc(), and String$()

- Picking substrings using Left$(), Right$(), and Mid$()

- Understanding how the Mid$() statement can change a string's internal value

- Using search strings for other values with InStr()

- Comparing strings with StrComp()

- Justifying strings with LSet and RSet

- Trimming strings with LTrim$(), RTrim$(), and Trim$()

- Changing case with LCase$() and UCase$()

After you learn the string functions in this chapter, you'll learn how to add your own functions to applications in the next chapter.

Note

Some of the material in this chapter covers statements—not functions. However, the statements taught here work hand in hand with string functions (such as the Mid$() function and the Mid$ statement). This chapter is the most logical chapter in which to group this material.

The *Len()* Length Functions

Len() returns the storage length of its argument.

The Len() function is one of the few functions that can take either a numeric or a string argument. Len() returns the number of memory *bytes* needed to hold its argument. A byte is one character of internal storage. Here are the formats of Len():

    Len(*StringExpression*)

and

    Len(*NumericVariable*)

Notice that Len() accepts any string value (variable, constant, or expression) but only numeric variables—not numeric constants or expressions—work as Len() arguments.

Programmers need to know the internal size each variable takes if there are going to be many variables (several hundred or more) used in the same program. If you're getting ready to store 200 single-precision variables and you want to see how much memory the data takes, you can code the following:

```
Dim testIt As Single
testIt = 0      ' A sample single-precision variable
storage = (Len(testIt) * 200.0)
```

This code stores the amount of memory needed to hold 200 single-precision values.

The Len() function is good to use when you want to know the length of a string. Len() returns the length (number of characters) of the string variable, string constant, or string expression inside its parentheses. The following statement stores 6 for the string length:

```
L = Len("abcdef")
```

> **Tip**
>
> If the string contains Null, Len() returns a value of 0. If the string contains an empty string (" "), Len() returns 0. Testing for an empty string lets you test to see if a user entered data in response to an InputBox() function or a field value.

The String-Conversion Functions

Several conversion functions work with string data. Str$() is a conversion function that can convert numeric arguments to strings so that you can print numbers with MsgBox statements.

Table 20.1 describes each of the string-conversion functions used in code that follows.

Table 20.1 The String-Conversion Functions

Function Name	Description
CStr()	Changes its argument to a string.
Str$()	Converts its numeric argument to a string. If you omit the dollar sign, the argument is converted to a Variant data type.
Val()	Converts its string argument to a number, assuming that a string-like number is passed.

> **Caution**
>
> Although they're easier to use, CStr() and Str$() aren't as powerful as Format$() (which you learned about in Chapter 14, "Formatting Data"). Format$() can do all the work of CStr() and Str$(), and more.

Both CStr() and Str$() convert their arguments to string values. The only difference is that CStr() does *not* add a leading blank before positive numbers converted to strings; Str$() does.

```
Dim s1, s2 As String
s1 = CStr(12345)
s2 = Str$(12345)
MsgBox "***" & s1 & "***"
MsgBox "***" & s2 & "***"
```

Figure 20.1 shows the first message box printed from this code and Figure 20.2 shows the second. Notice that no blank appears before the first string because the CStr() function was used, not Str$().

Fig. 20.1

The message box created with CStr().

The space appears for an implied plus sign

Fig. 20.2

The message box created with Str$().

> **Note**
>
> If you use Str() in place of Str$(), the results are the same, but the resulting value is of the Variant data type and not String.

The ASCII Functions

Appendix A lists the ASCII table used by the ASCII functions. You've already seen how Chr$() converts numbers to ASCII character values. Asc() performs the opposite job of Chr$() because Asc() converts a character to its ASCII number. String$() uses the ASCII table to generate lists of characters.

As a review, by putting a number inside the Chr$() parentheses, you can produce the character that corresponds to that number in the ASCII table. Using Chr$(), you can generate characters for variables and controls that don't appear on your computer's keyboard but that *do* appear in the ASCII table.

> **Note**
>
> If you omit the dollar sign from Chr$(), Chr() returns its argument as a Variant data type.

The Asc() function is the mirror-image function of Chr$(). Whereas Chr$() takes a numeric argument and returns a string character, Asc() requires a string argument and converts the first character of that argument to its corresponding ASCII table number.

The String$() function also uses the ASCII table to do its job. You generally use this function to create strings for output and storage. The String$() function requires two arguments:

String$() replicates the second argument.

- An integer followed by a second argument.

- The second argument can be a character, a character string, or another integer in the range of 0 to 255.

Depending on the values that you pass, String$() has two formats. They are as follows:

```
String[$](Number, ASCIIcode)
```

and

```
String[$](Number, string)
```

If you omit the dollar sign, String() returns a Variant data type. Otherwise, String$() returns a string.

When you enclose an ASCII number inside the Chr$() parentheses (its argument), Visual Basic substitutes the character that matches the ASCII value. Therefore, an A is stored in aVar in the following assignment statement because the ASCII value of A is 65:

```
aVar = Chr$(65)      ' Stores an A in aVar
```

Of course, it makes more sense to store an A directly in the aVar variable in the preceding code's statement. However, what if you want to ask a Spanish question inside a message box? Spanish questions always begin with an upside-down question mark, but there isn't an upside-down question mark on your keyboard. Therefore you can resort to using Chr$() as follows:

```
Dim myQuest As String
myQuest = Chr$(191) & "Se" & Chr$(241) & "or, como esta?"
MsgBox myQuest
```

Figure 20.3 shows the message box displayed from this code.

Asc() returns the ASCII number of the character argument that you give it. The argument must be a string of one or more characters. If you pass a string of more than one character to Asc(), it returns the ASCII number of only the *first* character in the string. For example, the following statement:

```
Print Asc("A"), Asc("B"), Asc("C")
```

produces the following output on the form:

```
65              66              67
```

Look at the ASCII table to see that these three numbers are the ASCII values for A, B, and C.

You also can use string variables as arguments.

```
letter1 = "A"
letter2 = "B"
letter3 = "C"
Print Asc(letter1), Asc(letter2), Asc(letter3)
```

This code produces the same output as the preceding code.

Fig. 20.3

Displaying characters not on the keyboard.

If you pass a string with more than one character to Asc(), Asc() returns the ASCII value of only the first character. Therefore, the statement:

```
aStrVar = Asc("Hello")
```

stores 72 (the ASCII value of H) in the aStrVar variable.

You can use the Asc() function to test for a specific user's response to a question, as done here:

```
ans = InputBox("Do you want to see the name")
If ((Asc(ans) = 89) Or (Asc(ans) = 121)) Then
    MsgBox "The name is " + aName
End If
```

The user can answer the prompt with y, Y, Yes, or YES. The If...Then test works for any of those input values because 89 is the ASCII value for Y and 121 is the ASCII value of y.

The best way to learn the String$() function is to see it used. Consider the following statement:

```
Print String$(15, "a")
```

This statement prints the lowercase letter a 15 times on the form like this:

```
aaaaaaaaaaaaaaa
```

If you use a string of characters (or a string variable) as the second argument, String$() replicates only the first character of the string. If the second argument is an ASCII number (from 0 to 255), String$() replicates the matching ASCII character. The following section of code illustrates this point:

```
Print String$(60, 43)
```

The preceding line produces the following row of 60 + signs:

```
++++++++++++++++++++++++++++++++++++++++++++++++++++++++++++++
```

This section demonstrates how well Visual Basic works with the ASCII table and gives you the power to manipulate characters and strings using their ASCII equivalents.

The Substring Functions

Right$() returns characters from the right side of a string. Right$()'s cousin function, Left$(), returns characters from the left side of a string. The strings can be variables, text controls, or constants enclosed in quotation marks. The Mid$() function takes up where Right$() and Left$() fail; Mid$() enables you to pick characters from the middle of a string.

You can access parts of a string.

> **Note**
>
> Actually, Mid$() can do the same thing as Right$() and Left$(), but Mid$() can accept an extra argument. Also, Right$() and Left$() are easier to use if you need characters from only one side of a string.

Here are the formats of the substring functions:

```
Left$(StringValue, NumericValue)

Right$(StringValue, NumericValue)

Mid$(StringValue, [StartPosition] [, Length ])
```

Both Left$() and Right$() require two arguments: a string variable, constant, or an expression followed by an integer constant or a variable. The integer determines how many characters are stripped from the left or right of the string and returned. If you do not specify the Length argument, Visual Basic uses a length of 1.

The following section of code explains Left$():

```
a$ = "abcdefg"
partSt1 = Left$(a$, 1)    ' Stores a
partSt2 = Left$(a$, 3)    ' Stores abc
partSt3 = Left$(a$, 7)    ' Stores abcdefg
partSt3 = Left$(a$, 20)   ' Stores abcdefg
```

Notice from the last statement that if you try to return more characters from the left of the string than what exists, Left$() returns the entire string and not an error message.

Right$() works in the same manner as Left$() except that it returns the rightmost characters from a string, as shown here:

```
a$ = "abcdefg"
partSt1 = Right$(a$, 1)    ' Stores g
partSt2 = Right$(a$, 3)    ' Stores efg
partSt3 = Right$(a$, 7)    ' Stores abcdefg
partSt3 = Right$(a$, 20)   ' Stores abcdefg
```

The Mid$() function accomplishes what Left$() and Right$() cannot: Mid$() returns characters from the *middle* of a string. Mid$() uses two or three arguments: a string followed by one or two integers separated by a comma. The first integer determines where Mid$() begins stripping characters from the string (the position, starting at 1), and the second integer, if used, determines how many characters from that position to return. If you don't specify two integers, Mid$() uses 1 as the starting position.

Mid$() can pull any number of characters from anywhere in the string. The following example shows how the Mid$() function works:

```
a$ = "QBasic FORTRAN COBOL C Pascal"
lang1 = Mid$(a$, 1, 6)    ' Stores QBasic
lang2 = Mid$(a$, 8, 7)    ' Stores FORTRAN
lang3 = Mid$(a$, 16, 5)   ' Stores COBOL
lang4 = Mid$(a$, 22, 1)   ' Stores C
lang5 = Mid$(a$, 24, 6)   ' Stores Pascal
langsome = Mid$(a$, 16)   ' Stores COBOL C Pascal
```

Mid$() doesn't require a *Length* argument. If you don't specify the length, Visual Basic returns all the characters to the right of the starting position. If the length is longer than the rest of the string, Visual Basic ignores the *Length* argument.

```
city = "Venice"
partial = Mid$(city, 3)        ' Stores nice
city = "Venice"
partial = Mid$(city, 3, 100)   ' Also stores nice
```

The following code includes several of the string functions described in this chapter. The goal of the code is to reverse a certain number of characters stored within a string named S with the number of characters to reverse stored in N. Here is the code:

```
' Accepts: a string, an integer indicating the number of
'          characters to reverse
' Purpose: reverses the specified number of characters in the
'          specified string
' Prints: the modified string

' Reverses the first N characters in S

    Dim Temp As String, Reverse As String, i As Integer
   DIM S as String
   DIM N as Integer
   S = "Visual Basic"
   N = 6

   If (N > Len(S)) Then
     N = Len(S)
   End If

   For i = N To 1 Step -1
       Temp = Temp + Mid$(S, i, 1)
   Next
   Reverse = Temp + Right$(S, Len(S) - N)

   MsgBox Reverse
```

Suppose the reversing code were executed with the following values assigned to S and N:

```
S = "Visual Basic"
N = 6
```

If all goes well, the string named Reverse will hold the characters lausiV Basic (the first 6 characters are reversed).

Here is how the code works. The first statement, Dim, declares two local variables, the first of which (a string variable named Temp) holds the reversed string as it's being built. The second variable, i, is used in the For loop.

The If statement makes sure that the integer used in the code for the reversing count isn't larger than the length of S. It's impossible to reverse *more* characters than what exists in the string. If more characters are attempted, If ensures that the entire string is reversed by changing the length to reverse to the exact length of the string via the Len() function.

The For loop then counts down, from the position to reverse (stored in N) to 1. Using the Mid$() function, Visual Basic concatenates one character from the string, at position N, to the new string being built. As N reaches 1, the reversed characters are sent to the new string. Once all the characters that need to be reversed are reversed, the rightmost portion of the passed string is concatenated *as is* to the reversed characters.

Figure 20.4 shows how the code operates on reversing the first six characters of Visual Basic.

Fig. 20.4
The reversing action.

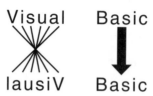

The *Mid$()* Statement

Mid$() **is also a command.**

Mid$() is *both* a command and a function. Mid$() works as a command when it appears on the left side of an assignment statement's equal sign. Mid$() is a function when it appears anywhere else. Here is the format of Mid$():

```
Mid$(String, Start [, Length])
```

When you use Mid$() as a command, Mid$() changes the contents of the string used inside the statement's parentheses. The following code initializes a string with three words and then changes the middle word with Mid$():

```
sentence = "Rain in Spain"
' Change the middle word
Mid$(sentence, 6, 2) = "on"
' After the change
MsgBox "After change: " & sentence   ' Prints Rain on Spain
```

The Mid$() statement gives you a powerful tool with which you can modify the contents of strings. Remember that as long as Mid$() appears on the left of the equal sign, Mid$() is a statement, not a function.

Searching with *InStr()*

InStr() is different from the other string functions you've seen in this chapter. InStr() is a *string-search* function. You use it to find the starting location of a string inside another string. InStr() returns the character position (an integer) at which one string starts within another string.

InStr() has two formats, depending on which version you want to use. Here are the formats:

```
InStr( [StartPosition, ] StringValue1, StringValue2)
```

and

```
InStr( StartPosition, String1, String2, Compare)
```

> **Caution**
>
> Remember that `InStr()` returns an integer, not a string.

`InStr()` looks to see whether the second string expression (`InStr()`'s third argument) exists within the first string expression. If it does, `InStr()` returns the starting position of the string within the first string. `InStr()` assumes a beginning position of 1, unless you override it by including the option integer as `InStr()`'s first argument. If you give `InStr()` a starting value of 5, for example, `InStr()` ignores the first four characters of the search string. If `InStr()` fails to find the first string within the search string, it returns a 0.

If you elect to use the second format of `InStr()`, the *Compare* value should be one of the following.

Compare Value	Description of the Comparison
0	Compare with case-sensitive strings (binary)
1	Compare without case-sensitivity

> **Note**
>
> If you don't specify a *Compare* option (using the first `InStr()` format), Visual Basic performs a binary compare (ABC compares differently from abc) or the compare specified by the `Option Compare` statement (if one exists).

The following lines help clarify `InStr()`'s operation:

```
a = "QBasic FORTRAN COBOL C Pascal"
n = InStr(a, "FORTRAN")         ' Stores 8
n = InStr(1, a, "FORTRAN", 0)   ' Not found due to case
n = InStr(a, "COBOL")           ' Stores 16
n = InStr(a, "C")               ' Also stores 16!
n = InStr(a, "PL/I")            ' PL/I not found, 0 stored
n = InStr(16, a, "FORTRAN")     ' 0 stored FORTRAN doesn't
                                ' exist past column 16
n = InStr(5, a, "PL/I")         ' 0 stored
n = InStr(a, "")                ' NULL is returned
n = InStr(5, a, "")             ' or start value
```

IV

Advanced VB Programming

The fourth assignment doesn't return 22 (the position of the c denoting the C language) because the c is also in COBOL. InStr() returns only the first occurrence of the string.

Comparing with *StrComp()*

As its name implies, the StrComp() function compares strings. Here is the format of the StrComp() function:

```
StrComp(String1, String2 [, Compare])
```

StrCmp() compares the two strings to each other. The comparison method is determined by the Compare value. The Compare value must be either 0 or 1, like that used by InStr() in the previous section.

If the first string compares less than the second string, StrCmp() returns a -1. If the strings are equal, a 0 is returned. If the second string is more than the first string, a 1 is returned.

> **Tip**
>
> Imagine a minus sign between StrCmp()'s first two arguments. If it were possible to subtract two strings, you'd get a negative result if the first string were less than the second. If the strings were equal, subtraction would produce zero. If the second string were less than the first, you'd get a positive result. Knowing this helps you remember the -1, 0, and +1 result of StrCmp().

The following statements store -1, 0, and +1 in the variables a, b, and c:

```
a = StrCmp("ABC", "XYZ")
b = StrCmp("NOP", "NOP")
c = StrCmp("XYZ", "ABC")
```

Customizing Strings

LSet and RSet aren't functions, but this chapter is a good place to introduce these two statements because they're similar to string functions. LSet and RSet let you right- or left-justify strings. Here are the formats of LSet and RSet:

```
LSet String1 = String2
```

and

```
RSet String1 = String2
```

Only apply LSet and RSet to fixed-length strings. The string lengths cannot vary.

After you declare a fixed-length string, you can use LSet to *left-justify* one string into another string. The RSet statement *right-justifies* one string into another string. When a string is left-justified or right-justified, its contents are pushed to the left or right of a string, and any leftover character positions are padded with blanks.

> **Tip**
>
> Remember that both LSet and RSet assign new strings to old strings but don't change the length of the target string from its previous value. Ordinarily, when you assign one string to another, the target string changes length to equal the string that you're assigning to it.

If you attempt to set a new string into another and the new string is longer than the target string, Visual Basic *truncates* (chops off) the extra characters and copies only as many characters as there are in the target string's length.

The string variables in each of the following statements are declared to have 10 characters. The length of that string value determines how many spaces have to be used to pad the strings.

```
Dim string1, string2 As String * 10
string1 = "1234567890"     ' 10 characters
LSet string1 = "left"      ' LSet "left" in those 10 characters
Print "¦"; string1; "¦"    ' Print lines between to see result
string2 = "1234567890"     ' 10 characters
RSet string2 = "right"     ' RSet "right" in those 10 characters
Print "¦"; string2; "¦"    ' Print between lines to see result
```

This section of code produces the following message in the first message box:

```
¦left      ¦
```

Here is the message that then appears in the second message box:

```
¦      right¦
```

Both LSet and RSet give you the ability to justify data within string variables that you may want to print or store on the disk at a later time.

Trimming Strings

The `LTrim$()` and `RTrim$()` functions trim spaces from the beginning or end of strings. `LTrim$()` returns the argument's string without any leading spaces. `RTrim$()` returns the argument's string without any trailing spaces. The `Trim$()` function trims both leading and trailing spaces from a string.

Here are the formats of the string-trimming functions:

    LTrim[$](*StringExpression*)

and

    RTrim[$](*StringExpression*)

and

    Trim[$](*StringExpression*)

> **Note**
>
> If you omit the dollar signs from the function names, the functions can accept a `Variant` data type, including the null value as an argument. If you pass null to the functions, a null value is returned.

`LSet` and `RSet` are statements that work almost like the `LTrim$()` and `RTrim$()` functions, except that instead of trimming spaces from strings, `LSet` and `RSet` insert spaces at the beginning or end of strings.

The following statements trim spaces from the beginning, end, or both sides of strings:

```
st1 = LTrim$("     Hello")    ' Stores Hello
st2 = RTrim$("Hello     ")    ' Stores Hello
st3 = Trim$("   Hello   ")    ' Stores Hello
```

Without the trimming functions, the spaces are copied into the target variables as well as the word `Hello`.

Earlier you learned how to use `Str$()` to convert a number to a string. Because `Str$()` always converts positive numbers to strings with a leading blank (where the imaginary plus sign appears), you can combine `LTrim$()` with `Str$()` to eliminate the leading blank. The first of the following two statements stores the leading blank in `st1`. The second uses `LTrim$()` to get rid of the blank before storing the string in `st2`.

```
st1 = Str$(234)           ' Stores " 234"
st2 = LTrim$(Str$(234))   ' Stores "234"
```

Changing String Case

You've already seen examples of the `LCase$()` and `UCase$()` functions. Just for a review, `LCase$()` returns its argument converted to lowercase and `UCase$()` returns its argument converted to uppercase. No change is made if the `LCase$()` argument contains one or more lowercase letters or if the `UCase$()` argument contains one or more uppercase letters.

You can omit the dollar sign from either function name if you want the return value to be the `Variant` data type.

Conclusion

You now have at your disposal several string functions that manipulate, change, and test string values. Many of the string-function names end with $ to show they can work with string data. Some, such as `Len()`, don't, however.

`Len()` serves as a bridge between the numeric and string functions. It's the only function that works with both string and numeric arguments by returning the length (the number of characters of storage) of the argument.

Many string functions return portions (such as the leftmost or rightmost characters) of strings. These functions are sometimes called the substring functions.

`RSet` and `LSet` aren't functions; instead they act a lot like Visual Basic's `Trim$()` functions by justifying strings within a certain length. You can test to see if one string resides inside another (with `InStr()`), and you can tell if one string is equal to another string (with `StrCmp()`).

Chapter 21

Modular Visual Basic Programming

In the preceding chapters you learned about some of Visual Basic's numeric and string handling functions. In this chapter you learn how to write your own functions. As you program, you create routines that you may need in the future. Perhaps your company calculates a net profit using a unique calculation. Instead of recoding that calculation in every program that uses it, you can save that routine in a module of functions that you write. When you need one or more functions from that module, you can add that module to your application and call any of its functions.

Remember that a module is just a set of Visual Basic code. Each form has its own module file associated with that form. There may be several code procedures inside each module. You now understand the essentials of event procedures. This chapter teaches you about general procedures that you can write and share between modules.

Here are some of the topics that will be discussed in this chapter:

- Understanding how local variable name clashes can occur

- Creating subroutine and function procedures

- Coding argument lists to pass values properly

- Handling the value returned from function procedures

When you begin a new COBOL program, you'll often find a similar COBOL program and modify it to suit your current application's requirements. In the same manner, by using general procedures, you'll take that code reuse to a higher and more productive level, very much like using a CALL statement in COBOL.

About Modular Programming the Visual Basic Way

The Visual Basic programs that you've written so far have contained a series of small event procedures. Also, you have called built-in functions once in a while. If you print a listing of a Visual Basic program (with File, Print), you will see a complete back-to-back listing of all procedures in the program. However, the Visual Basic editor usually keeps the procedures separated in the Code window to maintain a modular approach.

> **Note**
>
> Depending on your version of Visual Basic, you may see more than one procedure at a time inside the Code window.

General procedures aren't linked to events.

If you need to write code that is not connected to an event but is available for execution when your program needs the code executed, you'll have to write a general-purpose procedure.

There are two kinds of general-purpose procedures:

Subroutines

Functions

> **Tip**
>
> Think of general-purpose procedures as mini-programs that your application can execute.

Your program executes event procedures when an event occurs. General-purpose procedures, however, are not executed when events occur. You must somehow request that a general-purpose procedure execute when you need it and this is done through code. Usually, an event procedure will contain code that requests the execution of a general-purpose procedure.

For example, suppose that your payroll application's form contains a command button named `cmdPrintCheck` and has an appropriate caption that the user can understand, such as `Press to Print Check`. The user will press the command button and, in doing so, trigger the automatic execution of `cmdPrintCheck_Click()`.

During the execution of cmdPrintCheck_Click(), the application needs to print a test check to make sure the printer's check paper stock is properly aligned. Two weeks ago, you finished a vendor accounts payable program that also needed a test check-printing routine. As a modular structured programmer, you put that test check-printing routine in its own module and you can now, in the payroll program, add that module to your payroll program and make cmdPrintCheck_Click() execute the test check-printing procedure.

It's important to master simple terminology before learning the specifics of general-purpose procedures. Figure 21.1 shows the process of cmdPrintCheck_Click() *calling* (a term that means *executing*) the general-purpose procedure named TestCheckPrint(). As you can see, execution of cmdPrintCheck_Click() halts for the duration of TestCheckPrint() and resumes execution as soon as TestCheckPrint() finishes. cmdPrintCheck_Click() is the calling procedure and TestCheckPrint() is the *called* procedure.

Calling procedures execute called procedures.

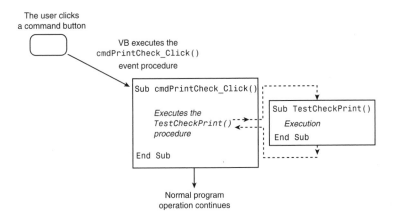

Fig. 21.1
The cmdPrintCheck_Click() procedure calls the general-purpose TestCheckPrint() procedure.

cmdPrintCheck_Click() is an event procedure and TestCheckPrint() is a general-purpose procedure. As mentioned earlier, a general-purpose procedure may be a subroutine or a function. The kind of procedure that you need to write depends on what you want the procedure to do when it completes its execution. Called subroutines execute code, terminate, and return to the calling procedure. Called functions execute code, terminate, and send a value back to the calling procedure.

You can easily relate to the difference between a subroutine and a function now. A subroutine is nothing more than a general-purpose procedure that works just like a COBOL paragraph. The COBOL paragraph finishes its job and returns to the calling code. A function, however, returns a value just like the built-in Visual Basic functions return values. In the following statement:

```
Ans = Int(23.422)
```

Visual Basic executes the called Int() function. Int() returns a value, the integer portion of the argument, and the assignment statement works with that value by assigning the integer value to Ans.

Creating General-Purpose Procedures

Before you create a general-purpose procedure, you must decide where you want to place the code for that procedure. If you want to place the procedure in a stand-alone file, along with a library of other general-purpose subroutine and function procedures that you may want to use in other applications, you'll have to create a new module with the file name extension .BAS (for *Basic*). Follow the steps below to create a new .BAS module:

1. Choose File, New Module from the menu bar. Visual Basic opens the new Code window, as shown in Figure 21.2, and opens a new code module with the default name MODULE1.BAS. Depending on the contents of your AUTOLOAD.MAK project file, you may or may not see the Option Explicit statement.

Fig. 21.2
The Code window for the new code module.

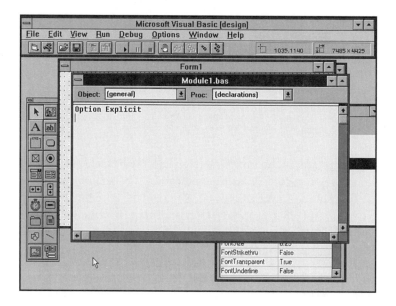

If you type the Option Explicit statement, as shown in Figure 21.2, Visual Basic assumes that you'll declare all variables before you use them. You can put the Option Explicit statement in the (declarations)

section of your AUTOLOAD.MAK code to ensure that the statement appears in all projects that you create.

2. Now you'll add one or more procedures to the new module. Remember that you will be adding either subroutine procedures, function procedures, or both to the module.

   Choose View, New Procedure from the menu bar. Visual Basic displays the New Procedure dialog box shown in Figure 21.3.

Fig. 21.3
Determining the kind of procedure to create.

3. Click Sub or Function to tell Visual Basic the kind of procedure you're creating. Also, you'll have to name the procedure using the same naming rules for variables that you learned in Chapter 10, "Visual Basic's Version of the *DATA DIVISION*." For example, to create a new subroutine procedure named CalcPay, you select Sub and type **CalcPay** for the name of the procedure.

   When you click OK, Visual Basic adds the surrounding wrapper lines for the new procedure that look like this:

   ```
   Sub CalcPay ()

   End Sub
   ```

4. After adding the body of the procedure, you can add additional procedures or save the module file. To save the file, choose File, Save File, and enter a new file name for the module (be sure to retain the .BAS file name extension). For the purposes of this example, you can use the name MYCODE.BAS.

   Now that you've created a new .BAS module, you can call the procedures within the module from whatever application you add the module file to.

Once you've created a module, you can reopen the module at any time from within any application that you've added the module file to. Click the name of the module file in the Project window and open the Code window to add additional procedures or to edit the procedures in the module.

Creating Application-Specific General Procedures

If you want to write general-purpose procedures that are application-specific and not tied to events, follow these steps:

1. Select the form whose Code window will contain the new procedures. As you already know, application Code windows go with form files. By first selecting a form, you'll determine which form's Code window to add code to.

2. Open the Code window.

3. Select the (general) object in the drop-down list box.

4. Choose View, New Procedure to display the New procedure dialog box.

5. Select the kind of procedure you're adding and enter a name for the procedure. When you click the OK command button, Visual Basic adds the wrapper code for the new procedure.

> **Note**
>
> Perhaps adding new procedures seems like a lot of work. It is. When you want to add a new paragraph to a COBOL program, you simply type the paragraph at the end of the code.
>
> If you want to, you can add procedures without first displaying the New Procedure dialog box. Go to the end of any procedure (after an End Sub or End Function statement) and begin typing a new procedure. Be sure that you add the enclosing Sub to the End statements, however. When you use the New Procedure command, you don't have to worry about coding the wrapper code yourself.

The next few sections explain how to use subroutines and the last part of this chapter explains how to write your own functions.

Executing a General Subroutine Procedure

There are two ways to call a general-purpose subroutine procedure. Keep in mind that a subroutine or procedure performs a specific job and then releases control back to the calling procedure. That calling procedure may be an event procedure or another general-purpose procedure. In other words, any kind of procedure can call any other kind of procedure.

The Call statement executes general-purpose procedures. Here is the format of the Call statement:

    [Call] *ProcedureName*

Notice that the keyword Call is optional. Therefore both of the following statements call the subroutine procedure named AProc:

    Call AProc

and

    AProc

> **Caution**
>
> Even though the subroutine has parentheses after its name in the subroutine's open-ing Sub statement, you don't necessarily use the parentheses when you call the subroutine.

Notice that you don't put parentheses after simple subroutine procedures when you call the procedures. If you put the empty parentheses after the subroutine procedure, Visual Basic will generate the error message shown in Figure 21.4. There are times, however, when the parentheses are required. The next section explains why you may have to use parentheses after a subroutine's name.

Fig. 21.4
Oops! Don't use parentheses after the subroutine's name.

Load the project named ADDSAL2.MAK. You created a version of ADDSAL2.MAK (called ADDSALES.MAK) in Chapter 12, "The Math Opera-tions." The original version requested three sales values from a company's three regions and added the region sales together and displayed the total.

In ADDSAL2.MAK, an extra factor is applied to the total sales right after the three regions are totaled. When the user clicks the <u>C</u>ompute Total command button, the following command button event procedure executes:

```
Sub cmdCompute_Click ()
' Convert the three regional sales values
' to numeric quantities before adding them
   lblSales.Caption = Val(txtSales1.Text) + Val(txtSales2.Text) +
   ➥Val(txtSales3.Text)
   Call ComputeFactor
End Sub
```

Notice that the second-to-last line calls a subroutine named `ComputeFactor`. Therefore, the `cmdCompute_Click()` event procedure computes the total and displays the total in the label named `lblSales`. However, immediately after displaying the total, the code in the following subroutine named `ComputeFactor` executes:

```
Sub ComputeFactor ()
' Multiply the total sales by an 8% factor
   lblSales.Caption = Val(lblSales.Caption) * 1.08
End Sub
```

Tip

You'll find the `ComputeFactor` subroutine in the `(general)` object of the Code window.

`ComputeFactor` raises the total just displayed in the label by 8 percent and stores the new factored total in the label once again. The original total appears in the label for such a short time (from the `cmdCompute_Click()` event procedure until the execution of `ComputeFactor`) that the user does not see the value before the second subroutine raises the value by 8 percent.

Calling Event Procedures

As you already know, Visual Basic automatically calls event procedures when the user triggers an event; for example, when the user clicks a command button.

If you need to, your subroutine (and function) procedures can trigger event procedures as well. For example, your application may have the need to generate an event to execute code that the user failed to trigger.

To call an event procedure from a subroutine or from another event procedure, use the `Call` statement just as you do when calling your own general-purpose procedures. Therefore there are two ways that the event procedure named `cmdButton_Click()` may execute: the user can click the command button named `cmdButton` or another procedure can call `cmdButton_Click()` like this:

```
Call cmdButton_Click
```

Arguments

The scoping rules of Visual Basic cause some problems when you begin to write general-purpose procedures. For example, what if you declare a local variable in one procedure, then you want another procedure to modify that variable? The second procedure will not have access to the first procedure's local variable.

The following sections explain how to get around the seemingly limited local variable problem.

Local data is much safer than global data. In previous chapters, you learned that the location of the variable's declaration is the primary determinant of a variable's scope. When you're writing an application with other programmers, using local variable data becomes even more critical. If two of you use many global variables, and you both happen to declare the same global variable, a name clash occurs.

Locals eliminate name clashes.

For example, if two global variables named `gi` (which stands for global variable) are declared, one for your procedure and one for someone else's, Visual Basic cannot know which `gi` you are initializing when you enter the following:

```
gi = 20
```

If you use a global variable and another programmer on the same application uses a local variable with the same name, the local variable always *hides the scope* of the global. Hiding the scope means that the local variable is used during that procedure and not the global variable. When the local variable goes out of scope (which means the variable is no longer available for use once the procedure ends), the global variable is then used whenever the name is referred to.

Figure 21.5 helps illustrate what happens when a local and a global variable have the same name. The best way to avoid name clashes and scoping considerations is to not use two or more variables with the same names. Nevertheless, there will be times when the same name does appear twice (possibly because of multiple programmers or you forget which variable names you've already used) and you must understand the ramifications of declaring multiple variables with the same name.

Fig. 21.5

Local variables overshadow globals with the same name.

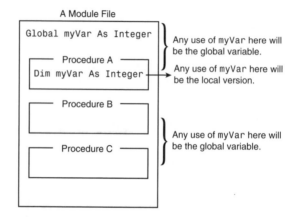

A Module File

Global myVar As Integer

Any use of myVar here will be the global variable.

Procedure A

Dim myVar As Integer

Any use of myVar here will be the local version.

Procedure B

Procedure C

Any use of myVar here will be the global variable.

Tip

Use only local variables to solve these problems: name clashes and local variables hiding the scope of globals.

Two or more local variables residing in two separate procedures can have the same name. You never have a problem with name clashes if you stick to local variables. The variables are known only in the procedures in which they *should* be known, and one procedure does not have improper access to other procedures' variables.

Why Share Data?

Local: Good; Global: Usually not good.

Given the premise that local variables are good, and given the fact that local variables can be used (in any manner) *only* in the procedure in which you declare them, a problem arises when you need to write modules that contain more than one procedure. Just because procedures are separate doesn't always mean they need to work with separate data.

One procedure may declare a work variable that *another* procedure is supposed to print the value of. Yet, if the variable is local in the first procedure, the second procedure cannot access the variable. Neither subroutine procedures nor function procedures can use each other's local data—at least, not until you set up a sharing mechanism between them.

As with built-in functions with which you pass data (called *arguments*, as you learned earlier in the book), your procedures can pass data between each other. By passing data, you maintain the advantage of local variables while allowing more than one procedure access to the same data.

When two procedures share local data, one procedure (the calling procedure) passes data to the second procedure (called the *receiving procedure*) as in Figure 21.6. If the receiving procedure computes or modifies a value that the calling procedure needs, the receiving procedure can return that value back to the calling procedure. The sole purpose of parentheses that follow subroutine and function names is to hold the argument lists that you pass to other procedures.

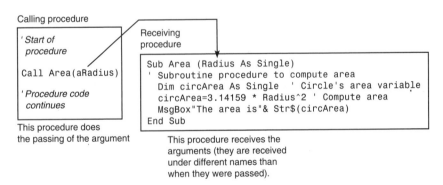

Fig. 21.6
Calling procedures pass local data, and receiving procedures work with that data.

Notice that you must declare the data type of the received argument. If you must pass and receive more than one argument, separate the passed arguments, and the received arguments (along with their declared data types) with commas. The following statement passes three values to a subroutine procedure named aProc:

```
Call aProc (x, y, s)
```

The following statement may appear at the start of the aProc subroutine procedure:

```
Sub aProc (x As Single, Value As Double, s As String)
```

Notice that the receiving arguments do not have to be named the same names as the passed arguments. The aProc subroutine procedure uses Value but is still working with the contents of the procedure's y variable.

Subroutine procedures look and work just like function procedures, with the following two exceptions:

- Subroutine procedures do not return values back to the calling procedure whereas function procedures do, as you'll see a little later in the section called "Functions Return Values."

Be careful with parentheses when calling subroutines.

- When you call subroutine procedures using the Call statement and pass arguments, you must use parentheses around the argument list. If you omit the Call keyword, you *don't* use parentheses around the argument list. Never use Call to call function procedures.

Suppose you wrote a procedure that called an Area subroutine and needed to pass to Area a radius value. Both of the following statements are identical:

```
Call Area(aRadius)
```

and

```
Area aRadius        ' No parens if no Call
```

It's easy to remember when you use parentheses around subroutine-calling argument lists: Remember, *if no Call, then no parens.*

Note

The built-in functions' arguments work *exactly* like subroutine procedure arguments, but because you didn't write the code for the built-in functions, you don't have to know as much about the functions' internals. The Left$() function, for example, cannot work with your local variables directly. That is why you must pass to Left$() the string that you want to work with and the number of characters to return from the left of that string. Left$() (although you can't see the code because it is already compiled and built into the Visual Basic language) receives your arguments into its own local variables, works with those variables, and then returns a value back to your program.

Suppose you're writing a set of programs for your company's consolidation. A requirement of each program is that you initially inform the user which method of depreciation is currently in use based on a code. In other words, you'll retrieve a depreciation code from a file upon starting the program and inform the user of the depreciation method with a message box. The following simple Select Case works well:

```
Dim Message As String
Select Case DepCode
  Case 1: Message = "Straight-line method"
```

```
      Case 2: Message = "Accelerated method"
      Case 3: Message = "Double-declining balance method"
      Case 4: Message = "Sum of the digits method"
      Case Else: Message = "The depreciation code is in error"
   End Select
   MsgBox Message
```

You find yourself needing to code this Select Case in every accounting program that you write for the consolidation effort. Instead of rewriting this code in each program, you decide to put the code in a stand-alone module named CONSOLID.BAS. Inside CONSOLID.BAS is the following general-purpose subroutine procedure:

```
Sub DispDepCode (DepCode As Integer)
   Dim Message As String
   Select Case DepCode
     Case 1: Message = "Straight-line method"
     Case 2: Message = "Accelerated method"
     Case 3: Message = "Double-declining balance method"
     Case 4: Message = "Sum of the digits method"
     Case Else: Message = "The depreciation code is in error"
   End Select
   MsgBox Message
End Sub
```

By putting this subroutine procedure in the module file, you only need to type the code *one time*. Afterwards, any application that you add the module file to (via the Project window) will be able to call the subroutine with this statement:

```
Call DispDepCode(DepCode)
```

By Address, by Value

Look back again at Figure 21.6. The Area subroutine does not change the value of Radius. The subroutine uses the value in the area calculation. If, however, Figure 21.6's Area procedure were to change the value of the argument in its code, the corresponding variable in the calling procedure *is also changed*. In all subroutines called and coded as Area (refer to Fig. 21.6), the subroutines are passed data that the subroutines have the power to change. Therefore, when the calling procedure regains control, the value (or values) that the calling procedure sent as an argument to the called subroutine may be different than before the call.

Arguments are passed by *address,* meaning that the passed arguments can be changed by their receiving procedure. If you want to keep the receiving procedure from being able to change the calling procedure's arguments, you must pass the arguments by *value.* To pass by value, precede any and all argument-receiving variable lists with the ByVal keyword. You can also enclose the passed arguments in parentheses.

In the following procedure (not all of the code is shown so that you can focus on the arguments), the variable r is received by address while v is received by value in the second procedure (RS()). If the RS() receiving subroutine changes r, the CS() calling subroutine r is changed as well. If the RS() receiving subroutine changes v, however, the CS() calling subroutine's argument retains its original value.

```
Option Explicit        ' All variables to be explicitly declared

                       ' Calling subroutine is next
Sub CS()
   Dim r, v As Variant ' Declare local variables named r and v
   Dim i As Integer    ' To hold the return value of function

                       ' Preliminary code would go here

   Call RS(r, v)       ' Call the subroutine and pass r and v
End Sub

                       ' Receiving subroutine is next
Sub RS(r As Variant, ByVal v As Variant)
                       ' Received r by address and v by value
                       ' Preliminary code would go here
   r = 50              ' Change r in both functions
   v = 20              ' Change v just here
End Sub
```

Instead of specifying the ByVal keyword in the receiving subroutine's argument list, you can put parentheses around the calling function's variable v to force it to pass by value like this:

```
Sub RS(r As Variant, (v) As Variant)
```

> **Note**
>
> In this book you often see more than one procedure listed after each other, with the declarations section appearing before the procedures as shown here. In most versions of Visual Basic's Code window, the procedures are windowed so that you see only one at a time. If you print a module on the printer, the declarations section and the procedures print together.

Functions Return Values

You'll recall that the built-in functions optionally accept arguments and always return values. There must be some way to capture or use that return value when you call the function. For example, you'd never code the following:

Functions receive and return data.

```
Right$(lblName, 3)    ' Invalid
```

The `Right$()` function does accept two arguments as shown, but `Right$()` also returns a value (the rightmost three characters of `lblName`). You can either assign the return value to another variable or control like this:

```
last3 = Right$(lblName, 3)
```

or you can display the value like this:

```
MsgBox Right$(lblName, 3)
```

The subroutine procedures that you write do not return values. That is why you can call the `Area()` function discussed in the previous section like this:

```
Area RadiusValue
```

The reason that you write a function instead of a subroutine is because you want that function to return a value. No matter how many arguments that a function accepts, a function only returns a maximum of one value. There are two primary differences in format between a subroutine and function procedure as well:

Functions that you write begin with `Function` *`FunctionName()`* and end with the `End Function` statement.

To return the function's value, assign the return value *to the name of the function.*

The example code in Listing 21.1 returns a value back to the calling procedure from a function named `RF()`. By studying this example, you can see how to specify the return value. The function named `RF()` returns a value because `RF` is assigned a value. When `CF()`'s execution resumes, the return value of `CF()` is assigned to `RF()`'s variable named `i`.

Listing 21.1   A Function Name Holds the Function's Return Value

```
                              ' Calling function is next
    Function CF ()
       Dim r, v As Variant    ' Declare local variables
       Dim i As Integer       ' To hold the return value

                              ' Preliminary code goes here

       i = RF(r, v)           ' Call the function and pass r
                              ' and v -- i gets RF()'s return
    End Function


    Function RF (r As Variant, ByVal v As Variant)
                              ' This is the receiving function
                              ' Received r by address and v by value
                              ' Preliminary code goes here
       r = 50                 ' Change r in both functions
       v = 20                 ' Change v only in this function
       RF = r * i             ' Return a value
    End Function
```

In Listing 21.1, the variable r is received by address while v is received by value in the second procedure, RF(). If the RF() receiving function changes r, the CF() calling function's r is changed as well. If the RF() receiving function changes v, however, the CF() calling function's argument retains its original value.

Instead of specifying the ByVal keyword in the receiving function's argument list, you can put parentheses around the calling function's variable v to force the function to pass by value.

Figure 21.7 illustrates how Listing 21.1 sends its arguments and returns a value. Study the figure to make sure you understand how the calling and returning mechanism works.

Fig. 21.7

Pass three values and return one value.

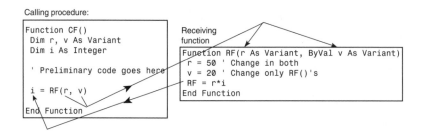

A function procedure does not *have* to return a value, but you must assign the function call to a variable, even if you do nothing with that variable, as if the called function were written to return a value.

Caution

Remember that a procedure can be passed many arguments, but a procedure can return only one value. Although the capability to return a maximum of one value may seem limiting, all the built-in functions can return a maximum of only one value. The limitation of a single return value poses no problem. Only function procedures can return values, not subroutine procedures. If the calling procedure calls another procedure that returns a value, the calling procedure must do something with that return value (such as print it or save it).

Here's one last short but useful function. You'll recall from Chapter 19, "Built-in Numeric Functions," that the Rnd function returns a random value between 0 and 1. Usually, however, you need a random number in a range of values. Therefore, you can write a function named RndRange() that receives the beginning and ending value of the range of randomness requested and then returns a value within that range.

```
Function RndRange(Low As Integer, ByVal High As Integer)
                ' Return a random number between Low and High
   RndRange = Int((high - low + 1) * Rnd + low)
End Function
```

If another procedure needed a random number from 1 to 6 (perhaps to simulate a dice roll), the procedure can call RndRange() like this:

```
DieRoll = RndRange(1, 6)
```

Conclusion

This chapter delved more deeply into the global versus local variable issue. Now, you should understand how global name clashes can occur and even if you don't *fully* understand why using local variables is important, at least you know to use them everywhere you can and what can happen at times if you don't use locals. You are fighting years of having a COBOL WORKING STORAGE division that contains global values available throughout the rest of the program.

Visual Basic lets you use the same local variable name in different procedures. Although you don't want to overdo the practice, using the same variable name for simple processing, such as counters in `For` loops, helps document your code and simplifies the number of variables that you have to keep track of. If, however, you have a global variable and a local variable with the same name, the local variable always hides the global's value.

If you use local variables, provide a way for your procedures to communicate with each other. When one procedure contains local data that another procedure needs to work with, pass the data from the calling procedure to the receiving procedure. The receiving procedure (if it is a function procedure) can return a single value back to the calling procedure. Normally, arguments pass by address. If you pass arguments by value (using the `ByVal` keyword), the receiving procedure cannot change the calling procedure's arguments.

In the next chapter you learn how to use the date and time functions. In most programming, you have to track the time and date when data is entered, printed, or updated.

Chapter 22

Using Dates and Times

This chapter teaches you about several functions that aren't available in most other languages. Time and date functions are critical when processing data, especially in a business environment. It may be important to record exactly when a field was edited for security or verification purposes. Also, all printed reports should have the time and date (often called *date-* and *time-stamping*) printed on the report, showing exactly when the report was produced. In a stack of similar reports, the time and date stamps show when the most recent report was printed.

To understand Visual Basic's time and date functions, you simply need to understand how Visual Basic stores time and date information internally. Until now, this book has said very little about time and date values. The time and date material warrants an entire chapter because its usage is so important and Visual Basic's support for time and date values is so superior to that of other languages.

Here are some of the topics that will be discussed in this chapter:

- Mastering the time and date retrieval functions: Date(), Now(), and Time()

- Using the time and date setting statements: Time and Date

- Using Timer to compute time between events

- Dating arithmetic with DateAdd(), DateDiff(), and DatePart()

- Learning how to work with serial time and date values

Starting with the 1974 ANSI COBOL standard language, you could use the DATE and TIME keywords to accept date and time values into data fields with the following statements:

```
ACCEPT TODAY-DT FROM DATE.

ACCEPT WS-TIME FROM TIME.
```

The `TODAY-DT` data field would then hold a date in the `YYMMDD` format and `WS-TIME` would hold a time value in the `HHMMSS` format. Visual Basic's time and date functions go far beyond the minor support given by COBOL, as you'll see in this chapter.

> **Note**
>
> In Chapter 20's discussion of string functions, you learned the `Mid$` statement because of its relation to the `Mid$()` function. Some of the material in this chapter consists of statements, not solely functions; however, the statements work hand in hand with the time and date functions, and this chapter is the most logical chapter in which to group all this material.

> **Note**
>
> You may have already heard of the *timer* control. Chapter 23, "Loose Ends: Scroll Bars and Timer Controls," discusses the timer control. The timer control doesn't relate directly to Visual Basic's time and date features discussed in this chapter.

Retrieving the Date and Time

Visual Basic can read your system's clock.

Inside most computers there's a clock and calendar that Visual Basic programs can read. The `Time$()` and `Date$()` functions support the access of your system clock and calendar through function calls. The dollar sign in each name is optional.

`Date$()` returns the system date in the `Variant` data type number 8 (see Chapter 19's discussion on the `VarType()` function) in the following format:

mm-dd-yyyy

mm is a month number (from 01 to 12), *dd* is a day number (from 01 to 31), and *yyyy* is a year number (from 1980 to 2099).

`Time$()` returns the system time in the `Variant` data type number 8 in the following format:

hh:mm:ss

hh is the hour (from 00 to 23), *mm* is the minute (from 00 to 59), and *ss* is the second (from 00 to 59).

> **Tip**
>
> Check at least weekly to make sure your computer's time and date values are set properly. You can check the time and date (and optionally enter new values) by typing the date or time at the DOS prompt before starting Windows and Visual Basic. You also can set the time and date from within Windows or from within a Visual Basic program, as shown in the next section, "Setting the Date and Time."

The Date$() function uses a 24-hour clock. Therefore all hours before 1:00:00 in the afternoon equate to a.m. time values, and all times from 1:00:00 until midnight have 12 added to them, so 14:30 is 2:30 in the afternoon. The military and several foreign countries use a 24-hour clock. To Visual Basic, 6:45 p.m. and 18:45 are the same time values.

The Now() function (a dollar sign is not allowed with Now()) combines the Date$() and Time$() functions. Now() returns a Variant data type 7 in the following format (if you were to print the Variant return value of Now() using Print, you'd see this format):

```
mm/dd/yy hh:mm:ss [AM][PM]
```

The placeholder letters correspond to those of the Date$() and Time$() functions with the exception that a 12-hour clock is used and either AM or PM appears next to the time.

The most important thing to remember about all three time and date retrieval functions is that they return time and date values that are stored internally as double-precision values (with enough precision to ensure that the time and date values are stored accurately), and it's up to your program to format the values and output them in whatever format you want. The best way to format time and date values is to use Format$() using the time and date formatting characters you learned in Chapter 14, "Formatting Data."

A cousin to Visual Basic called *Visual Basic for Applications* (which goes by the abbreviation *VBA*) requires parentheses when you use these functions in certain programs. Therefore if you get used to using the parentheses, your time and date retrievals always work whether or not you're working in Visual Basic.

Include the parentheses for consistency.

The Date$() and Time$() functions are extremely easy to use. Assuming that it's exactly 9:45 in the morning, the statement:

```
currentTime = Time$()
```

stores 9:45:00 in the variable currentTime.

If the date is 2/23/94, the statement:

```
currentDate = Date$()
```

stores 2/23/94 in the variable `currentDate`.

The statement:

```
currentDateTime = Now()
```

stores 2/23/94 9:45:00 AM in the variable named `currentDateTime`.

If it's exactly 9:45 at night, this statement:

```
currentTime = Time$()
```

stores 21:45:00 (subtract 12 to get the p.m. time in 12-hour format) in the variable named `currentTime`.

As you've seen, it is extremely easy to request that Visual Basic look at your computer's internal clock and calendar and return the time and date values found there.

Setting the Date and Time

Using `Date` and `Time` statements, you can set the computer's current date and time from within Visual Basic. Once you set your computer's date and time, they remain in effect until you change them again.

`Date` and `Time` statements can't have parentheses following them (the parentheses serve to distinguish between the functions and the statements), unlike the `Date$()` and `Time$()` functions and the equivalent `Date()` and `Time()` functions.

Here are the formats of the `Date` and `Time` statements:

```
Date[$] = dateExpression
```

and

```
Time[$] = timeExpression
```

The *Date* Expression Format

If you don't specify the trailing dollar sign (`Date`), you must enter the *dateExpression* as an unambiguous date value and the *dateExpression* must be a string or date data type. Each of the following sets the computer's current date to November 21, 1996:

```
Date = 11/21/1996

Date = 11/21/96
```

```
Date = November 21, 1996

Date = Nov 21, 1996

Date = 21-Nov-1996

Date = 21 November 1996

Date = 21 November 96
```

Although Visual Basic allows a lot of freedom in your *dateExpression*, the date must be a valid date between January 1, 1980 and December 31, 2099, or Visual Basic generates an error. (Wonder what those Visual Basic programmers will do in the year 2100?)

Caution

Depending on the Short Date format you've set in the International section of your Windows control panel, you may have to specify the date in your country's format if it differs from the American order described here.

If you do specify the trailing dollar sign (Date$), you can enter only the *dateExpression* in the following formats:

```
Date$ = 11-21-96

Date$ = 11-21-1996

Date$ = 11/21/96

Date$ = 11/21/1996
```

Because there are several date formats, Visual Basic recognizes just about any way you're used to specifying the date.

The following procedure tells the user the currently set date and lets the user enter a new date if the internal time and clock settings are incorrect. If the user presses Enter without entering a date, the previous date is kept.

```
Sub enterDate ()
  Dim newDate As Variant
  MsgBox "The current date is " & Date$     ' Calls function
  newDate = InputBox("What do you want to set the date to?")
  If IsDate(newDate) Then
    Date$ = newDate
  End If   ' Don't do anything if a new good date isn't entered
  MsgBox "The date is now " & Date$

End Sub
```

The IsDate() function ensures that the value entered by the user is a valid date. If the user didn't enter a valid date, the IsDate() function returns a false value.

Check all time and dates entered by the user!

The *Time* Expression Format

If you don't specify the trailing dollar sign (`Time`), you can enter *timeExpression* as either a 12-hour clock or a 24-hour clock with quotation marks, as follows:

```
Time = "1:30 PM"
```

or

```
Time = "13:30"
```

Again, your International setting in the Windows control panel controls how you specifically set the date for your country. If you do specify the trailing dollar sign (`Time$`), you can enter *timeExpression* in any of these formats:

```
hh
hh:mm
hh:mm:ss
```

hh is an hour number (from 00 to 23), *mm* is a minute number (from 00 to 59), and *ss* is a second number (from 00 to 59). You must use a 24-hour clock with `Time$`.

Tip

Using these `Time$` formats, you change only what you want to change. If the time zone has just turned to daylight savings time, for example, you can change just the hour.

Here is a time-setting procedure that works like the date-setting procedure shown in the previous example:

```
Sub enterTime ()
  Dim newTime As Variant
  MsgBox "The current time is " & Time$     ' Calls function
  newTime = InputBox("What do you want to set the time to?")
  If IsDate(newTime) Then
    Time$ = newTime
  End If   ' Don't do anything if a good time isn't entered
  MsgBox "The time is now " & Time$

End Sub
```

Note

Notice that the `IsDate()` function returns true or false if a good or bad time value is passed to it.

Consider the user's input shown in Figure 22.1. Why does Visual Basic indicate that an error occurred as soon as the user clicks OK?

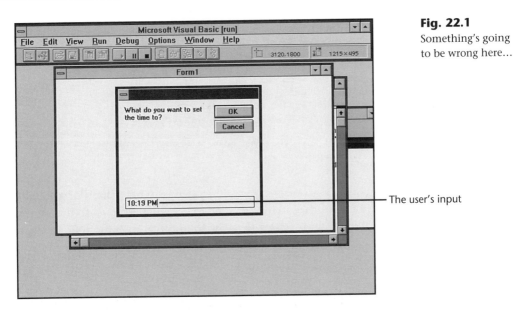

Fig. 22.1
Something's going to be wrong here...

The user's input

The `IsDate()` function thinks that the user entered a valid time value because the time shown in the figure is correct. Remember, though, that `Time$` requires a 24-hour clock and no AM or PM value is allowed. You can use the `Right$()` function to see if the user entered AM or PM.

Computing the Time between Events

The `Timer` function returns the number of seconds that have passed since your computer's internal clock struck midnight. Here is the format of `Timer`:

```
Timer
```

As you can see, `Timer` doesn't use parentheses. You may wonder why you'd ever need to know how many seconds have elapsed since midnight. The `Timer` function is perfect for timing an event. Suppose that you want to ask the user a question and determine how long it takes the user to answer. First, save the value of `Timer` before you ask the question. Then subtract that value from the value of `Timer` *after* the user answers. The difference of the two `Timer` values is the number of seconds the user took to answer.

Here is a procedure that determines how long the user takes to answer a math question:

```
Sub CompTime ()
' Procedure that times the user's response
  Dim Before, After, timeDiff As Variant
  Dim mathAns As Integer
  Before = Timer     ' Save the time before asking
  mathAns = InputBox("What is 150 + 235?")
  After = Timer      ' Save the time after answering
  ' The difference between the time values
  ' is how many seconds the user took to answer
  timeDiff = After - Before
  MsgBox "That took you only" & Format$(timediff, " ## ")
➥& "seconds!"
End Sub
```

The following procedure is a waiting procedure that pauses for a certain number of seconds as determined by the argument passed to the subroutine. If the calling routine passes 10 to the subroutine, the procedure loops for 10 seconds.

```
Sub pauseSecs (secs As Long)
' Procedure that pauses for a specified time
  Dim procEntryTime As Long
  procEntryTime = Timer    ' Get the time now
  Do
      ' Nothing is really done but wait...
  Loop Until (Timer >= procEntryTime + secs)
  Beep
End Sub
```

Note

Technically, Visual Basic lets you use parentheses after Timer() to indicate that Timer is a function. However, as soon as you press Enter at the end of typing a statement that uses Timer(), Visual Basic immediately deletes the parentheses, leaving only Timer from the statement that you just typed! Obviously, Visual Basic prefers that you leave off the parentheses.

More Date Arithmetic

The Timer() function does find the number of seconds between time values, but only for those time values that fall on the same day. The DateAdd(), DateDiff(), and DatePart() functions begin where Timer() leaves off. Table 22.1 lists the three date arithmetic functions and their descriptions.

Table 22.1   The Date Arithmetic Functions

Function Name	Description
DateAdd()	Returns a new date after you add a value to a date
DateDiff()	Returns the difference between two dates
DatePart()	Returns part (an element) from a given date

All three date arithmetic functions can work with the parts of dates listed in Table 22.2. Table 22.2 contains the parts of dates these functions work with as well as their *interval values* that label each part. You use the interval values inside the date arithmetic functions to get to a piece of a date or time.

Table 22.2   The Time Period Interval Values

Interval Value	Time Period
yyyy	Year
q	Quarter
m	Month
y	Day of year
d	Day
w	Weekday (Sunday is 1, Monday is 2, and so on for Day(), Month(), Year(), and DateDiff())
ww	Week
h	Hour
n	Minute (careful, not m)
s	Second

The *DateAdd()* Function

Despite its name, the DateAdd() function works with both dates and times (as do all the date functions) because the date passed to DateAdd() must appear in the VarType number 7 (date) format, and the number 7 VarType data type holds both date *and* time values. Here is the format of DateAdd():

```
DateAdd(interval, number, oldDate)
```

The *interval* must be a value (in string form) from Table 22.2. The *interval* you specify determines what time period is added or subtracted (a second value, minute value, or whatever). The *number* value specifies how many of the *interval* values you want to add. Make the number positive if you want to add to a date, and make the number negative if you want to subtract from a date. The *oldDate* is the date or time from which you want to work (the date or time you are adding to or subtracting from). The DateAdd() function then returns the new date.

Suppose you buy something today with a credit card that has a 25-day grace period. The following statement adds 25 days to today's date and stores the result in intStarts:

```
intStarts = DateAdd("y", 25, Now())
```

Note

If you're adding days to a date, you can use "y", "d", or "w" for the interval.

Suppose you work for a company that requires you to work 10 years before you can be vested in the retirement program. The following statement adds 10 years to your start date and stores the vested date in vested:

```
vested = DateAdd("yyyy", 10, hired)
```

Notice that the interval string value determines the value that DateAdd() adds to the date.

Note

If you don't specify a year in any of the date arithmetic functions, the current year (the year set on the system's clock) is returned.

The *DateDiff()* Function

The DateDiff() function returns the difference between two dates. The difference is expressed in the *interval* that you specify. Here is the format of DateDiff():

```
DateDiff(interval, date1, date2)
```

Caution

DateDiff() returns a negative value if *date2* is more than *date1*.

The following statement determines how many years an employee has worked for a company:

```
beenWith = DateDiff("yyyy", hireDate, Now)
```

The *DatePart()* Function

The DateDiff() function returns a part of a date (the part specified by the *interval*). With DatePart(), you can find what day, month, week, or hour (or whatever other interval you specify) on which a date falls. Here is the format of DatePart():

```
DatePart(interval, date)
```

The following statement stores the day number that an employee started working:

```
DatePart("w", hireDate)
```

Working with Serial Date and Time Values

Although you may not know about *serial values*, the time and date functions you have been reading about all work with serial values. A serial value is the internal representation of a date or time, stored in a VarType 7 (the Date data type) or a Variant data type. Visual Basic actually stores these values as double-precision values to ensure the full storage of time and date so that accurate date arithmetic can be performed.

All time and date functions work with serial values.

> **Note**
>
> Visual Basic uses 8 bytes (characters) of storage for double-precision values, which is enough room to hold the combined time and date value.

The functions explained in this section—DateSerial(), DateValue(), TimeSerial(), TimeValue(), Day(), Month(), and Year()—convert their arguments to serial dates, which really means they take their arguments and convert those arguments to the internal date format.

Here is the format of the DateSerial() function:

```
DateSerial(year, month, day)
```

year is an integer year number (either 00 to 99 for 1900 to 1999 or a four-digit year number) or expression, *month* is an integer month number (1 to 12) or expression, and *day* is an integer day number (1 to 31) or expression. If you include an expression for any of the integer arguments, you specify the number of years, months, or days from or since a value. To clarify the serial argument expressions, use the following two `DateSerial()` function calls, which return the same value:

```
d = DateSerial(1990, 10, 6)
```

and

```
d = DateSerial(1980+10, 12-2, 1+5)
```

The `DateSerial()` functions ensure that your date arguments don't go out of bounds. For example, 1992 was a leap year, so February of 1992 had 29 days. However, the following `DateSerial()` function call appears to produce an invalid date because February, even in leap years, cannot have 30 days:

```
d = DateSerial(1992, 2, 29+1)
```

Nothing is wrong with this function call because `DateSerial()` adjusts the date evaluated so that d holds `March 1, 1992`, one day following the last day of February.

> **Note**
>
> You probably will not deal with constant values such as 29+1 in your expressions. Your `DateSerial()` function calls will hold expressions with variables and field values from which you need to produce dates.

The `DateValue()` function is similar to `DateSerial()` except that the `DateValue()` function accepts a string argument, as the following format shows:

```
DateValue(stringDateExpression)
```

The *stringDateExpression* must be a string that Visual Basic recognizes as a date (such as those for the `Date$` statement described earlier in this chapter). If you ask the user to enter a date a value at a time (asking for the year, then the month, and then the day), you can use `DateSerial()` to convert those values to an internal serial date. If you ask the user to enter a full date (that you capture into a string variable) such as **October 19, 1996**, `DateSerial()` converts that string to the internal serial format needed for dates.

The `TimeSerial()` and `TimeValue()` functions work the same as their date counterparts. If you have three individual values for a time of day, `TimeSerial()` converts those values to an internal time format (the `Variant` or `VarType 7`). Here's the format of `TimeSerial()`:

```
TimeSerial(hour, minute, second)
```

The `TimeSerial()` function accepts expressions for any of its arguments and adjusts those expressions as needed, just as the `DateSerial()` function does.

If you have a string with a time value (maybe the user entered the time), the `TimeValue()` function converts that string to a time value with this format:

```
TimeValue(stringTimeExpression)
```

The `Day()`, `Month()`, and `Year()` functions convert their date arguments (of `Variant` or the `VarType 7` data type) to a day number, month number, or year number. These three functions are simple. Here are their formats:

```
Day(dateArgument)

Month(dateArgument)

Year(dateArgument)
```

In addition, the `Weekday()` function returns the number of the day of the week (see Table 22.2) for the date argument passed to it.

Pass today's date (found with `Now()`) to the `Day()`, `Month()`, and `Year()` functions, as shown here:

```
d = Day(Now())

m = Month(Now())

y = Year(Now())
```

The current date's day of week number (see Table 22.2), month number, and year number are respectively stored in the three variables `d`, `m`, and `y`.

The following function contains an interesting use of the `DateSerial()` function:

```
Function Weekend(anyDate As Variant)
' Accepts: a Date value
' Purpose: Calculates the first weekend day of the month
'          following the specified date
' Returns: the calculated date
   Dim Result
   Result = DateSerial(Year(anyDate), Month(anyDate) + 1, 1)
   If (Weekday(Result) <> 1) And (Weekday(Result) <> 7) Then
      DueDate = Result
   Else
      ' Adjust until the next Saturday
      DueDate = Result + (7 - Result)    ' Increment to Saturday
   End If

End Function
```

When this function is called, it's passed a date value stored in the `Variant` or `VarType 7 Date` data type. As the remarks tell, the function computes the day number of the first weekend of the next month (the first weekend day of the month following the argument).

Notice that the `DateSerial()` function is passed the date broken into three parts. The `Year()` and `Month()` functions are used (and a `1` is used as the day to trigger the beginning of the month) so that `1` can be added to the month number. In effect, the statement:

```
Result = DateSerial(Year(anyDate), Month(anyDate) + 1, 1)
```

breaks the date into three parts, increments the month, and then assembles the new date with the new month number and stores the new date in the variable named `Result`.

The `If-Then` test uses the `Weekday()` function to see if the first day of the next month falls on a Saturday or Sunday. If the day isn't Saturday or Sunday, the code increments the day number by the number of days needed to reach Saturday's day number.

Conclusion

Apparently, Microsoft thought well ahead when designing Visual Basic so that you have available to you every time and date function you'll ever need. This chapter taught you the time and date functions and the related statements that enable you to retrieve and set the date and the time.

Almost all of the functions and statements described in this chapter work with an internal `Variant` or `VarType 7 Date` data type. Visual Basic recognizes most formats of dates, and whether or not you spell out a month name when entering a date is up to you because Visual Basic can interpret the date.

The next chapter, "Loose Ends: Scroll Bars and Timer Controls," describes two additional controls: the scroll bar control and the timer control. You can combine timer control and this chapter's time and date functions to achieve real-time program processing such as the display of a digital clock on the screen or timing games.

Chapter 23

Loose Ends: Scroll Bars and Timer Controls

This chapter explains two Visual Basic features that have no equivalents in the COBOL language. Actually, there is no language that includes scroll bars, except for the newer versions of languages that support graphical environments such as Windows. Until the advent of graphical environments, there was simply no need for scroll bars.

There are ways to duplicate Visual Basic's timer control in many languages, but none offers consistency and ease of programming. The timer control lets you force execution of events at specific times, such as every few seconds or minutes. For example, Microsoft Word for Windows offers an *auto save* feature that saves your document every few minutes. Word uses a control identical to Visual Basic's timer control to trigger the automatic saving of the document.

Here are some of the topics that will be discussed in this chapter:

- Learning the parts of vertical and horizontal scroll bars

- Understanding how to operate scroll bars

- Placing and resizing scroll bars

- Programming your scroll bars to control portions of a running application

- Adding the timer control to your applications for controlling timed events

- Running an application that uses both a scroll bar and the timer control

About Scroll Bars

There are two scroll bars.

Visual Basic supports both vertical and horizontal scroll bars. You've probably seen both in your use of Windows. The choice of which to use depends on your application. If the user scrolls through a list of items (such as in a scrolling, drop-down list box), the vertical scroll bar is the best scroll bar to use. If the user selects from a range of values, often the horizontal scroll bar works best.

Before learning how to program with scroll bars, you should master the language of scroll bars. Figure 23.1 shows a vertical scroll bar and labels the important parts.

Fig. 23.1
All scroll bars have similar properties.

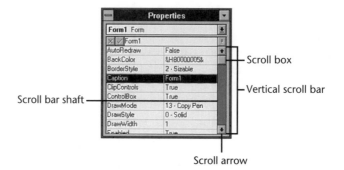

Scroll box

Vertical scroll bar

Scroll bar shaft

Scroll arrow

> **Note**
>
> The moving scroll box is sometimes called the *elevator bar* because the scroll box moves up and down the scroll bar the way that an elevator moves from floor to floor. Sometimes, the elevator bar is also called a *thumb button*.

Scroll bars provide your users with the graphical ability to run through a list of items or a range of values. By clicking on the scroll bar arrows or dragging the scroll box, the user is, with the mouse, moving forward or backward in the selection range. If the user clicks within the scroll bar shaft (the blank area on either side of the scroll box), the scroll box moves forward or backward more than one value. For example, if a vertical scroll bar represents a list of possible age values from 18 to 105, clicking the bottom or top scroll arrow increases or decreases the scroll bar value by one unit. Clicking on the scroll bar shaft increases or decreases the scroll bar value by more than one unit.

Tip

Think of a scroll box as the mercury in a thermometer. As the mercury moves up and down the thermometer, the temperature reading increases and decreases. As the user moves the scroll box throughout the scroll bar, the value of the scroll bar control changes. You can use that value in your programs.

Clicking a scroll arrow changes the scrolling unit by a value (often, but not always, by one unit) known as the *small change*. Clicking a scroll bar shaft changes the scrolling unit by a larger value known as the *large change* value. You'll learn more about these two values when you study the scroll bar properties later in this section.

Note

As you will soon learn, you control how many units each scroll represents.

When you place scroll bars on your Form window, you can resize the scroll bars. They can extend as far (lengthwise) and as wide as you need, covering whatever area you need them to cover.

Caution

Although you can change the thickness of scroll bars, you should be careful about resizing the width of scroll bars. The scroll bars become bloated looking and can take away from the effectiveness of your user interface.

Resist the temptation to widen scroll bars too much. When you widen scroll bars too much, they take on a comical appearance that takes away from their effectiveness. Also, Visual Basic keeps you from thinning scroll bars too much. You can only slightly decrease the thickness of scroll bars from their default width. If you were to make scroll bars too thin, the user could not easily see or use the scroll box.

Figure 23.2 shows several scroll bars of different thickness and lengths. I'm sure you'll agree that a standard thickness (such as the vertical scroll bar at the left and the horizontal scroll bar on the bottom of the figure's window) appears more professional and effective than the larger ones.

Fig. 23.2
Various sizes of
scroll bars.

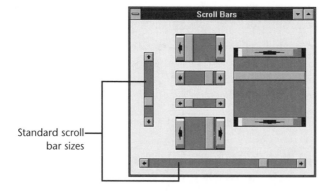

Standard scroll
bar sizes

You cannot change the color of scroll bars. Actually, the scroll bars have
fewer properties than most of the controls. Table 23.1 describes the most
common properties with which you'll work.

Table 23.1	Common Scroll Bar Properties
Property	**Description**
Enabled	Determines whether the user's scroll bar actions will be respected or ignored. Through coding, you may want to disable (set the Enabled property to False) the scroll bar until the user first responds to another event.
Height	Describes the height, in twips, of the scroll bar.
Index	Contains the subscript value of the scroll bar if you store the scroll bar in a control array with other scroll bars.
LargeChange	Indicates the number of units the scroll bar is to change when the user clicks within the scroll bar shaft.
Left	Indicates the number of twips from the window's left edge to the scroll bar's upper-left corner.
Max	Dictates the maximum value returned from the scroll bar (the maximum allowed value is 32767). When the user sends the scroll box to the bottom of a vertical scroll bar or to the far right of a horizontal scroll bar, the scroll bar returns the Max value. All other values fall between Max and Min.
Min	Dictates the minimum value returned from the scroll bar (the minimum allowed value is –32768). When the user sends the scroll box to the top of a vertical scroll bar or to the far left of a horizontal scroll bar, the scroll bar returns the Min value. All other values fall between Max and Min.
MousePointer	Describes the shape of the mouse when the user moves the mouse over the scroll bar.

Property	Description
Name	Contains the name of the scroll bar. Prefix the name with hsb or vsb indicating a horizontal or vertical scroll bar.
SmallChange	Indicates the number of units the scroll bar is to change when the user clicks either scroll arrow.
Top	Indicates the number of twips from the top of the window to the top of the scroll bar.
Value	Describes the current value of the scroll bar. When the scroll box is at its minimum point, the Value will be the same as the Min property. When the scroll box is at its maximum point, the Value will be the same as the Max property. When the scroll box is between the two end points, the Value will fall somewhere between Min and Max.
Visible	Indicates whether or not the user can see and access the scroll bar. The Visible property can be either True or False.
Width	The width, in twips, of the scroll bar.

Tip

By setting an initial Value property, you can control the initial placement of the scroll box when the user first sees the scroll bar.

Figure 23.3 shows where the horizontal and vertical scroll bars appear on the toolbox. Again, you'll almost always lengthen the scroll bars after you place them on the form.

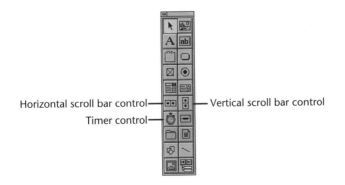

Horizontal scroll bar control —— Vertical scroll bar control
Timer control ——

Fig. 23.3
The scroll bar controls.

The Change event is by far the most common event used with scroll bars. If a scroll bar is named hsbBar1, that scroll bar's event procedure you're most likely to program will be named hsbBar1_Change().

Looking at a Simple Scroll Bar Application

This book's disk contains a simple scroll bar application that demonstrates how scroll bars work. The application uses a horizontal scroll bar to change the background color value of a label. To see this application, load and run the project file named SCROLL.MAK.

Figure 23.4 shows the running SCROLL.MAK application. As the user clicks the left and right scroll arrows, the color in the large label changes. Also, the value of the lower label's QBColor() function call changes as well. The QBColor() is a built-in Visual Basic function that accepts an argument between the values of 0 and 15 and generates one of 16 colors accordingly. Change the scroll bar to see how its various color changes occur.

Fig. 23.4
Running
SCROLL.MAK.

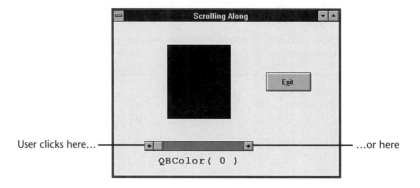

If you stop the program and analyze the scroll bar properties, you'll find the following key values:

LargeChange: 3

Max: 15

Min: 0

Name: hsbBar1

SmallChange: 1

Value: 0

Run the program once again, and you can see how these property value settings affect the use of the scroll bar. The scroll bar initially begins at 0 due to
the Value property. In response to the initial value, the scroll box initially
appears in the scroll bar shaft's leftmost minimum position.

As the user changes the scroll bar, the hsbBar1_Change() event procedure
executes. Here is that complete procedure:

```
Sub  hsbBar_Change()
' Each time the user changes the scroll bar setting,
' this procedure executes. The background color of
' the big label changes to the color value of the
' scroll bar and the text label containing the
' color value updates as well.
  lblColor1.BackColor = QBColor(hsbBar1.Value)
  lblDesc1 = "QBColor(" & Str$(hsbBar1.Value) & " )"
End Sub
```

The scroll bar can return only an integer value from 0 to 15 due to the corresponding Min and Max scroll bar property settings. The QBColor() function
accepts any value from 0 to 15 as well (the limits of QBColor() were the sole
reason for the scroll bar's Min and Max settings to begin with). Each time the
user scrolls the scroll box, the value of the scroll bar, from 0 to 15, is used to
change the background color of the large color label with the following assignment statement from hsbBar1_Change():

```
  lblColor1.BackColor = QBColor(scrBar1.Value)
```

The description in the text label at the bottom of the screen also changes to
reflect the new scroll bar value. The scroll bar's integer value is first converted
to a string value and then appended to a description of the QBColor() function in the following assignment statement from hsbBar1_Click():

```
  lblDesc1 = "QBColor(" & Str$(hsbBar1.Value) & " )"
```

If you run the program and click the scroll arrows, the QBColor() function
call updates by a value of 1 (either incremented or decremented, depending
on the direction of the scroll bar change) due to the value of SmallChange
(which is 1) in the property settings. If, however, you click in either scroll
bar shaft area, the QBColor() function call updates by a value of 3 due to the
value of LargeChange (which is 3) in the property settings.

List Boxes Take Care of Themselves

When you add list boxes to your applications, whether or not those list boxes are combo, simple, or drop-down list boxes, Visual Basic automatically takes care of the scroll bars for you if there are more items in the list than will fit in the list box.

For example, Figure 24.5 shows two list boxes. The list box on the right has a vertical scroll bar but not the list box on the left. The property settings for the list boxes are the same. However, the list box on the right contains more items (added with the AddItem method) than will fit in the list box; the list box on the left doesn't need scroll bars because it's large enough to display all of its items.

If the application later adds additional items to the list box on the left, Visual Basic will automatically add scroll bars—eliminating the need for you to worry about them. Therefore you'll be adding scroll bars for controlling values that *you or the user* need to control (as in SCROLL.MAK). When the user needs to indicate a value from a large range of values, and there's a strong possibility the value will change, a scroll bar makes it easy for the user to specify values and change the values when needed.

Fig. 23.5
You never have to
add scroll bars to
list boxes.

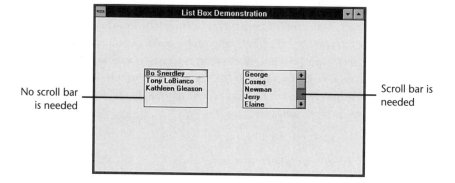

No scroll bar
is needed

Scroll bar is
needed

The Timer Control

A *millisecond* is
one-thousandth
of a second.

The timer control is the stopwatch icon in the toolbox (refer to Fig. 23.3). The timer control is responsible for triggering a Timer event. Instead of the Timer event waiting for the user to trigger it by moving the mouse, clicking, or some other action, the Timer event occurs every time a certain interval of time passes—regardless of what the user is doing. A Visual Basic timer interval is one millisecond. Therefore you can execute an event procedure every millisecond if you so desire. (Given today's computer speeds, an event every millisecond would bring your PC to a screeching halt!)

If you've ever written PC programs before and needed to pause the computer for a second or more, you may have attempted to write nested loops such as the following:

```
For i = 1 To 1000
  For j = 1 To 500
    ' This loop wastes time
  Next j
Next i
```

By the time the 1,000 outer loops each process 500 inner loops, a little wasted time passes on the computer. Perhaps you'll add even another outer loop and print a message or ring the PC's bell every few seconds. There are two big problems with writing such timing loops:

- Timing loops work differently on every computer whose speed differs from your computer's speed.

- Such timing loops are meaningless in the multi-user mainframe world because your program doesn't have complete (or in a GUI's case, even partial) control of the computer's environment.

Suppose that you're writing a game program that needs to count down the seconds to the end of the game. Not only do you have to design your loops to update the screen every second, but such loops are dependent on several other factors such as memory management, which may take place in the background.

The timer control eliminates the need for such timing loops that rarely work as expected. Using the timer control, you'll be able to write procedures that you know will execute after a preset time interval passes. You won't have to manage this interval of time—Visual Basic takes care of the time management for you.

The timer control doesn't work like the other controls—not only in the way that it times intervals and automatically triggers events, but in the way it resides on your form. Instead of studying a prewritten example supplied with this book, you'll understand how to use timer controls much better if you create an application from scratch.

Creating a Digital Clock

The following steps walk you through the creation of an on-screen digital clock. The digital clock application is extremely easy to create, thanks to the timer control's help. Follow these steps to get started:

1. Open a new project.

2. Double-click the timer control to place a timer control in the middle of your Form window. Your screen should look like the one shown in Figure 23.6.

Fig. 23.6
After placing the timer control.

The placed timer control—

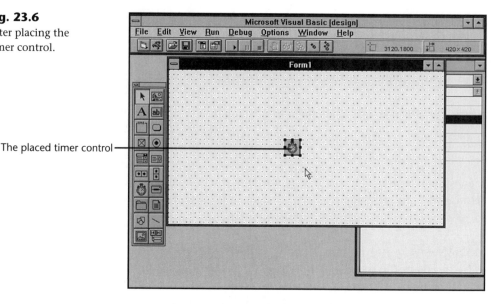

3. Move the timer control to the lower-left corner of the Form window. In moving the control, you're simply clearing the middle of the Form window so you can see other controls that you place there.

The user never sees the timer control.

The timer control *never appears on the user's form*. More accurately, the user never sees the timer control. Even though you place the control on the form, and even though you can move the control to a different location on the form, the control remains invisible to the user when the user runs the program. The timer control, unlike the other controls, is *not* a user control.

If you attempt to resize the timer control by dragging any of its eight resizing handles, the control immediately snaps back to its original size when you release the mouse button. There is no need to resize the timer control since the control never physically appears in the end user's application. Table 23.2 lists the property values and descriptions available for the timer control.

As you can see in Table 23.2, there are very few property values needed for the timer control because the control never appears to the user.

4. Press F4 to view the Properties window. Change the Interval property to **1000**. This interval ensures that a timer event occurs every second (a second is equal to 1,000 milliseconds and the Interval value is set in milliseconds).

5. Change the Name property to **tmrSecond**.

6. Click in the white area of the Form window and change the Caption property to **Digital Clock**.

7. For completeness, change the form's Name property to **frmClock**.

Table 23.2 The Timer Control's Property Values	
Property	**Description**
Enabled	Describes whether or not the control is currently in operation. The values for Enabled are True and False.
Index	Contains the control array subscript if the timer control is part of an array of timer controls.
Interval	Indicates the number of milliseconds until the timer control is to trigger the next Timer event.
Left	Describes the position of the timer control's left edge from the Form window's left edge.
Name	Contains the name of the timer control. Use the prefix tmr.
Tag	Every control has a Tag property, but this book has yet to address the Tag. The Tag acts like a second name that you can use to identify the control when you pass a control to a procedure through the procedure's argument list.
Top	Describes the number of twips from the top of the timer control to the top edge of the Form window.

You've now added the timer and forced a timer event to occur every second. The name of the timer control is now tmrSecond. Therefore the timer event procedure will be named tmrSecond_Timer(). You'll write the code for tmrSecond_Timer() as soon as you add the clock face.

Adding the Clock Face

This application's clock will be digital, so its *face* is really just a display of hours, minutes, and seconds in the format *hh:mm:ss*. If your Windows International setting isn't set for North America, your display may differ slightly from this example. Follow these steps to add the digital readout:

1. Double-click the label control to add one to your application.

2. Press F4 to change the property settings of the label. Use the following values (you will have to type **72** for the FontSize property because 72 will not appear in the scrolling list of available font sizes):

   Alignment: **2 - Center**

   BorderStyle: **1 - Fixed Single**

   FontName: **Courier New**

   FontSize: **72**

   Height: **1695**

   Left: **240**

   Name: **lblTime**

   Top: **960**

   Width: **6855**

> **Note**
>
> You may not have the Courier New font on your system. If not, choose another font. Make sure that you enter a FontSize of 72 for whatever font you select so the digital readout is large enough to be seen clearly.

3. Add an exiting command button by double-clicking the command button on the toolbox and setting the following command button property values:

   Caption: **E&xit**

   Height: **495**

   Left: **3000**

   Name: **cmdExit**

   Top: **3360**

   Width: **1215**

After setting the command button's property values, your screen should look like the one shown in Figure 23.7.

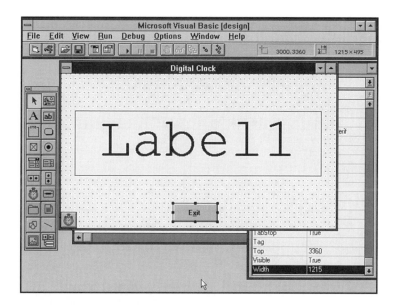

Fig. 23.7
The digital readout
is large.

Connecting the Timer Event

You must now code the event procedure that Visual Basic automatically runs
during every timer interval. Double-click the timer control on the Form window. Visual Basic opens the tmrSecond_Timer () procedure. Listing 23.1 contains the procedure that you should type.

Listing 23.1   The Timer's Event Procedure

```
Sub tmrSecond_Timer ()
' This timer event procedure occurs every second.
' This timer event procedure occurs every 1000 milliseconds.
' Updates the value of the label that holds the current time.
  lblTime.Caption = Time
End Sub
```

The remarks consume more space than the body of the function. The function simply assigns the time (using the Time function that you read about in
the previous chapter) to the large label's caption.

Double-click the cmdExit command button and insert the End statement in
the cmdExit_Click() procedure body so the user can easily terminate the
application when the user gets tired of seeing the clock on the screen.

**Always supply
an easy exit.**

If you now run the program, you'll see the large digital clock shown in Figure 23.8. Every second, the clock's time changes to reflect the new time.

That's because the timer's event procedure executes every 1,000 milliseconds as controlled by the timer control's Interval value.

Fig. 23.8
You can set your
watch by it!

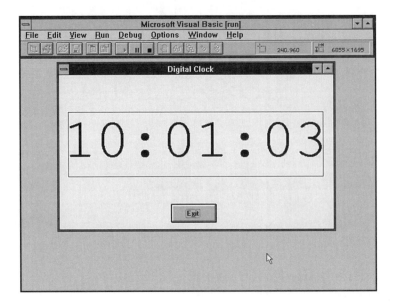

Fig. 23.8
You can set your
watch by it!

This digital clock application appears on this book's disk under the project name of DIGITAL.MAK.

Combining the Timer and Scroll Bar Control

This book's disk contains a simple and even rather silly application stored under the project named TIMEBEEP.MAK. When you load and run the application, you'll see the single beeping window with the scroll bar and labels shown in Figure 23.9.

Fig. 23.9
A simple applica-
tion with a scroll
bar and timer.

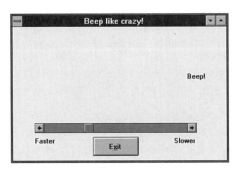

If you study the application, you'll see that it combines the use of a scroll bar with the timer control and Rnd() function to produce a controllable beeping sound with Beep! messages flashing on and off randomly in the form's background.

One of the tricky parts of the program involves the flashing of the Beep! labels. There are a total of 12 labels stored in a label control array named lblBeep. As you can see from the Form window in Figure 23.10, these labels appear all over the top portion of the form. The labels' initial Visible properties are set to False so the labels don't all appear when the user starts the application.

Fig. 23.10
The label control array contains 12 labels.

When the program first begins executing, the Form_Load() procedure, shown next, forces an initial execution of the scrBeep_Change() procedure (the procedure controlled by the scroll bar's change).

```
Sub Form_Load ()
' Force an initial beep
  Call scrBeep_Change
End Sub
```

The code for scrBeep_Change() only sets the timer's Interval property as shown here:

```
Sub scrBeep_Change ()
' Change the interval of the beep to a random
' value and select a new "Beep!" label to display
  Dim ctr As Integer
  tmrTimer.Interval = scrBeep.Value * 50
End Sub
```

When the application first begins, the timer's Interval property is set to 1 in the Properties window. Therefore when the form initially loads and executes this scrBeep_Change() procedure, the timer's Timer() event procedure, named tmrTimer_Timer(), executes every 50 milliseconds. Listing 23.2 contains the code for the tmrTimer_Timer() event procedure.

IV

Advanced VB Programming

Listing 23.2 Controlling the Beeping and Flashing

```
Sub tmrTimer_Timer ()
' Make a different "Beep!" label visible
  Dim ctr As Integer
  For ctr = 0 To 11
    lblBeep(ctr).Visible = False ' Set all to invisible
  Next ctr
  ' Select a random "Beep!" label to make visible
  ' from the control array of 12 labels
  ctr = Int(Rnd * 12)  ' From 0 to 11
  lblBeep(ctr).Visible = True
  ' Beep the speaker before leaving this interval
  Beep
End Sub
```

The For loop simply hides the appearance of all 12 Beep! labels. The Rnd function call and subsequent assignment of the ctr variable then display one of the 12 random Beep! labels from the control array. Depending on the value of the random number, the end result is that a new Beep! label turns on what was previously off. Of course, if the same random number from 0 to 11 appears twice in a row, the Beep! label doesn't flash during that 50-millisecond interval. Finally, the Beep statement at the end of the subroutine procedure forces the beep sound that you hear every 50 milliseconds.

There's one final procedure that you need to see. Here's what happens when the user changes the scroll bar:

```
Sub scrBeep_Change ()
' Change the interval of the beep to a random
' value and select a new "Beep!" label to display
  Dim ctr As Integer
  tmrTimer.Interval = scrBeep.Value * 50
End Sub
```

The scroll bar value, whose property settings ensure that the value ranges from 1 to 11, controls the speed of the beeping. The tmrTimer_Timer() procedure executes every interval, and scrBeep_Change()'s assignment statement changes the interval to match the scroll bar's value.

Conclusion

This chapter taught you how to program scroll bars and use the timer control. You first learned how the two scroll bars—the horizontal and vertical scroll bars—operate. You also learned the names of the parts of the scroll bars.

The Properties window determines a lot about how the scroll bar operates and sends values to the program. Through the Properties window, you set the scroll bar's minimum and maximum range values as well as the initial setting for the scroll bar. Once you set the properties, the user changes the scroll bar, causing a scroll bar `Change()` event procedure to execute.

The timer control is one of the most unique Visual Basic controls that you'll use. The timer control doesn't appear on the form but rather controls a specially timed event procedure through the Interval property. The Interval property controls how many milliseconds pass before the next timer event occurs.

With the timer control, you can pause the program for a preset time period. Such pauses might give the user a chance to read something on the screen. You can give the user a certain time period to answer a question and take a default answer if the user doesn't answer within a certain time period.

Now that you've mastered almost everything there is to master with Visual Basic's screen tools, it's time that you learned how Visual Basic controls the printer. As you'll see in the next chapter, you already know a lot about one of the primary printer commands, `Print`. With `Print`, you can write to both the printer and the screen.

Chapter 24

Controlling the Printer

This chapter teaches you how to produce printed output from Visual Basic. Your days of COBOL's line-oriented PIC clauses are over. Visual Basic offers several ways to send output to the printer.

Not all of your printed output will be reports. Sometimes, you may want to print a program listing so you can scan through a module's procedures debugging a program over coffee instead of over the keyboard. Also, Visual Basic lets you print copies of forms.

Here are some of the topics that will be discussed in this chapter:

- Printing code and forms for any and all modules within an application

- Using the Printer object for output

- Understanding how Windows Print Manager eliminates tedium from your program's printing chores

- Learning the various properties and methods associated with the Printer object

- Specifying various font attributes to print

- Controlling the number of lines that you print on each page

- Warning the user before sending printed output to the user's printer

Printing Program Information

When working on a program, you can print either a form, a textual description of a form, or code from the current module or from the entire project. To see how to print such information, load this book's CHKIF2.MAK project so that you can follow along.

Print program information during development.

You'll be printing form and code information during your program's development for documentation purposes or for debugging sessions. You may also participate in *structured walkthroughs* in your company where you and your peers analyze program code to improve its correctness and maintainability. Everybody at a structured walkthrough needs a listing of all code and forms so the committee can review the program's elements.

When you want to print program information, use the File, Print (Ctrl+P is the access key) command. Visual Basic needs to know exactly what you want to print. When you choose the File, Print command, Visual Basic displays the dialog box shown in Figure 24.1.

Fig. 24.1
Visual Basic needs to know what you want to print.

You must fill in an option on both sides of the Print dialog box. Visual Basic needs to know if you want to print only from the current form or from every form in the entire module. Select Current for the current form file or All if you want to print from the entire module. Also, select Form if you want to print a visual copy of your form (or forms if you first selected All).

> **Note**
>
> Depending on your printer and its resolution, your printed forms may not be extremely clear when you print visual representations of the forms.

Select Form Text if you want to print a textual description of the form. The textual description lists every property value from the form. Listing 24.1 contains the description that you'll get if you print the form text for the CHKIF2.FRM form.

Listing 24.1   The Form Text that Describes CHKIF2.FRM

```
CHKIF2.FRM - 1

VERSION 2.00
Begin Form frmIf
   Caption        =    "Working With If Statements"
```

```
ClientHeight      =     4020
ClientLeft        =     585
ClientTop         =     1515
ClientWidth       =     7350
Height            =     4425
Left              =     525
LinkTopic         =     "Form1"
ScaleHeight       =     4020
ScaleWidth        =     7350
Top               =     1170
Width             =     7470
Begin CommandButton cmdExit
   Caption        =     "&Quit"
   Height         =     495
   Left           =     5160
   TabIndex       =     7
   Top            =     2640
   Width          =     1215
End
Begin CommandButton cmdPress
   Caption        =     "&Press Me"
   Height         =     495
   Left           =     5160
   TabIndex       =     0
   Top            =     1320
   Width          =     1215
End
Begin CheckBox chkTravel
   Caption        =     "I travel a lot"
   Height         =     495
   Left           =     1080
   TabIndex       =     3
   Top            =     3000
   Width          =     1455
End
Begin CheckBox chkVote
   Caption        =     "I vote"
   Height         =     495
   Left           =     1080
   TabIndex       =     2
   Top            =     2040
   Width          =     1215
End
Begin CheckBox chkOver18
   Caption        =     "I'm  over 18"
   Height         =     495
   Left           =     1080
   TabIndex       =     1
   Top            =     1080
   Width          =     1455
End
Begin Label lblMess
   Caption        =     "Your personalized message:"
   Height         =     615
   Left           =     3000
   TabIndex       =     6
```

(continues)

Listing 24.1   Continued

```
            Top             =   1320
            Width           =   1215
        End
        Begin Label lblUserMsg
            BackColor       =   &H00C0C0C0&

CHKIF2.FRM - 2

            BorderStyle     =   1   'Fixed Single
            Height          =   735
            Left            =   3120
            TabIndex        =   5
            Top             =   2160
            Width           =   1575
        End
        Begin Label Label1
            BorderStyle     =   1   'Fixed Single
            Caption         =   "Using If Statements"
            FontBold        =   -1  'True
            FontItalic      =   -1  'True
            FontName        =   "MS Sans Serif"
            FontSize        =   12
            FontStrikethru  =   0   'False
            FontUnderline   =   0   'False
            Height          =   375
            Left            =   2280
            TabIndex        =   4
            Top             =   360
            Width           =   2655
        End
    End
End
```

Select Code if you want to print a listing of the form's or forms' (if you selected All) code. Listing 24.2 shows a listing of CHKIF2.FRM's code module. Instead of showing just a single procedure at a time, as most versions of Visual Basic do in the Code window, the printed listing contains all the procedures sequentially following each other in the listing so you can look at the entire program at once.

Listing 24.2   The Printout of CHKIF2.FRM's Code

```
CHKIF2.FRM - 1

Sub cmdExit_Click ()
    End
End Sub

Sub cmdPress_Click ()
```

```
' Builds a short or long user message
' depending on the user's selected statistics.
' The message appears in a label on the screen
'
' Create a line feed/carriage return variable
  Dim NewLine As String
  NewLine = Chr$(13) & Chr$(10)

' Empty the message string
  lblUserMsg.Caption = ""        ' Assign a null string

  If chkOver18.Value Then
    lblUserMsg.Caption = "You're an adult!"
  End If

  If chkVote.Value Then          ' Append a string
    lblUserMsg.Caption = lblUserMsg.Caption & NewLine
    lblUserMsg.Caption = lblUserMsg.Caption & "You get involved!"
  End If

  If chkTravel.Value Then        ' Append a string
    lblUserMsg.Caption = lblUserMsg.Caption & NewLine
    lblUserMsg.Caption = lblUserMsg.Caption & "You're lucky!"
  End If

End Sub
```

Note

Visual Basic makes sure that its printed reports break correctly on each page when printing to your printer.

Close the CHKIF2.MAK project now because you will not need the project for the rest of the chapter.

Printing a Form at Runtime

Visual Basic includes a printer output method named PrintForm. Here is the format of PrintForm:

```
frmName.PrintForm
```

You may want to print a form for manual data-entry. Data-entry personnel can later take the manually filled forms and enter that data directly into a Visual Basic application that displays the same form on-screen.

As with printing visual forms from the File, Print command, your visually printed forms may not always print clearly due to the resolution of your printer.

The *Printer* Object

Visual Basic includes a special object named `Printer` that represents your printer. Unlike non-GUI applications, neither you nor Visual Basic has to know anything about your printer. Visual Basic writes to this generic `Printer` object. Instead of talking directly to your printer, however, `Printer` represents the Windows Print Manager. Print Manager is a program that knows all about your printer and makes sure that the information sent to `Printer` by Visual Basic comes out correctly for your printer. Figure 24.2 illustrates how the `Printer` object collects Visual Basic program output, routes that output to the Windows Print Manager, and Print Manager converts that output to output that's fully compatible with your printer's format and resolution.

Fig. 24.2
The Windows Print Manager routes the `Printer` object's output to your specific printer.

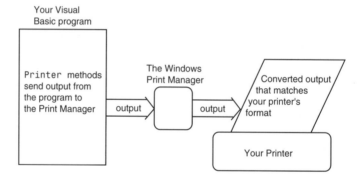

When you write code that outputs to the printer, you must use special methods that work with the `Printer` object. These methods manipulate all the properties associated with the `Printer` object. The next section offers an overview of many of the `Printer` object's properties and methods.

Printer's Properties and Methods

As with all of Visual Basic's objects, the `Printer` object contains several properties that you, through the execution of methods, can initialize and change. The `Printer` is not a control in the same sense that a text label or the timer is a control because you never place a printer object on your form. Therefore you cannot set the `Printer` object's properties through the Properties window. When you want to change one of the `Printer`'s properties, you'll have to use code to do so.

Table 24.1 contains several of the more common `Printer` properties. Look through the table to get an idea of the ones you'll use in your own programs.

IV

Advanced VB Programming

As with most property values, there are many properties that you'll rarely use, if ever. Most of the time, you'll want to output text to the printer for reports and you'll only need a handful of methods (and properties) to output reports.

Note

Several of the properties relate to graphics output that is not covered in detail in this book. You'll learn how to handle screen graphics in Chapter 25, "Controlling Graphics."

Table 24.1 The *Printer* Object's Properties

Property	Description
CurrentX	The horizontal print position (the column), from the top left corner of the page, measured either in twips or the scale defined by Scale properties.
CurrentY	Indicates the vertical print position (the row), from the top left corner of the page, measured either in twips or the scale defined by Scale properties.
DrawMode	Determines the appearance of drawn graphics.
DrawStyle	Specifies the style of graphical lines drawn.
DrawWidth	Indicates the width of lines drawn, from 1 to 32,767 screen-related pixels.
FillColor	Describes the color of printed shapes.
FillStyle	Describes the style pattern of printed shapes.
FontBold	Holds either True or False and determines whether or not subsequent output will be boldfaced.
FontCount	Indicates the current printer's number of installed fonts.
FontItalic	Holds either True or False and determines whether or not subsequent output will be italicized.
FontName	Specifies the name of the current font.
Fonts	Describes a table of properties that works like a control array. Fonts(0) to Fonts(FontCount - 1) holds the names of all installed fonts on the target computer.
FontSize	Indicates the size, in points, of the current font.

(continues)

Table 24.1 Continued	
Property	**Description**
FontStrikeThru	Holds either True or False and determines whether or not subsequent output will be printed with strikethrough.
FontTransparent	Holds either True or False and determines whether or not subsequent output will be transparent.
FontUnderline	Holds either True or False and determines whether or not subsequent output will be underlined.
ForeColor	Describes the foreground color of printed text and graphics. (The paper determines the background color.)
hDC	A Windows device context handle for advanced Windows procedure calls.
Height	Indicates the height, in twips, of the current page.
Page	Indicates the page number currently being printed.
ScaleHeight	Specifies how many ScaleMode units high that each graphic will be upon output.
ScaleLeft	Specifies how many ScaleMode units from the left of the page output will be placed.
ScaleMode	Sets the unit of measurement for all subsequent output.
ScaleTop	Specifies how many ScaleMode units from the top of the page output will be placed.
ScaleWidth	Specifies how many ScaleMode units wide that each graphic will be upon output.
TwipsPerPixelX	Indicates the number of twips each printer dot (called a *pixel*) height consumes.
TwipsPerPixelY	Indicates the number of twips each printer dot (called a *pixel*) width consumes.
Width	Indicates the size of the page width (measured in twips).

Table 24.1 is rather lengthy. This book presents the table here, in full, so you'll have the reference in one location when you want to manage advanced print jobs. Again, mostly you'll use just a handful of the printer's properties.

Use the Printer methods to work with the printer properties and direct output to the Printer object. Table 24.2 contains a list of all Printer methods and their descriptions. Usually, you'll use EndDoc, NewPage, and Print for most of your report printing needs.

Table 24.2 The *Printer* Object's Methods	
Method	**Description**
Circle	Draws a circle, ellipse, or arc on the printer.
EndDoc	Releases the current document, in full, to Print Manager for output.
Line	Draws lines and boxes on the printer.
NewPage	Sends a page break to the printed output so subsequent output appears on the next page.
Print	Prints numeric and text data on the printer. The Print method works for the Printer object in the same way that the Print method worked for form objects as described in Chapter 17, "Screen I/O: Message and Input Boxes."
PSet	Draws a graphical point on the printed output.
Scale	Determines the scale used for measuring output.
TextHeight	Specifies the full height of text given in the scale set with Scale.
TextWidth	Specifies the full width of text given in the scale set with Scale.

Suppose that you want to print the following poem on the printer:

The time has come
for me to change
from COBOL to GUI
and expand my range.

The following Print methods, applied directly to the Printer object, do just that:

```
Printer.Print "The time has come"
Printer.Print "for me to change"
Printer.Print "from COBOL to GUI"
Printer.Print "and expand my range."
```

You can use all the form's `Print` options. As a review, here is the format of the `Print` method for the `Printer` object:

```
Printer.Print [Spc(n) ¦ Tab(n)] Expression [; ¦ ,]
```

`Print` respects values you've stored in variables and also prints numeric literals as well as the string literals shown previously. The following section of code:

```
Dim Hello As Integer
Hello = 18
Printer.Print "Hello"
Printer.Print Hello
Printer.Print "Hello"
Printer.Print 18
```

sends this to the `Printer` object:

```
Hello
 18
Hello
 18
```

As with form objects, `Print` precedes each printed positive number with a space where the plus sign would normally go. If you print negative values, Visual Basic replaces the space with the negative sign.

You can combine variables and literals:

```
Dim Age As Integer
Age = 33
Printer.Print "I am"; Age; " years old."
```

Here is the printer's output for the previous `Print`:

```
I am 33 years old.
```

Using a semicolon suppresses a carriage return and line feed generation, so output stays on the same line if there is room for the output. Using a comma, however, forces the printer to space over to the next print zone. Each print zone is 14 spaces. The following loop will produce a table of values with each value aligned in columns every print zone:

```
For Line = 1 To 5
  Printer.Print Prod(Line, 1), Prod(Line, 2), Prod(Line, 3),
  ➥Prod(Line, 4)
Next Line
```

Here is the output of the table that appears in printed form (assuming that the `Prod()` array contains these string values):

```
X1IU2        A3          ET44-1      PL900PI
C4           W333ERF     ET231       M390II-12
FSE344DSS2   QQ49E-2     O02         KI01
LK890        CV7         UHGH77T     D7
WOP99        AS2E56      LP12A       MNWII9
```

Use `Spc()` to space printed values apart from each other an exact number of spaces determined by your argument to `Spc()`:

```
Printer.Print "Hi"; Spc(4); "there"; Spc(2); "you!"
```

Here is the output of the previous `Print`:

```
Hi    there  you!
```

Unless you terminate a `Print` with a semicolon, each subsequent `Print` starts a new line on the printer. For example, the following statement prints a total of *three* lines:

```
Printer.Print "I am ";
Printer.Print "going to be"
Printer.Print "an excellent"
Printer.Print "Visual Basic programmer!"
```

Here is the output from the previous set of `Print` methods:

```
I am going to be
an excellent
Visual Basic programmer!
```

The semicolon at the end of the first `Print` tells Visual Basic to stay on the same line of output for the subsequent `Print` to occur.

The `Tab()` works a lot like `Spc()` except instead of spacing each output value apart by a given value, `Tab()` instructs Visual Basic to print the values at specific columns on the line. The following `Print`:

```
Printer.Print "One"; Tab(10); "Ten"; Tab(25); "Twenty-five"
```

prints this output:

```
One     Ten            Twenty-five
```

Add special effects to your printed text by setting font modifying properties. The following code first puts the printer in a boldfaced, italicized, 72-point font (a print size of one full inch), and then prints a message:

```
Printer.FontBold = True
Printer.FontItalic = True
Printer.FontSize = 72
Printer.Print "A   B-i-g   M-e-s-s-a-g-e"
```

Note

There are still some printers in use, such as daisy-wheel and fixed-type printers, that do not support the changing of font sizes and styles through code.

Adding Page Breaks

Windows Print Manager ensures that each page properly breaks at the end of a physical page. Therefore, if the printer's page length is 66 lines and you need to print 67 lines, the 67th line will appear at the top of the second page of output.

There are times, however, when you need to print less than a full page on the printer. You should release that incomplete page for printing using the NewPage method (from Table 24.2). Listing 24.3 shows a program that uses the NewPage method to print halves of a poem on two separate pages. The first half of the poem prints on one page and the second half prints on the next page.

Listing 24.3   Using *NewPage* To Force a Page Break

```
Printer.Print "The time has come"
Printer.Print "for me to change"
Printer.Print "from COBOL to GUI"
Printer.Print "and expand my range."

' Force a page break here
Printer.NewPage

Printer.Print "I like visual programming..."
Printer.Print "I really do"
Printer.Print "but when I mess it up"
Printer.Print "I get very blue."
```

Caution

No criticism of the author's poetry will be tolerated!

In COBOL programming, you would keep track of the number of lines printed and force a new page break if you reach that limit. There is much more to determining how many lines will fit on a printed page in Visual

Basic, however. You've got to remember that you're working with printers that support many fonts and font sizes.

You can always determine, in advance, how many lines of output will fit on a single page as long as you first check the value of the following formula:

```
numLinesPerPage = Printer.Height / Printer.TextHeight("X")
```

As explained in Table 24.1, the `Height` property determines the height, in twips, of the page. The `TextHeight` property determines the full height of a printed character (including *leading*, which is the area directly above and below characters). `TextHeight` measures the height in twips if you haven't changed the scale using the `ScaleMode` property.

Note

For printed reports, you'll rarely use the `ScaleMode` method. If you need to change the scale of measurement, however, you'll have to change the scale back to twips before calculating the number of output lines per page, like this:

```
Printer.ScaleMode = TWIPS
```

The `ScaleMode` accepts values defined in Table 24.3. As long as you add the CONSTANT.TXT file to your application's Properties window, you can use the named constants in place of the numeric values if you want to change the scale measurement.

Table 24.3   The *ScaleMode* Values

Value	Named Constant	Description
0	USER	A user-defined value
1	TWIPS	Measured in twips (the default)
2	POINTS	Measured in points
3	PIXELS	Measured in pixels (the smallest unit addressable by your printer)
4	CHARACTERS	Measured in characters (120 by 240 twips)
5	INCHES	Measured in inches
6	MILLIMETERS	Measured in millimeters
7	CENTIMETERS	Measured in centimeters

Initiating the *Print* Method

As you send `Print` methods to Print Manager, via the `Printer` object, Print Manager builds the page or pages of output but does not release that output until you issue an `EndDoc` method. `EndDoc` tells Print Manager, "I'm done sending output to you; you can print now."

Listing 24.4 prints part of a poem and then signals to Print Manager that the output is ready to go to paper.

Listing 24.4   The *EndDoc* Releases the Output for Actual Printing

```
Printer.Print "I like visual programming..."
Printer.Print "I really do"
Printer.Print "but when I mess it up"
Printer.Print "I get very blue."

' Now, release the job for actual printing
Printer.EndDoc
```

Note

If you fail to execute an EndDoc method, Visual Basic releases all printed output for printing automatically when your application ends. For better programming and maintenance, however, show that your output is complete by sending an EndDoc method when you're completely finished printing.

Warn Your User before Printing!

Before printing anything, it's always best to remind your user to turn on the printer and to make sure that the printer has paper and is online. The function procedure in Listing 24.5 provides you with a sample `MsgBox()` call that you may want to incorporate into your own programs.

Listing 24.5   Ask the User before Printing

```
Function PrReady()
' Make sure the user is ready to print
  PrReady = MsgBox("Make sure the printer is ready", 1,
➥"Printer Check")
  If (PrReady = 2) Then
    PrReady = 0      ' Turn a Cancel press to False
  End If
End Function
```

Figure 24.3 shows the message box generated by Listing 24.5. Once the user reads the message and responds to the message box, the procedure's return value determines if the user wants to see the output (and has properly prepared the printer, we assume) or cancel the printing. The return value of zero (meaning false, the user wants to cancel the printing) or one (meaning true) can be checked as follows from another procedure that prints based on the user's response:

```
If (PrReady() = True) Then
   Call PrintRoutine
End If
```

Fig. 24.3
Prepare the user for printing before you send output to the `Printer` object.

Note

If the user has not prepared the printer yet but goes ahead and indicates that the printer is ready, Windows Print Manager will display the error message shown in Figure 24.4. The user must fix the printer problem and switch to Print Manager to release the job. It's much easier for most users to get the printer set right *before* printing and Listing 24.5's routine helps ensure that the user has no trouble.

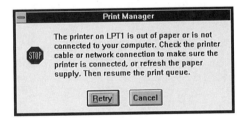

Fig. 24.4
Print Manager may not be able to print.

Conclusion

This chapter explained how to work with the printer. You send data not directly to the printer, but to the `Printer` object. After your print job is finished and you're ready to release the output for actual printing, you send an `EndDoc` method to the `Printer` object so Visual Basic knows to release the printing and Windows Print Manager can finish sending the output to paper.

Despite the buffer between you and the printer, you must still be able to get information from the printer so that you'll know how many lines per page you can print before forcing a new page break. Also, it would be nice to know what fonts are available on the user's printer so that your program can select a font if your program recognizes one of the fonts in the list. The methods and properties work both ways and from the properties currently set; you can gather information about the user's printer and change that information, such as a font size, through Visual Basic's methods and properties.

The next chapter begins the most advanced and final part of this book by introducing you to Visual Basic's graphic commands and capabilities. Many of the graphic commands work for both forms as well as the printer as long as your printer supports graphics. Most importantly, graphics are fun for both you as the programmer and for the user.

Part V

Your Next Step with VB

Chapter 25

Controlling Graphics

This chapter teaches you how to add graphics to your applications. The graphics will spice up your forms and add pizzazz to your applications. Graphics are not just for games anymore. Corporate boardrooms all around the world use graphics to display sales trends and cost projections. A picture is worth a thousand words.

There are several ways to add graphics to your programs. Programmers often take advantage of the many images supplied with Visual Basic. You can add supplied images to your forms and resize those images to fit the area needed.

Not only can you use pre-supplied images, you can draw any drawing that you want on your application's forms. Visual Basic offers line, circle, and dot-drawing features with which you can draw color graphics. You'll have fun working with Visual Basic's graphics capabilities.

Here are some of the topics that will be discussed in this chapter:

- Loading graphic file images into your own applications

- Understanding the differences between the image control and the picture box control

- Using the line control to draw lines of all lengths and directions

- Drawing shapes on your application's form

- Animating your graphics using the timer event

The Graphical Controls

Visual Basic supports two graphical controls that display images stored on the disk: the picture box control and the image control. Figure 25.1 shows the location of these graphical controls on the toolbox.

Fig. 25.1

The picture box and image controls on the toolbox.

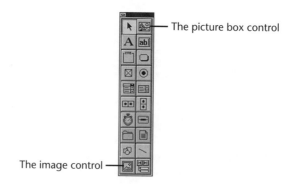

The picture box control

The image control

Basically, you can use either the picture box or the image control to place graphic images, from disk files, onto your form. The primary difference between the two controls is that the picture box control provides a few advanced features that you can tap into if you ever write *MDI* (*multiple document interface*) applications; however, the picture box control does not support as many methods and properties as the image box control does. The image box control is more efficient and displays images faster.

> **Tip**
>
> Either control handles the placement and arrangement of virtually all your graphic images. Therefore, use the *image box* control because of its efficiency. If you ever need the advanced properties offered by the picture box, you can use it.

Table 25.1 describes several of the images that come with Visual Basic and the directory where you can find the images. Sometimes, you have to try an image to see if it suits your needs. For example, if you know you want to use an arrow, you just have to load one arrow at a time, from the long list of graphics files stored in the /ARROWS directory. The directories listed in Table 25.1 all reside in your PC's Visual Basic directory.

> **Note**
>
> See your Visual Basic documentation for a listing of all the images that come with Visual Basic.

Table 25.1 The Images that Come with Visual Basic

Directory	Type	Description
ASSORTED	Bitmap	A miscellaneous collection of pictures
GAUGE	Bitmap	Pictures of gauges such as thermometers
OUTLINE	Bitmap	Outlines of some symbols
TOOLBAR3	Bitmap	Toolbar icons you may want to place in your applications
ARROWS	Icon	Arrows going in all directions and sizes
COMM	Icon	Communications-related icons such as networking pictures
COMPUTER	Icon	Computer-related icons
DRAGDROP	Icon	Icons you may want to use for drag-and-drop cursor shapes
ELEMENTS	Icon	Weather element symbols
FLAGS	Icon	Flags from around the world
INDUSTRY	Icon	Industry-related icons such as hammers, planes, and cars
MAIL	Icon	Postal-related icons that don't require an extra 3 cents postage when you use them
MISC	Icon	A miscellaneous collection of icons that don't fit in other categories
OFFICE	Icon	Office-related pictures such as desktop items
TRAFFIC	Icon	Traffic-related icons
WRITING	Icon	Book and writing-related icons
ARROWS	Metafile	Arrows going in all directions and in all sizes
BUSINESS	Metafile	Pictures used in business such as calculators, calendars, books, money symbols, and more

> **Note**
>
> Table 25.1 lists the type of graphic file as well as the description and storage directory. Visual Basic supports these three image file types:
>
> - Bitmap files that end with the .BMP and .DIB file name extensions and whose directories fall inside the /BITMAP directory
>
> - Icon files that end with the .ICO extension and whose directories fall inside the ICONS directory
>
> - Metafiles that end with the .WMF extension and whose directories fall inside the /METAFILE directory
>
> You can use any of these files with either the picture box control or the image control.

> **Tip**
>
> You're not limited to the file types that come with Visual Basic. You can supply your own icon, bitmap, and metafiles if you have access to any.

Placing Pictures

When you want to put a graphic image on your form, you only need to place an image (or picture box) control on the form and specify a file name for the image that you want the control to display. Open a new form and follow these steps to create an application with an image:

1. Double-click the image control to place the control in the middle of the form.

2. Press F4 to display the Properties window.

3. Single-click the Picture property. You see an ellipsis appear where you normally enter property values as shown in Figure 25.2.

4. If you click the ellipsis, Visual Basic opens a Load Picture dialog box. (You could also double-click on the picture property and save a step.) In the dialog box, you specify the file (from any directory in Table 25.1), including its path, that holds the image you want to display on your form.

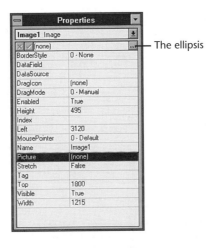
— The ellipsis

Fig. 25.2
The ellipsis gives
you the ability to
specify an image
file.

Note

Instead of selecting from the Load Picture dialog box, you could type the full
path and file name for the Picture property value.

5. For this example, select the /ICONS directory and double-click, then
point to the COMPUTER directory and double-click, and finally double-
click the icon file named DISK04.ICO. When you double-click the file
name, Visual Basic transfers that file's image to the form and closes the
Load Picture dialog box. Your form should now look like the one in
Figure 25.3. You see a picture of the disk in the center of the form. Once
you place the picture, you then can move the control to any point on
the form.

Load through Code

If you need to replace an image at runtime using Visual Basic code, use the
LoadPicture() function. The following statement replaces the picture file
used for an image control named imgPic:

```
imgPic.Picture = LoadPicture("C:\VB\ICONS\COMPUTER\FORM.ICO")
```

The LoadPicture() function lets you erase graphics as well. By using a null
string, "", for the LoadPicture() argument, you can erase a picture from
view.

Fig. 25.3
The form contains
the image once
you load the image
from the disk.

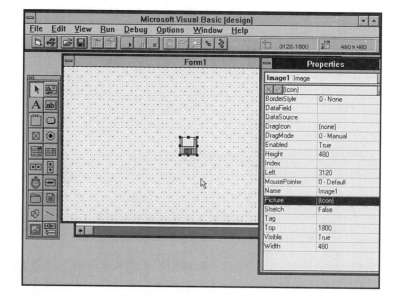

Resizing Images

You can only resize bitmaps and icons that reside on image controls. The
picture box control will not give you access to the resizing handles no matter
what you do to resize the image.

Eight resizing handles appear around the image control on your form. If you
attempt to drag one of the handles, however, Visual Basic refuses to let you
resize the image. You may change the size of the image control but the picture will stay the same. By default, Visual Basic keeps you from resizing icons
and bitmap images. To resize an icon or bitmap image, first set the Stretch
property to True. Follow these steps to resize the disk on your form:

1. Set the Stretch property to True.

2. Grab one of the resizing handles and enlarge the disk to a larger square
    (about 1,575 by 1,680 twips as measured in the upper-right corner of
    the toolbar).

3. When you release the resizing handles, your image will be enlarged as
    shown in Figure 25.4. (Move your image to the left so it's out of the
    way of subsequent controls that you'll place.)

    If you were to change the Stretch property back to False, Visual Basic
    would immediately shrink the stretched image down to its original size,
    but don't do this now.

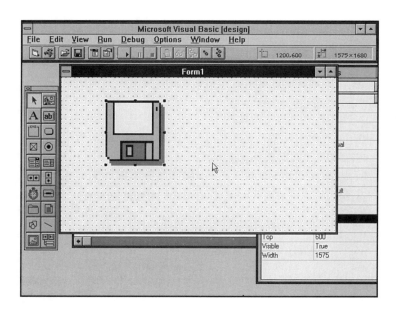

Fig. 25.4
You've just
enlarged the
image.

If you place metafile graphics, Visual Basic initially uses the file's original image size to place the graphic. Follow these steps to place a metafile and watch how the file's original image size dictates the size of the placed image:

1. Double-click the image control to place a second image on the form.

2. Press F4 to display the control's Properties window.

3. Double-click on the Picture property to open the Load Picture dialog box.

4. Select the /METAFILE directory (which resides directly under the VB directory) and then select the /BUSINESS directory under /METAFILE. Double-click the file named CALCULTR.WMF and Visual Basic displays the metafile on your form.

   The original calculator image was so large, the calculator will not fit the entire form. Depending on your video card's resolution, you may not be able to expand the bottom of the form enough to hold the full calculator image. Figure 25.5 shows a form that holds as much of the calculator as possible.

   As you can see from Figure 25.5, you rarely have to enlarge metafiles. Many times, you'll have to shrink them to fit in the form's area. To resize metafile images, you don't have to change the Stretch property first unlike the icon and bitmap files.

V

Your Next Step with VB

Fig. 25.5
Metafiles can be
quite large.

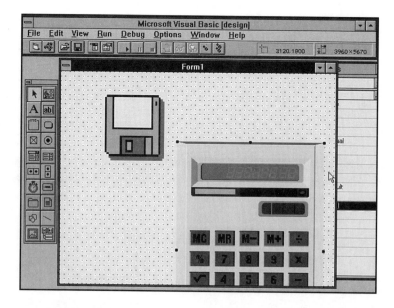

Resizing the Control

An image that you place will not automatically fill the image or picture box control's size. If you place images onto picture box controls, however, you can request that Visual Basic resize the control's outline to fit the actual image's size. By setting the AutoSize picture box control property to True before loading an image file, the picture box control will immediately shrink around the image no matter what size you originally specified for the control.

There is not an AutoSize property for image controls. If you don't specify a BorderStyle of 1 - Fixed Single, the user will never know that an image or picture box control is larger than the image's actual area.

If you want to load the PIC.MAK file from this book's disk, you can do so to look at the two icons loaded in this chapter. The project contains nothing more than what has been described here and the pathname links used in the project's image files may not match your Visual Basic installation. If the pathname does not match and Visual Basic cannot find the images on your disk drive, you may have to change the Picture property values for the two images before running the program.

The Shape of Graphics

You're not limited to the graphic images stored in files. You can draw your own graphics using the line and shape controls. Figure 25.6 shows you where these two controls are located.

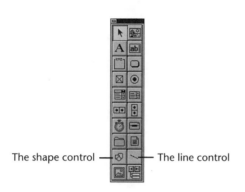

The shape control —   — The line control

Fig. 25.6
The graphic tools you can use to draw your own pictures.

The line control is the simplest of the two graphics controls but you will see in the next section, "Clean Your Paintbrushes," that the shape control is not difficult. The line control can draw lines on your form. The shape control can draw the following shapes:

> The shape control draws many shapes.

Circle

Oval

Rectangle

Rounded edge rectangle

Rounded edge square

Square

By using the shape controls, you'll save yourself lots of tedious drawing time. Visual Basic draws the fundamental shapes and you then can edit those shapes and their property values to look the way you want them to.

Clean Your Paintbrushes

You can use the line and shape controls to add a swinging pendulum to the digital clock application created in Chapter 23, "Loose Ends: Scroll Bars and Timer Controls." After each passing second, the pendulum will swing the opposite direction.

To begin, load the DIGITAL.MAK application. As soon as the application loads, choose File, Save Project As to save the file under the new name, DIGITAL2.MAK. This keeps the first application away from the changes you make in this chapter.

Note

If you get a `File already exists` warning when you attempt to save DIGITAL2.MAK, you probably copied the entire disk from this book to the same directory where you're attempting to save the file. This book's disk contains the DIGITAL2.MAK application with all the modifications you'll make here. Go ahead and save this chapter's application under a different name, such as DIGITAL3.MAK, so that you can follow these instructions and learn about graphics without modifying the book's file.

You can draw lines of all sizes and lengths using the line control. The lines can point in any direction. To place a line, you only need to anchor the line in one position, then extend the line to its end point by dragging with the mouse.

Before drawing the pendulum, you should know in advance that you really must draw *two* pendulums. One will point in the direction of one swing and the other will point in the opposite direction. After drawing the pendulums, you use Visual Basic code to place them at the same form location and display them one at a time.

The following steps get you started by drawing the line of both pendulums:

1. Double-click the line control to place a line on your form.

2. Change the properties of the line to these values:

    Name: **linLeft**

    X1: **5520**

    X2: **5280**

    Y1: **3120**

    Y2: **3480**

    When you change the properties, your Form window should look like the one in Figure 25.7.

    The X1 and Y1 coordinates indicate the starting screen coordinate (in twips) and X2 and Y2 indicate the ending screen coordinate.

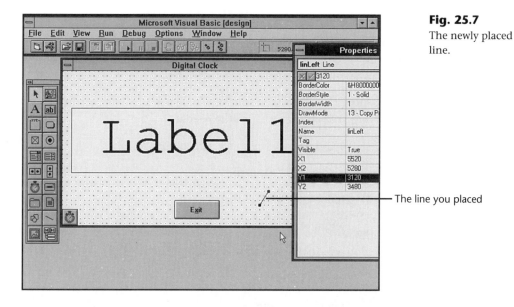

Fig. 25.7
The newly placed
line.

The line you placed

Tip

There's really an easier way to place a line. You can click the line control once, point to the starting point of the line, and press and hold the mouse button. Drag the new line to its ending point and then release the mouse button to anchor the line. This chapter uses property values to ensure that you place your lines so that they match the figures.

3. Now you should create the line for the pendulum's right swing. Basically, you'll add a mirror-image line to the right of the line that you just placed.

Double-click the line control again. Change the line control's property values to these settings:

> Name: **linRight**
>
> X1: **6000**
>
> X2: **6240**
>
> Y1: **3120**
>
> Y2: **3480**

Now that you've drawn the lines, you can draw the circles beneath them.

Using the Shape Control for Circles

The shape control draws circles of all sizes. The shape's property values determine the size-and-look properties the shape takes on. To complete your left and right pendulum swings, follow these steps:

1. Double-click the shape control. You see a square appear in the center of the form where the shape now resides.

2. Press F4 and change the shape's properties to these values:

   BackStyle: **1 - Opaque**

   DrawMode: **1 - Blackness**

   Height: **495**

   Left: **5040**

   Name: **cirLeft**

   Shape: **3 - Circle**

   Top: **3360**

   Width: **300**

3. Place another shape on the form and set its properties to these values:

   BackStyle: **1 - Opaque**

   DrawMode: **1 - Blackness**

   Height: **495**

   Left: **6240**

   Name: **cirRight**

   Shape: **3 - Circle**

   Top: **3360**

   Width: **300**

   Your screen should look like the one in Figure 25.8.

Note

The right pendulum's circle may not fully connect with the pendulum's line unless you turn off the grid alignment and modify the coordinates used here.

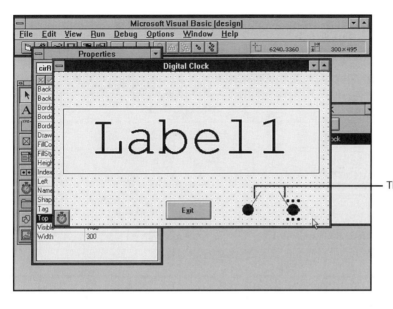

Fig. 25.8
You've just added the left and right pendulums.

—— The swinging pendulums

The two most important properties of any shape are the FillStyle and Shape properties. Table 25.2 lists the possible FillStyle properties. The FillStyle property determines how the middle (the inner body) of the shape will be patterned.

Table 25.2 The FillStyle Property Values	
Value	**Description**
0 - Solid	Completely fills the center of the shape
1 - Transparent	Shows only the shape's outline
2 - Horizontal Line	Lines appear across the body of the shape
3 - Vertical Line	Lines appear down the body of the shape
4 - Upward Diagonal	Diagonals heading from the upper-right corner to the lower-left
5 - Downward Diagonal	Diagonals heading from the upper-left corner to the lower-right
6 - Cross	Cross hairs throughout the body of the shape
7 - Diagonal Cross	Diagonal cross hairs throughout the body of the shape

Table 25.3 lists the kinds of shapes possible when you select the Shape property value.

Table 25.3 The Shape Property Values	
Value	**Description**
0 - Rectangle	A four-sided shape
1 - Square	A perfect square
2 - Oval	A rounded shape
3 - Circle	A perfectly round shape
4 - Rounded Rectangle	A rectangle with rounded corners
5 - Rounded Square	A square with rounded corners

Swing with Code

All you must do now is to make sure that the two pendulums swing from the same pivot point and that only one pendulum appears at any one time. The Form_Load() procedure is a great place to position the two pendulums from the same pivot point and to make both pendulums invisible initially. Double-click on the body of the form. You will see the Form_Load() screen. Here is the code for Form_Load():

```
Sub Form_Load ()
' Initialize the label and pendulum
  lblTime.Caption = Time

  ' Put the two pendulums on top of
  ' each other and hide each one
  linLeft.X1 = 5760
  linLeft.X2 = 5520
  linLeft.Visible = False
  cirLeft.Left = 5280
  cirLeft.Visible = False
  linRight.X1 = 5760
  linRight.X2 = 6000
  linRight.Visible = False
  cirRight.Left = 5910
  cirRight.Visible = False
End Sub
```

Once you set up the initial pendulum values, you only need to "turn on" (display by making the pendulum visible) the correct pendulum every second. Here is additional tmrSecond_Timer() event code that does just that.

```
Sub tmrSecond_Timer ()
' This timer event procedure occurs every second.
' This timer event procedure occurs every 1000 milliseconds.
' Updates the value of the label that holds the current time.
   lblTime.Caption = Time
   If (Timer Mod 2) = 0 Then      ' An even clock tick
       cirLeft.Visible = False    ' Show the right pendulum
       linLeft.Visible = False
       cirRight.Visible = True
       linRight.Visible = True
     Else                         ' An odd clock tick
       cirLeft.Visible = True     ' Show the left pendulum
       linLeft.Visible = True
       cirRight.Visible = False
       linRight.Visible = False
   End If
End Sub
```

The timer named `tmrSecond` is set to trigger this event procedure every second so the time display updates every second. The timer's Interval property value of 1000 makes sure this occurs faithfully. The `tmsSecond_Timer()` event procedure turns on the left or right pendulum line and circle (and turns off the other by making it invisible) every second. The `Mod` operator finds out if the current `Timer` value is odd or even. You'll recall from Chapter 22, "Using Dates and Times," that `Timer` returns the number of seconds since midnight.

When you run the application, your screen should look like Figure 25.9 every other second.

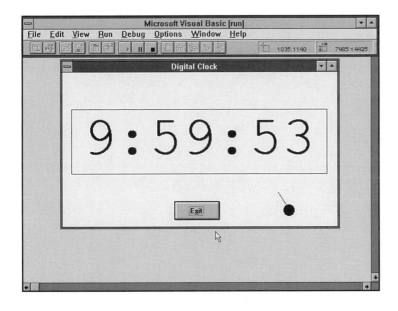

Fig. 25.9
The swinging pendulum.

V

Your Next Step with VB

> ## Add a Beep?
>
> Want to spice the digital clock up and really annoy your coworkers? Insert a Beep statement right before `tmrSecond_Timer()`'s `If` statement. Every time the clock ticks off one second, the beep sounds. Run your application and take a break!

Conclusion

Now you can add fancy graphics to your applications. Actually, this chapter only scratched the surface of graphics fundamentals but you're now on your way to sprucing up applications and even animating them a bit if you like.

There are two approaches to adding graphics to your applications: you can either load an image from disk using the picture box or the image control. The image control is more efficient but doesn't add as much future flexibility as the picture control. You can load bitmaps, icons, and metafile images into your applications using either the picture or image control.

If you want to draw your own graphics, use the line and shape controls. The line control lets you draw lines of all sizes and directions while the shape control produces circles, ovals, squares, and rectangles of all shapes, sizes, and patterns.

You're really veering away from your COBOL days now. There's very little at this point to relate to your COBOL experience because most mainframe and minicomputer COBOL applications are textual in nature and have no capabilities for graphic displays. The next chapter, "Working with the Mouse," takes you yet another step away from your COBOL days by explaining how to track and capture mouse events as the user controls the mouse.

Chapter 26

Working with the Mouse

This chapter teaches you how to access the user's mouse movements and clicks. The mouse is incredibly adept at handling graphical interfaces. Unlike text environments, the keyboard does not adequately handle user selections in Windows. There are too many screen elements, pushbuttons, arrow clicks, and dragging requirements for the keyboard to produce effective user results.

Not only are you concerned with the user's mouse movements and clicks, you'll also have to manage the mouse cursor. Many programmers and texts are lenient in their terminology. The mouse cursor is the true Windows *cursor*, while the vertical text cursor is more accurately known as the *caret*. This book will usually call the two cursors *mouse cursor* and *text cursor* just to keep things simple and obvious.

Here are some of the topics that will be discussed in this chapter:

- Learning about the many mouse cursors

- Changing the mouse cursor within the Properties window and through code

- Responding to the three primary mouse events

- Learning about event procedure arguments

- Writing code that responds to mouse movements and button presses

- Looking at the mouse button information to see which button the user pressed

- Understanding how to check for the user's keyboard presses while analyzing mouse events

The Multiple Mouse Cursors

The mouse cursor takes on several shapes.

Almost every control has a property named MousePointer. The MousePointer can take on one of the 13 values shown in Table 26.1. No doubt, you've seen several of these mouse cursor values in your own use of Windows.

Table 26.1 The Thirteen Mouse Cursor Values	
Value	**Description**
0 - Default	The cursor assumes its default shape. Each control has its own default mouse cursor shape. Most controls use the arrow for the default shape.
1 - Arrow	The typical arrow mouse pointer.
2 - Cross	A cross-hair pointer.
3 - I-Beam	The vertical mouse cursor most often used as a text cursor.
4 - Icon	A small black square within another square.
5 - Size	The sizing cursor that looks like a plus sign with arrows pointing in the four directions.
6 - Size NE SW	A diagonal arrow pointing northeast and southwest.
7 - Size N S	A vertical arrow pointing north and south.
8 - NW SE	A diagonal arrow pointing northwest and southeast.
9 - W E	A vertical arrow pointing west and east.
10 - Up Arrow	An arrow pointing straight up.
11 - Hourglass	The hourglass shape.
12 - No Drop	The familiar roadsign "No" circle with a slash through it.

This book contains an application that steps through each of the mouse cursors and displays each one in sequence. Load and run the application named MOUSE1.MAK. When you do, you'll see the screen shown in Figure 26.1.

As you press Alt+N (thereby selecting the first command button), you'll see the mouse cursor change shape. Be sure to follow the form's directions by placing the mouse under the center label so you can see the shape change.

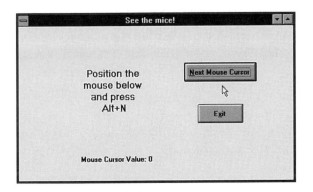

Fig. 26.1
A program that lets
you look at any
mouse cursor.

V

Your Next Step with VB

> **Note**
>
> If you leave the mouse cursor positioned over the command button, you won't see
> any shape change. The mouse is always an arrow over command buttons (unless, of
> course, you change the command button's MousePointer property).

The heart of MOUSE1.MAK lies in the cmdNext_Click() procedure shown in
Listing 26.1. The procedure executes every time the user clicks the top command button.

Listing 26.1   The Procedure that Changes the Mouse Cursor

```
Sub cmdNext_Click ()
  Static MouseCurNum As Integer
  ' Set the mouse cursor's initial value
  ' MouseCurNum will initially be zero
  ' and won't change between procedure executions
  ' due to the Static keyword
  lblValue.Value = MouseCurNum   ' Show user the value
  frmMouse1.MousePointer = MouseCurNum

  ' Increment the mouse cursor
  ' number so the next time the user
  ' clicks the command button, the
  ' cursor takes on the next shape
  '
  ' Make sure the cursor stays
  ' within the range, 0-12
  If (MouseCurNum < 12) Then
      MouseCurNum = MouseCurNum + 1
    Else
      MouseCurNum = 0
  End If
End Sub
```

The first action that the procedure takes is to update the value of the label at the bottom of the screen so you'll know the number of the form's MousePointer value. Then, the form's mouse cursor value is assigned the new value.

The second half of the procedure ensures that the value stays within the range of 0 to 12. If you were to assign a MousePointer a value more than 12 or less than 0, Visual Basic would issue the error message shown in Figure 26.2. Therefore be sure that you protect the mouse cursor's value so it does not go outside its range.

Fig. 26.2

Don't let the MouseCursor value go outside its range.

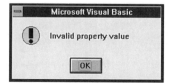

What's that *Static* All About?

In the cmdNext_Click ()'s event procedure, you'll see a statement that you've never seen before. The following statement:

```
Static MouseCurNum As Integer
```

declares an integer variable named MouseCurNum. The variable is used throughout the rest of the procedure to update the value of the MousePointer mouse cursor value.

Dim would not work in this instance because Dimed variables are always initialized when the event procedure starts execution, so a special variable-declaration statement, Static, has to be used. Static works just like Dim and declares variables of any data type. Unlike Dim, however, Static declares local variables whose values *don't go away when the procedure ends*.

If you declare MouseCurNum using Dim, the procedure can use the local variable and assign values to the variable. However, when the procedure ends, the local variable loses its value and disappears. (All local variables disappear when their procedures end unless you declare them with Static.) If you reenter a procedure that uses Dim to declare local variables, the variables are declared *and re-initialized all over again*.

With Static, Visual Basic declares the variable only the first time the procedure executes. The variable does not lose its value when the procedure ends. Therefore, the variable will, upon reentering the procedure, retain the last value it had when the procedure previously ended. The Static variable is still local and accessible only from within its procedure.

The CONSTANT.TXT data file contains the following `MousePointer` named constant assignments:

```
' MousePointer
Global Const DEFAULT = 0          ' 0 - Default
Global Const ARROW = 1            ' 1 - Arrow
Global Const CROSSHAIR = 2        ' 2 - Cross
Global Const IBEAM = 3            ' 3 - I-Beam
Global Const ICON_POINTER = 4     ' 4 - Icon
Global Const SIZE_POINTER = 5     ' 5 - Size
Global Const SIZE_NE_SW = 6       ' 6 - Size NE SW
Global Const SIZE_N_S = 7         ' 7 - Size N S
Global Const SIZE_NW_SE = 8       ' 8 - Size NW SE
Global Const SIZE_W_E = 9         ' 9 - Size W E
Global Const UP_ARROW = 10        ' 10 - Up Arrow
Global Const HOURGLASS = 11       ' 11 - Hourglass
Global Const NO_DROP = 12         ' 12 - No drop
```

Instead of assigning the `MousePointer` property a specific integer value, such as 2, you can assign the `MouseCursor` property the named constant like this:

```
frmName.MouseCursor = CROSSHAIR
```

Suppose that you were needing to sort a huge array of string data. Such a sort can take a few seconds. To show that the user must wait a bit, change the mouse cursor to an hourglass shape with this assignment statement:

```
frmName.MouseCursor = HOURGLASS
```

As you've seen, changing the mouse during certain events adds yet another interface element for the user that helps him ascertain the status of the program's operation. You can change the mouse to an hourglass when your program needs some computing time, you can change the mouse to an arrow when the user moves the mouse, and you can change the mouse to a warning sign when the user moves the mouse over an area of the screen in which the mouse has no function.

Capturing Mouse Movements

Every time the user moves the mouse or clicks a button, a mouse event occurs. Table 26.2 lists the mouse-related events that can trigger procedure calls.

Sometimes it helps to follow the user's mouse.

Table 26.2 The Mouse Events	
Event	**Description**
MouseDown	The user presses the mouse button.
MouseMove	The user moves the mouse.
MouseUp	The user releases the mouse button.

Although these mouse-related events are common and occur after the user performs standard mouse operations, they do require extra effort at times. For example, you'll often want to get answers for the following questions:

What event occurs if the user double-clicks the mouse button?

Which mouse button (left, center, or right) did the user press if the user uses a multi-button mouse?

Did the user press a Shift, Alt, or Ctrl key while pressing a mouse button?

Where did the user move the mouse cursor?

These questions and more can be answered through the three mouse events along with combinations of events and properties discussed in the following sections.

Capturing Mouse Clicks

The mouse events generally require event procedures that Visual Basic passes arguments to. Most of the event procedures that you've seen so far have had no argument values. For example, here is the common Exit command button event procedure that you've seen so often:

```
Sub cmdExit ()
    End
End Sub
```

The empty parentheses mean that the event never gets values sent to the subroutine.

Some event procedures require arguments.

Suppose, however, that you need to take an action every time the user clicks a mouse button over the form. You'll have to write an event procedure for the form that takes on the following name:

```
frmName.MouseDown (argument list)
```

The `MouseDown()` event procedure requires an argument list. Visual Basic automatically supplies the argument list for you when you code the `MouseDown()` event procedure.

To learn more about the creation of such event procedures, open a new project and press F7 to display the Code window. Visual Basic always opens the Code window to the `Form_Load()` event procedure.

Display the `Proc:` drop-down list. Click the `MouseDown` procedure name. As soon as you do, Visual Basic codes the wrapper code for `Form_MouseDown()` as shown in Figure 26.3.

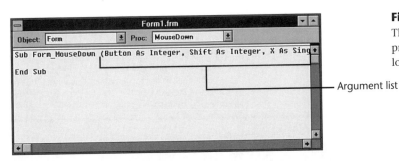

Fig. 26.3
This event procedure requires lots of arguments.

— Argument list

V

Your Next Step with VB

> **Note**
>
> Unless you use an exceptionally large monitor, you won't be able to see the entire argument list at one time. Scroll with the Code window's horizontal scroll bar to see the rest of the argument list.

Notice that the first line (called the *procedure declaration line*) does not contain the usual event procedure's empty argument list. Instead, you'll see the following (if you scroll the Code window) declaration line:

```
Sub Form_MouseDown (Button As Integer, Shift As Integer,
➥X As Single, Y As Single)
```

The `MouseDown()` event procedure requires four arguments. These arguments are described in Table 26.3. The `MouseMove` event procedure is available for controls other than forms. This section's discussion applies whether you are dealing with a form's `MouseMove` event or another control's.

Table 26.3 The *MouseDown()* Arguments	
Argument	**Description**
Button	The number of the mouse button pressed. Button is sent 1 for the left button, 2 for the right button, and 4 for both the middle button on a three-button mouse.
Shift	The Shift key (if any) pressed at the same time as the mouse button. Shift is sent 1 for the Shift keypress, 2 for the Ctrl, and 4 for the Alt key. If Shift contains another number, that number is the sum of two or more key-presses. For example, if Shift is passed 5, you know that the user pressed the Shift (1) and the Alt (4) keys at the same time as the user pressed the mouse button.
X	The horizontal twip form measurement where the user clicked the mouse button. The twip measurement is relative to the form's upper-left corner.
Y	The vertical twip form measurement where the user clicked the mouse button. The twip measurement is relative to the form's upper-left corner.

Note

If the form is part of a control array, there will be an additional integer argument, Index, at the start of the argument list that contains the index of the form where the user clicked the mouse.

The CONSTANT.TXT file contains the following assignment statements for named constants:

```
' Shift parameter masks
Global Const SHIFT_MASK = 1
Global Const CTRL_MASK = 2
Global Const ALT_MASK = 4

' Button parameter masks
Global Const LEFT_BUTTON = 1
Global Const RIGHT_BUTTON = 2
Global Const MIDDLE_BUTTON = 4
```

Instead of using the numeric literals, you can use the named constants as long as you add the CONSTANT.TXT file to your application's Project window.

Listing 26.2 contains a Form_MouseDown() event procedure that you should type into your Code window. The procedure prints a message directly onto the form that displays information about the user's mouse click over the form.

Listing 26.2   Display the Mouse Information

```
Sub Form_MouseDown (Button As Integer, Shift As Integer,
➡X As Single, Y As Single)
' Display text on the form that
' describes the mouse button press
' The semicolon at the end of the Print statements
' causes VB to keep the cursor on the same Print
' line. In a way, you are building the output one
' line at a time as you do in COBOL when sending data
' values to a print record.
  Print "Down: The button you pressed was the ";
  Select Case Button
    Case 1: Print "Left ";
    Case 2: Print "Right ";
    Case 4: Print "Middle ";
  End Select
  Print "button"
  If (Shift <> 0) Then
    Print "The key you pressed was the ";
    Select Case Shift
      Case 1: Print "Shift ";
      Case 2: Print "Ctrl ";
      Case 4: Print "Alt ";
    End Select
    Print "key"
  End If

  Print "The mouse was at X position: ";
  Print X;
  Print "and Y position: ";
  Print Y
  ' Print a blank line to separate for subsequent output
  Print
End Sub
```

Before running the program, add two command buttons to the right of the form. Add the first command button and set the following property values:

Caption: **&Erase form**

Left: **5520**

Name: **cmdClear**

Top: **840**

Add the second command button and set the following property values:

Caption: **E&xit**

Left: **5520**

Name: **cmdExit**

Top: **2040**

Double-click the first command button and add the following
cmdClear_Click() event procedure:

```
Sub cmdClear_Click ()
  Form1.Cls
End Sub
```

The Cls method erases whatever form you apply the method to. Cls only
erases the background of a form, not the controls from the form. This program prints two lines on the form every time the user presses the mouse.
The first command button named cmdClear erases the form when you want
to make room for additional output with Print.

Double-click the second command button and add an End statement to the
body of the cmdExit_Click() event procedure.

Run the program. Move the mouse around the form and click a mouse button. Click another mouse button. Click two at once. You'll see output that
looks like that of Figure 26.4.

> **Note**
>
> If you have a two-button mouse, press both at the same time. You'll see that Visual
> Basic generates both a left *and* right button event.

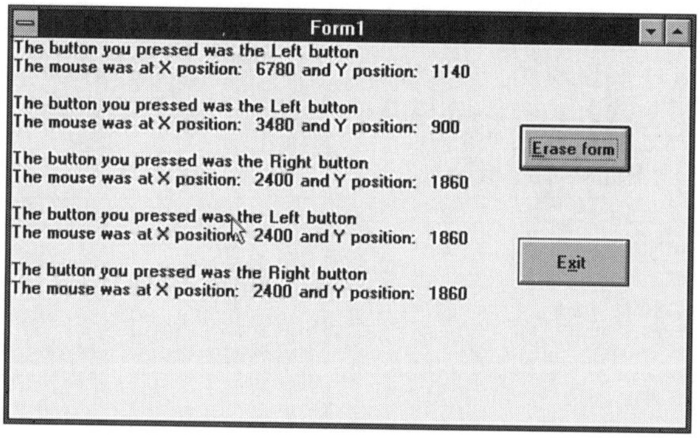

Fig. 26.4
Clicking the
mouse to see
information.

Save the form file and project to disk so your changes remain safely stored.

The Double Mouse Click

When you run the mouse application and double-click a mouse button, the program only prints the description for the first of the two clicks. As soon as you click the mouse a second time, quickly enough for Visual Basic to realize that a double-click occurred, Visual Basic does not call the MouseDown event again. Instead, Visual Basic calls both the DblClick and MouseUp events.

Therefore, from the Code window, display the form's DblClick procedure from the Proc drop-down list box and add the following code that executes only when Visual Basic realizes that a double-click took place:

```
Sub Form_DblClick ()
   Print "You just double-clicked the mouse!"
   Print       ' Prints a blank line
End Sub
```

Run the program again to see how the new DblClick event changes things a little. The first click of the double-click generates a regular MouseDown event because Visual Basic has no idea if you'll follow that first click with another. Therefore Visual Basic has to treat the first of a double-click as if it's a single click. As soon as Visual Basic receives the second of your two clicks, Visual Basic calls the Form_DblClick() procedure and prints the additional message that a double-click took place.

The *MouseUp* Event

Whether or not you double-click the mouse, the MouseUp event occurs *every time you release a mouse button*. To see how the MouseUp event works, add Listing 26.3 to the form's MouseUp Code window:

Listing 26.3 Display the *MouseUp* Information

```
Sub Form_MouseUp (Button As Integer, Shift As Integer,
➥X As Single, Y As Single)
' Display text on the form that
' describes the mouse button press
' The semicolon at the end of the Print statements
' causes VB to keep the cursor on the same Print
' line. In a way, you are building the output one
' line at a time as you do in COBOL when sending data
   Print "Up: The button you released was the ";
   Select Case Button
     Case 1: Print "Left ";
     Case 2: Print "Right ";
     Case 4: Print "Middle ";
   End Select
   Print "button"
```

(continues)

V

Your Next Step with VB

Listing 26.3   Continued

```
Print "The mouse was at X position: ";
Print X;
Print "and Y position: ";
Print Y
' Print a blank line to separate for subsequent output
Print

End Sub
```

This event procedure code matches that of the MouseDown event procedure except for the name and the Up: label that appears at the start of the output.

Moving the Mouse

When the user moves the mouse, Visual Basic generates a MouseMove event. The Form_MouseMove() procedure handles the mouse movement. The arguments for the MouseMove event procedure are the same as for the MouseDown and MouseUp event procedures because you'll sometimes need the same information about the keyboard and mouse button when the user moves the mouse.

To see how the MouseMove event works, add Listing 26.4 to the form's Code window:

Listing 26.4   Display the Mouse Movement Information

```
Sub Form_MouseMove (Button As Integer, Shift As Integer,
➥X As Single, Y As Single)
  Print "Move: ";
  ' Perhaps no button was pressed
  If (Button <> 0) Then
    Print "The button you pressed was the ";
    Select Case Button
      Case 1: Print "Left ";
      Case 2: Print "Right ";
      Case 4: Print "Middle ";
    End Select
    Print "button"
  End If

  If (Shift <> 0) Then
    Print "The key you pressed was the ";
    Select Case Shift
      Case 1: Print "Shift ";
      Case 2: Print "Ctrl ";
      Case 4: Print "Alt ";
    End Select
    Print "key"
  End If
```

```
        Print "The mouse was at X position:";
        Print X;
        Print "and Y position:";
        Print Y
        ' Print a blank line to separate for subsequent output
        Print

    End Sub
```

This event procedure code matches that of the MouseDown and MouseUp event procedures except for the name and the Move: label that appears at the start of the output.

When you run the program, you may have to expand the height of your Form window because the mouse movement events occur often when you move the mouse. Usually, Visual Basic generates a mouse movement event every time the user moves the mouse 15 twips or so.

You'll fill up the Form window with lots of mouse movement messages if you're not careful as shown in Figure 26.5.

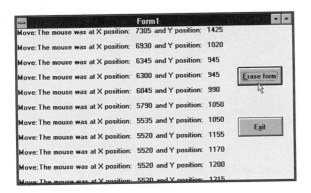

Fig. 26.5
Mouse events can really happen fast.

This completed mouse event application is stored on this book's disk under the name MOUSE2.MAK.

Conclusion

This chapter taught you all about mousing around inside a Visual Basic program. There are only a handful of mouse events that you need to respond to. You'll often want to know when the user presses a button, releases a button, and moves the mouse.

Not only will you want the fundamental button and movement event information, but you'll also want to know which button the user pressed and whether or not the user also held down a Shift, Alt, or Ctrl key while using the mouse. The mouse event procedures generate arguments that you can test to find out more details on mouse events that take place.

A mouse event can occur over virtually any control. Although programming around mouse events is fairly straightforward as this chapter showed you, your application might demand some additional coding. For example, the user might press the mouse button over one control but release the mouse button after moving the mouse to another control. Depending on your application, you may want to respond to the mouse up event or ignore it (by not coding a MouseUp event procedure.

The next chapter shows you how to work with dialog boxes. Dialog boxes are perfect collection vehicles for Windows programs. The user can fill out needed options and select from lists of items in a single dialog box, giving your program a lot of information in one place.

Chapter 27

Common Dialog Boxes

This chapter teaches you about *common dialog boxes*. Common dialog boxes are dialog boxes that you've seen in virtually every Windows program. There is a dialog box for selecting files, colors, and other standard options that the user often has to make. A dialog box is a group of two or more controls that appear together when the user needs to give sets of information to programs. The dialog box gets its name from the fact that users interact with them by supplying information as if there was a "dialog" going on between the user and the program.

In learning about the common dialog boxes, you'll not only learn how to display the boxes, but also how to respond to them when the user fills out the fields inside the dialog box. Your Visual Basic code must be able to look at the user's dialog box selections and make decisions based on those selections.

Here are some of the topics that will be discussed in this chapter:

- Adding the common dialog box control if you don't currently have the control on your toolbox

- Understanding the advantages of common dialog boxes over custom dialog boxes

- Recognizing these four kinds of common dialog boxes: color, file, font, and print selection dialog boxes

- Using the Action property to specify one of the four dialog box displays

- Controlling the dialog box display through named constants in the CONSTANT.TXT file

Note

Have you ever asked the user for a file name in COBOL? Suppose that the user must enter a file name so that your COBOL program can read data from the file. Does the user know how to enter the file name correctly? If you use a mainframe system, does the user know the proper dataset naming conventions? If you're using a UNIX-based COBOL compiler, does the user know that file names are case-sensitive and that SALES92 is much different from Sales92 on such systems?

The common dialog boxes eliminate all guesswork from such chores as getting user file names. The user can select drives, file names, and directories with a few simple clicks of the mouse.

Which Dialog Boxes Are Common?

Microsoft recommended and implemented the use of common dialog boxes to add even more consistency to Windows programs than was already present. Before Microsoft approved the common dialog box designs, it was possible and even common for software developers to create their own versions of file selection dialog boxes, color selection dialog boxes, and so on. All of the different dialog boxes added confusion to a graphical user environment which was attempting to be consistent and *non*-confusing.

Note

Developers didn't always use dialog boxes for common tasks such as file selections. Sometimes, the programmers would request a file name with an input box and display a drop-down list box for a directory selection. Every time a user learned a new Windows program, the user would have to master yet another interface to accomplish familiar tasks.

Here are the four kinds of common dialog boxes you'll work with:

- Color dialog box
- File dialog box
- Font dialog box
- Print dialog box

There are several versions of most of these dialog boxes. For example, you can use the file dialog box for file opening and saving operations.

Figures 27.1 through 27.4 each show a version of these common dialog boxes. You'll probably recognize some or all of the common dialog boxes.

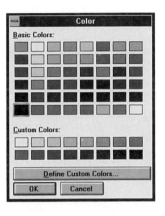

Fig. 27.1
The Color dialog box.

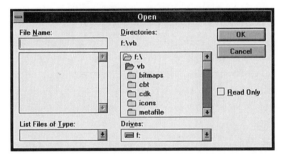

Fig. 27.2
The Open dialog box.

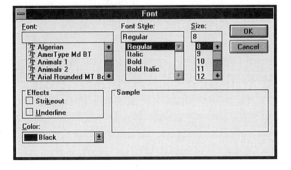

Fig. 27.3
The Font dialog box.

V

Your Next Step with VB

Fig. 27.4

The Print dialog box.

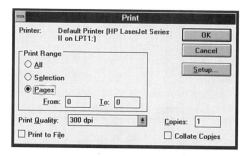

You'll notice that some of the options in the Open dialog box, such as the File Name field, are blank. Before displaying a common dialog box from your program, you'll have to set some default values, such as the file name list and type of file to open.

The options that you set also determine what kind of file dialog box that the program opens. For example, using a file dialog box, the user may be opening or saving the file, and the dialog box differs slightly for those two operations.

Prepare for Common Dialog Boxes

Not every Visual Basic programmer can add dialog boxes without modifying his or her Visual Basic system. Before using the common dialog box control, you'll have to make sure that your WINDOWS or WINDOWS\SYSTEM directory contains the file named COMMDLG.DLL. If you need to copy this file to your Windows directory, you may find it in your Visual Basic directory. If not, copy the file from your Visual Basic distribution disks.

Also, the standard Visual Basic setup does not put the common dialog box control on your toolbox. You need this control to add common dialog boxes. To add the control, choose the File, Add File command from Visual Basic's menu bar and add the CMDIALOG.VBX file to your Visual Basic application.

Tip

If you want to add the common dialog box control permanently to your toolbox, add the CMDIALOG.VBX file to your AUTOLOAD.MAK file.

Figures 27.5 and 27.6 show what the common dialog box control looks like. The location of this control may differ on your system from the figure's location, so learn how the control looks.

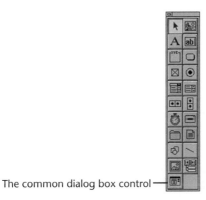

Fig. 27.5
The location of the common dialog box control.

The common dialog box control ——

Fig. 27.6
The common dialog box control.

V

Your Next Step with VB

Working with the File Dialog Box

This section lets you practice using the common dialog box by displaying a file dialog box. Open a new project and make sure that you have the common dialog box control in your toolbox. Add the common dialog box to the form.

The common dialog box acts a little like the timer. The user will not see the common dialog box, so it does not matter where on the form you place it. Therefore after placing a common dialog box, move the control out of the way so that you have room for the rest of the controls on the form.

> **Note**
>
> When your application, through code, eventually displays the dialog box, you will have no control over the size or placement of the dialog box. Therefore you don't have to resize common dialog boxes or worry about where to place the control.

The Common Dialog Box Properties

The default name for the first common dialog box is CMDialog1. It's important to know that you use the same dialog box for *all* of the common dialog boxes listed previously. Therefore the common dialog box controls are perhaps the few controls you *won't* want to rename. After all, it wouldn't make sense for you to name a control comFileOpen when you might also use the control for file saving.

The Action property tells Visual Basic, through programming, exactly what kind of dialog box you want displayed on the form. Table 27.1 lists the Action values available to your code. When you assign a value to the Action property, Visual Basic displays that action's dialog box.

Table 27.1   The *Action* Values for Common Dialog Boxes

Value	CONSTANT.TXT	Description
1	DLG_FILE_OPEN	Displays a file open dialog box
2	DLG_FILE_SAVE	Displays a file save as dialog box
3	DLG_COLOR	Displays a color selection dialog box
4	DLG_FONT	Displays the font dialog box
5	DLG_PRINT	Displays the print dialog box
6	DLG_HELP	Invokes the help system

Add a command button to the form where you've placed the common dialog box control. Name the control cmdDialog. Double-click the control to open the cmdDialog_Click() command button so you can place practice code that you can later trigger by clicking the command button.

Suppose that you want to display a file open dialog box. To display a file open dialog box when you click the cmdDialog command button, you only have to add this assignment statement to the body of the cmdDialog_Click() procedure:

```
CMDialog1.Action = DLG_FILE_OPEN
```

The file open dialog box that you see contains file name fields and a file types field as shown in the same Open dialog box in Figure 27.2. Before displaying the dialog box, you should set some initial default values. Of course, the user can always override these default values, but you should offer initial values.

Use the Filter property to set default values.

Suppose that you were writing a program that accesses binary data files whose file name extensions end in either .BIN or .DAT. If so, you would probably want to display those file names only (those on the disk that end in the .BIN or .DAT extensions) and those file type descriptions in the file type field. The `Filter` property determines the file name and file type fields that display.

Use a string value for the `Filter`. Here is the format for the `Filter` value:

```
"Description (*.ext) [ ; (*.ext)]¦*.ext [; *.ext]"
```

The `Filter` format looks difficult, but it's not. Start easy. The `Filter` code line must go *before* the `Action` assignment. To display a file type field value of `Binary (*.BIN)`, and to display a list of .BIN files in the file name field, you'll assign the `CMDialog1.Filter` the following value:

```
CMDialog1.Filter = "Binaries (*.BIN)¦*.BIN"
```

> **Note**
>
> `*.BIN` is called a *file mask*. `*.BIN` means *all files that end with the .BIN extension.*
> In other words, all other files are masked from the list.

The ¦ symbol (called the *pipe*) separates the file type field value from the file name field value. If you want to display two types of files (both .BIN and .DAT files), separate the file masks with semicolons like this:

```
CMDialog1.Filter = "Binaries (*.BIN; *.DAT)¦*.BIN;*.DAT"
```

Do not put spaces on either side of the pipe symbol.

Figure 27.7 shows the Open dialog box that you'll see if you insert this assignment before the `Action` assignment inside your command button's procedure. If you precede the `Filter` file name masks with a full drive and pathname, the drive and directory fields will be set accordingly. Otherwise, the drive and directory will be set to the active disk drive last selected from a file open dialog box.

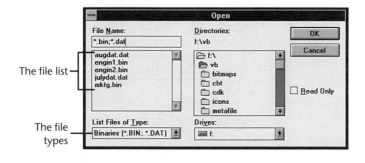

The file list ──

The file types ──

Fig. 27.7
The Open dialog box contains default values.

Of course, there are other field values besides the file type and file name fields that you may want to set. Use the `Flags` property for controlling the way a file open dialog box operates. Table 27.2 contains several CONSTANT.TXT values that you can use to modify the behavior of the file open dialog box. (Both file open and file save dialog boxes use values from Table 27.2.)

Table 27.2 *Flags* **Values for File Dialog Boxes**

CONSTANT.TXT	Description
OFN_ALLOWMULTISELECT	Lets the user select more than one file name using the Shift and arrow keys.
OFN_CREATEPROMPT	Asks the user if he or she wants to create a file if the user selects a file that does not already exist. If the user's file selection is supposed to open only a file that already exists, don't use this FLAGS value.
OFN_EXTENSIONDIFFERENT	A possible file open dialog box return value that indicates that the user's file name extension does not match one of the file name extensions you specified in the file type field.
OFN_FILEMUSTEXIST	The user can only enter a valid file name that already exists.
OFN_READONLY	Hides the Read Only checkbox.
OFN_NOCHANGEDIR	The original default directory that was set before the user selected from the dialog box (and possibly changed in the file dialog box to open a file in a different directory) is returned to the original default value.
OFN_NOREADONLYRETURN	Ensures that the selected file's read-only attribute will not be set or be write-protected.
OFN_NOVALIDATE	Indicates that the user's file name can contain invalid characters.
OFN_OVERWRITEPROMPT	Used when displaying a file save as dialog box to force the user to indicate whether or not the file should replace one if another with the same name already resides on the disk.
OFN_PATHMUSTEXIST	The user can enter only valid pathnames.
OFN_READONLY	Forces the dialog box's Read Only checkbox to be selected.
OFN_SHAREAWARE	Ignores any and all file-sharing violations the user's selection may cause.
OFN_SHOWHELP	Adds a Help command button to the dialog box.

To specify more than one value, add the named constants together. For example, the following cmdDialog_Click() procedure selects the Read Only checkbox and requires that the user's select file path must exist:

```
Sub cmdDialog_Click ()
  CMDialog1.Flags = OFN_READONLY + OFN_PATHMUSTEXIST
  CMDialog1.Filter = "Binaries (*.BIN; *.DAT)¦*.BIN;*.DAT"
  CMDialog1.Action = DLG_FILE_OPEN
End Sub
```

If the user is to save a file instead of open one, you only need to change the Action property. Changing the assignment of the previous code's Action property to DLG_FILE_SAVE (see Table 27.1) produces the Save As dialog box shown in Figure 27.8.

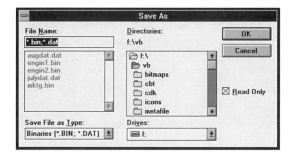

Fig. 27.8
The Save As
dialog box.

V

Your Next Step with VB

Tip

Be sure to add the Open and Save menu commands to the File menu in your application.

Receiving Values

Once the user closes the file dialog box, you can check and use various values from the fields described in Table 27.3.

Table 27.3 Returned Values from File Dialog Boxes	
Value	**Description**
File name	The user's selected file name

(continues)

Table 27.3 Continued	
Value	**Description**
Flags	Checks against the various Flags (see Table 27.2) with an If or Select Case statement to see results of the user's file selection
Path	The user's selected path

You've now learned how to generate dialog boxes and respond to the user's selection. The remaining common dialog boxes vary those procedures just a little.

Displaying the Color Selection

Once you learn how to program one kind of common dialog box, the others are easy. By specifying an Action property with the value of 3 (or DLG_COLOR), Visual Basic displays a color selection list (such as the one shown in Figure 27.9) from which the user selects a color. The following code displays the color selection list, then sets the form's background color to the selection chosen by the user:

```
CMDialog1.Action = DLG_COLOR
Form1.BackColor = CMDialog1.Color
```

As you can see, the Color property contains the color value (the hexadecimal value of the color selected by the user) that the user chose.

Table 27.4 lists some CONSTANT.TXT values that you can use to set initial color dialog box default values.

Table 27.4 *Flags* Values for Color Dialog Boxes	
CONSTANT.TXT	**Description**
CC_FULLOPEN	Displays a full color selection dialog box (as shown in Figure 27.9) instead of the shortened form that requires that the user press the Define Custom Colors command button to define custom colors
CC_PREVENTFULLOPEN	Keeps the user from being able to select the custom color command button
CC_RGBINIT	Sets the initial color value for the dialog box
CC_CCSHOWHELP	Displays a help button on a color dialog box

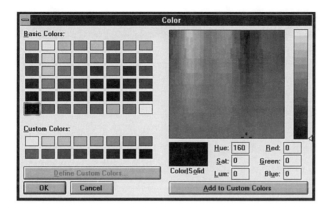

Fig. 27.9
The full Color
dialog box.

A color selection dialog box offers the user a simple way to choose from various system colors. There is no reason the user should ever know about hexadecimal color values. When the user needs a color, provide a color selection dialog box to let the user choose from among the colors in the dialog box.

Displaying the Font Dialog Box

Here's just more of the same. (See why they call it the *common* dialog box control?) By setting the Action property to DLG_FONT, you can display a font selection dialog box to let the user select a font from the list of available fonts. Table 27.5 lists the CONSTANT.TXT named values for setting the font selection dialog box properties.

Table 27.5 *Flags* Values for Font Dialog Boxes

CONSTANT.TXT	Description
CF_APPLY	Displays the Apply command button on the font dialog box. Sometimes, you'll want to offer the user a chance to apply a font to currently selected text, and the Apply command button is a nice way to let the user do so.
CF_ANSIONLY	Requires that the user select a font that contains characters from the Windows character set.
CF_BOTH	Lists both the printer and screen fonts.
CF_EFFECTS	Ensures that the dialog box contains options for strikethrough, underlining, and coloring effects.

(continues)

| **Table 27.5 Continued** | |
CONSTANT.TXT	Description
CF_FIXEDPITCHONLY	The dialog box only displays fixed-pitch (non proportional) fonts.
CF_FORCEFONTEXIST	Displays an error message if the user selects a font that does not exist.
CF_LIMITSIZE	Makes sure that the dialog box displays only fonts within a range given by the dialog box's Min and Max property values.
CF_NOSIMULATIONS	The dialog box will not allow GDI simulations but only actual fonts.
CF_NOVECTORFONTS	The dialog box will not allow vector-drawn fonts to be available.
CF_PRINTERFONTS	Displays only printer-supported fonts.
CF_SCALABLEONLY	Displays only scalable fonts.
CF_SCREENFONTS	Displays only screen fonts.
CF_SHOWHELP	Displays the Help command button.
CC_TTONLY	Displays only Windows TrueType fonts.
CF_WYSIWYG	Requires that both CF_BOTH and CF_SCALABLEONLY flags are set. The setting of this Flag's value limits the font selection to those fonts available both on the printer and on the screen.

> **Caution**
>
> You must describe, with the Flags property, which font selection list the dialog box should display or an error appears.

You can test the values of the following properties to determine what font information the user selected: FontName, FontSize, FontBold, FontItalic, FontStrikeThru, FontTransparent, FontUnderline.

The following code displays the font dialog box and displays information about the user's in message boxes:

```
CMDialog1.Flags = CF_WYSIWYG + CF_BOTH + CF_SCALABLEONLY
CMDialog1.Action = DLG_FONT
MsgBox "You chose: " & CMDialog1.FontName
MsgBox "Size: " & CMDialog1.FontSize
```

```
If (CMDialog1.FontBold = True) Then
  MsgBox "Boldfaced"
End If
```

Displaying the Print Dialog Box

When you direct output to a printer, you should make a print dialog box available to let the user select a printer and possible resolution and number of copies values. The print dialog box simply gives your user one final chance to cancel the print job or direct the output to a printer of his or her choosing.

Table 27.6 lists the Flags CONSTANT.TXT values you'll need for the print dialog box.

Table 27.6 _Flags_ Values for Print Dialog Boxes

CONSTANT.TXT	Description
PD_ALLPAGES	Sets or returns the value of the All Pages option button.
PD_COLLATE	Sets or returns the value of the Collate check box.
PD_DISABLEPRINTTOFILE	Disables the Print to File check box so the user cannot use the option. Use this Flag when you don't want the user to send output to a disk file.
PD_HIDEPRINTTOFILE	Keeps Visual Basic from displaying the Print to File check box.
PD_NOPAGENUMS	Doesn't allow the user to edit the Pages option button and control.
PD_NOSELECTION	Disables the Selection option button so the user cannot use the option.
PD_NOWARNING	Doesn't allow Visual Basic to display a warning message when there is no default printer selected.
PD_PAGENUMS	Sets or returns the value of the Pages option button.
PD_PRINTSETUP	Displays the printer setup dialog box so the user can change the printer selection and settings.
PD_PRINTTOFILE	Sets or returns the value of the Print to File check box.
PD_RETURNDC	Returns the handle of the printer device context. (For advanced internal Windows function calls that require such a handle.)

(continues)

Your Next Step with VB

V

Table 27.6 Continued	
CONSTANT.TXT	**Description**
PD_RETURNIC	Returns the information context for the printer. (For advanced internal Windows function calls.)
PD_SELECTION	Sets or returns the Selection option button.
PD_SHOWHELP	Displays the Help command button in a print dialog box.
PD_USEDEVMODECOPIES	Disables the Copies control if the printer does not support multiple copies. Otherwise, the user's Copies control value is stored in the dialog box's Copies property for subsequent printing of those copies.

Before printing from your application, give the user a chance to select printer settings by first displaying the Print dialog box.

Conclusion

As you learned in this chapter, the common dialog boxes give your users access to generic Windows dialog boxes that appear in many applications. Whenever the user is to specify a color, font, file, or printer, you can ask the user for the information through a series of input boxes. You'll eliminate tedious programming and get more accurate responses which you can further control by setting a few flags.

In using the common dialog boxes, you add consistency to your user's interface. The users will be selecting from entry forms or screens that they have used before in other Windows programs. The dialog boxes are safe (the user cannot mess them up unless you allow him or her to by setting bad Flags values), and the user's answers to the dialog boxes' fields will be complete.

Now that the user can specify a file name, don't you think it's time to master file I/O? The next chapter introduces you to the database access feature of Visual Basic. In today's computing environment, there is simply no reason to perform tedious COBOL-like READ and WRITE statements, especially when the user needs to access file data as you'll see when you master the database control.

Chapter 28

Database Access

This chapter teaches you how to access database files from your Visual Basic application. More importantly, this chapter discusses the *data control*. With the data control, your user can read and manage database records without knowing anything about the database program that created the data.

In the PC world, there are several advanced database applications with which you can create and manage large repositories of data. You may have worked with 4th generation database applications on the larger mainframe systems. When a company must manage a vast resource of data, a database manager runs circles around the old indexed-sequential and random-access storage methods that we used to use.

Here are some of the topics that are discussed in this chapter:

- Discussing the database products supported by the Visual Basic data control

- Learning some terminology of a relational database system

- Placing the data control on the form and setting its properties

- Determining the correct controls needed for read-only and read/write field access

- Writing a database updating program that uses *no code* to read, scroll, or change a database file

Reviewing Various Databases

Visual Basic supports the access of all the database products listed in Table 28.1. As you can gather from the table's first entry, Microsoft Access is the premiere product for Visual Basic. Access works hand in hand with Visual Basic and it is the easiest to manage from a Visual Basic program.

Table 28.1 The Visual Basic-supported Database Products	
Product	**Description**
Microsoft Access	The most compatible of all the Visual Basic-supported databases. Access includes a Visual Basic-like language that interacts with Visual Basic quite well.
Microsoft FoxPro	A secondary database product offered by Microsoft. FoxPro has been around longer than Access. It is not as fancy, but is a solid product in use by many.
dBASE	Perhaps the first database product offered for PC users was dBASE. dBASE still has the largest installed user base for PC users.
Paradox	Borland, International's Windows database product designed with a well-featured Windows interface. The Paradox programming language (named *PAL*) is one of the most powerful database programming languages in existence but PAL is not compatible with Visual Basic.
Btrieve	A Novell database retrieval system that offers full access support for the famous *Btrieve* file structure that speedily accesses any record in the database.
ODBC	An industry standard database format. ODBC stands for *Open DataBase Connectivity*. The ODBC standard allows any database product that supports ODBC to work with Visual Basic's data control.

Non-database data systems are redundant.

Most companies keep their industry information in a database so that the employees can manage, edit, add, delete, and report information. Information is often considered a company's second most important asset (the first is the collection of employees). Managing that important information through the use of a database, as opposed to the scores of unrelated, redundant, and disorganized files that companies kept data in years ago, means that the company can view the information in ways that were never possible before.

Note

Creating database files from within Visual Basic is possible but not recommended. Use Visual Basic to write wrapper applications that use the data generated from within a database to get the most productivity from your information systems.

The standard organization of a database should pose no problem for you as a COBOL programmer. You've been working with records and fields for years. Perhaps you do or do not have access to a PC database program. If not, run don't walk, to your nearest software vendor and get a copy of one of the database products listed in Table 28.1. You'll add some free time to your schedule by using the database product for data management as opposed to writing long lists of COBOL PIC clauses. Without the database, you'll make changes to scores of applications every time your data changes.

Just in case you don't have a database product at your disposal, this book's disk contains a copy of a small Microsoft Access database file used in this chapter. You can use the database file in this chapter's sections as you learn more about the data control.

Note

Although Microsoft Access is the easiest database format for Visual Basic to work with, you'll have to keep the following in mind: Visual Basic versions 1 and 2 do not support the data control. Visual Basic version 3 supports Microsoft Access version 1.0 and 1.1. If you have a later version of Visual Basic, you can manage Microsoft Access 2.0 databases. The Access database supplied with this book is a version 1.1 database so that all Visual Basic versions 3.0 and later will be able to access the file.

Figure 28.1 shows an outline of the sample Microsoft Access database stored in INVENT.MDB. Table 28.2 contains a list of the database file's values so you can see the format before accessing the data later in this chapter.

Table 28.2   The INVENT.MDB Database File's *Inventory* Field Values

IDCode	Desc	Quant	Order	Price	Reorder
C1E4A	Widget-A	22	50	4.34	16
P92LO	Widget-B	80	150	2.19	45
L92Y6	Gadget-A	27	10	21.54	20

(continues)

V

Your Next Step with VB

Table 28.2 Continued					
IDCode	**Desc**	**Quant**	**Order**	**Price**	**Reorder**
U98PP	Washer-X	10	12	.81	12
TY98O	Mount	5	10	5.64	8
P192U	O-Seal	45	80	1.26	60
T2R2Q	Wing Nut	70	65	2.78	50
KP92M	Washer-Y	56	25	.75	42

Fig. 28.1
The sample
database format.

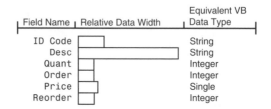

Using the Data Control

Figure 28.2 shows the location of the data control on your toolbox. Despite its name, the data control does not display data. The text box and label controls you've been using for displaying data work for database data as well as program data. The data control simply lets the user decide *which* data appears in text box and label controls that you use for the data's display.

Fig. 28.2
The data control
on the toolbox.

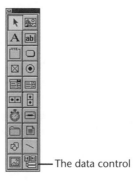

The data control

You must link the data control to your database from where you want to access data. The data control, although *data-aware*, must still have lots of database information that you'll set in the data control's properties, for proper database access. Remember, the data control links your Visual Basic environment to the database and its tables. The following sections explain how to access the INVENT.MDB data from a Visual Basic program.

Setting Data Control Properties

Open a new Visual Basic project and get ready to add some controls to the Form window. Double-click the data control to place the control on the form. You can drag the data control's resizing handles to extend the length of the control. To make sure that you get the control sized to match this chapter's application, press F4 and set the Width property to **2535**. While viewing the Properties window, change the name of the data control to **dtaInvent**. Your form should look something like the one in Figure 28.3.

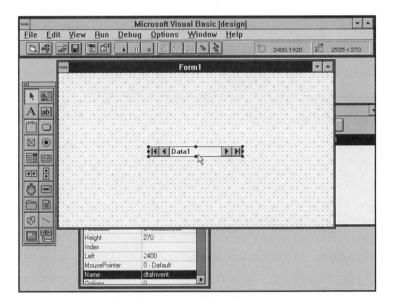

Fig. 28.3
The form now contains the data control.

Note

Your data control may not be centered as it is in the figure. Later, you'll move the data control to another location, so its current spot is not important.

Think for a moment what kind of information the data control needs to attach your application to the Microsoft Access INVENT.MDB database. The data control will need to know the database name, table name, and field names that you want to access.

V

Your Next Step with VB

Tables in a Database?

You may or may not be familiar with the way that Microsoft Access stores data in a database file. Most database applications store data differently from other database applications.

Microsoft Access uses a single file, called a *database file,* to store all of its contents. The single database file can contain one or more *database tables.* A database table is often what we think of when we think of a data file. Access gets its terminology from *relational database* theory, which Access supports. In a relational database, there is one single database with lots of tables that relate to each other in some manner.

We're keeping things simple here. The INVENT.MDB database file has only two tables. The table of interest here is called `Inventory`. The other table is named `ObjectBasis` (just a placeholder table). Unlike database files, internal Access database tables don't have to follow DOS- and Windows-based file-naming conventions.

Follow these steps to connect data control to the inventory database table:

1. Press F4 again to see the data control's Properties window.

2. Change the Caption property to **Inventory View**. The words `Inventory View` appear in the middle of the data control's body.

3. Highlight the DatabaseName property. The DatabaseName property holds the file name of the database you want to access. Click the ellipsis to display a `DatabaseName`'s File Open dialog box.

The selection you make depends on where you copied the database file from this book's disk. Determine the drive and directory where you copied this book's data files and select that drive and directory in the `DatabaseName`'s file open dialog box.

Caution

This chapter's example application is stored in the file named DATA.MAK. The drive and pathname for DATA.MAK's data control DatabaseName property may *not* match your computer's setup. Therefore if you want to load DATA.MAK instead of creating this example yourself, change the DatabaseName property value to match the drive and directory of your own data files.

When you select the database's name and directory, you see the INVENT.MDB file name in the File Name field. Select the INVENT.MDB file and click the OK command button to close the dialog box. You'll see the full path and file name inside the DatabaseName property as soon as the dialog box goes away.

> **Note**
>
> There are several property values you'll want to explore further if you connect Visual Basic applications to database applications often. This chapter stays rather simple so that you can learn the fundamentals. A lot of details may hinder you more than help at this point. Check out Visual Basic's online help system (search for Data Control, then click the Properties cross-referenced topic).

4. There are two tables in the INVENT.MDB database, so you'll also need to tell the data control which table to access. Highlight the RecordSource control (or select in the Properties window drop-down selection box) and type **Inventory**.

5. Move the data control to the bottom of the form by setting these property values:

   Left: **2640**

   Top: **3120**

6. Change the form's Caption property to **Inventory Update**.

You've now done all you need to do with the data control. Your form is not yet fancy. Figure 28.4 shows your lone data control form, set up to access the Inventory table in the INVENT.MDB database.

Remember that the data control itself cannot display data. The data control can only manage the user's selection of data from the database as you'll see in the next section. The data control establishes the link between Visual Basic and the database.

Fig. 28.4

The data control appears at the bottom of the form.

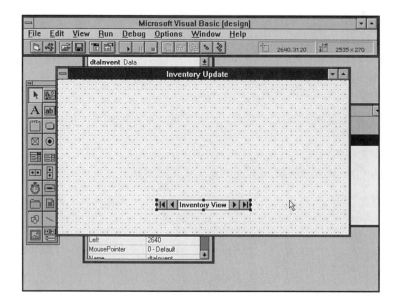

Connecting the Fields

You've now got to determine exactly what fields from the file you want the user to be able to see. Also, you'll need to decide whether or not the user can change the data or simply look at the data in a read-only form. This application will stay extremely simple so we'll display only three fields from the six in the table: the IDCode field that contains a unique product code, the Desc field that contains a description of the product, and the Price field that contains the product's price.

Protect read-only fields.

There is a handy way to protect read-only fields from the user's prying keyboard: use the label control to display read-only data and use the text box control to display data fields that the user can change.

Throughout your COBOL programming, you faced the day-to-day challenges of writing file-maintenance routines so the user could change data. By using ISAM (*indexed sequential access method*) files and proprietary filing systems, you were able to access records based on a key supplied by the user. You probably also wrote scores of programs that displayed records in a file, moving forward or backward in the file as the user pressed keys (the old PF7 and PF8 terminal keys often paged back and forth through files).

All of the tedious programming that required key matching and record searching in response to the user's paging keystrokes are behind you!

You won't believe how easy displaying records and letting the user update field values can be until you follow these steps to see for yourself (what a lead-in, right?):

1. Double-click the label control. Press F4 and highlight the DataSource property. When you use a label control to display database values, the DataSource property holds the name of the data control that manages the database in the Visual Basic application. Therefore, type **dtaInvent** for the DataSource value so that the label can use the data control you placed earlier for the data access.

2. Now the label needs to know which field to display from the data control's table. Highlight the DataField property and type **IDCode**. (You can also select from a drop-down list of available database fields by clicking the down arrow of the property value entry field.) This label displays the product code for each inventory item.

3. Set the remaining property values as follows:

    BackColor: **&H00C0C0C0&**

    BorderStyle: **1 - Fixed Single**

    Caption: (blank)

    FontSize: **12**

    Height: **375**

    Left: **1800**

    Top: **2040**

    Width: **975**

    The BackColor property changes the background to a light gray to separate the label from the text box that you'll place later.

4. Add a second label to the form, press F4, and set these property values:

    BackColor: **&H00C0C0C0&**

    BorderStyle: **1 - Fixed Single**

    Caption: (blank)

    DataField: **Desc**

DataSource: **dtaInvent**

FontSize: **12**

Height: **375**

Left: **3120**

Top: **2040**

Width: **1575**

This label control displays the inventory item's description.

5. Add a text box control to the form and set these properties:

BorderStyle: **1 - Fixed Single**

DataField: **Quant**

DataSource: **dtaInvent**

FontSize: **12**

Height: **420**

Left: **5040**

Text: (blank)

Top: **2040**

Width: **855**

The text box control lets the user change inventory quantity values as she or he steps through the display of the inventory records. Your screen should look like the one in Figure 28.5.

6. Add a command button with the following property values:

Caption: **E&xit**

Left: **6480**

Name: **cmdExit**

Top: **3360**

7. Double-click the command button and add the End statement to the body of the cmdExit_Click() procedure.

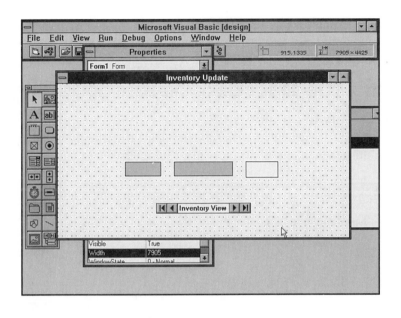

Fig. 28.5
You've almost
completed the
form.

8. All you now must do is add some descriptive labels above the controls you've got on the form. Add a label and set these properties:

>   Caption: **Product ID**
>
>   Height: **255**
>
>   Left: **1800**
>
>   Top: **1680**

Add another label with these values:

>   Caption: **Description**
>
>   Height: **255**
>
>   Left: **3120**
>
>   Top: **1680**

Add the final label with these values:

>   Caption: **Quantity**
>
>   Height: **255**
>
>   Left: **5040**
>
>   Top: **1680**

You're now completely done with the program. Save the application if you want. This application is stored on the book's disk file as DATA.MAK.

Using the Database Access

When you run the program, you'll see the form appear just like the one in Figure 28.6. You're actually looking at the product ID, description, and quantity for the first item in the inventory file (Table 28.2 verifies this).

Fig. 28.6
Viewing the first
database inventory
record.

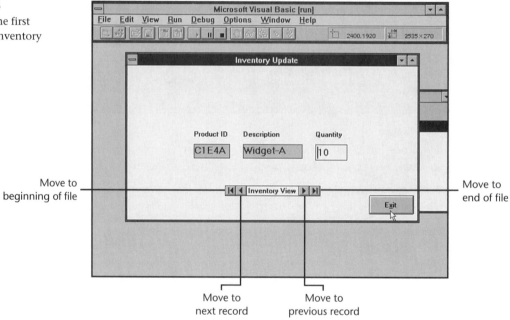

Move to beginning of file

Move to end of file

Move to next record

Move to previous record

Figure 28.6 shows how the user can move through the file. By clicking on either end data control arrow (the arrows that each point to straight bars), the application displays either the very first or last record in the file. By clicking on either of the two inner arrows, the user can page through the file one record at a time.

Changes require no programming. If the user changes the quantity field, that field changes *directly in the database itself*. The text control is a read/write control. When the user changes the value in the control, the value is linked directly to the database file itself. Therefore, if you were to change the quantity of the third record to 199, you could exit Visual Basic, start Microsoft Access, and the third record's quantity would still contain 199.

> **Note**
>
> Did you notice that *no programming* was required on your part, other than the terminating command button's End statement, to produce a fully updateable database access application?

> **Tip**
>
> Check box controls work well when displaying true or false data values.

What about long PIC clauses? What about using the Type command to generate record layouts and write programs that piece together records and display fields through loops and control statements? Visual Basic supports all that through the use of *recordsets* (simply a collection of table records that you define) and database-related commands.

If you need to use Visual Basic for such tedious access, you'll learn more about the recordset and database commands in the next chapter. These offer an easy database record-level access through programming but without the traditional file I/O problems.

Conclusion

This chapter explained how to access database files through the use of the data control. The data control is one of the most powerful controls on the Visual Basic toolbox. Not only is the control aware of multiple vendor databases, but the control performs *complete* data access, management, paging, and updating of records from a database system through your Visual Basic application.

As this chapter mentioned, Visual Basic programmers rarely use detailed file I/O commands as you would in a COBOL program. In addition, database users often use the database's native language to program extremely complicated database-related updates. If you use Microsoft Access, the Access programming language works a lot like Visual Basic, and you'll virtually feel at home in that environment. Once you tell the data control the name of the database that you need to access, then supply text boxes and labels for displaying data the user can and cannot change.

In the next chapter, "Database Commands, Properties, and Methods," you'll learn about other database-related commands, properties, and methods with which you can access database information with code.

Chapter 29

Database Commands, Properties, and Methods

This chapter introduces you to the world of database access through Visual Basic. Whereas the previous chapter explained the use of the data control, this chapter shows you how to program Visual Basic code to access, read, write, and search for data from within a database you associate to a Visual Basic program.

Many database management system development companies have decided that their database product's native language offers a better selection of database-retrieval commands. It's true that a database product almost always offers the best access language for that particular database. Nevertheless, the language that comes with Microsoft Access, Access Basic, looks and acts a lot like Visual Basic. You can use Visual Basic to retrieve information from an Access database (or almost any other database listed in Table 29.1) easily and store that information in variables for use within your program.

Here are some of the topics that will be discussed in this chapter:

- Using object variables to interact with tables

- Declaring and assigning Database variables

- Using the recordset object variables: Table, Dynaset, and Snapshot

- Using the Move methods to move through recordsets

- Reordering recordset data

- Finding specific records with Find and Seek

- Creating QueryDefs to see only fields of information

- Changing table data from within your Visual Basic program

Note

You'll find very little similarity between Visual Basic's database commands and COBOL's file I/O commands. Visual Basic uses numerous property settings and methods for its database access.

Note

If you use Visual Basic version 3.0, you must use the Professional Edition to utilize the database routines described in this chapter.

Object Variables

In a nutshell, an *object variable* is a lot like any other kind of variable. Object variables have names, and you can store or retrieve data with them. However, unlike `Integer`, `Single`, and the other types of regular variables, object variables represent database-like things such as databases, tables, *queries*, and *dynasets*. You'll learn about the special terms, such as query, dynaset, and recordsets, later in this chapter.

Object variables don't hold data in the same sense that regular variables do. Object variables are often associated with their database counterparts, so that when you work with an object variable, you are really working with the database table, query, or whatever the object variable represents. Object variables are Visual Basic's way of interacting with your data in the database. Think of the object as a database table and the variable as a field from within that table.

Database Variables

The `Database` keyword lets you specify when you need a `Database` variable. The `Dim`, `Static`, and `Global` keywords all declare database object variables just as they do other kinds of variables.

The following statements declare `Database` variables:

```
Global myDB As Database    ' Global is only in declarations section
Dim yourDB As Database
Static ourDB As Database
```

There is nothing unusual about these variable declarations. They work just like other variable declarations except they create `Database` type variables instead of variables of the other data types such as `Integer`.

Associating *Database* **Variables**

Obviously, before you can work with a table, there must be a database. You must associate `Database` variables (with `Set`) to actual databases before you can have access to the variables.

Database **variables associate to databases.**

The `OpenDatabase()` function works closely with `Database` variables. The `Close` method (which works like a built-in function in many ways and acts upon `Database` objects), works with `OpenDatabase()` to clean up memory reserved by `OpenDatabase()`. `Close` is described in the last section of this chapter. The `OpenDatabase()` function and the `Close` method operate on database files just as COBOL's `OPEN` and `CLOSE` provide and remove file access.

Here is the format of the `OpenDatabase()` `Database` object function:

```
OpenDatabase(dbFile, [, exclusive [, readOnly [, connectDB]]] )
```

The `OpenDatabase()` function lets you specify the database to open. The `dbFile` is any valid file with optional drive and path. `exclusive` is a `True` or `False` value that specifies networked environment arguments. If you want access to the database and want nobody else to have any access while you have it open, pass `True` for this argument. If you want your access to be read-only so you don't inadvertently change important data, pass `True` as the third argument as well. The `connectDB` must be a value from Table 29.1. Be sure to match the `connectDB` value exactly or Visual Basic will not recognize the database. Notice that you don't need to specify this fourth argument if you use a Microsoft Access database.

Table 29.1 The *connectDB* String Argument for *OpenDatabase()*

connectDB	Database Product
(none)	Microsoft Access
"dBASE III"	dBASE III
"dBASE IV"	dBASE IV
"Paradox"	Borland Paradox
"Paradox 3.x"	Borland Paradox

(continues)

V

Your Next Step with VB

Table 29.1 Continued	
connectDB	**Database Product**
`"Btrieve"`	Novell Btrieve
`"FoxPro 2.0"`	Microsoft FoxPro 2.0
`"FoxPro 2.5"`	Microsoft FoxPro 2.5
`"ODBC"`	An ODBC-compliant database

The following code opens three database files and associates them with appropriate `Database` variables.

```
Dim payrDB As Database
Dim acctDB As Database
Dim engDB As Database
' Associate databases to these variables
Set payrDB = OpenDatabase("C:\PAYROLL.MDB")
Set acctDB = OpenDatabase("D:\ACOUNTNG.MDB")
Set engDB = OpenDatabase("D:\ENGINEER.FOX", False, False,
➥"FoxPro 2.5")
```

In the following code, a network is being used. The first database associated to a `Database` variable is located on the server named `\\CHILD\BOYS` and the second is on the local drive C:. The first file can only be used by the application (until code later closes the database to release the database to other users) and the second file is read-only.

```
Set boysDB = OpenDatabase("\\CHILD\BOYS\BLUE.MDB", True)
Set girlsDB = OpenDatabase("PINK.MDB", False, True)
```

> **Note**
>
> In the second `Set` statement, the database can be used by other people on the network because of the `False` second argument.

Recordset Variables

Recordsets are Table, Dynaset, or Snapshot.

A *recordset* literally defines a set of zero or more records. A recordset is a generic term given to these three kinds of data collections:

- Tables

- Dynasets

- Snapshots

A `Table` variable is associated to a table in an open database. Through programming, you can reorder a `Table` variable and the underlying table is reordered as well. `Table` variables are extremely dynamic and changes that you or others make to the underlying table are immediately reflected in the `Table` variable.

A `Dynaset` is a collection of records from a table, a query for records that meet a specific criteria, or another `Dynaset` variable. You can filter and sort `Dynaset` records. If the underlying table data is changed (not added to or deleted from, but changed from one value to another), the `Dynaset` record collection's data changes too. If, however, another user or action deletes records from the underlying table, the `Dynaset` contains null values for those deleted records. If another user or action adds records to the underlying table, you have to re-create the `Dynaset` again to use those new records. Therefore, `Dynaset` variables are not quite as dynamic as `Table` variables because changes made to the database aren't always reflected in the actual database file.

A `Snapshot` is like a frozen picture in time of a table or query of particular records that meet a criteria match. If the underlying table changes in any way, *no* change is made to the `Snapshot`'s collection of records.

> **Note**
>
> Changing the record sets of `Table` and `Dynaset` variables can change the underlying table data. Changing a `Snapshot` variable, however, does not change the underlying table in any way.

Three more tables are critical in understanding these recordset kinds of variables. Table 29.2 lists the methods for `Dynaset`, `Table`, and `Snapshot` variables. Table 29.3 lists recordset properties that we'll discuss in the section called "Working with Records." The `D/S/T` column indicates whether the method applies to a `Dynaset`, `Snapshot`, or `Table`.

> **Note**
>
> This book cannot cover *all* the methods and properties listed in the tables due to space limitations. Some of the table entries require a lot of internal database understanding, which is not a goal of this book.

Table 29.2   Recordset Methods

Method	D/S/T	Description
AddNew	D,T	Prepares a new record so it can be inserted
Clone	D,S,T	Creates duplicate recordset objects
Close	D,S,T	Closes an object
CreateDynaset	D,S,T	Creates a dynaset object from a table, QueryDef, or SQL string
CreateSnapShot	D,S,T	Creates a snapshot object from a table, QueryDef, or SQL string
Delete	D,T	Deletes the current record in a table or dynaset
Edit	D,T	Copies the current record into a buffer area for editing
FindFirst	D,T,S	Makes current the first record that satisfies a search criteria
FindLast	D,T,S	Makes current the last record that satisfies a search criteria
FindNext	D,T,S	Makes current the next record that satisfies a search criteria
FindPrevious	D,T,S	Makes current the previous record that satisfies a search criteria
ListFields	T	Creates a snapshot with a record or each field in the database
ListIndexes	T	Creates a snapshot with a record for each index in the database
MoveFirst	D,S,T	Makes current the first record in a recordset
MoveLast	D,S,T	Makes current the last record in a recordset
MoveNext	D,S,T	Makes current the next record in a recordset
MovePrevious	D,S,T	Makes current the previous record in a recordset
Seek	T	Makes current a record in an indexed table that satisfies a search criteria for the current index

Method	D/S/T	Description
Update	D,T	Saves the contents of the editing buffer to a table or dynaset

---

Note

The SQL associations with these methods are not discussed in this book.

Table 29.3   Recordset Functions

Property	D/S/T	Description
BOF	D,S,T	Contains True (-1) if the current record is at the beginning of the recordset.
Bookmark	D,S,T	Sets a bookmark that marks a recordset's location so you can return to it later.
Bookmarkable	D,S,T	Contains True (-1) if recordset supports the use of Bookmarks.
DateCreated	D,T	Contains the date and time when a table was created.
EOF	D,S,T	Contains True (-1) if the current record is at the end of the recordset.
Filter	D,S	Sets a filter when you create a dynaset or snapshot. *
LastUpdated	D,T	Contains the date and time when a table was last changed.
LockEdits	D,T	Locks records during editing sessions. (Used in network environments.)
Name	D	Specifies a name to use for a form, control, or database object.
NoMatch	D,S,T	Indicates the success (with -1 for True or 0 for False) of a Find or Seek method.
Sort	D,S	Sets the order of records in a dynaset or snapshot.
Transactions	D,T	Contains True (-1) if a series of changes to a table or dynaset can be reversed. *

These methods do not apply to Snapshots created with these database-information methods: ListFields *and* ListIndexes.

V

Your Next Step with VB

Creating *Table* Variables

The `Table` keyword lets you create table variables within your Visual Basic programs. Before associating a `Table` variable to a table, you must declare and associate a `Database` variable to a database. The `OpenTable` method works like the `OpenDatabase()` function and lets you associate a table within the open database to a `Table` variable.

The following code first declares a `Database` and `Table` variable. The user is asked for the name of a table. The table name is then used to associate the table variable to the `Table` in this book's INVENT.MDB database.

```
Dim userDB As Database
Dim userTB As Table
Dim userAns As String
Set userDB = OpenDatabase("f:\vb\invent.mdb")
' Ask the user for the table to open
userAns = InputBox("Which table do you want to work with?")
' Use the OpenTable method to associate the actual table
Set userTB = userDB.OpenTable(userAns)
```

Creating *Dynaset* Variables

Create dynaset variables from tables, dynasets, forms, snapshots, and `Clone`.

Dynaset variables are as easy to declare and use as `Table` variables. The `CreateDynaset` method runs an existing query to store the result of the query in a `Dynaset` variable. Your database should support queries. A query is nothing more than a request for particular records that meet a certain condition. You'll later create queries from within Visual Basic with the `QueryDef` statement.

The following code declares a `Database` variable and a `Dynaset` variable, opens a database, and creates a dynaset from a table within the database.

```
Dim userDB As Database
Dim userDS As Dynaset
' Open the database or you cannot get the dynaset from it
Set userDB = OpenDatabase("RENTALS.MDB")
' Create the dynaset from the table
Set userDS = userDB.CreateDynaset("TENANTS")
```

In this example, `TENANTS` is a table from the RENTALS.MDB database. In place of `TENANTS`, you could have stored the name of a query such as `Find OutOfTown Tenants` (assuming the query is already defined through the Visual Basic `QueryDef` statement or from within your database) and the resulting `Dynaset` variable would have contained that query's data.

Creating *Snapshot* Variables

Creating Snapshot variables works the same way as Dynaset variables, but you must remember that a snapshot is a still-frame dynaset—if the data changes in any way, the Snapshot variable's contents will never change (unless you reassign the variable a new snapshot). The CreateSnapshot method retrieves the actual snapshot and associates the variable to it.

Snapshots **are dynasets "frozen in time."**

Tip

At first, Snapshot variables seem too limiting because they save only the current image of the data and not an ongoing image that changes as the data in the table changes. There are many times, however, when you'll want to save the current image of a dynaset. For example, you may want to save a set of records exactly as they appear *before* you perform a large update on the data.

The following example creates and associates a Snapshot variable:

```
Dim userDB As Database
Dim userDS As Dynaset
Dim userSS As Snapshot
Set userDB = OpenDatabase("c:\data\mydata.mdb")
' Create a dynaset from a query
Set userDS = userDB.CreateDynaset("Under16Customers")
' Create a snapshot of that dynaset
Set userSS = userDS.CreateSnapshot()
```

Notice that no argument was used in the CreateSnapshot method because userDS was not a database but a dynaset object. The snapshot (and the initial dynaset) contained all records which had fewer than 16 customers.

Cleaning Up When Done

Almost every programming language includes some way for the programmer to *close* a file when that file is no longer needed in the program. If you don't close files, the programming language will usually close them for you; however, it is always recommended that you explicitly close files when finished with them.

Use the Close method when you are done with recordset variables. Even though the Close will eventually happen automatically, it may be a while and valuable resources are being used while the recordsets are still open.

V

Your Next Step with VB

> **Caution**
>
> Closing your recordset variables in a networked environment is most critical because other users might be scrambling for resources that you still have open but no longer need.

After statements such as these:

```
Set db = OpenDatabase(DatabaseName)
Set dsTable = db.CreateDynaset(TableName)
```

you'll find these closing statements at the end of the module:

```
dsTable.Close
db.Close
```

Working with Records

Now that you can declare and associate recordset variables, it is time to use them to get to your database data and bring that data into your Visual Basic programs. Often, you want to load specific data from a table into your Visual Basic programs. Other times, you may want to work with all the data in a table.

Reading Table Data into Variables

As you assign data from tables to recordset variables, you must keep in mind the position of the recordset pointer in the table. For example, when you declare a Dynaset variable and load data from the table into the Dynaset variable, what prints if you printed a field in the Dynaset variable? The entire dynaset? One record? All the records from a query? The answer depends on many factors, but the primary consideration is the position of the recordset pointer.

After associating recordset variables to tables, you then must control a recordset position pointer within the recordset to access different records. If you do nothing special, the first record in the recordset will remain the current position. No matter how many times you print or store data from the recordset into other variables, they will always hold the first recordset record's data.

The following program performs two tasks: it shows you one way to access data from a table and store that data in a recordset variable (myTable) and it also shows that the recordset's position pointer does not change on its own.

```
Sub getContact ()
' Read three contact names from the Customers table into an array
  Dim myDB As Database, myTable As Table
  Set myDB = OpenDatabase("C:\data\mydata.mdb")
➥' Assumes Northwind Traders
  Set myTable = myDB.OpenTable("Customers")
  ' Declare three array variables to hold data from the table
  Static ContName(3) As Variant   ' An array

  ' The next 3 lines appear to store the first 3 contacts
  ContName(1) = myTable("ContactName") ' a Contact field
  ContName(2) = myTable("ContactName")
  ContName(3) = myTable("ContactName")

  Print ContName(1)    ' All three Prints
  Print ContName(2)    ' prints the SAME
  Print ContName(3)    ' names!
End Sub
```

This procedure appears to store the first three contact names in a three-element array. However, each access of the Table variable grabs the *same* record. When the first assignment statement stores the first record's Contact Name field value into ContName(1) like this:

```
ContName(1) = myTable("ContactName")
```

the *only* thing to happen is that the assignment takes place. Visual Basic does not automatically move the Table variable's record pointer forward. Therefore the next two lines:

```
ContName(2) = myTable("Contact Name")
ContName(3) = myTable("Contact Name")
```

also store the first record's Contact Name value in the array elements.

To shift the currency of the recordset pointer, you have to use one of these four methods described in Table 29.2: MoveFirst, MoveLast, MoveNext, and MovePrevious. Remember that a recordset variable can be a Table variable (as in this code), a Dynaset variable, or a Snapshot variable, and these methods are available to each.

Note

This section is devoted to reading data from a table, not storing data in the table. To change table data, you'll need the information from the later sections of this chapter.

The BOF property will be True if the current position of the recordset pointer is the first one in the recordset (the beginning of the file). The EOF property will be True if the current position of the recordset variable is *past* the last record (at the end of the file). If both properties are True, there are no records in the recordset.

> **Note**
>
> The order of the records in a Table variable is random unless you use a primary key or index as explained in the following sections. The data you retrieve is in the same physical order that the data was entered into the underlying table. There is no logical order.

The following code properly uses MoveNext to move the recordset position ahead one record after each assignment of the Contact Name field to variables.

```
Sub getContact ()
' Read three contact names from the Customers table into an array
  Dim myDB As Database, myTable As Table
  Set myDB = OpenDatabase("C:\data\mydata.mdb")
  Set myTable = myDB.OpenTable("Customers")
  ' Declare three array variables to hold data from the table
  Static ContName(3) As Variant   ' An array

  ' The next 3 lines appear to store the first 3 contacts
  ContName(1) = myTable("Contact Name")
  myTable.MoveNext        ' Move the recordset  pointer
  ContName(2) = myTable("Contact Name")
  myTable.MoveNext        ' Move the recordset  pointer
  ContName(3) = myTable("Contact Name")

  Print ContName(1)     ' All three Prints
  Print ContName(2)     ' prints the SAME
  Print ContName(3)     ' names!
  myTable.Close         ' You cannot close a current database
End Sub
```

If you run this code on a database, the form will display the first three contact names from the Customers table.

Finding *Table* Records in a Different Order

All the databases supported by Visual Basic let you set index values for the database tables. Use the index defined for the table to retrieve table records in a logical order different from the arbitrary, physical order that regular data retrieval provides. If there are no index files defined for the table, you can use the primary key to retrieve the records.

The Table variable's Index property tells Visual Basic which index to use for the Table variable retrieval. Use either PrimaryKey, or Index1, Index2, Index3, Index4, Index5 (for each of the subsequent multiple key values), or the specific name of the index-key field when assigning the Index property.

The following code prints the first three products of a database in random order, then uses the primary key to print the first three products as defined by the key.

```
Sub indexPrint ()
' Read three product descriptions in their random, physical
' order, then read the 1st three in logical key order
  Dim myDB As Database, prodTable As Table
  Dim subsc As Integer    ' Loop subscript
  Set myDB = OpenDatabase("f:\vb\invent.mdb")
  Set prodTable = myDB.OpenTable("Inventory")
  ' Print the first 3 lines
  Print "Without using the index:"
  For subsc = 1 To 3
    Print prodTable("Desc")
    prodTable.MoveNext
  Next subsc
  prodTable.MoveFirst              ' Reset the position
  ' Now, use the index
  prodTable.Index = "PrimaryKey"   ' Use the primary key
  Print "Using the index:"
  For subsc = 1 To 3
    Print prodTable("Desc")
    prodTable.MoveNext
  Next subsc
  prodTable.Close
End Sub
```

Ordering *Dynaset* and *Snapshot* Records

If you want to reorder a Dynaset or Snapshot variable, you must do so at the *source* of that variable. The order depends on whether you get the data from a table or from another Dynaset or Snapshot variable.

The source determines order.

If you create a Dynaset or Snapshot variable from a table, the order will be in the underlying table's primary key order if the table has one (if not, the records will be random in the Dynaset or Snapshot variable).

If you create a Dynaset or Snapshot variable from a Dynaset or Snapshot, the Sort property of the Dynaset or Snapshot determines the order of the resulting records. You can set the Sort property yourself to have more than one Dynaset or Snapshot variable with different views of the same data.

The following procedure creates a dynaset from a Customers table. The Customers table is ordered by its Customer ID primary key field, and so will the resulting Dynaset variable custDY. The first three customer IDs and names are printed directly on the form and the names appear in Customer ID order.

```
Sub dynaPrint ()
' Print 3 dynaset records ordered by the table's primary key
  Dim myDB As Database
  Dim custDY As Dynaset
```

```
    Dim subsc As Integer    ' Loop subscript
    Set myDB = OpenDatabase("C:\DATA.MDB")
    Set custDY = myDB.CreateDynaset("Customers")
    ' Print the first 3 lines
    For subsc = 1 To 3
      Print custDY("CustomerID"), custDY("CompanyName")
      custDY.MoveNext
    Next subsc
    custDY.Close          ' You cannot close a current database
End Sub
```

The following example creates the same Dynaset variable as the previous example. A second Dynaset variable is then created after the Sort property is set to the Postal Code field. The resulting five records printed are in Postal Code order. You could not order these Dynaset records in Postal Code order if they came directly from a table unless the table was originally ordered by Postal Code.

```
Sub sortDY ()
' Print 3 dynaset records ordered by the Postal Code
    Dim myDB As Database
    Dim custDY As Dynaset
    Dim postDY As Dynaset   ' The second dynaset variable
    Dim subsc As Integer    ' Loop subscript
    Set myDB = OpenDatabase("C:\DATA.MDB")
    Set custDY = myDB.CreateDynaset("Customers")
    custDY.Sort = "PostalCode"
    Set postDY = custDY.CreateDynaset()
    ' Print the first 3 lines
    For subsc = 1 To 3
      Print postDY("CustomerID"), postDY("CompanyName")
      postDY.MoveNext
    Next subsc
    postDY.Close
    custDY.Close              ' You cannot close a current database
End Sub
```

Finding Specific Records

Whereas the Move methods described in the previous section are useful for moving the recordset's pointer, the FindFirst, FindLast, FindNext, and FindPrevious methods are better at zeroing-in on the records you want and only those records. Here is the general format of the Find methods:

```
Find... criteria
```

The *criteria* expression must be a string expression. The sole purpose of the Find methods is to move the recordset position to the record you want to work with next.

If a Find method cannot locate a record in the Dynaset or Snapshot, Visual Basic sets a NoMatch property to True and you have to assume that no valid record pointer is set. (In actuality it will be the most recent position or record.)

The following code prints customers that have no fax numbers from a Customers table. Unlike the previous example, this one uses FindNext to position the recordset position only to those records that have Null for the Fax field, therefore improving the efficiency from the previous example that printed the Customer IDs that have Null for the fax field.

```
Sub noFax ()
' Print Customer IDs of all without fax numbers
' Use the FindNext method to improve efficiency
  Dim myDB As Database
  Dim custDS As Dynaset
  Dim faxNum As Variant    ' To hold incoming fax values from
                           ' dynaset
  Set myDB = OpenDatabase("C:\DATA.MDB")
  Set custDS = myDB.CreateDynaset("Customers")
  custDS.FindNext "Fax = Null"
  Do Until custDS.nomatch        ' Loop until reach no more matches
    Print custDS("CustomerID")   ' Prints only if no fax
    custDS.FindNext "Fax = Null"
  Loop
  custDS.Close
End Sub
```

Seek and You'll Find *Table* Data

Use the Seek method if you want to locate records in a Table variable instead of the Find methods that work with Dynaset and Snapshot variables. Here is the format of Seek:

```
tableVariable.Seek comparison, key [, key] [...]
```

The *comparison* argument can be any of the string expressions from Table 29.4. The Seek method also accepts a variable number of arguments depending on the number of fields in the index you use for the table. The argument (or arguments) following *comparison* is the value you are comparing to a field in the index (or values being compared to more than one field in the index).

Table 29.4 The *Seek* Comparison Argument Values

String	Description
"="	Is equal to the key
">"	Is greater than the key

(continues)

Table 29.4 Continued	
String	**Description**
">="	Is greater than or equal to the key
"<"	Is less than the key
"<="	Is less than or equal to the key

Note

You cannot change records with either the Move, Find, or Seek methods without using the Edit and Update methods described later in the section, "Changing a Record."

Listing 29.1 looks through the Customers table storing all company names that fall within the first half of the alphabet in one array and storing the last half in another array.

Listing 29.1   Split the Company Names into Two Arrays

```
Sub halfNames ()
' Store Customers whose ID is in upper and lower halves of alphabet
Dim custDB As Database
Dim custTB As Table
Dim subscr As Integer          ' Array subscript variable
Set custDB = OpenDatabase("C:\CUSTS.MDB")
Set custTB = custDB.OpenTable("Customers")
Static highCusts(100) As String  ' To hold  A-M names
Static lowCusts(100) As String   ' To hold  N-Z names
subscr = 1  ' First subscript
' Set the index to the right field
custTB.index = "Company Name"
custTB.Seek  "<", "N"        ' Seek out customers  A-M
Do Until custTB.nomatch      ' Loop until reach no more matches
  highCusts(subscr) = custTB("Company Name")
  subscr = subscr + 1
  custTB.Seek "<", "N"       ' Seek again
Loop
custTB.MoveFirst             ' Reset position at beginning
Do Until custTB.nomatch      ' Loop until reach no more matches
  custTB.Seek ">",  "M"      ' Seek out customers  N-Z
  lowCusts(subscr) = custTB("Company Name")
  subscr = subscr + 1
  custTB.Seek  ">", "M"      ' Seek again
Loop
custTB.Close
End Sub
```

An Introduction to *QueryDefs*

Once you create a `QueryDef` variable, you can create your own query from within your Visual Basic programs. Unlike the recordset variables, a `QueryDef` variable contains the query instructions but not any data. The query is a selection criterion that you want Visual Basic to use when searching for a particular set of records.

You must understand *SQL* (pronounced *sequel*) statements to create queries from within Visual Basic, and this book doesn't go into detail on that. SQL is a common query language supported by most of today's database products. Sorry, but SQL is a complete book in itself. Nevertheless, if you need to know how to create queries and use a product such as Microsoft Access that supports *SQL*, you probably have all the SQL references that you need to write queries.

> **Note**
>
> QueryDefs contain no data, so you must create a Dynaset or Snapshot variable if you want to access data that the QueryDef generates. Do not create Dynaset or Snapshot variables from your QueryDef if the query is an updating query because the query is used to change or remove data and not produce a recordset as the selection queries are. (You can run updating queries using QueryDef variables, but don't create recordset variables from such queries.)

As with other recordset variables, close your `QueryDef` variables with the `Close` method when your program is done with them.

Use the `QueryDef` keyword to declare `QueryDef` variables. The following statement declares a `QueryDef` variable named `QD`:

```
Dim QD As QueryDef
```

Here is a possible query created and stored in the `QD` query variable that you can later use when you need the query's selected records (all records whose child ages are over 12 years old):

```
Set MyQuery = MyDB.CreateQueryDef("Older Kids",
➥"SELECT >12 FROM Children;")
```

Again, you must understand the SQL language before you'll be skilled at writing your own queries to retrieve selected data from a database file.

Changing a Record

Once you locate a record of interest, you may want to change the data in that record. Updateable queries can change table data, but the change you want to make might be too complex for a query to provide.

Visual Basic makes sure that you *want* to change a record before the change is made. First, you must tell Visual Basic that you want to change the record (with the Edit method), make the change, then use the Update method to save those changes.

> **Caution**
>
> If you leave out any step when changing records, Visual Basic will not let you make the change.

The procedure in Listing 29.2 creates a dynaset of a company's Customers table. Suppose that several records in the table have blank fax numbers. This procedure displays the company name of each company without a fax number, one at a time, and asks the user to fill in the number. Once the user types a fax number, that number is written to the dynaset (and the underlying table) until all fax numbers have been entered. The user can press Enter if a fax number is not yet available for a particular company.

Listing 29.2 Creates a Dynaset by Searching the *Customers* Table

```
Sub changeFax ()
' Ask the user for fax numbers to replace those that are Null
' in the Customer table
  Dim myDB As Database
  Dim custDS As Dynaset
  Dim faxNum As Variant    ' To hold incoming fax values from
                           ' dynaset
  Dim msg As String        ' For message box
  Set myDB = OpenDatabase("C:\CUSTS.MDB")
  Set custDS = myDB.CreateDynaset("Customers")
  custDS.FindNext "Fax = Null"
  Do Until custDS.nomatch ' Loop until reach no more matches
    msg = "Enter a fax number for " & custDS("CompanyName")
    custDS.Edit              ' Prepare for edit
    custDS.Update            ' Make the actual change
    custDS.FindNext "Fax = Null"
  Loop
  custDS.Close
End Sub
```

Adding and Deleting Records

The AddNew method creates new records in a Table or Dynaset variable. AddNew creates a new blank record that your code can initialize. The Update method then saves the new record in the table or dynaset.

The position of the new record in a Table variable depends on the active index you are using at the time. The record is always added to the end of a Dynaset variable but you can create a new sorted Dynaset variable to hold the data in a correct position.

If you want to delete the record at the current position, use the Delete method. No Update method is needed or allowed after a Delete method, and you *must* use Move to move the record position to the next record of interest.

Suppose that a customer data table included orders from three countries: USA, Canada, and the UK. Suppose that the company created a European sales office that handled all the orders in the UK. Listing 29.3 deletes all the order records that reside in the UK from the company's table so that the overseas office can take over the UK operations.

Listing 29.3   Removes All Order UK Records from the Database

```
Sub RemoveUK ()
' Remove the UK orders so the newly formed
' European division can handle them.
  Dim DB As Database
  Dim ordTB As Table
  Set DB = OpenDatabase("D:\COMPANY.MDB")
  Set ordTB = DB.OpenTable("Orders")
  ordTB.MoveFirst
  Do Until ordTB.EOF
    If ordTB("ShipCountry") = "UK" Then
      ordTB.Delete
    End If
    ordTB.MoveNext
  Loop
  ordTB.Close
End Sub
```

There is a second way you could accomplish the removal of the UK records and, at the same time, eliminate the need for the European office to re-enter the data. You can create a new table for those records that are part of the UK and then delete those records from the original database while creating the new table. There are usually several ways to accomplish the same task with database methods.

Conclusion

You are now much more familiar with the declaration and association of object variables within Visual Basic. This chapter set the groundwork to let you explore the use of Visual Basic with a database.

The recordset variables are extremely important because when using them, Visual Basic can manipulate, sort, input, and output an entire set of data. A recordset contains either table, dynaset, or snapshot data. A database must be open before you can associate recordset variables to actual data within the database.

As you learned in this chapter, the world of database access and management is fairly complicated and requires an understanding of new terms. You may need to read up on your database product before this chapter really sinks in.

If you want to write fairly involved database applications, the database's own language is probably the best place to do so. Que offers a book called *Access 2 Programming By Example* that you might find handy for getting familiar with programming using Access. Also, for more advanced information, check out *Creating Access Applications* or *Access 2 Power Programming* for in-depth coverage of the Microsoft Access language.

Whereas the last two chapters brought database access into your Visual Basic application, the next chapter lets you give spreadsheet-like control over data using the grid control.

Chapter 30

Using the Grid Control

COBOL is not known for its mathematical strength, but COBOL handles the business world's financial calculations with adequate ease. Despite its excellence in the business world, however, COBOL is not typically a language one would target for mathematical modeling. Even if you were going to model financial calculations and variance scenarios, COBOL would not be one's long-shot choice for languages. The spreadsheets available on microcomputers and the mainframe modeling systems such as IFPS (*Interactive Financial Planning System*) make much better "what if" tools.

As you've seen, Visual Basic handles the business world well. In addition, the Visual Basic language contains mathematical functions that perform fairly complex mathematical and trigonometric operations. Well, hang on to your hats because this chapter will show you how Visual Basic can perform spreadsheet-like analysis with the ease of Lotus 1-2-3 and the programmability of Microsoft Excel!

This chapter introduces you to Visual Basic's *grid* control. The grid control lets you place a grid of spreadsheet-like cells on an application's Form window. The user has the power of a Visual Basic program and, in addition, the user can analyze numerical and textual values in a grid of rows and columns.

Here are some of the topics that will be discussed in this chapter:

- Learning how to find and place the grid control
- Setting the grid size using the Properties window
- Analyzing the number of fixed rows and columns that your grid needs
- Adding graphics and text to the grid's cells
- Locating the user's selected grid cells and modifying the selected cells

The user can select a cell or a range of cells and scroll through a grid of cell values. The user cannot, however, enter values into the cells. The grid control displays data but does not let the user enter or change that data directly.

Preparing for the Grid Control

Figure 30.1 shows the placement of the grid control on your toolbox. Alas, not all of you will have the grid control. There are three requirements for using the grid control:

- You must have Visual Basic version 3.0 or later.

- If you use Visual Basic version 3.0, you must use the Professional Edition because the Standard Edition does not contain the grid control.

- The grid control is an add-in control that may not appear on your toolbox until you add the GRID.VBX custom control to your application. For a review about adding custom controls, see the discussion on CMDIALOG.VBX in Chapter 27, "Common Dialog Boxes."

Fig. 30.1
The grid control
on the toolbox.

The grid control——

Learning the Grid Control's Properties

Spreadsheet users love the grid control!

The grid control is a two-dimensional control. In lots of ways, the grid created by a grid control operates a lot like a two-dimensional table of data. The grid control contains rows and columns of data. The user can move through the grid's spreadsheet-like values.

Tip

Many Visual Basic programmers forget the grid control when displaying table data. If you need to display table data, such as a table of division price codes from several salespeople in each division, collect the data in a grid of cells instead of using `Print` or labels.

Figure 30.2 illustrates the grid control's layout. A grid can contain fixed rows and columns. The fixed rows and columns often contain labels that describe the data in the rows and columns. The fixed rows and columns always remain in place, whereas the user can scroll the non-fixed rows and columns to see additional data (if your application supports scrolling the grid's rows and columns).

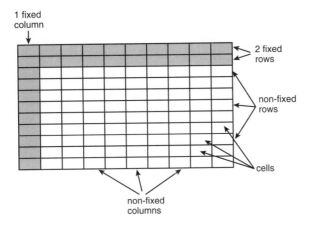

Fig. 30.2
A grid's layout.

V

Your Next Step with VB

Note

The figure's fixed rows and columns are shaded light gray. Visual Basic also shades the fixed rows and columns so that the user can tell the fixed from the non-fixed cells. Also, you can control whether or not Visual Basic displays vertical or horizontal (or both) scroll bars through properties if the grid control is not large enough to hold all the rows and columns.

Table 30.1 describes the grid control's important properties that you can set both at runtime and from the Properties window.

Table 30.1   The Grid Control's Major Properties

Property	Description
About	The custom controls contain an About box that indicates the version and creator of the control.
BackColor	Specifies the background color of the non-fixed cells.
BorderStyle	Holds either 0 - None or 1 - Fixed Single to describe the border around the grid.
Cols	Indicates the number of columns (the total of fixed and non-fixed).
FillStyle	Contains either 0 - Single or 1 - Repeat depending on whether a value is to be assigned to a selected cell or to a range of selected cells.
FixedCols	The number of fixed columns (must be at least one less than the value of Cols).
FixedRows	The number of fixed rows (must be at least one less than the value of Rows).
FontBold	Contains either True or False indicating that the cell value is boldfaced.
FontItalic	Contains either True or False indicating that the cell value is italic.
FontName	The name of the font's file.
FontSize	The size of the cell's font.
FontStrikeThru	Contains either True or False indicating that the cell value is strikethrough.
FontUnderline	Contains either True or False indicating that the cell value is underlined.
GridLines	Contains True or False to either display the dividing lines between cells or not to display the dividing lines.
GridWidth	Indicates the width, from 1 to 9 twips, of the grid lines.
Height	The height, in twips, of each cell.
HighLight	Contains either True or False and determines whether or not the selected cell or cells are highlighted.
Left	The number of twips from the left edge of the window to the grid's left edge.
Name	The name of the grid.

Property	Description
Rows	The number of rows in the grid.
ScrollBars	Determines the style of scroll bars that appear around the grid by containing either 0 - None, 1 - Horizontal, 2 - Vertical, or 3 - Both.
Top	The number of twips from the top of the window to the top edge of the grid.
Width	The width, in twips, of the grid.

There are several additional properties that you can only set at runtime. These properties will be discussed as this chapter progresses.

Working with a Grid

Load this book's application named MYGRID.MAK. When you run the program, you'll see the grid shown in Figure 30.3. Notice that the grid control contains horizontal and vertical scroll bars with which the user can look at all the cells within the grid. You can resize this particular grid so the scroll bars aren't needed because the grid is fairly small. However, MYGRID.MAK contains a fairly small grid window so that you can see the effects of the scroll bars. Scroll the grid to see that the titles (located within fixed columns and rows) don't scroll away.

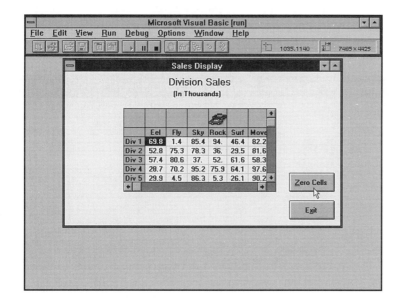

Fig. 30.3
The form after running the MYGRID.MAK application.

Exit the program and press F4 to display the grid's Properties window. The following property values uniquely identify this grid:

Cols: 10

FixedCols: 1

FixedRows: 2

Height: 2175

HighLight: True

Left: 1560

Name: grdSales

Rows: 8

ScrollBars: 3 - Both

Top: 960

Width: 4095

The two fixed rows let the application display a picture in the center of the top row and display the column descriptions in the second row. The single fixed column labels each row in the application.

Use code to initialize cells.

The Form_Load() procedure is the catalyst for initializing and preparing the grid for display. The Properties window cannot assign values to the grid's cells. You can only assign values to a grid through code. Remember that each application executes a Form_Load() procedure at the start of each program run. Listing 30.1 shows the Form_Load() procedure for the MYGRID.MAK application.

Listing 30.1 The *Form_Load()* Event Procedure

```
Sub Form_Load ()
    Call CenterCells    ' Center all cell alignments
    Call PicCell        ' Put picture of car in top row
    Call CellTitles     ' Insert column titles
    Call DivTitles      ' Add division titles
    Call FillCells      ' Fill cells with random values
End Sub
```

The Form_Load() procedure works like a controlling COBOL paragraph that calls the other procedures in the program. All of the procedures are general subroutine procedures. Although all of these procedures' code could be folded into one long Form_Load() event procedure, the called subroutines offer a better and more structured approach. Each of the following sections explains the general procedures and teaches you how to manage grid controls as well.

Centering Cell Values

As with most major spreadsheets, you can left-justify, right-justify, or center text data within a cell. The following two grid properties control cell alignment (also known as *justification*):

`FixedAlignment()` (for the cells in fixed columns)

`ColAlignment()` (for the cells in non-fixed columns)

You can assign the alignment properties one of these three values:

0   for left alignment (the default)

1   for right alignment

2   for center alignment

> **Note**
>
> You can control alignment by columns only, not rows.

Listing 30.2 contains the code for the MYGRID.MAK's `CenterCells()` procedure. An integer subscript named `Cars` steps across each of the nine columns and sets both the fixed cells and the non-fixed cells within the columns. (Although there are ten columns total, the first column's labels fill the fixed column without needing to be centered.)

Listing 30.2   The Cell Alignment Procedure

```
Sub CenterCells ()
' Ensures that all future cells are center aligned
  Dim Cars As Integer
  ' Center all values in the grid
  For Cars = 1 To 9
    grdSales.Col = Cars
    grdSales.FixedAlignment(Cars) = 2
    grdSales.ColAlignment(Cars) = 2
  Next
End Sub
```

Without the centering procedure, the grid looks less professional as proved by Figure 30.4's labels and data.

Fig. 30.4
The cells need to
be aligned.

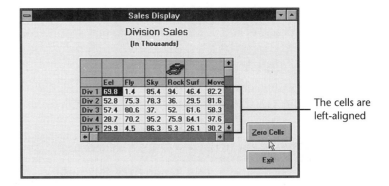

The cells are
left-aligned

Adding Graphics to the Grid

You can display both icon and bitmap images in the grid's cells. The Picture
property contains the path and file name of the graphic that you want to
display in the grid. You can display graphics in one or more cells in a grid by
inserting the graphic in the cell or cells at runtime.

> **Caution**
>
> You cannot adjust individual cells, only full column and row sizes. Be sure the grid
> cells' height and width values are large enough to hold the graphic. You can use the
> ColWidth(*columnNumber*) and RowHeight(*rowNumber*) to adjust the width and
> height if you need to.

The PicCell() procedure, shown in Listing 30.3, displays the car image that
appears in the grid's first row. After setting the first row's height and the fifth
column's width, the Col and Row properties are set to indicate the intersection
of the cell that will be filled next. Therefore the subsequent LoadPicture()
function stores the image in the cell.

Listing 30.3 Adding a Graphic to the Grid

```
Sub PicCell ()
  ' Put a picture in the middle cell of the top row
  grdSales.RowHeight(0) = 475
  grdSales.ColWidth(4) = 475
  grdSales.Col = 4
  grdSales.Row = 0
  grdSales.Picture = LoadPicture("f:\vb\icons\industry\cars.ico")
  ' Be sure F:\ is replaced by where you have VB installed
End Sub
```

Anytime you need to assign an individual cell a value (whether that value is text or a graphic), set the grid's Row and Col properties to the row and column that forms an intersection of the specific cell you want to initialize. The Properties window's Rows and Cols values are different from the (singular) Row and Col properties. Rows and Cols hold the total number of rows and columns in the grid and the Row and Col values target a specific cell at any one time.

Tip

The user can resize cell width and height values at runtime by placing the mouse cursor between the columns and rows of the fixed cells. The cursor shape changes to a vertical bar with which you can drag the mouse to resize the row and column width.

Adding Titles to the Non-Fixed Cells

Always place labels inside the grid's cells so that the user knows what kinds of information appear in the grid. The CellTitles() procedure fills the MYGRID.MAK's fixed row and column with labels that indicate what each row and column contains. Listing 30.4 lists the CellTitles() procedure.

Listing 30.4   Adding the Column Titles

```
Sub CellTitles ()
  ' Fill in the column titles
  grdSales.Row = 1    ' All car titles are in row #1
  grdSales.Col = 1
  grdSales.Text = "Eel"
  grdSales.Col = 2
  grdSales.Text = "Fly"
  grdSales.Col = 3
  grdSales.Text = "Sky"
  grdSales.Col = 4
  grdSales.Text = "Rock"
  grdSales.Col = 5
  grdSales.Text = "Surf"
  grdSales.Col = 6
  grdSales.Text = "Move"
  grdSales.Col = 7
  grdSales.Text = "Wow"
  grdSales.Col = 8
  grdSales.Text = "Zap"
  grdSales.Col = 9
  grdSales.Text = "Power"
End Sub
```

V

Your Next Step with VB

Use the Text
**property to store
cell values.**

The Row is set to 1 early in the procedure so that the row directly beneath the graphic image receives the titles. The rest of the procedure sets the Col value for each of the next columns' values and assigns labels to each of the columns. The Text property receives the value that the cell will hold. The code is a little tedious. In a larger application, you might store the titles in a file or in a secondary .TXT file, initialize them in a string array, and assign them from that string array.

Each of the rows needs titles as well, and the DivTitles() procedure fills the first column (Col number 0) with the division number titles. Listing 30.5 contains the DivTitles() procedure. As you can see, the procedure first sets the Col value to the column that will receive the labels and subsequently assigns the division titles.

Listing 30.5 Adding the Row Titles

```
Sub DivTitles ()
  ' Add titles to the divisions
  grdSales.Col = 0  ' Division titles in first column
  grdSales.Row = 2
  grdSales.Text = "Div 1"
  grdSales.Row = 3
  grdSales.Text = "Div 2"
  grdSales.Row = 4
  grdSales.Text = "Div 3"
  grdSales.Row = 5
  grdSales.Text = "Div 4"
  grdSales.Row = 6
  grdSales.Text = "Div 5"
  grdSales.Row = 7
  grdSales.Text = "Div 6"
End Sub
```

Filling Cells with Data

Once you've assigned titles to cells, assigning data values is simple. Generally, putting data in a cell requires these steps:

1. Set the Col value to the column in which you want to initialize the cell.

2. Set the Row value to the row in which you want to initialize the cell.

3. Format the value using the Format() function so the cell holds data stored in a correct format.

4. Assign the Text property the formatted value.

Listing 30.6 contains the code that randomly fills the grid with data values. The listing uses the Rnd function to generate the data values although you would normally read the data from a database.

Listing 30.6 Adding the Data to the Grid

```
Sub FillCells ()
' Fill all data cells with random values
  Dim Cars, Divs As Integer
  Dim SalesRand As Single
  For Cars = 1 To 9     ' 10 columns of cars
    For Divs = 2 To 7  ' 8 rows of divisions
       grdSales.Col = Cars
       grdSales.Row = Divs
       SalesRand = Rnd * 99
       grdSales.Text = Format(SalesRand, "##.#")
    Next Divs
  Next Cars
End Sub
```

Selecting Cells

If you want the user to be able to select one or more cells, Visual Basic makes it easy to do. Use the five properties described in Table 30.2 to tell your program how the user selected cell values.

Note

A user can select a range of cells with the Shift and arrow keys or by dragging the mouse. The selected range can either be the currently highlighted cell or multiple cells. The selected range *must* be contiguous; that is, the selected cells must appear together as a partial or full row or column of cells, or a rectangular shape of selected cells.

Table 30.2 Properties Related to the User's Selection of Cells	
Property	**Description**
HighLight	Becomes True when the user selects a cell or a range of cells and remains False otherwise
SelEndCol	The rightmost column of the selected range
SelEndRow	The bottom row of the selected range
SelStartCol	The leftmost column of the selected range
SelStartRow	The top row in the selected range

Tip

As long as a fixed row or column exists, the user can click any fixed column's cell to select the entire column or click any fixed row cell to select the entire row.

The MYGRID.MAK application contains a command button named cmdZero that the user can click to assign zeros to any selected range of cells. Listing 30.7 contains the command button's range-zeroing code for you to review.

Listing 30.7 Zeroing the Selected Range

```
Sub cmdZero_Click ()
' Zero user-selected cells
  Dim SelRows, SelCols As Integer
  If (grdSales.HighLight) Then    ' If true...
    For SelRows = grdSales.SelStartRow To grdSales.SelEndRow
      For SelCols = grdSales.SelStartCol To grdSales.SelEndCol
        grdSales.Row = SelRows
        grdSales.Col = SelCols
        grdSales.Text = "0.0"
      Next SelCols
    Next SelRows
  End If
End Sub
```

When the user clicks the Zero Cells command button (refer to Fig. 30.4), the event procedure first checks to make sure there is a range of cells selected. If there is a range selected, the nested For loop steps through each of the selected cells, given the enclosing values fenced by Table 30.2's range-fencing properties, and assigns each of the selected cells the string value 0.0.

Conclusion

Although this chapter has seemed easy, you now know the essentials of Visual Basic's grid control. The grid control is easy to use and acts like a spreadsheet with which you can display tables of values. Although the user cannot change data directly within the cells, you can write the application to update the cell values and read the user's selected cell range when needed to determine where changes should take place.

You can store both text and pictures in the grid cells. If you store numeric values, format the values with the `Format()` function to add consistency to the appearance of the grid. After running the program, the user then can scroll through the grid and select values as required by the application.

The grid control is an extremely powerful control that requires very little programming. The grid control is a good place to end this book because the grid control epitomizes the entire Visual Basic system as an easy and *fun* approach to Windows programming. Windows programming is traditionally labor intensive but not Visual Basic. As you've seen in this book, writing advanced interactive Visual Basic programs that take advantage of the Windows environment takes less effort than writing COBOL programs for textual environments. The Visual Basic environment often manages the tedious details for you so that you can concentrate on an effective user interface and on the primary goals of the application.

V

Your Next Step with VB

Appendix A

EBCDIC's Cousin: The ASCII Table

ASCII (American Standard Code for Information Interchange) is a widely used standard that defines numeric values for a common set of alphabetic characters. The first 32 characters are reserved for formatting and hardware control codes. Following these codes are 96 "printable" characters. IBM defined symbols for the final 128 ASCII values when it released the IBM PC, and referred to the additional characters as *Extended ASCII codes*.

Dec X_{10}	Hex X_{16}	Binary X_2	ASCII Character	Ctrl	Key
000	00	0000 0000	null	NUL	^@
001	01	0000 0001	☺	SOH	^A
002	02	0000 0010	☻	STX	^B
003	03	0000 0011	♥	ETX	^C
004	04	0000 0100	◆	EOT	^D
005	05	0000 0101	♣	ENQ	^E
006	06	0000 0110	¬	ACK	^F
007	07	0000 0111	•	BEL	^G
008	08	0000 1000	◘	BS	^H
009	09	0000 1001	○	HT	^I
010	0A	0000 1010	◙	LF	^J
011	0B	0000 1011	♂	VT	^K
012	0C	0000 1100	♀	FF	^L
013	0D	0000 1101	♪	CR	^M

(continues)

Dec X_{10}	Hex X_{16}	Binary X_2	ASCII Character	Ctrl	Key
014	0E	0000 1110	♪	SO	^N
015	0F	0000 1111	☼	SI	^O
016	10	0001 0000	►	DLE	^P
017	11	0001 0001	◄	DC1	^Q
018	12	0001 0010	↕	DC2	^R
019	13	0001 0011	‼	DC3	^S
020	14	0001 0100	¶	DC4	^T
021	15	0001 0101	§	NAK	^U
022	16	0001 0110	▬	SYN	^V
023	17	0001 0111	↨	ETB	^W
024	18	0001 1000	↑	CAN	^X
025	19	0001 1001	↓	EM	^Y
026	1A	0001 1010	→	SUB	^Z
027	1B	0001 1011	←	ESC	^[
028	1C	0001 1100	∟	FS	^\
029	1D	0001 1101	↔	GS	^]
030	1E	0001 1110	▲	RS	^^
031	1F	0001 1111	▼	US	^_
032	20	0010 0000	Space		
033	21	0010 0001	!		
034	22	0010 0010	"		
035	23	0010 0011	#		
036	24	0010 0100	$		
037	25	0010 0101	%		
038	26	0010 0110	&		
039	27	0010 0111	'		
040	28	0010 1000	(		
041	29	0010 1001	)		
042	2A	0010 1010	*		
043	2B	0010 1011	+		
044	2C	0010 1100	,		
045	2D	0010 1101	-		

Dec X_{10}	Hex X_{16}	Binary X_2	ASCII Character
046	2E	0010 1110	.
047	2F	0010 1111	/
048	30	0011 0000	0
049	31	0011 0001	1
050	32	0011 0010	2
051	33	0011 0011	3
052	34	0011 0100	4
053	35	0011 0101	5
054	36	0011 0110	6
055	37	0011 0111	7
056	38	0011 1000	8
057	39	0011 1001	9
058	3A	0011 1010	:
059	3B	0011 1011	;
060	3C	0011 1100	<
061	3D	0011 1101	=
062	3E	0011 1110	>
063	3F	0011 1111	?
064	40	0100 0000	@
065	41	0100 0001	A
066	42	0100 0010	B
067	43	0100 0011	C
068	44	0100 0100	D
069	45	0100 0101	E
070	46	0100 0110	F
071	47	0100 0111	G
072	48	0100 1000	H
073	49	0100 1001	I
074	4A	0100 1010	J
075	4B	0100 1011	K
076	4C	0100 1100	L
077	4D	0100 1101	M

(continues)

Dec X_{10}	Hex X_{16}	Binary X_2	ASCII Character
078	4E	0100 1110	N
079	4F	0100 1111	O
080	50	0101 0000	P
081	51	0101 0001	Q
082	52	0101 0010	R
083	53	0101 0011	S
084	54	0101 0100	T
085	55	0101 0101	U
086	56	0101 0110	V
087	57	0101 0111	W
088	58	0101 1000	X
089	59	0101 1001	Y
090	5A	0101 1010	Z
091	5B	0101 1011	[
092	5C	0101 1100	\
093	5D	0101 1101	]
094	5E	0101 1110	^
095	5F	0101 1111	–
096	60	0110 0000	`
097	61	0110 0001	a
098	62	0110 0010	b
099	63	0110 0011	c
100	64	0110 0100	d
101	65	0110 0101	e
102	66	0110 0110	f
103	67	0110 0111	g
104	68	0110 1000	h
105	69	0110 1001	i
106	6A	0110 1010	j
107	6B	0110 1011	k
108	6C	0110 1100	l
109	6D	0110 1101	m

Dec X_{10}	Hex X_{16}	Binary X_2	ASCII Character
110	6E	0110 1110	n
111	6F	0110 1111	o
112	70	0111 0000	p
113	71	0111 0001	q
114	72	0111 0010	r
115	73	0111 0011	s
116	74	0111 0100	t
117	75	0111 0101	u
118	76	0111 0110	v
119	77	0111 0111	w
120	78	0111 1000	x
121	79	0111 1001	y
122	7A	0111 1010	z
123	7B	0111 1011	{
124	7C	0111 1100	¦
125	7D	0111 1101	}
126	7E	0111 1110	~
127	7F	0111 1111	f
128	80	1000 0000	Ç
129	81	1000 0001	ü
130	82	1000 0010	é
131	83	1000 0011	â
132	84	1000 0100	ä
133	85	1000 0101	à
134	86	1000 0110	å
135	87	1000 0111	ç
136	88	1000 1000	ê
137	89	1000 1001	ë
138	8A	1000 1010	è
139	8B	1000 1011	ï
140	8C	1000 1100	î
141	8D	1000 1101	ì

(continues)

Dec X_{10}	Hex X_{16}	Binary X_2	ASCII Character
142	8E	1000 1110	Ä
143	8F	1000 1111	Å
144	90	1001 0000	É
145	91	1001 0001	æ
146	92	1001 0010	Æ
147	93	1001 0011	ô
148	94	1001 0100	ö
149	95	1001 0101	ò
150	96	1001 0110	û
151	97	1001 0111	ù
152	98	1001 1000	ÿ
153	99	1001 1001	Ö
154	9A	1001 1010	Ü
155	9B	1001 10211	¢
156	9C	1001 1100	£
157	9D	1001 1101	¥
158	9E	1001 1110	₧
159	9F	1001 1111	ƒ
160	A0	1010 0000	á
161	A1	1010 0001	í
162	A2	1010 0010	ó
163	A3	1010 0011	ú
164	A4	1010 0100	ñ
165	A5	1010 0101	Ñ
166	A6	1010 0110	ª
167	A7	1010 0111	º
168	A8	1010 1000	¿
169	A9	1010 1001	⌐
170	AA	1010 1010	¬
171	AB	1010 1011	½
172	AC	1010 1100	¼
173	AD	1010 1101	¡

Dec X_{10}	Hex X_{16}	Binary X_2	ASCII Character
174	AE	1010 1110	«
175	AF	1010 1111	»
176	B0	1011 0000	▒
177	B1	1011 0001	▓
178	B2	1011 0010	█
179	B3	1011 0011	│
180	B4	1011 0100	┤
181	B5	1011 0101	╡
182	B6	1011 0110	╢
183	B7	1011 0111	╖
184	B8	1011 1000	╕
185	B9	1011 1001	╣
186	BA	1011 1010	║
187	BB	1011 1011	╗
188	BC	1011 1100	╝
189	BD	1011 1101	╜
190	BE	1011 1110	╛
191	BF	1011 1111	┐
192	C0	1100 0000	└
193	C1	1100 0001	┴
194	C2	1100 0010	┬
195	C3	1100 0011	├
196	C4	1100 0100	─
197	C5	1100 0101	┼
198	C6	1100 0110	╞
199	C7	1100 0111	╟
200	C8	1100 1000	╚
201	C9	1100 1001	╔
202	CA	1100 1010	╩
203	CB	1100 1011	╦
204	CC	1100 1100	╠
205	CD	1100 1101	═

(continues)

Dec X_{10}	Hex X_{16}	Binary X_2	ASCII Character
206	CE	1100 1110	╬
207	CF	1100 1111	╧
208	D0	1101 0000	╨
209	D1	1101 0001	╤
210	D2	1101 0010	╥
211	D3	1101 0011	╙
212	D4	1101 0100	╘
213	D5	1101 0101	╒
214	D6	1101 0110	╓
215	D7	1101 0111	╫
216	D8	1101 1000	╪
217	D9	1101 1001	┘
218	DA	1101 1010	┌
219	DB	1101 1011	█
220	DC	1101 1100	▄
221	DD	1101 1101	▌
222	DE	1101 1110	▐
223	DF	1101 1111	▀
224	E0	1110 0000	α
225	E1	1110 0001	β
226	E2	1110 0010	Γ
227	E3	1110 0011	π
228	E4	1110 0100	Σ
229	E5	1110 0101	σ
230	E6	1110 0110	μ
231	E7	1110 0111	γ
232	E8	1110 1000	Φ
233	E9	1110 1001	θ
234	EA	1110 1010	Ω
235	EB	1110 1011	δ
236	EC	1110 1100	∞
237	ED	1110 1101	$\varnothing$

Dec X_{10}	Hex X_{16}	Binary X_2	ASCII Character
238	EE	1110 1110	$\in$
239	EF	1110 1111	$\cap$
240	F0	1111 0000	$\equiv$
241	F1	1111 0001	$\pm$
242	F2	1111 0010	$\geq$
243	F3	1111 0011	$\leq$
244	F4	1111 0100	$\lceil$
245	F5	1111 0101	$\rfloor$
246	F6	1111 0110	$\div$
247	F7	1111 0111	$\approx$
248	F8	1111 1000	$\circ$
249	F9	1111 1001	$\bullet$
250	FA	1111 1010	$\cdot$
251	FB	1111 1011	$\sqrt{}$
252	FC	1111 1100	^{n}
253	FD	1111 1101	^{2}
254	FE	1111 1110	$\blacksquare$
255	FF	1111 1111	

Index

Symbols

PLUG YOURSELF INTO...

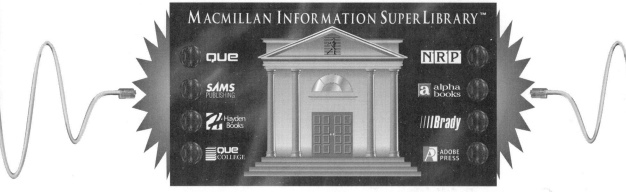

THE MACMILLAN INFORMATION SUPERLIBRARY™

Free information and vast computer resources from the world's leading computer book publisher—online!

FIND THE BOOKS THAT ARE RIGHT FOR YOU!

A complete online catalog, plus sample chapters and tables of contents give you an in-depth look at *all* of our books, including hard-to-find titles. It's the best way to find the books you need!

- **STAY INFORMED** with the latest computer industry news through our online newsletter, press releases, and customized Information SuperLibrary Reports.

- **GET FAST ANSWERS** to your questions about MCP books and software.

- **VISIT** our online bookstore for the latest information and editions!

- **COMMUNICATE** with our expert authors through e-mail and conferences.

- **DOWNLOAD SOFTWARE** from the immense MCP library:
    - Source code and files from MCP books
    - The best shareware, freeware, and demos

- **DISCOVER HOT SPOTS** on other parts of the Internet.

- **WIN BOOKS** in ongoing contests and giveaways!

TO PLUG INTO MCP: →   WORLD WIDE WEB: **http://www.mcp.com**

GOPHER: gopher.mcp.com

FTP: ftp.mcp.com

GET CONNECTED
to the ultimate source of computer information!

The MCP Forum on CompuServe

Go online with the world's leading computer book publisher!
Macmillan Computer Publishing offers everything
you need for computer success!

Find the books that are right for you!
A complete online catalog,
plus sample chapters and tables of contents
give you an in-depth look at all our books.
The best way to shop or browse!

- ► Get fast answers and technical support for MCP books and software

- ► Join discussion groups on major computer subjects

- ► Interact with our expert authors via e-mail and conferences

- ► Download software from our immense library:
  - ▷ Source code from books
  - ▷ Demos of hot software
  - ▷ The best shareware and freeware
  - ▷ Graphics files

Join now and get a free CompuServe Starter Kit!

To receive your free CompuServe Introductory Membership, call **1-800-848-8199** and ask for representative #597.

The Starter Kit includes:
- ➤ Personal ID number and password
- ➤ $15 credit on the system
- ➤ Subscription to *CompuServe Magazine*

Once on the CompuServe System, type:

GO MACMILLAN

for the most computer information anywhere!

MACMILLAN
COMPUTER
PUBLISHING

CompuServe

Licensing Agreement

By opening this package, you are agreeing to be bound by the following:

This software product is copyrighted, and all rights are reserved by the publisher and author. You are licensed to use this software on a single computer. You may copy and/or modify the software as needed to facilitate your use of it on a single computer. Making copies of the software for any other purpose is a violation of United States copyright laws.

This software is sold *as is* without warranty of any kind, either expressed or implied, including but not limited to the implied warranties of merchantability and fitness for a particular purpose. Neither the publisher nor its dealers or distributors assume any liability for any alleged or actual damages arising from the use of this program. (Some states do not allow for the exclusion of implied warranties, so the exclusion may not apply to you.)